Marketing Financial Services

Mary Ann Pezzullo

AMERICAN
BANKERS
ASSOCIATION ®

1120 Connecticut Avenue, N.W.
Washington, D.C. 20036

This publication is designed to provide accurate and authoritative information in regard to the subject matter covered. It is sold with the understanding that the publisher is not engaged in rendering legal, accounting, or other professional service. If legal advice or other expert assistance is required, the services of a competent professional person should be sought.

From a Declaration of Principles jointly adopted by a Committee of the American Bar Association and a Committee of Publishers and Associations.

CONTENTS

PREFACE

Changes in this Edition

"Marketing must be an integral part of everything the bank does," said Tom Brown, a senior banking industry analyst for Donaldson, Lufkin and Jenrette in New York City, in 1996. At the time, his words shocked the financial services world, which had remained complacent and low key in its approach to marketing. Brown backed up his statements by evaluating banks' marketing strategy as part of his analysis of the bank's worth. He no longer analyzed banks' overall performance, growth rate, and risk level alone because success in the race against competitors would be much more than a numbers game in the future.

Brown's philosophy has been taken seriously by a growing number of financial services providers. Many are investing in database research tools such as marketing information systems and segmentation software to learn how to market to their customers one to one. To provide services tailored to individual customers' needs and wants, banks are developing home banking software and Internet web sites to allow customers to bank 24 hours a day from home. Advances in technology have allowed tremendous advances in customer call centers, allowing 24-hour loan processing and virtually instantaneous approvals. Automated teller machines have been updated to include additional services to meet consumers' needs, and automated loan machines have been added as yet another convenience.

Advances in technology have been dynamic since the fourth edition of this textbook was printed, but dramatic changes have also occurred in customer relations. Financial services providers take extensive training in communication and selling, as well as marketing, to ensure that customers receive the service and attention they need. The industry's perspective on personal selling has changed tremendously, and the importance of selling as a business strategy has gained acceptance in an industry that never needed to sell before.

All these changes and more have been included in the fifth edition of this textbook. You'll also find extensive lists of new resources and updated exhibits. New case studies reflect the changes in advertising and describe the effect of mergers and acquisitions and the importance of community relations.

To reflect the rapid evolution of the industry, particularly in the field of marketing, we have changed the title of the book from *Marketing for Bankers* to *Marketing Financial Services*. We believe this title more accurately reflects the scope and importance of the movement in which entire banking organizations wear the mantle of marketing. *Marketing*

Financial Services, even more than *Marketing for Bankers*, stresses the marketing concept of providing a full range of financial services, including management and advisory services, desired by customers.

Marketing Financial Services also contains much new material pertaining to the advances in technology that affect the financial services industry. Among these changes are marketing information systems and the Internet. Because the Internet is promising to be a useful tool for research, training, advertising, and many more of the functions important in marketing financial services, a list of useful Web sites has been included at the end of the book. Many, many more worthwhile sites exist, and we encourage you to explore.

About the Author

Mary Ann Pezzullo, a bank marketing consultant specializing in strategic marketing planning and the development and execution of advertising, sales promotion, product development, staff cross-selling, and customer relations programs, has also been director of marketing at United Jersey Banks, Princeton, New Jersey, and Industrial Valley Bank, Philadelphia, Pennsylvania, and director of advertising at Fidelity Bank in Philadelphia.

Ms. Pezzullo holds an M.A. in economics from Boston College, where she completed all course work for a doctorate degree, and is past president of the Penn-Jer-Del Chapter of the Bank Marketing Association. Besides *Marketing for Bankers*, Ms. Pezzullo has written several sales training courses for the American Institute of Banking.

About the Editor

Tanja Lian Sablosky, working with the reviewers listed below and with Susan Siegel, an instructional designer experienced in the financial services industry, updated and revised the fourth edition of *Marketing for Bankers*. Currently she is an independent writer and editor in Reston, Virginia. Ms. Sablosky was the editor of *Bank Marketing,* the magazine published by the Bank Marketing Association, from 1992 to 1996. Previously, she held several positions at the American Bankers Association, including assistant division manager for the retail, consumer credit, bank card, and human resources divisions, and editor of American Institute of Banking textbooks.

Ms. Sablosky holds a B.A. in English from Carleton College and has completed graduate work at George Washington University. She also earned a Publications Specialist Certificate from George Washington University and graduated from the Essentials of Bank Marketing School, which is sponsored by the Bank Marketing Association. She has also attended many banking and marketing conferences and seminars.

Acknowledgments

We want to thank all the organizations that granted permission for use of their advertisements and provided information for *Marketing for Bankers* and *Marketing Financial Services*: Carl Schmitt, University National Bank & Trust Co., Palo Alto, California; Texas Commerce Bancshares, Houston, Texas; Peterson Bank, Chicago, Illinois; Key Bank of New York, Albany, New York; Key Bank of Washington, Seattle, Washington; Silo and its advertising agency, Saatchi & Saatchi; St. Louis Bank for Savings, Duluth, Minnesota; The Bank of Boston, Boston, Massachusetts; Florida First Federal Savings Bank, Panama City, Florida; BankAmerica Corporation, San Francisco, California; Magnolia Federal Bank for Savings, Hattiesburg, Mississippi; Chemical Bank, New York; American National Bank, Omaha, Nebraska; First National Bank and Trust Company, Stuart, Florida; Fleet

Bank, Providence, Rhode Island; Deposit Guaranty National Bank, Greenville, Mississippi; Mark Twain Bank, St. Louis, Missouri; Southside State Bank, Tyler, Texas, and its advertising agency, Sachnowitz & Company, Houston; and Albert F. Appleton, Commissioner of the New York City Department of Environmental Protection. For permission to print images from its Home Page, Bank Online page, and HomeBanking Page from its Web site, we thank Bank of America. For permission to print its logos, we thank LaSalle State Bank, LaSalle, Illinois.

Many bankers were consulted during the revision process, and we are grateful to all of them. The editor wishes to thank Ann Kessler and the rest of the professional staff of the ABA/BMA Center for Banking Information for their invaluable research support and guidance. The following banking professionals reviewed the entire manuscript of *Marketing Financial Services*, and the American Bankers Association especially wishes to thank them for their dedication to maintaining the accuracy, thoroughness, and usefulness of ABA's publications. Their help was invaluable.

Don Anderson
Vice President, Marketing
Community National Bank
Grand Forks, North Dakota

Sheila Bacon
Director, Business Development, New Media
GTE Corporation
Dallas, Texas

Diane Beukelman
Director of Marketing
Merchants Bank
Aurora, Illinois

John Delmhorst
Vice President
Lafayette American Bank
Fairfield, Connecticut

Susan Goodwin
Assistant Vice President
Norwest Bank Texas, N.A.
Kerrville, Texas

Part I

WHAT IS MARKETING?

Part I of *Marketing Financial Services* focuses on the term *marketing:* how it is defined, what it means conceptually, what its goal is, what tasks it entails, what its history is in this country, and what its place is in the history of banking. This information forms the foundation for all that follows and establishes the overriding importance of customer satisfaction to the business of marketing. Bear in mind that marketing—as a concept and as a practice—continually evolves. Just as lifestyles, technology, and the environment change, so, too, do the methods of marketing.

After studying part I, you will understand that marketing is not just one of the many routine tasks that a bank performs in its daily operations. Rather, it is a way of thinking and doing business that, in the ideal situation, permeates the bank and helps the bank focus on the customer and the sales process.

1

Introduction to Marketing and Key Marketing Concepts

Learning Objectives

After studying this chapter, you should be able to

- define marketing and explain each element of the definition,
- describe the marketing concept and explain its four elements,
- list five factors that lead organizations to adopt the marketing concept,
- describe the stages through which the banking industry has passed in its growing awareness of marketing,
- explain the importance of marketing definition and differentiate among product, production, selling, and customer orientation in a business, and
- describe the five service elements that are most important to bank customers.

Introduction

Marketing permeates our daily lives and influences many of our decisions—especially our selection of brands of products. But what exactly is marketing? And what role does it play in the banking industry? This chapter begins to answer these questions and illustrates why banks, like other businesses, need to see themselves as marketing organizations.

Chapter 1 opens with a basic definition of marketing and a discussion of each of the elements in that definition. Next, it addresses a way of conducting business known as the marketing concept and explains when, why, and how marketing has evolved in the banking industry. Finally, it focuses on why it is critically important for any bank to have a market definition of its business.

The Definition of Marketing

The American Marketing Association's board of directors defines *marketing* as "the process of planning and executing the conception, pricing, promotion, and distribution of ideas, goods, and services to create exchanges that satisfy individual and organizational objectives."[1] This definition of marketing encompasses five key elements that will be expanded on throughout this text:

1. Marketing is a planning process.
2. Marketing involves the conception, pricing, promotion, and distribution of something.
3. Marketing's object can be a tangible good, a service, or an idea.
4. Marketing seeks to meet the objectives of both individuals and organizations.
5. Marketing works through exchange processes.

Let's look at each of these elements more closely.

Key Elements of the Definition

1. *Marketing is a planning process.* As later chapters will describe, marketing entails an ongoing process of developing plans, executing them, monitoring their results, and modifying them as needed to stay on course. In other words, marketing is a strategic management process; the business of marketing must be organized, directed, measured, and controlled to be effective.

2. *Marketing entails the conception (product), pricing, promotion, and distribution (place) of something.* The daily activities of people who work in marketing departments revolve around designing, developing, and enhancing products; setting the prices for those products; promoting the products' features and benefits to the target markets; and distributing the products to the markets. These activities constitute the four elements of what is known as the *marketing mix*. For ease in memorization, they are often referred to as "the four Ps" of marketing:

- product,
- price,
- promotion, and
- place (a convenient synonym for distribution).

Subsequent chapters present these four elements in some detail.

3. *Marketing's object can be a tangible good, a service, or an idea.* In fact, any good, service, idea, or place that satisfies the needs or desires of customers is referred to as the product. The term *product* can cover anything from cereal to certificates of deposit; from a tropical island to the idea that drugs can damage your brain; from a hospital to a presidential candidate. Although the product is but one of the four ingredients in the marketing mix, it is the central element around which the other three revolve. (See exhibit 1.1.)

4. *Marketing seeks to satisfy the objectives of individuals and organizations.* Put another way, marketing seeks to satisfy its own objectives and those of customers. The objective of the customer (who may be an individual or an organization) is to satisfy certain needs and wants. The terms *needs* and *wants* tend to be used inter-

Exhibit 1.1   **The Four Ps of the Marketing Mix**

Product

Pricing

Promotion

Place (Distribution)

changeably, although most businesses today are really in the business of satisfying wants. People need shelter, but they want a contemporary house on a third of an acre. They need clothing, but they want designer jeans. They need a safe place for their savings, but they want the maximum rate of interest on their certificates of deposit.

The objective of the marketer, who may be either an individual or an organization, is to reach goals. These goals might involve attaining the leading share of the cereal market, increasing tourism, reducing the number of drug abusers, increasing the number of hotel beds occupied, getting the candidate elected, or increasing the bank's share of the consumer loan market.

5. *Marketing works through exchange processes.* The existence of two parties with objectives to be satisfied is essential to the marketing mix, but it is not the sole condition necessary for marketing to occur. Marketing can occur only when the party with the need for a certain product (the customer) is capable of offering something of value that will also satisfy the marketer's objectives. In other words, an exchange of value must be possible. Thus, the cereal manufacturer (the marketer) must be capable of exchanging its product

for money, and the customer must be capable of exchanging money for cereal. Similarly, a bank exchanges its checking, savings, and credit products in return for fees, service charges, and interest payments paid by customers. A drug-abuse prevention organization exchanges the idea that it is okay to say no to drugs (that is, moral support) in return for public awareness that will help alleviate the drug problem. (See exhibit 1.2.)

To effect a successful exchange, a marketer must understand what the customer wants and be able to elicit an appropriate response, whether that be buying a product, voting in an election, joining an organization, or refraining from an activity. Exchange processes have existed since that time in primitive civilization when people realized that bartering or trading among themselves made it easier to satisfy their needs. Marketing as a business discipline, however, did not develop until the twentieth century.

A discussion of exchange processes leads to the concept of the market. "A market consists of all the potential customers sharing a particular need or want who might be willing and able to engage in exchange to satisfy that need or want."[2] The word *able* is included because it is

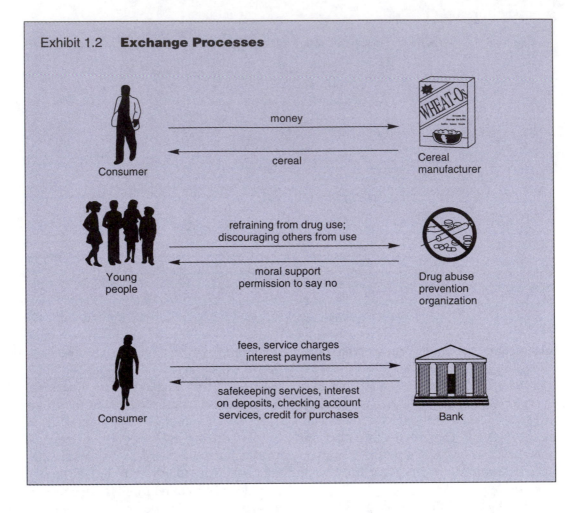

Exhibit 1.2 **Exchange Processes**

money →
← cereal

Consumer — Cereal manufacturer

refraining from drug use; discouraging others from use →
← moral support permission to say no

Young people — Drug abuse prevention organization

fees, service charges interest payments →
← safekeeping services, interest on deposits, checking account services, credit for purchases

Consumer — Bank

possible for a customer to influence the buying decision and to have access to purchasing power while not actually possessing purchasing power. For example, a child who asks a parent to buy a specific brand of cereal or toy is a customer, even though the cereal and toy are bought with the parent's purchasing power. For an example of how marketers respond to this reality, one need only watch the advertisements surrounding Saturday morning television cartoon shows. Applying this definition to banking, the market for retail banking services consists of people and organizations with the capability, actual or potential, to satisfy their financial management needs.

Marketers use the term *market* to encompass various groups of potential customers. Bank marketers, for instance, talk about product markets ("the certificate of deposit [CD] market"), demographic markets ("the Generation X market"), geographic markets ("the suburban market"), and psychographic markets ("the sophisticated investor market").

Just as there are many different management styles and management philosophies, there are a number of different philosophies to guide marketing management. Only one of them, the marketing concept, generally leads to long-run marketing success.

The Four Pillars of the Marketing Concept

The particular school of thought that has emerged over several decades as the guiding philosophy of the most successful marketing firms is known as the marketing concept. (See exhibit 1.3.) The marketing concept is a recognition that the objectives of an organization can best be reached by identifying the needs and wants of customers who make up the target market and meeting those needs and wants through an integrated, efficient, organization-wide effort. Additionally, since the marketer and the consumer do not exist in a vacuum but rather are part of society, another element may be added to this concept: marketing should be carried out in a socially responsible manner.

The marketing concept is a philosophy and a frame of mind; it is also a basis for decision making and a guide for effectively managing resources. Marketing, then, is not an activity that a business undertakes; instead, it is an organizational philosophy that influences and directs all the operations of a bank or other business. The four pillars that support the marketing concept are customer orientation, profit, total company effort, and social responsibility. When they are in place, these pillars help ensure the success of a business. The following section covers each of the four elements of the marketing concept in detail and shows how it applies to the business world.

Customer Orientation

The marketing concept recognizes that customer satisfaction is the business that all businesses are in. A truly marketing-oriented company believes that its financial objectives will be best served by identifying its target market and recognizing and responding to that market's needs and wants. Marketing expert J. B. McKitterick once said that, under the marketing concept, it is not important to be skillful in making the customer do what suits the interest or convenience of the firm,

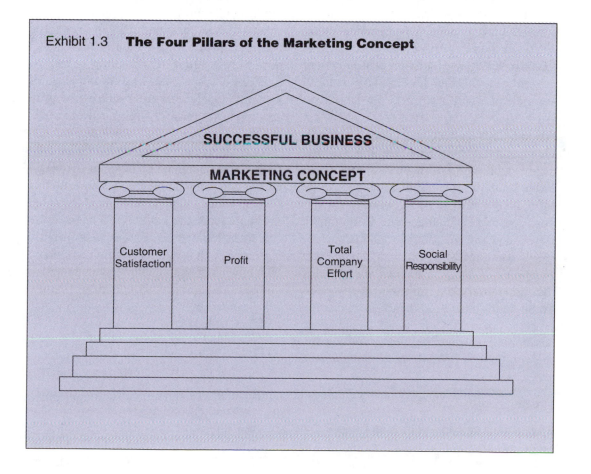

Exhibit 1.3   **The Four Pillars of the Marketing Concept**

SUCCESSFUL BUSINESS

MARKETING CONCEPT

Customer Satisfaction | Profit | Total Company Effort | Social Responsibility but to be skillful in inducing the firm to do what suits the interest of the customer.[3] This skill has been in short supply in American business. McKitterick's observation was made in the late 1950s; 30 years later, the federal government instituted the Malcolm Baldrige National Quality Award in an effort to motivate American companies to improve the quality of their goods and services. This award can be won only by firms that demonstrate a company-wide, organized, integrated commitment to customer satisfaction—firms that are customer—driven and that have adopted the marketing concept.

Although customer satisfaction has always been a principal element of the marketing concept, the understanding of what it means has been evolving in the American business world. Several companies have taken the lead in pursuing a high level of service quality as defined by the customer. There are several good business reasons for operating this way. Highly satisfied customers tend to be repeat purchasers, and it is much more expensive to generate a new customer than to provide additional service to an existing one. Satisfied customers are also more loyal, thus less likely to stray to competitors, and less price-sensitive than are customers who are not highly satisfied. Some recognized leaders in customer service (as noted by their Malcolm Baldrige award–winning performance) are the mail-order house Lands' End, Inc.; Motorola, Inc.; AT&T Consumer Communications Services; and GTE Directories Corporation. Renowned and often-cited retailers such as Nordstrom's are also pointed to as excellent examples of how companies should treat their customers and train their employees. Some banks have used the experiences and practices of these companies as guides to developing their own programs for improving the quality of their customer-focused services.

Profit

The marketing concept does not imply that customer satisfaction is the only objective of an organization. It is not a philanthropic philosophy aimed at helping customers at the expense of the business institution. Rather, it recognizes that to reach profit objectives there must be a balance between customer satisfaction and profitability. Indeed, the market concept believes that profit objectives can best be met by providing customer satisfaction. (See exhibit 1.4.)

The highly successful marketing organization finds ways to use its resources in the most efficient way possible consistent with customer wants and needs. A bank might improve its customers' satisfaction with its services by offering a checking account with no fees, service charges, or minimum-balance requirements. However, a checking account is one of the most costly products offered by a bank, and it would be inadvisable to price the product this way. From a marketing perspective, the ideal approach would be to design checking products to meet the customers' needs and wants and then to select the service charges and minimum-balance combinations that come closest to meeting consumers' desires while earning a profit for the bank. Many banks now offer a range of checking accounts, from basic low-cost, minimum-services accounts to elaborate, interest-bearing accounts that require high minimum balances and provide numerous additional services, such as bonus rates or preferred loan rates. The concept of value is an important part of consumer satisfaction. The bank that builds more value into its checking accounts from the customer's perspective can attract more customers at a slightly higher price than can its competitors whose checking accounts offer fewer benefits. Greater customer satisfaction should improve earnings by increasing fee income and deposit balances.

Total Company Effort

The marketing concept must become the philosophy of the entire organization, not just the marketing department. In banks, as in other organizations, the importance of effectively integrating and coordinating the activities of employees is based on a sim-

Exhibit 1.4   A Customer-Oriented Bank: University National Bank & Trust Co., Palo Alto, California

In 1980, former California banking commissioner Carl Schmitt established a new bank to prove that a small, creative bank that emphasized customer service could be financially successful. From the outset, he endeavored to rethink the business of banking from the viewpoint of the customer: What does the customer want? How do we look to the customer? What do we sound like to the customer? How is the customer reading what we are communicating?

Schmitt used his 14 years of experience in banking and his customer orientation to create one of the most profitable small banks in California. He proved that the marketing concept works. Note some of the customer-focused marketing strategies that Schmitt used:

- If customers are waiting in line, nonteller staff assist with noncash transactions to help move things along.
- If a customer is waiting to enter the bank before it opens, the customer gets assistance; and if regular banking hours are inconvenient, customers can make appointments to do their banking, regardless of the size of their balances.
- Customers can buy stamps at cost or get a free shoeshine in the bank.
- The bank has six courier vans to collect noncash deposits from business clients located at a distance from the two "banking floors." (The banking term "branch" is not used.)
- The bank promises customers that all checking statements will be in the mail on the second business day of the month. Production-oriented banks stagger statement production and mailing throughout the month, but Schmitt believes that customers prefer to keep their records by calendar month. As a result, all 120-plus bank employees, from the chairman down, work late on the first business night of the month to get the statements out on time.
- Each customer is assigned to one of several "bank within a bank" teams, which have their own client list and manage their own loan portfolios, giving staff a sense of ownership. However, the teams do not compete; rather, all compensation is tied to the performance of the entire bank.

Did it work? The bank grew to $355 million in assets in its first 12 years. In 1992, its return on assets, a measure of profitability, was greater than 1 percent, and was 45 percent higher than the national average. Successful customer-oriented banks like this one are prime targets for regional and superregional banks. In February 1996, University National merged with Comerica Bank, California, and became part of a $2.6 billion corporation.

Source: Elizabeth Conlin, "Small Business: Second Thoughts on Growth," *Inc.*, March 1991, pp. 60–66; Terence P. Paré, "Bankers Who Beat the Bust," *Fortune*, November 4, 1991, pp. 159–165; and interview with Roberta Washburn, Assistant Vice President, University National Bank & Trust Co. Updated 1997.

ple truth: The people who work for the business *are* the business. A firm is marketing itself every time a customer interacts with an employee. A teller is engaged in marketing when greeting a customer. If the teller is rude, then, as far as the customer is concerned, the bank is rude. The question is not whether the teller should engage in marketing; marketing is inherent in the job. The question is whether the teller will market the bank's services effectively. Effective integration of the marketing concept throughout the bank's operations increases the likelihood that the teller's job, and all other jobs, will be performed in a manner consistent with the marketing concept.

This customer-oriented attitude does not develop naturally; it must be fostered by management. The commitment to customer satisfaction must be made and supported by top management and implemented in the form of a corporate culture that places the customer at the center of all the bank's activities. The marketing concept implemented in this way ties together the various staff divisions in the bank by giving them a common focus. Every department of the bank sees itself, in some way, as serving the bank's customers. While employees who work in branch offices and, say, business development deal directly with customers, employees who do not have this direct contact understand how the work they do affects the customer. For example, the proof operator knows that an encoding error will lead to an error on the statement, which will cause a problem for the customer. The customer will then call or visit the bank to get the problem resolved, creating additional work for customer-service staff. This experience, and the way the error is corrected, affects the customer's satisfaction with the bank. The computer programmer knows that modifications to the savings statement that might be required by a new regulation must reflect a sensitivity to the way the customer will perceive the change. Back-office staff who provide service to customer-contact staff

see them as needing a level of service that will help them provide excellent service to their customers. (See exhibit 1.5.) In a marketing-oriented, customer-focused bank, all employees understand that "if you aren't serving the customer directly, you're serving someone who is."

Social Responsibility

Social responsibility is an important part of the marketing concept, especially for banks, which provide a quasi-public service. It is quite possible for a company to satisfy its customers yet be in conflict with the well-being of society as a whole. For example, a firm might market a product that satisfies a number of consumers but dangerously pollutes the environment or harms some type of wildlife. Increased sensitivity to social responsibility has resulted in some fast-food chains switching from Styrofoam to paper containers in recognition of the environmental harm caused by nonbiodegradable waste and in some tuna canning companies promoting their change to a system of harvesting tuna that does not kill dolphins.

Banks, like other firms that are respected institutions in the community, are expected to play an active, socially responsible role in civic affairs. It is not unusual for a bank to mandate that its officers be involved with local service organizations. Through their community relations programs, banks often support the arts, scholastic achievement, and amateur sporting events. Frequently, a bank will take the initiative in addressing a specific cause, such as promoting neighborhood improvement or developing recreational opportunities for youth.

Some aspects of social responsibility have been mandated by banking regulation. Since the passage of the Community Reinvestment Act, banks are subject to periodic examinations and are rated on the extent to which they meet the credit needs of all segments of the communities they serve.

Unfortunately, not all firms conduct their business with a social conscience.

All too often newspapers report on businesses that abuse the environment, use misleading advertising or labeling, discriminate in hiring employees, and manufacture unsafe products. Some banks have been, and continue to be, guilty of *redlining,* the intentional or unintentional practice of not encouraging or not approving loans from certain geographic areas within their community because they are seen as poor risks. Sooner or later, companies that commit irresponsible acts are exposed by consumer advocates, ecologists, politicians, or community leaders. Often, this exposure leads to the passage of restrictions that are applied to all firms regardless of culpability. The passage of Truth-in-Savings legislation is an example of how all banks can be profoundly affected by the irresponsible actions of a few banks that engage in misleading advertising.

The existence of "consumerism" and the consumer protection movement may be proof that businesses have not genuinely integrated the marketing concept into their overall organizational philosophies, that they are still too focused on selling and achieving the company's goals and not focused enough on meeting customers' needs. To quote author Peter Drucker: "Consumerism demands that business start out with the needs, the realities, the values of the customer. It demands that business define its goals as the satisfaction of customer needs. It demands that business base its reward on its contribution to the customer. That after twenty years of marketing rhetoric consumerism could become a powerful popular movement proves that not much marketing has been practiced. Consumerism is the 'shame of marketing.'"[4]

In the 1970s, consumer service firms—including banks, insurance companies, and brokerage houses—began to display a heightened marketing awareness. At the onset of the 1980s, nonprofit organizations also recognized the need for effective marketing. Colleges instituted modern marketing techniques to help boost enrollments, hospitals used them to raise funds, and police departments used them to improve their public image.

Why has it taken many organizations so long to adopt the marketing concept, and what is it that prompts businesses to realize its importance?

Evolution of the Marketing Concept

Firms usually discover—or rediscover—the marketing concept when they find that their profits are declining or stagnating because of one or more of the following situations:

- a decline in sales or market share,
- slow growth,
- a change in consumer buying patterns,
- increased competition, or
- increased marketing expenses.[5]

Following is a discussion of these five key factors in the evolution toward adopting the marketing concept.

Declining Sales or Market Share

Diminishing demand for its products or services is the most likely cause of a business' heightened marketing awareness. Many small private colleges faced with declining enrollments turned to marketing research to help them understand how high school seniors made the decision to "buy" a college. The colleges then used this information to recruit the caliber of students they were seeking.

The commercial banking industry began losing *market share* of financial institution deposits in the late 1940s. (See exhibit 1.6.) Initially, it lost market share to thrift institutions. By analyzing what the competition was offering that banks were not, banks realized that the thrifts, which by law were permitted to pay higher rates of interest on deposits than commercial banks were permitted to pay, were more effectively meeting customer demand for higher returns on savings.

More recently, both commercial banks and thrift institutions have been losing market share of financial assets to such nonbank financial institutions as insurance companies and brokerage firms. These institutions offer a broader range of financial services for individuals who are willing to risk losing some principal in return for a higher return on their investment. These two instances of loss of market share to competitors led the banking industry to lobby for deregulation of interest rates and expansion of banking powers so that banks would be legally free to use the marketing tools of product development and pricing. As a result, the Depository Institutions Deregulation and Monetary Control Act (DIDMCA) was passed in 1980, eliminating interest rate ceilings on bank deposits. The banking industry has continued to lobby for further deregulation and for expanded banking powers; as a result, banks now may offer discount brokerage service and nontraditional products.

Exhibit 1.6   Factors in the Development of Marketing Awareness in the Banking Industry

1.   *Declining Market Share.* From the end of World War II to the end of the 1970s, commercial banking's competition came primarily from other deposit-taking financial institutions: savings and loans, savings banks, and credit unions ("thrift institutions"). Whereas commercial banks held about 55.9 percent of domestic deposits in 1948, over the succeeding 32 years they have lost over 30 percent to non-banks.

Percentage of Financial Assets Held by

	Commercial Banks	S&Ls, Savings Banks, & Credit Unions	Other Financial Institutions
1948	55.9	12.3	31.8
1960	38.2	19.7	42.1
1980	34.8	21.4	43.4
1993	25.4	9.4	65.0

Source: Data for 1948 from Raymond W. Goldsmith, *Financial Structure and Development* (New Haven, CT: Yale University Press, 1969), Table D-33, pp. 548–549. Data for 1960–1993 from Board of Governors of the Federal Reserve System, "Flow of Funds, Accounts," various years.

2.   *Increasing Competition.* In the early 1980s, commercial banks continued to lose market share to the thrifts, but the real competition came from nonbank financial institutions: money market funds, mutual funds, securities brokers and dealers, and others (insurance companies, pension funds, investment companies, finance companies, and real estate investment trusts). Since 1980, the banking industry (both commercial banks and thrifts) has lost share to other financial institutions, whose share of the total market has increased substantially.

3.   *Slow Growth.* From 1980 to 1989, financial assets held by the banking industry grew by 8 percent per year while those held by other financial institutions grew by 14 percent per year. The banking industry's growth lagged behind the growth of the total market for financial assets.

	Compound Annual Growth Rate of Financial Assets by Type of Institution, 1980–1989 Percent
All financial assets	11
Domestic commercial banks	8
S&Ls, savings banks, & credit unions	8
Other financial institutions	14

Source: *Statistical Abstract of the United States,* 1989.

In addition to seeking expanded powers and broader product lines, banks have also learned from their competitors and from other industries that to recapture market share they will need to focus on the customer. Understanding the wants and needs of their customers, adding the technology to identify and satisfy those needs, and improving service standards to a level where customers develop a long-term loyalty to the bank will be critical factors in the banking industry's struggle to regain market share.

Slow Growth

The demand for goods and services is not infinite. Sooner or later, markets become saturated. This condition leads marketers to search for other related consumer needs that can be met and, in the process, increase sales.

McDonald's is a good example of how successful marketers respond to slow growth. Increased competition, a reduction in hamburger consumption by health-conscious consumers, and a decline in the overall growth of the fast-food market considerably slowed McDonald's corporate growth. That led the company to take a number of steps to find new ways to meet changing consumer needs. It gave its local franchisees freedom to experiment with new menu items based on the preferences of their local consumers. Consequently, McDonald's offered a breakfast menu, which led to new business and increased sales. Following that success, it focused on increasing the appeal of its restaurants as places to eat dinner and as an adult meal restaurant and deemphasizing its children's meals.[6] The hope is that this experimentation will lead to new products or delivery methods that will further increase sales. In the hope of encouraging customer loyalty, McDonald's developed a television campaign around the theme "That's My McDonald's" and again featured satisfied adult customers eating breakfast, lunch, and dinner at the golden arches.

In banking, when sales decline or when a bank wishes to boost sales it is time to create a new promotional campaign or a sale to recapture customers' attention. For example, some banks tie CD sales to events. Every year, the Bank of Boulder sponsors a 10K race. In 1996, it decided to tie a CD promotion to the race. The bank named its new CD "The Race CD." The promotion was for a $1,000 minimum deposit with an annual percentage yield (APY) of 5.5 percent. However, customers could increase their APY up to 10 percent by correctly guessing numerous final tallies relating to the race. Depositors were awarded 0.25 percent for correctly predicting the winning man's time, winning woman's time, winning wheelchair competitor's time, and 15 other numbers. The six-week promotion drew 100 CD customer and new deposits estimated at nearly $3 million.[7]

Changing Buying Behavior

Customer wants and needs are not static, but constantly changing. An increase in consumers' personal disposable income and changes in values have brought about a change in their lifestyles. The movement toward health and fitness in this country has affected the marketing of health clubs, weight training machines, exercise shoes and attire, and low-fat foods. Advances in electronics and telecommunications have increased the interest in home entertainment products and, to some extent, have reduced the popularity of movies and live theater. Similarly, the growing number of working mothers has led to a swell in the demand for day-care centers for children as well as for convenience foods and microwaveable meals. Marketers must respond to these changing needs in order to continue to prosper.

Banks are no different than other businesses. They must monitor changes in the market in order to adapt their products and their distribution accordingly. For example, many banking customers have come to place a greater value on saving time than on being loyal to their bank. To take advantage of this trend, many banks have begun offering 24-hour telephone banking, personal computer (PC) banking services, and automated loan machines (ALMs). The ultimate in speed and convenience for customers seeking loans, for example, are instant loan approvals by telephone. A bank that offers the customer this service is in a position to charge a higher interest rate than one that requires customers to come into the bank to apply, again demonstrating the positive effect that a customer-oriented marketing concept can have on pricing and, thus, on profitability.

Buying patterns for consumer financial services have undergone dramatic changes in the past several years. Consumers are seeking a greater range of investment products and services, including mutual funds and insurance. The availability and success of stock and bond mutual funds have drawn customers away from safer but lower-yielding bank products. Since deregulation has blurred the differences between commercial banks and other financial institutions, customers now have numerous alternatives when selecting financial services. Because of the changes in buyer behavior and the increasing number of competitors, bank marketers are finding it more difficult than ever to compete in the financial services arena.

To combat the blurred distinction between financial services providers, banks have aggressively worked to add new products such as brokerage services, mutual funds, insurance products, and investment products and services. Unfortunately, consumers are often unaware of the broad range of products banks now offer. Bank marketing efforts to communicate the existence and value of these products must be increased to capture the sophisticated investor and high-balance customer.

Increased Competition

The situations described above—declining market share, slow growth, and changing buyer behavior—often result from increased competition. When it confronts these situations, a firm becomes more marketing conscious. In some cases, the mere presence of a new competitor increases a bank's marketing awareness. Probably nothing more effectively stirs up a staid community bank than the sudden presence of a new competitor's branch nearby.

Every bank in the United States faces competition from other banks—community banks, large banks, regional banks, superregional banks, and nationwide banks. In addition, the entire banking industry faces competition from mutual funds, brokerage houses, insurance companies, nonbank banks, and captive finance companies. Now more than at any time in the past, banks need strategic marketing planning and the legal right to compete. The increase in competition has made the financial services industry a buyer's market in which the customer has a huge selection of highly competent and competitive providers to choose from.

Increased Marketing Expenses

Marketing consciousness sometimes results from budgetary concerns. An organization whose marketing expenses absorb an increasing share of its operating budget is likely to look more closely at its marketing activities. While the typical result might be to cut the marketing budget, a more reasonable response would be to reorganize so that marketing principles are better integrated into the entire operation. However, this is probably the least common path by which a firm becomes marketing conscious.

Stages in the Adoption of the Marketing Concept

Regardless of why or how a company or an industry discovers the need for the marketing concept, the process takes time and involves several stages. These stages can be seen by looking back at the history of bank marketing. In the early 1950s, marketing had not yet dawned on the traditionally conservative banking community. This was the pre-marketing era. (See exhibit 1.7.) Banks operated in a seller's market. Customers needed the basic financial services that banks provided, so banks had no need to develop marketing savvy to sell their services. Bankers waited for customers to come to them. Bank staff were order-takers, not salespeople.

In the late 1950s, competition for savings accounts increased, and some banks took a cue from the consumer goods industries and started using advertising and sales promotion techniques to attract customers and differentiate themselves from the competition. This was the sales promotion stage.

The growing battle for customers taught banks that getting people to come to them was one thing, but keeping them was another. So, bank marketing took on a new dimension—that of trying to make banking more pleasant for the customer. Tellers began to smile, and the bars came off their windows. Banks were remodeled to create a warm and friendly atmosphere. This was the friendly bank stage.

As all of them came to look alike, some banks recognized the need to find new ways of differentiating themselves from their competition. In the late 1960s, many banks responded by recognizing that their customers' changing financial needs called for new and improved services. At this stage, bank credit cards, overdraft credit lines, and other innovative products were developed. This was the product proliferation stage.

Inevitably, the new banking services became widespread; so again, in the 1970s, there was a need for a competitive advantage. Banks began to think less in terms of being all things to all people and more in terms of appealing to specific segments of the market. Some banks established their pricing and designed their services and advertising to appeal heavily to the very well-to-do segment of the population. Others aimed at the 25- to 45-year-old age group. Still others made a special effort to attract senior citizens. Many worked at developing distinct personalities or images for their banks through the use of slogans or mascots. This was the image and positioning stage.

In the 1980s, as strategic business planning became more widely accepted as a management tool, many bankers recognized the importance of applying that tool to the marketing of the bank's services. Bank marketers began developing annual marketing plans, identifying target markets, researching the market's needs, offering products and services to meet those needs, establishing goals, and developing systems for measuring and controlling the plan's progress. They prepared business plans for proposed new products and services. This stage significantly improved the way banks marketed themselves, but it did not go far enough.

At the start of the 1990s, members of the banking industry joined the movement to provide better-quality, customer-oriented services. This movement represented an important stage in the evolution of the marketing concept and gave new meaning to the term *customer orientation*. Banks now focused on "marketing to the individual" and "one-to-one marketing." Some banks are quite involved in implementing these concepts, but many commercial banks are still in the early stages of marketing enlightenment. Some are still in the sales promotion stage.

Several significant legislative and regulatory events that occurred in the early and mid-1990s have enhanced banks' ability to compete. Among the most notable were the Inter-Agency Statement by Bank Regulators on Retail Securities Sales, which took effect in February 1994. This statement allowed banks to offer financial products that are not insured by the Federal Deposit Insurance Corporation (FDIC). The Fair Credit Reporting Act, which took effect in September 1996, authorized banks and their affiliates to centralize customer information. By

Exhibit 1.7 The Evolution of Marketing in the Banking Industry

Key Events in the U.S. Market Environment	Decade	Key Events in Bank Marketing
Brand names appear; Ford unveils Model T; start of hard-sell era in marketing	1900s	Business and industry are principal bank customers; banking operates in a seller's market
First long-distance phone call; United States enters World War I	1910s	Federal Reserve System established
Radio becomes tool for mass communication; first talking movie; stock market crash	1920s	Increased banking regulation
Depression; New Deal initiatives; television invented	1930s	Banking panic and bank "holiday"; bank failures
World War II; pent-up demand fuels economy; first calculation by computer; television flourishes; advertising expenditures skyrocket	1940s	Commercial banks hold 80 percent of industry deposits; thrifts hold 20 percent
Economic growth; emergence of marketing research; suburban sprawl begins; convenience foods; sales promotion era—giveaways, contests, trading stamps; brand image building; public relations becomes popular	1950s	Banks get into advertising, public relations, sales promotion; first bank credit card; thrifts grow quickly
Ecology awareness begins; first satellite TV relay; consumerism begins with auto safety push; Vietnam involvement	1960s	Friendly, personal banking emerges; premium promotions; product innovation: mass credit cards, automated teller machines (ATMs)
Gasoline price escalation; Vietnam pullout	1970s	IRAs introduced; Keogh plans instituted; banks begin positioning and image creation; expansion through branching
Record inflation; recession begins; real estate values decline	1980s	Marketing planning spreads; NOW accounts introduced; pricing becomes more of a concern; account packages proliferate; money market accounts introduced Reg. Q phase out; interstate banking; commercial banks hold 60 percent of industry deposits—thrifts 40 percent; banking industry holds 60 percent of total financial assets—non-banks hold 40 percent; S&L crisis; more than 1,000 banks closed or assisted

Exhibit 1.7, *continued*

Key Events in the U.S. Market Environment	Decade	Key Events in Bank Marketing
Record low interest	1990s	Nonbank financial institutions reach 65 percent share of financial assets; megamergers—consolidation of big banks across state lines; on-line banking gains popularity; introduction of Internet banking; marketing's role gains value and recognition in banks; June 1997 interstate branching takes effect; Sept. 1992 Reg. DD takes effect requiring APY disclosure; advances in deregulation

merging all information at one location, banks are able to segment their markets better. In June 1997, interstate branching legislation took effect, which expands the ability of banks to have a presence across state boundaries. These and other improvements in banks' regulatory environment signal important opportunities for bank marketers to expand banks' market share in the years to come.

If banks are to be successful in the rapidly changing and increasingly competitive era that lies ahead, both individual banks and the banking industry as a whole must adapt quickly to changing environments and adopt the marketing concept as it is defined today. This topic is addressed in chapter 15, which deals with the implementation of bank marketing plans.

The Importance of Market Definition

When a firm adopts the marketing concept, it must redefine its identity. When asked "What business are you in?" a marketing-oriented executive will answer in terms of what needs or wants the firm is satisfying. (See exhibit 1.8.) Although this answer

might seem obvious, it is not. Many businesses define themselves in other than marketing-oriented terms. They choose such terms as *product oriented, production oriented, selling oriented,* and *customer oriented.* Following are examples of four different business definitions.

The Product Orientation

A marketing and management scholar named Theodore Levitt wrote a seminal article related to how businesses define themselves.[8] In "Marketing Myopia," he suggested that the decline of one-time growth industries (such as the railroad industry) was the result of management failure rather than market saturation. The principal failure of management, Levitt wrote, lies in defining a business in terms of current products instead of changing markets. In other words, because consumers' buying habits often change, firms should not define their businesses in terms of products currently being sold to fill consumer needs, but rather in terms of the underlying—and rapidly changing—customer needs that are being met.

For example, the railroads defined themselves as being in the railroad business,

	Exhibit 1.8	**Examples of a Market Definition of the Business, "Which Answers the Question, "What Business Are You In?"**	
Company	**Product-Oriented Answer**	**Marketing-Oriented Answer**	**Advertising Message**
AT&T	We run a telephone company	We meet our customers' need to stay close to people who are far away	"Reach out and touch someone"
GE	We make appliances	We meet our customers' desires for easy and convenient ways to accomplish household tasks	"We bring good things to life"
U.S. Army	We defend the nation's security	We meet the needs of young people for training, education, and experience	"Be all that you can be"

when in fact they were in the transportation business. Consequently, they failed to branch into new business sectors such as air and highway transport and lost their leading edge in the transportation business. A similar problem occurred in the American automobile industry. Automobile manufacturers defined their business in terms of the large, gas-guzzling cars they were accustomed to producing rather than in terms of meeting the changing needs of consumers for personal transportation. Foreign car manufacturers, more in touch with these changing needs, exported smaller, more-efficient cars to the United States. Twenty years later, the American auto industry is still trying to recover.

More recent is the example of IBM, which saw itself as being in the business of providing mainframe computers for businesses. It let other hardware and software companies take over the market for personal computers, which eventually were able to handle much of the work formerly done by mainframe computers, and IBM's market leadership eroded. In the early and mid-1990s, IBM experienced a turnaround. By aggressively refocusing its lines of business and streamlining its staff, IBM is regaining some of the ground it lost in the 1980s.

How does this idea apply to banking? To prosper in a rapidly changing market, banks must see themselves not simply as providers of such traditional banking services as checking, savings, certificates of deposit, loans, and mortgages, but rather as providers of *whatever* financial services are needed by individuals and by businesses and other organizations.

More and more, banks see the need for the market concept. Banking regulations have limited the ability of banks to design products that respond to changing customer needs, though not as much as they once did. The first major change in bank regulations in recent times occurred in the early 1980s. At that time, consumer financial behavior was undergoing more rapid change than it had in decades.

During 1981, interest rates were at an all-time high and money market mutual funds offered by brokerage firms and investment companies grew by $108 billion, largely at the expense of bank certificates of deposit and savings accounts. (Growth in the previous two years had been about $30 billion a year.) That significant increase was a strong signal that financial needs were changing and that consumers were seeking and finding a way to take advantage of the record high interest rates. Banks were not permitted to match the money market funds' product or rates. However, in response to lobbying by the banking industry, the money market deposit account was authorized by the Garn–St Germain Act in December 1982. This groundbreaking product has effectively replaced the old regular savings account for many savers.

The growth during the late 1980s and early 1990s of mutual funds that invest in stocks and bonds has signaled an even greater willingness of consumers to trade some of the safety of their principal for higher interest rates. Banks have been managing mutual fund portfolios since 1987, and, while prohibited from underwriting and distributing such funds, many banks are able to offer customers affiliated mutual funds and the funds of third-party providers. Banks can retain their customers and earn fees by offering these products—deposits and customers they might have lost if they did not offer products with higher rates of return.

The Production Orientation

The production-oriented firm is more concerned with the method used in producing the product than with the product itself, the selling of it, or the needs of the consumer. This orientation channels the firm's energies into achieving greater efficiency. In a production-oriented bank, new products are developed by data processing or systems personnel and designed so that, first and foremost, they work for the bank.

The monthly checking account statement generally indicates the extent to which a customer focus has permeated the computer operations of a bank. A customer-oriented bank designs the statement from the customer's perspective and makes it easy for the customer to read it and to balance his or her account without confusion. A production-oriented bank sees the statement as a required report of the activity in the customer's account deposits, checks cleared, transfers, automated teller transactions, and service charges. It uses banking terminology (such as "debits" and "credits") or obscure abbreviations (such as "chk chg") rather than words that customers would use (such as "reductions," "additions," and "check reorder"). In a production-oriented bank, policies and procedures are likely to result in behavior toward customers that is anything but customer oriented. (See exhibit 1.9.)

The Selling Orientation

Some firms define themselves in terms of their sales efforts (for example, "We sell insurance"). This raises an important issue that warrants further discussion: the difference between a selling orientation and a marketing orientation. Many people confuse the two or think they are related. Traditionally, they have been opposites. A sales-oriented business focuses on making a product or delivering a service, then attempts to sell it. The company's product may meet a customer's needs, but that is not the company's primary focus. In contrast, a marketing-oriented firm does research to find out what customers need or want, and then provides appropriate products and services. Broadly speaking, a sales-oriented firm emphasizes convincing consumers to do what the firm desires; a marketing-oriented firm focuses on doing what the consumer desires. For a detailed discussion of the contrast between selling and marketing and how sales orientation is evolving, turn to chapter 12.

In their progress along the path toward full adoption of the marketing concept, many banks go through a selling-oriented phase. After years of expecting customer service representatives to do nothing more than take customers' orders for new accounts and services, some banks teach their customer service representatives about their products and about sales techniques that are oriented toward finding out customer needs and satisfying them. Both types of knowledge are essential for the customer service job in a marketing-oriented bank. However, many of these banks continue to emphasize increasing the number of new accounts opened rather than identifying and meeting customer needs and wants. They set numerical goals and may even institute an employee incentive program. This often leads to attempts by staff to sell additional banking services to customers who don't need them. (See exhibit 1.10.) Despite its avowed interest in customer-oriented products, the bank's emphasis remains on selling rather than on being of service.

The Customer Orientation

In an organization committed to the marketing concept, the entire organization is oriented toward identifying and meeting customer needs and wants. To continue the sales training example given above, as they are trained in selling skills, customer-service representatives are taught ways to engage customers in conversations that may reveal unmet needs for banking services or opportunities for customers to profit by moving accounts from competing banks. The focus is on understanding the customer and meeting customer needs, not on selling a specific number of services to each customer. Sales performance data may be kept to motivate staff to improve their customer-oriented selling skills, but the numbers are not an end in themselves. The ultimate goal is maximum customer satisfaction. In a bank with a customer-focused approach to selling, the new customer who comes into the bank simply to open a checking account may leave having signed up for other types of accounts and services. However, if that is the case, it is because the customer actually needs and wants them and will receive value from them. The customer also leaves with the name of the person to call when any other financial need arises and with an impression that the bank believes its customers' business is important.

If the ultimate goal is to maximize customer satisfaction, it is essential to understand what it is that customers want from a bank. This new focus on understanding and meeting the needs of each customer has come to be known as one-to-one marketing. Research has shown that customer expectations for quality service can be categorized into five areas: responsiveness, assurance, empathy, reliability, and tangibles.[9]

1. *Responsiveness.* Customers want bank staff to be ready and willing to take care of their needs. They expect prompt and accurate resolution of any errors that might occur. It is interesting that bank customers

do not expect a completely problem-free relationship with a bank. They do, however, expect that any error will be taken care of promptly and professionally, and they expect staff to be accessible or a system to be in place whenever they need service.

2. *Assurance.* Customers expect bank staff to be courteous and competent. They expect to be reassured through bank employees' actions that staff members not only are nice and treat them with respect but are able and willing to help. They want to hear expressions of courtesy, such as "please" and "thank you." They expect bank staff to be considerate of their feelings and sensitive to the privacy of their financial transactions. They want to be treated as though they matter to the bank. Customers often react with surprise and delight when a bank employee, whether a teller or a customer service representative, somehow communicates that the bank is genuinely glad to be of service. Some bank employees treat customers in that fashion because it is their nature to do so. However, many bank employees are not cognizant of how their demeanor appears to customers, and their employers have obviously not required that they treat customers in a way that promotes positive relations between customers and employees. In some banks, the emphasis seems to be on completing transactions with no errors and no deviations from policies rather than on satisfying the customer's emotional and financial needs.

3. *Empathy.* Showing a genuine interest in customers' financial needs and wants is one way to gain their confidence. Apologizing for an inconvenience, acknowledging customers' frustrations, and listening attentively to customers to help find solutions add the "human touch" to each transaction. Attempting to understand and meet the customer's needs in the best way possible is part of following the marketing concept.

4. *Reliability.* Bank staff members must always work to maintain their credibility and dependability. That means completing tasks and requests right the first time. Customers appreciate staff who call when they promise to call, follow up after sending information to see that it arrived, and inform them when they will not be able to carry out a request.

5. *Tangibles.* The most competent, courteous bank staff can fail to satisfy customers if the bank appears disorganized, dirty, or unprofessional. While it may seem to be a less important element, giving a positive first impression through the bank's physical layout is critical in delivering quality service. Automated teller machines (ATMs) must be clean and well lit, brochure racks must be well stocked and tidy. The attention to detail makes a clear and positive impression on customers.

Very few banks give the level of attention to ongoing customer service that is provided by many consumer goods firms. Although many banks have a customer service department that customers can call to get account information and to resolve problems, employees may not be trained to handle dissatisfied customers with the appropriate degree of diplomacy. In a product-oriented bank, the prevailing attitude is that if there is a monetary dispute, the customer is wrong until the bank proves otherwise (except in the case of electronic funds transfers, which are governed by Regulation E, the Federal Reserve regulation that protects consumers using electronic funds transfer systems).

Bank customers, especially in urban areas, dislike waiting in long lines. Some banks use technology to monitor the length of time customers wait in line throughout the day. On the basis of these findings, they modify the manner in which they staff the teller line. One bank uses flextime: half of the tellers report for work at 10 A.M., but they work through the lunch hour so that the maximum number of tellers can be on duty at that peak period. Many banks, however, place the desire of the tellers to eat lunch between 11 A.M. and 1 P.M. ahead of the customers' need to be served quickly during those same hours.

In conclusion, although some individual banks have demonstrated an unusual degree of orientation toward customer needs and wants (see exhibit 1.4), the above observations suggest that the banking industry as a whole lags behind many other industries in adopting the customer focus necessary in a truly marketing-oriented environment.

Summary

Marketing involves the conception, pricing, promotion, and distribution of a product, a service, or an idea. The goal of marketing is to satisfy customer needs and wants and, in the process, to meet the company's objectives as well. Marketing works through exchange processes, in that each party involved in the transaction receives something of value from the other. A market encompasses all potential customers with a particular need or want who might be willing and able to engage in some form of exchange to satisfy that desire.

Marketing requires an ongoing process of planning, executing plans, monitoring their results, and modifying strategies. In other words, marketing is a management process, and the process that can best ensure long-term marketing success is known as the marketing concept. The marketing concept states that an organization's goals for profitability are best met by satisfying customers' needs and wants through an integrated, efficient system and in a socially responsible manner.

Most industries and individual firms discover the truth of this concept and adopt it gradually. The stimulus for marketing enlightenment may come from any number of sources. The principal ones include a decline in sales or market share, slow growth, a change in consumer buying patterns, and increased competition and marketing expense. The evolution of the marketing concept in banking has been stimulated considerably by (1) the loss of market share to nonbank financial institutions, (2) slow growth brought on by changes in consumer buying patterns that banks were unable to respond to due to regulation, and (3) increased competition from other banks and nonbank sources.

A firm that has adopted the marketing concept will define its business in terms of the needs or wants it is satisfying. In other words, it will have a customer orientation. Firms that have not yet reached that level of marketing sophistication may have a product orientation, a selling orientation, or a production orientation. In each of these cases, some objective other than customer satisfaction is the primary guiding force in determining how the business allocates its resources.

Banks are prevented by regulation from responding to some changing financial needs of customers. However, the lack of response by certain banks to customers' stated needs for responsiveness, assurance, empathy, reliability, and tangibles suggests that the industry as a whole is still just beginning to adopt the marketing concept as it has been defined here. Banking, like many other American industries, has taken a short-term focus and made decisions on the basis of their effect on this year's earnings. It takes vision and a leap of faith to believe that long-term success will result from committing to customer- and quality-oriented service, and in recent years more banks have made that leap.

A growing number of banks now provide systems to promptly resolve customer complaints and problems, improve aspects of service quality, train customer-service personnel in methods for dealing effectively with customers, improve the efficiency and reliability of service, or implement procedures for staying in touch with customers and monitoring their changing needs. But not enough have made the major commitment to doing all these things and focusing the whole bank on the customer. As a whole, the industry has been slow to enter the era of enlightened customer-oriented marketing, but it appears to be working hard to put one-to-one marketing in place.

Points for Review

1. Define or briefly explain the following key terms:
   - marketing
   - the market
   - the marketing concept
   - the product
2. Explain each of the four elements in the definition of the marketing concept.
3. What five situations might cause a business to become more marketing conscious?
4. Describe the difference between selling and marketing.
5. What are the five stages through which the banking industry has passed in its growing awareness and understanding of marketing?
6. What is meant by "a market definition of the business"?
7. What are the five elements of service that customers most desire of their banks?
8. What are the differences between businesses that have a product orientation, a production orientation, a selling orientation, and a customer orientation?

Notes

1. *Marketing News,* March 1, 1985, p. 1.
2. Philip Kotler, *Marketing Management: Analysis, Planning, Implementation, and Control,* 7th edition (Englewood Cliffs, N.J.: Prentice-Hall, 1991), p. 8.
3. J. B. McKitterick, *The Frontiers of Marketing Thought* (American Marketing Association, 1957), pp. 71–82.
4. Peter F. Drucker, *Management: Tasks, Responsibilities, Practices* (New York: Harper & Row, 1974), p. 62.
5. Kotler, *Marketing Management,* p. 22.
6. "McRisky," *Business Week,* October 21, 1991, pp. 114–122.
7. "Strange Estimates Yield Dividends for Bank of Boulder Customers," *Bank Marketing Magazine,* August 1996, p. 10.
8. Theodore Levitt, "Marketing Myopia," *Harvard Business Review,* July-August 1960, pp. 45–56.
9. Leonard L. Berry, David R. Bennett, and Carter W. Brown, *Service Quality: A Profit Strategy for Financial Institutions* (Homewood, Ill.: Dow Jones–Irwin, 1989), pp. 26–33. See also the AIB course *Customer Service: Achieving Results in Your Bank* (1996).

Part II

STRATEGIC MARKETING

Everyone has remarked at one time or another, "Everything is changing so fast these days!" Due to advances in communications and the accelerating pace of scientific and technological discoveries, the environment in which we live changes more quickly than ever. This continual change dictates that the marketer be a strategic thinker. *Strategy* was once a term used primarily by the military in tactical planning. But today, as a result of the proliferation of new products and services, marketing has become a battleground where only the strategists survive.

The strategic marketer is a planner who looks at where the company is today, gives careful thought to where it wants to be at some time in the future, and then develops strategies and tactics for getting there. This part of the text presents the basics of marketing planning: why planning is needed and what it entails. It introduces the six-step marketing planning process: (1) situation analysis, (2) objective setting, (3) target market selection, (4) strategy and tactics development, (5) implementation, and (6) evaluation. It then looks more closely at the early stages of that process: conducting a situation analysis and establishing strategic marketing objectives that accurately reflect management's objectives for the future.

2

MARKETING PLANNING: THE BASICS

Learning Objectives

After studying this chapter, you should be able to

- describe the macroenvironmental forces that shape the market for an organization's goods and services,
- give examples of how economic, demographic, social and cultural, political and legal, technological, and natural environments affect bank marketing,
- describe the microenvironmental forces that shape the market for an organization's goods and services,
- describe the customers, producers and suppliers, marketing intermediaries, competitors, publics, and markets that constitute the microenvironment for bank marketers, and
- name two characteristics that differentiate strategic planning from annual planning and budgeting.

Introduction

In any organization, marketing managers work with and within two broad sets of variables: those that relate to the marketing mix and those that relate to the marketing environment. The *marketing mix* variables—product, pricing, promotion, and place (distribution)—are within the control and direction of the organization. The marketing manager selects from among alternative marketing mix strategies on the basis of what the target market needs and wants and the objectives of the organization. (Part IV deals extensively with those marketing mix decisions.)

This planning does not take place in a vacuum. Rather, it occurs in a multifaceted and ever-changing *marketing environment*. That environment, in turn, is affected by two broad groups of external forces over which the organization has little or no control. The first group comprises those forces that make up the *macroenvironment:* demographics, economics, social and cultural factors, political and legal factors, technology, and the natural environment. Organizations have no control over the macroenvironment. The second group comprises the elements that make up an organization's *microenvironment:* its markets, competitors, producers and suppliers, marketing intermediaries, and publics. Organizations have a modicum of control over their microenvironment. While all marketers must deal with these macro- and microenvironmental realities, bank marketers are faced with some unique challenges that are not faced by manufacturers of tangible goods.

In light of the above, it should be apparent that marketing management means managing change, or more specifically, adapting to change that is outside the company's control and initiating change that is within its control. Adapting to change in the macro- and microenvironments is the only viable option open to firms that hope to achieve economic success in a constantly changing world. The effective marketing manager uses the changing environment to make things happen; the mediocre manager lets things happen. The only way to market effectively under such changing circumstances is through a carefully thought-out process of planning along with the ability to remain flexible and open to change.

This chapter reviews some of the major macro- and microenvironmental factors facing bank marketers and shows how dealing with them requires strategic planning. Numerous external forces shape the market for any organization's goods and services. (See exhibit 2.1.) Some of these forces are broadly based—even global—while others are closer to the firm and may be directly affected by it.

The Macroenvironment

The macroenvironmental forces that all marketers, including bank marketers, must cope with are economics; demographics; society and culture; politics; legislation and regulation; technology; and even Mother Nature.

Economic Environment

The business cycle, changing levels of disposable income, inflation, fluctuating interest rates, stock market performance, the rate of unemployment, shortages of raw materials—all of these have a far-reaching influence on markets.

The energy crisis of the 1970s, which arose from shortages of oil and, to a lesser extent, natural gas, provides a vivid example of this concept. The gasoline shortages and resulting high prices of fuel reduced the demand for large automobiles, houses, and recreational vehicles and placed a constraint on long-distance family vacations. These factors, in turn, led to a drop in consumer demand for hotels, motels, restaurants, and other travel-related services. Conversely, sales of many other goods and services got a sudden boost: wood-burning stoves, solar heating systems, warm clothing, passenger rail service, and smaller automobiles. Later,

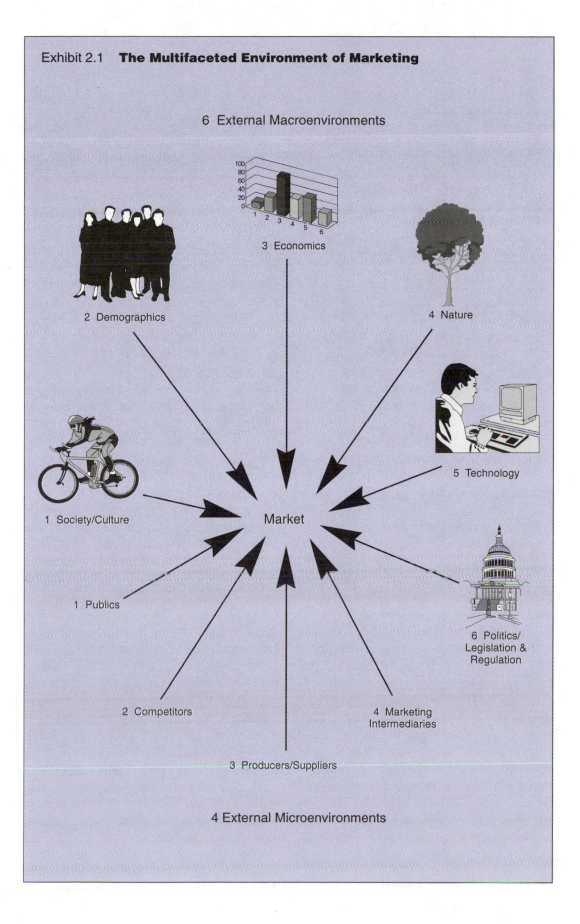

Exhibit 2.1   **The Multifaceted Environment of Marketing**

6 External Macroenvironments

3 Economics

2 Demographics

4 Nature

5 Technology

1 Society/Culture

Market

1 Publics

6 Politics/
Legislation &
Regulation

2 Competitors

4 Marketing
Intermediaries

3 Producers/Suppliers

4 External Microenvironments

when the energy crisis abated, many of the affected markets did not return to their previous levels of consumer demand; buying patterns had changed permanently.

One of the economic variables that bank marketers must deal with daily is the interest rate environment and consumers' short- and long-term expectations concerning the level of interest rates. Banks compete for interest-bearing deposits with alternative investment possibilities, such as the stock and bond market. This combination of external environmental factors—interest rates and competition—creates marketing challenges.

For example, in the early 1990s, interest rates reached lows that had not been seen since the early 1950s. Consumers with maturing certificates of deposit found that the rates at which they would be rolling them over were well below the rates they had been earning. Many consumers, especially those who relied on monthly or quarterly interest checks to supplement their income, were faced with a serious choice: whether to suffer an income reduction by leaving the money in the federally insured certificate or to take some risk and invest in a potentially higher-yielding mutual fund. Many chose mutual funds, and banks found their consumer deposit balances eroding. Some banks responded by making it possible for their customers to achieve their investment goals without leaving the bank. The banks created services that enabled consumers to invest in mutual funds available through the banks' own investment subsidiaries or from third parties. Although the banks lost the deposit funds, they earned fee income for the mutual fund sales, met the customers' needs, and retained their customers. The rationale is that when interest rates improve and customers wish to invest again in bank certificates, the customers will continue to do business with the banks that provided the investment assistance rather than go to competitors.

While low interest rates posed problems for savers, they provided a positive marketing opportunity for banks to attract borrowers. Most banks actively promoted the refinancing of home mortgages. With fixed-rate mortgage rates near 7.5 percent and one-year adjustable-rate mortgages at 5 percent, customers paying 2 or more percentage points over those rates on their existing mortgages could save considerable interest expense and accelerate the build-up of equity in their homes by refinancing. Banks that were especially aggressive in promoting refinancing could hardly keep up with the volume. In addition to generating new income-producing mortgages, banks profited from the points and other fees paid by the refinancing applicants.

A midwestern community bank seized the opportunity provided by low interest rates to develop a creative variation on the refinancing theme. The bank held a one-day sale offering consumers the opportunity to refinance their car loans at single-digit interest rates. In addition to increasing its loan volume, the bank earned noninterest income by selling credit life insurance to the borrowers. It also cross-sold a number of checking and savings accounts with an automatic monthly loan payment option, as well as certificates of deposit. Soon other banks followed suit.

Demographic Environment

Demographics is the science dealing with the vital statistics of populations, and population groups make up markets. Some of the major demographic changes taking place in the United States are the aging of the population, the declining birth rate, the changing makeup of the family, the differing levels of education achieved, the shifting of population from the rustbelt to the sunbelt, and the growing diversity of the population.

One of the demographic factors that banks have had to deal with is the shift in population from the cities to the suburbs. When customers of banks in urban areas first started moving to the suburbs in the 1950s, banks adapted their distribution strategy in order to be able to continue to serve their customers and retain market share. This meant establishing branches in the newly developing areas and, eventually, providing other means of service distribution, such as automated teller machines (ATMs).

Another demographic trend affecting banking is the rising level of education in this country. In 1970, only 10.7 percent of adults were college graduates. Less than 20 years later, this proportion had risen to 21.1 percent. This has resulted in a more financially astute bank customer than in years past. Consequently, banks must train customer-service personnel so they can deal knowledgeably with better-educated customers.

The fact that Americans are now living longer and having fewer children, combined with the aging of the postwar baby-boom generation, is causing considerable growth in the number of adults aged 35 to 65. These people are either in their peak wage-earning years or have accumulated their maximum amount of assets. Many banks have targeted the "seniors" market by, for example, creating special packages of services that include such features as travel discounts, newsletters, and supplementary medical insurance and offering them to their mature customers who maintain sizable savings or certificate balances on deposit. (See exhibit 2.2.)

Whereas a household was once most likely to consist of a husband, wife, and two children, the household of today may consist of a single parent with children or two unmarried individuals of the same or different sex, with or without children. Adults in such households may want to purchase a house jointly or to open joint accounts, which requires bankers to adjust their policies so that they can meet the needs of their customers while safeguarding the soundness of the bank.

Another major demographic trend is the increasing proportion of Hispanics, Asians, and other cultures in the population. As a result, ethnic marketing is growing in importance for banks in metropolitan areas where large concentrations of these ethnic groups live. Banks are hiring multilingual employees, providing telephone customer-service systems that communicate in multiple languages, printing advertising in second languages in minority newspapers and magazines, and making brochures and other bank documents available in multiple languages.

One Chicago bank created a special department to serve the 150,000 Koreans living in that city. It installed a voice-response customer-service system in Korean and designed a savings account based on forced savings plans offered by banks in Korea. Named the Blossom Account because of the Korean regard for flowers, the account is designed so that the customer sets a savings goal and the banker opening the account explains how much money must be contributed regularly to reach it. The product is advertised on Korean cable television, on Korean-language radio, and in Korean-language newspapers.[1] (See exhibit 2.3.)

Social and Cultural Environment

The social and cultural environment in which banks operate includes such factors as changing lifestyles and social values. One recent social development is a concern for reducing the amount of fat and salt in the foods we eat. This concern has led food marketers to expand or modify their product lines. Low-fat and no-fat alternatives for everything from ice cream to hamburgers are now marketed widely, and the sodium content has been reduced in many products—including table salt itself.

Another social trend of which banks are very much aware is the growing need for convenience and for time-saving services. On the retail front, this has led to the growth of catalog companies and cable television home-shopping networks, whose

One bank's response to a demographic phenomenon. Targeting customers over 50 years old is gaining popularity as the baby-boomer generation ages (next page).

Exhibit 2.2

OnePlus50.℠ The Best Deal In Banking, By All Accounts.

OnePlus50 from Texas Commerce puts all your accounts together to help you make more money, save more, and manage your money smarter. And it does all that better than any other program for people age 50 and over. Plus, join by August 31, with a $2,000 opening deposit combined among your OnePlus50 accounts, and you'll receive all of these valuable benefits:

OnePlus50™
Free Checking.
Free First Order of Checks.
Free Traveler's Checks, Money Orders and Cashier's Checks.
Free Special Events and Seminars.
Higher Rates on Savings and CDs.
Lower Rates on Loans and Credit Cards.
Discounts on Travel, Pharmacy, Eye Care and More.
Consolidated Monthly Statement.

Come by Texas Commerce for the best deal in banking – OnePlus50. Just one more way Texas Commerce is working for your success.

510 Park
6363 Phelan

838-0234

Texas Commerce Bank

Working For Your Success.℠

To join OnePlus50, simply open a checking account plus savings or a CD. Member: Texas Commerce Bancshares, Inc., FDIC.

Exhibit 2.3

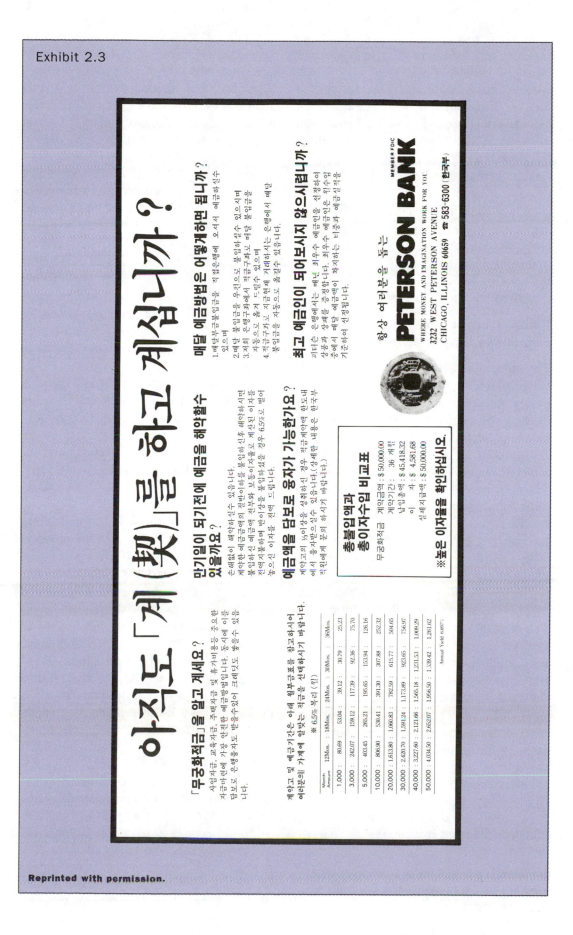

services let customers shop at home and over the phone. Banks are very much aware of their customers' need for convenience. Some institutions have extended their hours of operation to weekends, and virtually all banks provide ATMs. Others have opened branches in supermarkets, as well as superstores such as Wal-Mart, to provide consumers with "one-stop shopping" for all their household and financial needs. An increasing number of banks take consumer loan applications over the phone and offer 24-hour telephone banking and PC banking so customers can get information about their accounts around the clock.

Political, Legal, and Regulatory Environment

The political and legal (or regulatory) environment refers to the way in which public policy affects markets. The government exerts a certain amount of influence on business to protect consumers, natural resources, the economy, and other entities from various kinds of harm. For example, the Federal Trade Commission (FTC), the Food and Drug Administration (FDA), the Civil Aeronautics Board (CAB), and the Securities and Exchange Commission (SEC) regularly issue rules that organizations in the private sector must follow.

Numerous agencies regulate the financial services industry. (See exhibit 2.4.) The rules laid down by regulators frequently discourage, limit, or eliminate certain bank product, pricing, promotion, or distribution alternatives. These regulations and the slow pace of deregulation have limited banks' ability to compete in the changing market for financial services. Until the early 1980s, regulations placed a ceiling on the interest rate that banks could pay on savings accounts, and banks had no discretion over the pricing or product design of their certificate of deposit offerings. This situation changed in 1980 when Congress

Marketing in a unique cultural environment can require a bank to be flexible and able to use foreign languages (previous page).

passed the Depository Institutions Deregulation and Monetary Control Act (DIDMCA), but not before banks had lost hundreds of millions of dollars of deposits to the unregulated money market mutual funds, whose interest rates were free to float with general market rates.

One result of DIDMCA was that banks were allowed to offer interest-bearing negotiable order of withdrawal (NOW) accounts, which allowed them to compete with the money market funds. DIDMCA also phased out Regulation Q, which limited the interest banks could pay on deposits. By offering NOW accounts in the 1980s and interest-bearing checking accounts and access to mutual funds in the 1990s, bank have kept customers they might have lost to nonbank competitors.

The Glass-Steagall Act of 1933, which was passed in the wake of the stock market crash and the ensuing Great Depression, prevents banks from competing on an equal footing with mutual funds and brokerage houses for investors' deposits. Bank lobbyists are working to have the Glass-Steagall Act repealed.

Two contemporary pieces of legislation that affect the distribution of bank products are the Community Reinvestment Act (CRA) and the Americans with Disabilities Act (ADA). The CRA has been mentioned already as an important stimulus to banks to make loans available to individuals of all income levels. Among other requirements, the ADA is causing banks to modify ATM installations so they can be reached from a wheelchair, to install high-contrast signs that can be read more easily by the visually impaired, and to make their telephone-based customer-service systems accessible to the hearing impaired.

In addition to its effect on banking's product, pricing, and distribution strategies, regulation affects a bank's advertising practices. Truth-in-Lending and Truth-in-Savings regulations affect the way banks advertise their products. In an effort to protect consumers from misleading advertising, these regulations establish rules for the way interest rates must be computed, presented, and explained. For instance, a loan ad that mentions any one of several items—a down payment amount, a statement of the payment period, a monthly payment amount, or the amount of the finance charge—triggers the need for additional Regulation Z disclosures. The ad must also show the down payment in dollars, the repayment terms, and the annual percentage rate. (See exhibit 2.5.)

The regulatory limits on banking are gradually lessening, creating new challenges for bank marketers. Interstate banking facilitated through bank holding companies is requiring marketers to adjust to broader and more diverse geographical markets. Banks are now able to provide consumers with a broadening range of financial services, such as mutual funds and insurance. However, as barriers to offering these services also fall, bank marketers will face expanding their product lines and competing, with no prior experience, with organizations that have been in those businesses for many years. The changes due to deregula-

tion are, indeed, the most important macro-environmental issues that bank marketers will encounter in the years ahead.

Technological Environment

The technological environment is a product of the wealth of technical knowledge and advances in our society. Genetic mapping, space and oceanographic exploration, fiber optics, and personal communication systems are a few positive examples. The reduction of privacy and the creation of such harmful by-products as air, water, and outer-space pollution are also part of the technological environment. The fruits of technology, whether constructive or potentially destructive, have significantly shaped our country. A high rate of personal consumption, a respect for higher education, the desire for excellence in all fields, and government support of basic research have all contributed to the rapidly changing technological environment in the United States.

Technology has given consumers a greater number of choices in the way they access

Exhibit 2.5

Our Home Equity options can be explained in one word:

Better.

Key Bank's Free and Easy home equity offer is back – and better than ever. It's still free, with no closing costs* if you apply by April 30, 1993. And easy, at the lowest rates in 20 years.

And now we're giving you *three* options to choose from: a Variable Rate Prime + 0 Line, a secure 3-Year "Fixed Rate" Line and a lump sum Fixed Rate Loan.

Absolutely no closing costs make this offer Free and Easy.

We're waiving all closing costs on lines and loans from $20,000 to $100,000. There are no application fees. No points. We even pay the NYS mortgage tax. With lines or loans below $20,000, you still pay no closing costs except the mandatory NYS mortgage tax. For lines or loans over $100,000, you only pay title insurance.

With our flexible payment plans, we'll help you get a repayment schedule you're comfortable with. For example, a line of credit offers convenient check access for up to 20 years, with up to 15 more years to repay. And your interest may be fully deductible (consult your tax advisor).

So get your Key Bank Home Equity Application Kit now and choose the options that can work *better* for you.

Monthly Variable Rate Line Prime + 0 for one year.

~~7.75%~~ APR Prime + 1.75%   6.00% APR Prime + 0%

Now is a great time to take advantage of this very special variable rate line. You'll only pay the Prime Rate for the first year your line is open (6.00% APR as of February 1, 1993). After that, your rate will go to a competitive Prime + 1.75% (7.75% APR as of February 1, 1993) and will never exceed 15.90% APR.

3-Year "Fixed Rate" Line.

8.50% APR   Get the benefits of our regular home equity line *plus* the security of a rate that remains fixed for 3-year periods for the life of the account. The rate may be adjusted only once at the end of each 3-year period and the maximum rate will never exceed 17.90% APR. The APR as of February 1, 1993 was 8.50%.

Fixed Rate Home Equity Loan.

Our Home Equity Loan offers you the security of a fixed rate and flexible payment options that can give you up to 15 years to repay. You get the convenience of a fixed monthly payment and the peace of mind that comes with knowing your interest rate will never increase.

8.95% APR Up to five year term

To get your FREE Home Equity Application Kit: a) return this coupon; b) stop by any Key Bank branch; or c) call toll-free: 1-800-8ANSWER.

☐ Yes. Please send me a Key Bank Home Equity Application Kit.

Send to: Key Express, P.O. Box 708, Buffalo, NY, 14240-0708.

NAME

ADDRESS

CITY   STATE   ZIP

KEY BANK
America's neighborhood bank.℠   BFB

(Enlarged footnote)
*Provided you maintain your line or loan for at least 3 years; should your line or loan terminate for any reason during that time, you will repay us the third party fees we incurred to open your plan. For credit limits between $20,000 and $100,000, these fees can range from $315 to $1,180. For lines and loans between $7,500 and $20,000, the mortgage tax ranges from $37.50 to $125; and on early termination, additional fees range from $252.50 to $580. For lines or loans over $100,000 to $2,000,000, title fees can range from $563.03 to $6,262.50; and on early termination, additional fees range from $715 to $15,380. Normally, we don't require new surveys for Home Equity lines and loans, but if one is required to resolve questions of title to the property securing the line or loan or flood hazard zone questions, then you must pay for the survey. Hazard insurance must also be carried on the property securing the line or loan. Offer available to new Home Equity customers only. The Key Bank logo is registered trademark of KeyCorp. Member FDIC.

Reprinted with permission.

their banking services. Automated teller machines enable customers not only to get cash, make deposits, and inquire about their account balances, but also to cash checks, obtain an account statement, and move funds among deposit and investment accounts. Point-of-sale terminals in stores allow consumers to pay for purchases and, at supermarkets, to get cash. The proliferation of personal computers both in the home and in business has stimulated banks to create new product and distribution strategies, and the rapidly growing popularity of the Internet and the World Wide Web has added a new dimension to banking and marketing. Through their personal computers, via modem connection or the Internet, consumers and businesses can access information about their accounts, initiate transfers between accounts, wire funds out of the bank, and pay bills. Technological advances have enabled banks to automate the teller workstation, streamlining customer service by eliminating the need to phone to obtain a customer's balance and to determine whether a hold must be placed on a customer's check. Automation in many banks is reducing the amount of paperwork involved in setting up a new account or changing addresses on existing accounts.

Technology is also helping some banks reduce the problems of returning canceled checks to customers. Through a process called image processing, banks can provide customers with up to 24 miniature images of checks per statement page. This cuts postage and processing costs for the bank, but the emphasis is on the customer's convenience: the customer has no more need to store shoe boxes full of checks, yet still has proof of payment.

Enhancements to computer programs that produce checking statements have enabled at least one bank to let its customers choose from three statement options: a chronological statement that lists transactions by date; a category statement that divides transactions into categories, such as deposits and withdrawals; or a summary statement that lists all activity in a summary format. The bank that makes these options available recognizes that while all customers need clear and understandable communications, what constitutes clear and understandable may vary from one individual to another.

In addition to affecting banking products and their distribution, technological advances can also affect the way a bank promotes its products. Many banks today are creating Web sites that contain information on products, services, rates, and even the history of the bank and its city or town. Web sites allow customers to search for the information they need 24 hours a day. Some sites are linked to an E-mail system to allow customers to send requests or fill out applications on-line. Some banks place in their lobbies terminals with touch screens. Customers who are comfortable interacting with computers use these terminals to inquire about the bank's services and to initiate the process of opening accounts.

The Natural Environment

In an era when air and water pollution, global warming, and other ecological concerns are becoming more widespread, all businesses must pay special attention to the environmental effects of their marketing efforts. As a service industry, banking only marginally adds to pollution, principally through the volume of paper that is used and disposed of in its daily operations. Many banks use recycled paper for printing their brochures and other information, and they recycle the paper trash that they generate. Banks also offer debit cards, which help save paper because there is no check writing. Smart cards also help save paper. Some banks support local organizations dedicated to environmental issues.

The natural environment is capable of creating situations—natural disasters—to which bank marketers must respond. In the fall of 1992, Hurricane Andrew devastated parts of south Florida, leaving thousands

The footnote in this ad contains disclosures required by Regulation Z (left).

homeless and destroying a number of banking offices. Customers needed access to their cash to pay for much-needed food, clothing, and temporary shelter. Individuals and businesses needed access to credit to begin rebuilding. Consumers also needed a safe place to deposit the proceeds of their insurance claims. Banks quickly devised new service-distribution techniques, setting up makeshift check-cashing facilities in modular buildings, mobile homes, or mobile banking vans for residents short of cash.[2] Their prompt response was made possible by compliance with the regulation that requires banks to have written disaster-recovery plans.

The marketer has no control over the macroenvironmental forces that continually change target markets. However, the marketer has a modicum of control over the microenvironmental forces affecting the market. Banks' speedy responses to the Red River floods in the winter and spring of 1997 also showed how banks can set up emergency assistance and funding operations. (See Case Study G.)

The Microenvironment

The microenvironment is external to the marketing organization but is related to its marketing efforts. The principal microenvironmental factors are the firm's customers, producers and suppliers, marketing intermediaries, competitors, and publics.

Customers

The market in which an organization operates, or the set of all its actual and potential customers, is affected by macro- and microenvironmental factors, as well as being a changing microenvironmental entity in itself. Banks have many types of customer groups. First are the consumers, the individuals and households that require banking products. Next are the business and institutional customers, for whom credit services are especially important for bridging gaps in the flow of cash into and out of the organization and

for financing expansion. The government market is made up of state, city, or municipal governments and such entities as sewer and water departments and housing authorities. Some banks operate in international markets, providing services to domestic customers doing business in foreign markets as well as to foreign customers. Trust customers constitute another market for banks that provide financial management and estate planning services. All of these customers and markets are affected by macroenvironmental factors and by their own set of microenvironmental forces. Thus, the market, as shown in exhibit 2.1, constantly changes in response to developments in its external environment as well as to changes intrinsic to the market itself.

Producers and Suppliers

Most marketing organizations depend on other producers or suppliers for raw materials and for services they need to produce and deliver their product. The cereal manufacturer depends on the grain farmer, the sugar processor, the packaging manufacturer, and the shipper. It must also obtain a labor force, electricity and other utilities, equipment, and other elements of production.

Although it is a service industry rather than a manufacturing industry, banking also has suppliers and vendors on whom it depends for accomplishing its objectives. Firms that enable banks to provide their customers with mutual funds, annuities, and brokerage services are suppliers to the banking industry. The printers who provide customers with their checks are suppliers, and bankers rely on them to fill customer orders promptly, accurately, and at a reasonable cost. In recent years, as a cost-cutting and efficiency measure, some banks have begun to outsource some of their back-office operations. The firms that take over these operations become extremely important to the banks because so much of what a bank does for its customers depends on these essential services.

Uncontrollable events that affect a firm's suppliers can seriously affect marketing management. For instance, shortages of raw materials can raise the producer's costs, which are then passed on to the consumer in the form of higher prices. Problems in labor and management relations can also affect product quality.

In most industries, marketing managers do not have to concern themselves much with the production and supply side of the business. Their efforts are focused on creating and meeting market demand for the product. This is one respect in which banking is very different from other businesses. Bank marketers must be doubly marketing oriented. They must use marketing techniques to acquire both the sources of raw material (depositors) and the users of the raw material (borrowers). The bank must implement a marketing strategy for each source market and each use market. This process is illustrated in exhibit 2.6.

Marketing Intermediaries

Marketing intermediaries are firms that assist in promoting, selling, and distributing products to consumers. The cereal manufacturer, for instance, might use such middlemen as brokers, manufacturers' representatives, wholesalers, and retailers. Product manufacturers also employ such firms as warehouse and transportation companies to distribute their products. Banking, however, is a service industry— its products are intangible. Therefore, bank marketers do not deal with traditional types of intermediaries. Rather, marketing intermediaries in the banking business are such organizations as credit card companies,

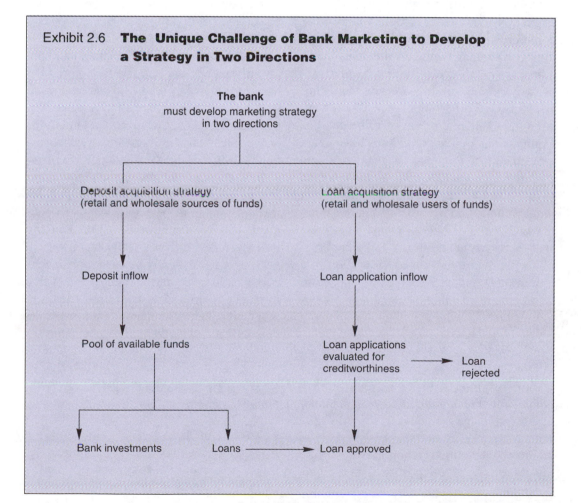

Exhibit 2.6   **The Unique Challenge of Bank Marketing to Develop a Strategy in Two Directions**

The bank
must develop marketing strategy
in two directions

Deposit acquisition strategy
(retail and wholesale sources of funds)

Loan acquisition strategy
(retail and wholesale users of funds)

Deposit inflow

Loan application inflow

Pool of available funds

Loan applications
evaluated for
creditworthiness → Loan rejected

Bank investments   Loans ⟶ Loan approved

operators of networks of automated teller machines, and the automated clearinghouse system. These intermediaries facilitate the delivery of a bank's credit and deposit services to its customers.

Competitors

The marketing manager must always keep a wary eye on competitors and formulate a strategy for responding to changes in the market. Competition occurs when two or more entities seek a similar result—for example, when students apply for a limited number of openings in medical school, political candidates seek the same public office, or firms seek a larger share of a defined market.

Banks that understand they are in the business of meeting financial service needs define the competition differently than do banks with a more myopic view. The latter might consider their competition to be other commercial banks, savings and loans, savings banks, and credit unions. But many nonbanking firms also hold consumer deposits, extend credit, provide checking accounts, and offer other services that were once the exclusive province of banks. For example, insurance companies have chartered banks so they can issue savings certificates and credit cards, and brokerage firms offer check-writing privileges on mutual funds that are invested in the stock market. With this kind of competitive pressure on banks, in addition to mitigating regulatory constraints, the need to adopt the marketing concept becomes all the more imperative.

Publics

In the business of pursuing its marketing objectives, an organization must be aware of and responsive to its various publics and to how these publics view it. A public is a group of people having something in common, and, as the word is used here, what they have in common may affect the ability of an organization to pursue its objectives.

A bank has both internal and external publics to consider. Its external publics include its stockholders and the investment community, especially bank stock analysts who are in a position to recommend the stock. Another public is the media—the newspapers and television and radio stations that serve its market and whose reporting on the bank can affect the way it is perceived by the general public. State and local government officials are a public with whom the bank must maintain good relations. Community action groups have become an increasingly important public since the passage of the Community Reinvestment Act. Acting as watchdogs for their minority interest groups, they call to the attention of the regulators and the media a bank's activities that are contrary to their interests. Finally, there is the general public in the area served by the bank, whose awareness and impression of the bank are related to its ability to attract new customers.

The bank's internal publics are its employees and directors. Their view of and attitude toward the bank can affect, either for good or for ill, the way they deal with customers and with one another. It is critical that a bank manage its communications and relations with all its publics in its efforts to establish a favorable image and to promote goodwill.

In an environment characterized by change and uncertainty, and with so many changes taking place in the external macroenvironments and microenvironments, the banking business is very different today than it was 10 years ago. It will surely be even more different in another 10 years. To survive in such a turbulent environment, banks must learn to adapt to considerable change. Planning is the process that enables them to cope with this situation.

Stages of Bank Planning Development

The focus of this section is on *strategic marketing planning*. But what is meant by this term, and how does strategic marketing planning differ from its alternatives?

Just as there are various stages of development of marketing awareness in the business world, there are stages in the level of sophistication in the planning effort. For instance, a bank might prepare for the upcoming calendar year a budget that projects each category of deposits and loans as well as each type of income and expense. The overall budget is the composite of the detailed budgets of each of the operating divisions of the bank. This type of budget-oriented planning is usually based on past trends and expectations about the level of interest rates in the upcoming year. But budgets do not qualify as plans in the sense used in this text. Banks whose planning is limited to budgeting are in an immature stage of planning.

Many institutions have implemented an annual planning process in which broad goals are set by senior management or by the directors. The various departments then establish plans to help achieve those goals. Kotler has called this process "goals-down, plans-up" planning.[3] It usually takes place in the late summer or early fall to allow time for the resulting budgets to be consolidated and adjusted as needed. Preliminary budgets are rarely accepted without modification because the expense side of the departments reflects the strategies that department heads would pursue in the ideal situation. These budgets may need to be trimmed and priorities may have to be adjusted to arrive at a total budget that accomplishes the organization's profit objectives.

Such annual planning is quite useful, but it addresses only short-range considerations. It also assumes continuation of the business along the same lines as those being currently pursued.

Many banks have graduated beyond the annual "goals-down, plans-up" stage and are engaged in strategic planning. Generally speaking, strategic planning has two unique characteristics:

1. *Emphasis on long-term goal setting.* The bank openly addresses the question, "What do we want to accomplish in the next five or more years?" While annual planning concentrates on the bank's business as it is, strategic planning looks at the business the bank is in and at other businesses in which it might operate. Then it considers which it should enter, grow, harvest, or exit. For example, a retail-oriented regional bank may decide, based on analysis of several possible alternatives, that it wants to strengthen its position as a corporate banking institution in its trade area. A money center bank may conclude that its current market cannot grow at a sufficient rate to ensure long-run profitability in the credit card area. Consequently, it might decide that in five years it wants to be generating 75 percent of its credit card business from residents of other states. Or, a regional bank might determine that the cost of being in the retail banking business does not provide a rate of return consistent with corporate objectives and decide to exit that area of its operation.

2. *Responsiveness to problems and opportunities generated by the changing environment.* Recognizing that the marketing environment constantly changes, the bank develops a five-year plan that it updates every year. In 1995, the five-year plan that includes 1999 is updated to take 2000 into account, and so on. This process forces the bank to review its current situation annually and to plan on a consistent and continual basis.

Strategic Marketing Planning

Armed with the mission and objectives set forth in the long-range plan for the organization, the marketing manager applies the steps in the strategic planning process to a marketing plan that encompasses each of the bank's markets. While the corporate plan identifies those businesses that the bank wants to enter, grow, harvest, or exit, the marketing plan sets forth the specific marketing strategies and tactics that will achieve those objectives. The stages in that process are discussed in the following chapter.

Summary

Marketing managers deal with two broad sets of variables: those that relate to the marketing mix and those that relate to the marketing environment. The marketing mix variables are product, price, promotion, and place (distribution). The marketing environment has two components: the macroenvironment and the microenvironment. Both of them pose numerous challenges to the marketing manager.

Macroenvironmental factors include demographics, economics, social and cultural factors, political and legal considerations, technology, and the natural environment—forces over which the marketing manager has no control. Microenvironmental factors, which are external to the marketing organization but which can be controlled to some degree, are producers and suppliers, marketing intermediaries, competitors, publics, and the market itself.

These and other factors contribute to a turbulent marketing environment and to constantly changing markets. To survive and prosper in the face of this turbulence and change, a firm must implement strategic planning. Strategic planning differs from other approaches in that it takes a long-range, exploratory view. It examines not only where the organization is, but also where it wants to be several years hence. The marketing manager then assembles the tools needed for strategic marketing planning and applies them toward the projected corporate objectives.

Points for Review

1. What is the difference between the macroenvironment and the microenvironment in which banks operate?
2. Give an example of each of the six types of macroenvironmental forces that affect the banking industry.
3. Who or what entities constitute the microenvironment for a bank? Give an example of each.
4. Indicate which elements of the marketing mix are affected by banking regulation and explain how such regulation limits banking's ability to respond to changing consumer needs and wants.
5. How does strategic planning differ from an annual planning and budgeting process?

Notes

1. "'Ethnic Marketing': A New Discipline Is Defined as Banks Zero In on Hispanic and Asian Americans," *Marketing Update* (Bank Marketing Association), January 1991, p. 12.
2. *American Banker,* September 1, 1992, p. 2.
3. Philip Kotler, *Marketing Management: Analysis, Planning, and Control,* 5th edition (Englewood Cliffs, N.J.: Prentice-Hall, 1984), p. 278.

3

THE STRATEGIC MARKETING PROCESS

Learning Objectives

After studying this chapter, you should be able to

- describe the process of management and, more specifically, the marketing management process,
- explain the marketing task of controlling marketing demand,
- explain the key difference between the marketing planning process and a marketing plan,
- describe the four steps involved in developing a marketing plan, and explain the reason for evaluating the results of a marketing plan,
- respond to some of the most common arguments against planning, and
- list five prerequisites for planning.

Introduction

Strategic marketing is a management process that involves the development of marketing plans, their careful implementation, evaluation of their results, and then the adjustment and fine-tuning of the entire package. It takes marketing beyond completing a product promotion campaign and creates a long-term business position and philosophy. The process begins with the critically important task of marketing planning, a discipline that consists of four key steps. These steps answer the following questions: (1) Where are we now? (2) Where do we want to go? and (3) How are we going to get there? Evaluating the results of the plan's implementation poses the final question: (4) How will we know when we have arrived?

This chapter introduces the marketing management process and each step that occurs in the planning stages. Since planning is so important to the marketer, the chapter concludes with a discussion of the necessity of the planning process, the most common objections to planning, and the prerequisites for a successful planning process.

The Marketing Management Process

All the employees of a bank are involved in marketing, whether they are conscious of it or not. Marketing takes place every time a customer contacts the bank. Even employees who never have direct contact with a customer can affect service to a customer through the quality of their service to their colleagues. Therefore, the trick to making the most of these marketing opportunities is for everyone in the bank to prepare for them in advance. To plan and prepare for marketing opportunities, the bank should implement a marketing management process.

Before discussing the marketing management process further, some key terms must be understood. Chapter 1 established that marketing is an activity directed at satisfying needs and wants through exchange processes. But what is management?

What Is Management?

For the purposes of this text, management is "the process of planning, implementing, and evaluating the efforts of a group of people toward a common goal."[1] Planning is that part of the management process that attempts to control the organization's future situation. It includes all of the activities that lead to the definition of goals and the determination of the appropriate means to achieve them.

Most people have been involved in the process of managing at one time or another, such as organizing the family for a week's vacation, planning a surprise party for a friend, or overseeing the operation of a bank branch. The three fundamental steps of managing—planning, implementing, and evaluating—were most likely involved. If the first two steps are completed but the results are not evaluated, the management job is incomplete. The evaluation step is critical for learning from the management experience and can improve the performance of similar tasks in the future.

Exhibit 3.1 illustrates the management process. The circle represents the process of planning, implementing the plan, and evaluating the results. It applies to managers of all functions—finance, operations, sales—as well as to marketing managers.

The management process is shown as a circular flow because managing should be dynamic and ongoing. Developing the marketing plan is not a one-time event, and the plan should not be cast in concrete once it is prepared. At any point during implementation and evaluation, unforeseen circumstances may require modification of the plan or the timetable for phasing it in. Specific marketing strategies may not function as originally intended. For example, a major change in the marketing environment might affect consumer demand for the product or service being marketed. The

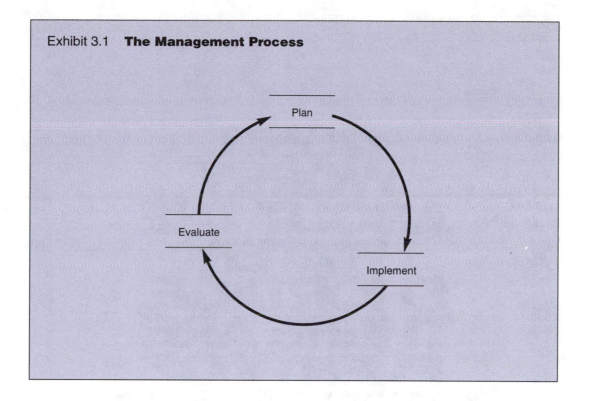

Exhibit 3.1 **The Management Process**

Plan

Implement

Evaluate

flexibility to change, modify, adapt, and fine-tune must be built into the process.

What Is Marketing Management?

Marketing management is "the marketing concept in action."[2] It involves planning, implementing, and evaluating activities aimed at meeting the objective of customer satisfaction at a profitable volume, carried out in an integrated framework and in a socially responsible manner. Philip Kotler's formal definition of marketing management takes it a step further:

> Marketing management is the analysis, planning, implementation, and control of programs designed to create, build, and maintain mutually beneficial exchanges and relationships with target markets.[3]

The Task of Marketing Management

What task is marketing management attempting to accomplish through the process of analysis, planning, implementation, and

control? Essentially, the goal is control of market demand. The term *control* is used instead of *increase* because the concept often goes beyond attempts to increase demand; marketing must sometimes decrease demand. This situation is referred to as *demarketing*. For example, electric utilities use marketing strategies to convince people to consume less energy. Water companies use marketing strategies to convince people to conserve water. (See exhibit 3.2.) Cruise lines use marketing strategies (especially pricing strategies) to shift demand to off-peak seasons. When the supply of money is limited, banks reduce the demand for loans by raising their interest rates. In doing this, they are regulating the timing of demand.

At other times, marketing management might want to counteract demand. For example, the American Lung Association tries to persuade cigarette smokers to stop smoking, and the Partnership for a Drug-Free America attempts to keep people from experimenting with drugs.

Marketing management, then, like all management, is a planning/implementing/

Exhibit 3.2

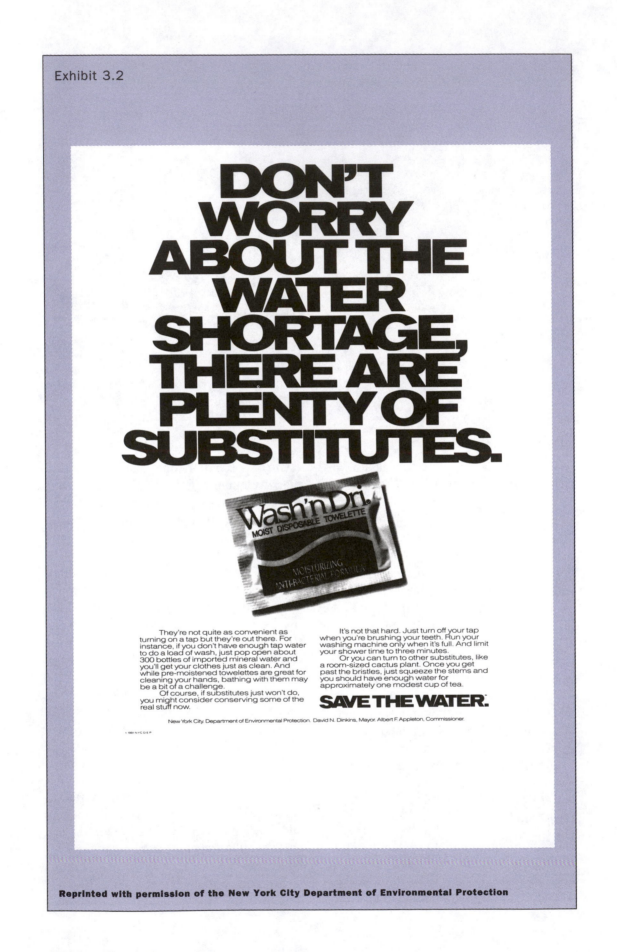

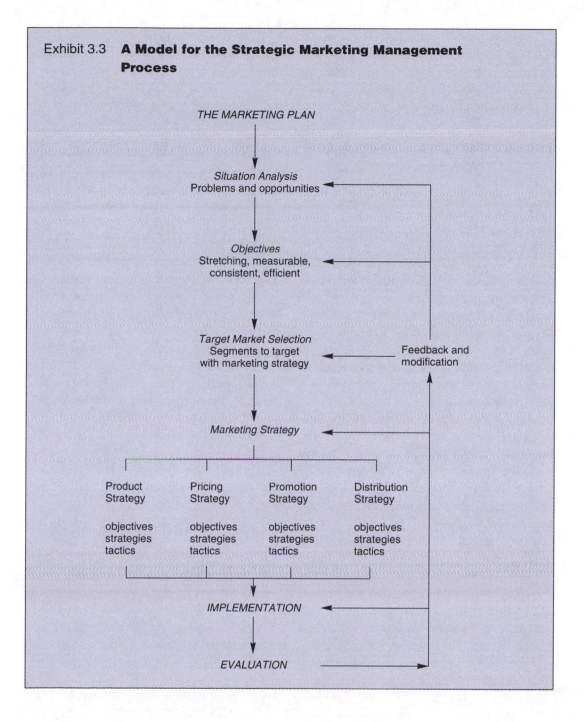

Exhibit 3.3 A Model for the Strategic Marketing Management Process

THE MARKETING PLAN

↓

Situation Analysis
Problems and opportunities

↓

Objectives
Stretching, measurable,
consistent, efficient

↓

Target Market Selection
Segments to target
with marketing strategy

Feedback and
modification

↓

Marketing Strategy

Product Strategy	Pricing Strategy	Promotion Strategy	Distribution Strategy
objectives	objectives	objectives	objectives
strategies	strategies	strategies	strategies
tactics	tactics	tactics	tactics

↓

IMPLEMENTATION

↓

EVALUATION

evaluating process. Exhibit 3.3 presents the model for the strategic marketing management process. The planning stage is a detailed process in itself, and developing a marketing plan requires four key steps:

- situation analysis,
- objective setting,
- target market selection, and
- strategy formulation.

This ad illustrates demarketing, which encourages customers to use less of a product or service (left).

The remainder of this chapter describes the elements of the marketing planning process and then expands on the implementation and evaluation stages involved in the strategic marketing management process.

The Marketing Planning Process

As mentioned above, planning is that part of the management process that attempts to control the organization's future situation by defining the appropriate goals and determining the most effective means to achieve them. It is critical for the marketing student to understand and recognize the importance of the planning process.

There is an important, albeit subtle, distinction between marketing planning and a marketing plan. Marketing planning is an ongoing process, whereas a marketing plan is the output of the planning process for a particular period—it is a document. Put another way, marketing planning involves devising the strategy for carrying out the business's goals and the marketing plan describes the specific tactics and time frames those strategies will require. (For more on goals, objectives, strategies, and tactics, turn to Chapter 5.)

Former president Dwight D. Eisenhower is reputed to have said, "Plans are nothing; planning is everything." In other words, it is the discipline of going through the process of creating, implementing, and evaluating a plan that is important—not the creation of a plan document.

Why is marketing planning so important? As an old adage says, "If you don't know where you're going, any road will take you there." What's more, "marketing research, advertising, and salespeople cannot work effectively for you unless they're asking the right questions, responding properly to the forces at work in the marketplace, and doing those things that are the most important to the owners and managers of your bank. And a marketing plan ensures the right questions are being asked."[4]

A great deal of energy is expended fulfilling the basic purpose of most organizations. Many people work 40 hours a week, or more. Resources are depleted and much expense is incurred carrying out routine activities. But without direction—an objective—this effort is likely to be less effective than it otherwise could be. At the same time, the effort a business exerts cannot be measured against some nebulous external standard because the structure and needs of various firms are unique. Consider, for example, the community bank that hired a new business development officer. In her first year, she increased loan volume by 35 percent, although a 10 percent increase had been considered an acceptable objective by the bank's management. Obviously, this bank had not developed a realistic marketing plan. Consequently, its loan volume before the arrival of the new loan officer was far lower than it should have been. The bank may have failed to answer the four essential marketing planning questions: (1) Where are we now? (2) Where do we want to go? (3) How are we going to get there? and (4) How will we know when we have arrived? The systematic answering of these four questions constitutes the process of planning.

Conducting the Situation Analysis

Before it is possible to set meaningful organizational and marketing objectives, a bank must go through a detailed self-examination in which data concerning the bank and its environment—past and present—are collected, summarized, and carefully evaluated. The bank must first answer the question, "Where are we now?" The situation analysis answers this question and involves

• gathering historical trend data on the bank and its competition,

• reviewing the markets and market segments in which the bank operates or would like to operate, and

• evaluating the external factors influencing the bank's markets (macroenvironmental factors—economic; demographic; social and cultural; political, legal and regulatory; technological; and natural—and microenvironmental factors, especially competition) in terms of their implications for the bank.

Not surprisingly, a situation analysis must be based on research. The conclusions reached about those forces affecting the market and the bank must be grounded in solid data. Collecting this type of information about the bank, its competition, the market, and the environmental forces affecting it is called marketing research.

The end product of the situation analysis is a summary of the bank's strengths and weaknesses. Armed with this type of information, the bank's management can make educated decisions that are in line with the bank's objectives. (The situation analysis is treated in greater detail in chapter 4.)

Setting Marketing Objectives

Once the bank has established where it is, the next question that must be answered is "Where do we want to go?" Evaluating the situation analysis provides the basis for developing marketing objectives, which are written statements detailing what the organization would like to accomplish within a specific period. Marketing objectives should have the following characteristics:

• They should help the bank strive to achieve excellence, yet be realistic and attainable.

• They should be measurable, regardless of whether the specific objective relates to something quantitative (for example, the volume of demand deposits) or qualitative (for example, awareness of the bank among the target audience). In the former case, a measurable objective might be to increase demand deposits by $12 million over the course of the year. Setting measurable objectives with regard to qualitative outcomes, however, is more difficult and requires the use of marketing research. To continue with the example above, the objective might be to increase unaided awareness of the bank among the target audience from 30 percent to 60 percent in one year. One marketing research survey would be required to determine the pre-planning level of awareness and to set the objective, and a second survey would be needed to measure whether the objective had been attained.

• They should be consistent with one another. For example, an objective to increase market share for checking accounts might not be consistent with an objective to increase fee income (which probably entails increasing service charges and fees on checking accounts).

• They should relate to the bank's strategic objectives. For instance, if a strategic objective is to achieve a 30 percent penetration of market-area households, a marketing objective might be to add two new branches in growth areas. Or the objective might be to increase awareness of the bank by some amount or to add to the number of personal transaction accounts by some percentage. Any one of the bank's overall objectives may translate into a number of marketing objectives.

Selecting the Target Market

Most firms, including banks, generally aim their marketing strategies at more than one target market at a time. To do so, they employ a variety of marketing mixes. For example, General Motors attempts to attract one sector of the automobile market with its Cadillac Seville, another with its Chevrolet Corvette, and a third with its Pontiac Le Mans. Similarly, a bank might have different but simultaneous marketing programs to attract senior citizens who want safe places to deposit their savings, college students seeking educational loans, newcomers to the community who need to open checking and savings accounts, and executives who require large lines of credit and highly personalized services.

Today's marketing customer information files (MCIF) systems allow banks to sort and select target markets in an infinite variety of ways. With an MCIF, it is possible to add information from outside sources and combine them with internal information on existing customers to create an even more comprehensive customer information file. That information can then be refined and sorted according to the needs of the marketing objectives.

Through situation analysis, the bank analyzes its customer base and compares it with the market at large. A bank might learn, for instance, that its marketing strategies are attracting an older clientele rather than the desired young, upwardly mobile professionals. Based on this information, the bank can identify within the market at large specific segments of its target audience toward which it will direct its strategies.

Designing the Marketing Strategy

Marketing strategy encompasses the four "Ps" of the marketing mix—product, price, promotion, and distribution (place)—and seeks to attract the target audience. The process of selecting a target market identifies potentially profitable market segments, each of which has relatively homogeneous needs that can be satisfied by using the same marketing mix. The design of the particular marketing mix that will be used is based on the distinctive needs of the targeted market segment.

Although each element of the marketing mix is important in itself, blending and coordinating the elements ultimately determines whether a marketing strategy is successful.

Product Strategy

For the target market, the product is the means to the end. More than just a physical object (toothpaste) or a service (extension of credit), it is a provider of benefits—a way of directly satisfying existing or latent needs. The success of a product is contingent on how well it compares with the competitions' products in satisfying the target market's needs or wants.

Firms that excel in product strategy develop and offer products designed specifically to solve the problems of their target markets. Much of IBM's initial computer marketing success was due to its decision to provide its customers with delivery, installation, operator training, warranty protection, preventive maintenance, and other services in addition to the computer itself.[5] Similarly, Maytag washing machines are designed for the target market that is willing to pay a premium for a reliable and durable product. Colgate is a market leader because it is attuned to the needs of its various target markets and introduces new products to meet changing needs. Some recent additions to its product lines are a dishwashing detergent for sensitive skin, a toothbrush with irregular-length bristles to compensate for poor brushing technique, and a toothpaste tube that returns to its original shape after being squeezed.[6]

Pricing Strategy

Selling a product at a price the target market sees as commensurate with the product's perceived benefits is the key to marketing success. Mercedes-Benz can sell its cars at a high price because of the workmanship and engineering that go into the automobiles and the willingness of the target market to pay a commensurate amount of money for those attributes.

For years, banks were limited in their use of pricing strategies by regulations governing interest rates on deposits and loans. Only since the onset of deregulation, for example, have banks had the opportunity to select a deposit pricing strategy. Some banks choose to pay consistently high, top-of-market rates. Some set their rates just under the market leader, and still others set their rates at the lower end of the market, perhaps believing that their target market is less responsive to interest rates and more responsive to such factors as superior service.

In addition to interest rates on loans and deposits, bank pricing consists of fees and charges levied for the performance of various services. In recent years, as noninterest expenses have increased, banks have paid increasing attention to fee income. They are more likely than in the past to raise service fees or institute fees on services previously provided at no charge, such as ATM transactions. Some banks even charge certain customers for every deposit and withdrawal, whether made through an ATM or in the bank. For some time, banks have been marketing fee-based services, such as offering annuities and mutual funds, through a third party.

The pricing of a bank's retail, commercial, and trust products dramatically affects the institution's bottom line. A bank's interest income from its retail and commercial loans plus its fee and service-charge income might constitute 70 percent or more of its total income from all sources. The interest paid on deposits is a major expense for banks, but it is usually only about half of a bank's total expenses, which include salaries and other operating expenses. Due to the bottom-line implications, a decision made on the pricing of loans and deposits is usually a joint process that involves the members of the bank's asset/liability management committee as well as the marketing management executive.

Promotion Strategy

Promotion strategy focuses on communicating the availability of products or services to the target market. Advertising campaigns, point-of-purchase materials, sales promotion activities, direct marketing, and product publicity are the main elements of promotion. Personal selling generally is considered to be a part of promotion strategy, but due to its importance in providing and delivering bank services, this function is regarded in this text as part of distribution strategy.

The development and implementation of attention-getting, informative, and persuasive communication techniques is vital to creating market awareness of a bank's product. A product's positive attributes, its price, and its means of distribution are meaningless unless the product's benefits are clearly and forcefully communicated to prospective customers.

Banks typically communicate with customers through print advertising in newspapers and magazines, broadcast advertising on radio and television, direct marketing through direct mail and statement inserts, and point-of-purchase advertising through brochures and posters in the bank. Now, due to the increasing use of personal computers, banks are also communicating with customers via PC banking programs and the Internet. In addition, banks and other marketers still use a limited amount of sales promotion techniques such as special offers, giveaways, contests, and packaging incentives.

Distribution Strategy

Distribution strategy is mainly concerned with making the product available at the desired time and place. Even the "right" product for a market segment provides limited satisfaction—or none at all—if it is not available when and where consumers want it.

For example, *TV Guide*'s perceived value would be considerably diminished if each week's issue arrived three days late. Similarly, a bank might have superior service and products, but if it is located where potential customers must pass by several other financial institutions to get to it, its ability to attract those customers will be greatly lessened. Accordingly, two important elements of distribution strategy for banks are site location and ease of access. Furthermore, the current social environment places a heavy emphasis on time as well as convenience. As a result, many banks have joined nationwide automated-teller networks to maximize the number of locations where customers can access their accounts. Many banks also provide telephone banking services and PC banking services that enable customers to perform transactions and make account inquiries 24 hours a day, 7 days a week.

Since banking products and services are largely intangible, they are often difficult to separate from the people who distribute them. This is especially true at the time the customer initiates the relationship with a bank, but it also applies to the day-to-day servicing of accounts. Although the use of technology has reduced contact with tellers, there will always be a need for personal customer service, whether it be in person or by phone. The growing implementation of customer-relations and sales training programs in banks reflects management's recognition of the importance of the human element in the bank's distribution strategy.

Implementing the Plan

Implementing a successful marketing plan requires the cooperation of both management and staff. For example, consider the implementation of a marketing plan for a new product—a home equity line of credit. (See Case B.) To develop the product and bring it to the market, the marketing manager needs the assistance and cooperation of the following divisions:

- *computer programming*—to modify the consumer loan or demand deposit accounting system to manage this special type of account;
- *operations*—to process the checks, payments, and other paperwork related to servicing the accounts;
- *legal services*—to write the credit application and loan agreement so they conform to the appropriate regulations;
- *accounting*—to establish the accounts and reporting systems necessary for tracking this product's performance;
- *bank investments*—to assist in the pricing of this particular use of funds;
- *training*—to instruct the branch staff in the operational and sales aspects of the product;
- *branch staff*—to sell and service the product;
- *customer service*—to understand and be prepared to handle customers' questions about any aspect of the new product; and

- *Web site staff*—to modify and update the Web site to include the product, whether an outside consultant or in-house staff.

Such cooperation will be more easily achieved if the planning process includes representatives from these areas. Many banks use the task force approach to implementing a marketing plan for a new product. Chaired by the product manager, the task force develops a list of tasks to be accomplished in each department in order to introduce the product. Each member of the task force has specific responsibilities and a timetable for completing them. The task force members are responsible for completing the required tasks and seeing that their individual departments are kept informed about the progress of the plan and its impact on them. The service-quality movement, which has gained acceptance in the banking industry, has its greatest effect on the implementation stage of a bank's planning.

When all the internal elements are in place and it is time to execute the marketing strategy, the bank is ready to communicate the offer to the target market and to begin monitoring the results.

Evaluating the Results

Before the implementation stage, the bank should determine how to measure progress toward attaining the marketing plan's objectives and who is responsible for that measurement. In other words, the plan itself should include the answer to the question, "How will we know when we have arrived?" It is essential to the marketing management process that the bank monitor the results of its marketing plan so that any needed adjustments to the plan may be made. Performance may be monitored through such internal sources of information as, say, daily, weekly, and monthly reports that show the number of applications received, the number of accounts opened and closed, the balance levels, and the source of new customers. To determine the target market's awareness of the product, the bank might obtain external data by surveying customers to find out how they learned of the new product and what their opinions of it are.

It is possible that the marketing strategy will not produce the results expected or that some part of the marketing mix will not perform as intended. The causes may be internal, or they may be the result of some activity on the part of a competitor or some change in the macroenvironment. Whatever the cause, evaluating the source of the problem and adjusting or fine-tuning the marketing mix are essential. That is why the model for the strategic marketing management process contains a feedback loop. The process does not stop at any one point—planning, implementing, or evaluating—but is ongoing and circular.

It is important to note that, while they might appear to be rational, logical, even undeniably sensible, the approaches presented in this chapter are not necessarily accepted and practiced by all banks as a matter of course. In fact, many marketing managers who attempt to use this process, especially those working for smaller banks, encounter resistance.

Why Plan? Some Specious Arguments

Bank marketers must be prepared to answer the question, "Why plan?" A bank's management may proffer many arguments to rationalize why planning is unnecessary. Several of the most common arguments follow, and responding to them will help define and clarify the importance of marketing planning:[7]

"This bank has done fine for 150 years without planning." Recall the example cited earlier in this chapter: The bank thought it was doing well with its annual loan growth of 10 percent until a new business development officer increased volume by 35 percent in one year. The point is that there is always room for improvement, even when the bank is apparently doing well. More to the point, with the environment constantly changing as it is today, merely projecting the accomplishments of the past onto the future is unwise. There is no assurance that the growth rates of the past will continue under their own momentum.

"We are a hometown bank. We know this community, what it wants and needs, and how best to serve it." Undoubtedly, local bankers get feedback from the people they meet and talk with, but this type of information contains built-in bias. What bankers hear depends very much on who they are and to whom they are talking. To fully understand the market, bankers need to hear from a wide cross-section of people. They need unbiased, objective feedback from the market, and this type of information can be obtained only through research.

"There are too many changes taking place. You can't anticipate them, so planning is a wasted effort." Formal planning forces the bank to define its assumptions about the future, so it places the bank in a better position to recognize variations when they take place. Planning improves the chances of making the right decision in the face of unexpected events. Using a systematic process of analysis and reasoning puts the marketer in a better position to understand previously unexplained results. In fact, this process might lead to better decision making in the future.

"The sign of a good manager is the ability to respond quickly and efficiently to unanticipated events and to change." This is true up to a point, but while one manager may be putting out brush fires, his competitor might be planning for the management of change. As chapter 2 pointed out, the effective marketing manager is a manager of change.

"Planning takes too much time." The time spent in planning should be seen as an investment in the future. Furthermore, planning is not a one-time activity, as has been shown. It is an ongoing process, and it

is part of the entire management approach. Any manager who is not planning is not managing properly.

"Things change too fast in this business. It is more important to stay flexible. A plan is too rigid." Here again, it must be stressed that planning is a process. It requires constant review and adaptation. This means changing the assumptions, or the objectives, or the strategies as needed. Furthermore, planning improves the chances of recognizing and adapting to forces of change before the competition does so.

"Planning means setting objectives and measuring results. My people are not used to being measured and they will not like it." On the contrary, employees will not mind being measured if they are given realistic goals, the tools to achieve them, and recognition for doing so. Employees also like to feel as if they are part of an organized effort. Therefore, it is important that all personnel be included in the objective-setting process and understand their role in the overall plan.

"Why plan if you cannot measure your results?" This objection is directed at a major weakness in much of the informal, and even some of the formal, planning that banks do. Objectives are set, but the procedure for measuring the results is not defined. In the absence of such measurement, the effect of planning cannot really be understood, so the planning process is perceived as being worthless when, actually, the objective-setting step is at fault. The point is, do not plan if you are not going to set measurable objectives.

In summary, the planning process results in a number of benefits:

1. It motivates executives to set marketing objectives and evaluate the bank's current situation in an explicit manner, and it forces them to plan ahead in a systematic fashion.

2. It inspires the bank to consider new opportunities, which tend to stimulate growth and profits.

3. It makes bank personnel more aware of their roles and responsibilities with respect to the bank's overall marketing program, and it encourages cooperation and coordination of efforts.

4. It leads to more efficient use of the bank's limited resources because it directs them toward specific targets.

5. It enables bank executives to evaluate and improve marketing efforts because the plan includes performance standards and control measurements.

6. It helps the bank to distinguish between those factors that are within its control and those that are not through analysis of the bank's current and anticipated market situation.

7. It leads to a more efficient use of time. There will be fewer brush fires to contend with and more attention paid to achieving goals.

8. The planning process typically results in a bank's being better prepared for responding to unexpected developments. Since the changes taking place in banking are making it more difficult to maintain the growth rates of the past, formalized planning can help anticipate problems, identify possible solutions, and develop strategies for achieving desired performance levels in the face of such challenges.

Prerequisites for Planning

Before initiating the planning process, the marketer must be aware of several factors that will ensure a favorable atmosphere. When planning fails, the roots can be traced to one or more of these factors:

*   *Senior management support and involvement.* Top management must convey the attitude that the planning process is important and that the firm is sincerely interested in the results. The chief executive officer must refer to the plan both in meetings and in correspondence and must communicate to the staff the bank's progress with respect to its goals.

• *Cooperation at all levels of the bank.* Most marketing programs affect many departments within the bank and, indeed, depend on the prompt and accurate performance of many jobs. It is essential for the bank to educate each employee about his or her role in implementing the marketing program. When employees see themselves as part of an overall plan, the innate desire to be part of a winning team takes over and cooperation results.

• *Willingness of management to conduct the required research.* The bank must continually gather information from the marketplace. It is necessary to study historical trends; the competition; market share; the local economy; and customer characteristics, attitudes, and behavior. This information forms the situation analysis—the foundation on which the plan is built. Some of it may be obtained from secondary sources, but certain crucial information can be obtained only through primary research. Using a marketing customer information system to collate this information and sort it to segment target markets yields much stronger customer targets for product promotions. (See Chapter 7.)

• *Designated responsibility for implementing the plan.* Setting measurable objectives and assigning the responsibility for reaching them to specific individuals increases the likelihood of accomplishing a task. Delegated responsibility often motivates employees, especially if good performance is recognized. Each manager should develop measurable objectives, consistent with the bank's plan, for which he or she is accountable. In the ideal situation, each employee should also develop or be given specific, measurable objectives that relate to the plan. Within this framework, objectives are more likely to be accomplished. If they are not accomplished, the reasons will be more easily identified, and corrective measures can be taken.

• *Recognition that the plan will not be perfect and unchanging.* Since markets are in a constant state of flux, the successful marketer must be able to manage change. Planning must be an ongoing process, with periodic reviews to measure progress and to make adjustments.

Summary

Strategic marketing is a management process that involves planning, implementing those plans, and evaluating their results. It is a circular, ongoing process that recognizes that because plans do not always turn out as expected, a mechanism for adjusting them must be built into the process.

The marketing manager creates, implements, and evaluates marketing plans to pinpoint target markets that desire the products and services the bank wants to sell to reach its strategic marketing objectives. The elements of a plan include situation analysis, marketing objectives, target market selection, and marketing strategy. The marketing strategy is the sum total of the marketing- mix strategies. For each target market, the marketing manager develops product, pricing, promotion, and place (distribution) strategies that will meet the needs and wants of the target market in a way that is superior to the competitions' offerings.

In many instances, implementing a marketing plan requires the cooperation of several departments within a bank. Achieving this level of cooperation requires that those departments be included in the planning process.

The evaluation stage of the marketing management process is critical. The marketing manager must be able to report on the effectiveness of the marketing strategy and, therefore, must include in the plan the various research techniques that will be used to measure results. On the basis of this information, the strategy can be changed or fine-tuned to attain the desired objectives.

Some executives do not believe in planning. Instead, they have a short-range view of the business. The marketing manager should be prepared to respond to the most common objections to planning and to pave the way for marketing planning's success by seeing that its foundation is firmly in place. The foundation stones are involvement of senior management, multilevel cooperation, willingness to do research and to delegate responsibilities to individuals, and recognition that the plan might need to be adjusted after implementation.

The next two chapters of this section present the steps involved in conducting a situation analysis, guidelines for setting objectives, and general concepts and techniques for formulating strategy.

Points for Review

1. Define or briefly explain the following:
   - the management process
   - the marketing management process
   - target market selection
   - marketing strategy
   - demarketing
2. Why is it the task of marketing management to regulate market demand?
3. What are the four steps involved in the marketing planning process?
4. Explain this statement: "Plans are nothing; planning is everything."
5. What is the end product of the situation analysis?
6. What are the characteristics of effective marketing objectives?
7. What are five prerequisites for planning?
8. Respond to the following statement made by a bank president: "We're growing at an acceptable annual rate that is in line with our peer banks. We don't need to plan."

Notes

1. William J. Stanton and Charles Futrell, *Fundamentals of Marketing,* 8th edition (New York: McGraw-Hill, 1987), p. 40.
2. *Ibid.,* p. 12.
3. Kotler, *Marketing Management,* p. 14.
4. James A. McComb, "Marketing by Design," *Bank Marketing,* January 1997, p. 16.
5. James S. Hensel, "The Essential Nature of the Marketing Management Process: An Overview," in Leonard L. Berry and L. A. Capaldini, eds., *Marketing for the Bank Executive* (New York: Petrocelli Books, 1974), p. 65.
6. "New Products Reward Colgate," *Marketing News,* July 13, 1992, p. 4.
7. This section, and especially the treatment of the benefits and prerequisites for planning, draws heavily on Robert W. Joselyn and D. Keith Humphries, *An Introduction to Bank Marketing Planning* (Washington, D.C.: American Bankers Association, 1974).

4

THE DEVELOPMENT OF A SITUATION ANALYSIS

Learning Objectives

After studying this chapter, you should be able to

- provide three reasons for conducting a formal situation analysis,
- describe the rationale for conducting a self-analysis and the sources of data for such an analysis,
- discuss the six elements of a macroenvironmental analysis and what each element contributes to the analysis,
- discuss the five elements of a microenvironmental analysis and what each element contributes to the analysis, and
- describe three characteristics of a summary of problems and opportunities.

Introduction

Previous chapters have discussed marketing planning and the four questions it addresses: (1) Where are we now? (2) Where do we want to go? (3) How are we going to get there? and (4) How will we know when we have arrived? The situation analysis answers the first of those questions.

Situation analysis is a formal, systematic procedure aimed at generating useful written information that will help management understand the bank's current situation. Its purpose is to establish a clear understanding of the bank's strengths and weaknesses to set meaningful objectives. It should provide an accurate picture of the environment in which the bank operates—not a still picture, but, rather, a moving picture that throughout the planning process reveals trends and forecasts the condition of the environment. The period covered by a plan may be as short as three months or as long as five years. Whatever the time frame, the situation analysis is a must in that it performs one critical function: it helps management understand what needs to be done.

Why Formalize the Situation Analysis?

Why is it necessary to formalize the situation analysis? There are three answers to that question.

First, essential research must be conducted. Implementing the situation analysis is similar to preparing for a trip to a distant place. Before mapping out a route, the planner must know what supplies he or she has, what else might be needed at the destination, the location from which the trip will begin, and what method of transportation is best for the trip. Knowing this information is essential for planning a successful journey. Likewise, the critical planning steps of setting objectives and measuring and evaluating the results cannot be accomplished without the baseline information provided by the formal situation analysis.

The situation analysis generates a variety of statistics (such as share of market, number of services used per customer, level of consumer awareness of bank services, rate of growth of accounts, average balances in each type of deposit account, average size for each type of loan, proportion of noninterest income derived from fees, and so on). These statistics become the raw material for the objective-setting process. Worthwhile objectives might include increasing the share of market by 2 percent, raising the average number of services per customer from 1.5 to 1.8, or increasing consumer recall of the bank's advertising message from 10 percent to 25 percent. After the plan is implemented, the measurement and evaluation of results may be seen as an updated situation analysis, one which concentrates on the specific areas targeted in the objective-setting process.

Second, the situation analysis is objective and thorough. Every bank manager has an opinion or impression of what is going on in the market, how the bank is doing in comparison with the competition, and what the bank's strengths and weaknesses are. However, these opinions may not be based on facts, and they may not be all-encompassing. Being forced to record the situation analysis in black and white ensures that the input to the goal-setting process will be factual, objective, and thorough. It reduces the likelihood that a real problem or opportunity might be overlooked.

Third, formalizing the situation analysis—putting it down in writing—can do wonders for internal public relations and motivation. There are many employees who are not personally involved in the development of marketing plans but whose cooperation will, nevertheless, be required for their execution. (An example in chapter 3 cites nine departments in the bank that should be involved in developing a marketing plan. This example illustrates the importance of gathering information from many sources.) Sharing information from the written situation analysis with these employees will give them an understanding of the bank's current situation, the need for an integrated marketing plan, and the importance of their cooperation.

Although the situation analysis is a critical first step in the planning process, the information generated by it need not be included in the plan document itself. A situation analysis generates a great deal of data as backup to the statement of strengths and weaknesses, problems and opportunities. If all of that data were placed at the front of a written plan, it could very well detract from the operational components of the plan—that is, the "to do's." The information should, of course, be referenced and available, but it is not an end in itself.

In the following pages, the steps involved in the process of developing a situation analysis—both on a bankwide scale and on a smaller scale (product)—are discussed. Throughout this chapter are references to Cases B and F. Case F is the annual marketing plan for a community bank; Case B is a marketing plan for a new product—specifically, a home equity credit line. These cases demonstrate how the basic elements of a situation analysis are treated differently depending on the scope of the particular marketing plan.

The Four Elements of a Situation Analysis

Developing a situation analysis requires four steps: self-analysis, analysis of macroenvironmental factors, analysis of microenvironmental factors, and analysis of problems and opportunities.

In chapter 2, the elements of the macroenvironment and microenvironment were covered in some detail to explain the variety of factors that influence marketing. In this chapter, the elements of both the macroenvironment and the microenvironment that are essential to the situation analysis are discussed in detail.

Exhibit 4.1 outlines a situation analysis for a bank, presenting many of the potential categories of information that might be included. However, not all of these categories will appear in every situation analysis. The scope of the particular marketing plan will dictate which of the many factors is relevant to the current situation. This will become clearer when studying Cases B and F while reading the following pages.

Self-Analysis

The purpose of the self-analysis step in the situation analysis is to learn as much as possible about a bank's performance, its current situation, and the condition of the market environment with respect to the particular marketing effort being planned. The self-analysis should include a review of the bank's current marketing-mix strategies—that is, how its current product, pricing, promotion, and distribution strategies are working. It should also include the bank's current market share and its position in the market. It might include feedback from market research surveys of the bank's customers or prospects.

Much of the information for the self-analysis is available from internal secondary sources and is stored in an MCIF. Secondary data are information that has been compiled for some other purpose. Internally generated reports and existing data provided by government bodies are examples of secondary data. Within the bank, internal data are available on trends in new and closed checking and savings accounts, new commercial and installment loans and mortgages, and demographic characteristics of new borrowers. The marketer's challenge is to locate this information within the bank, since it is collected for operational or credit rating reasons and is not generally compiled for or disseminated to the marketing department. For this reason, a useful first step in the self-analysis of a bank is to determine what information is available within the bank and to establish a system for its up-to-date dissemination to appropriate marketing personnel.

The planner should also look at the bank's financial statements in comparison with the statements of competing banks and banks in its peer group—that is, banks that are of the same size but that are not necessarily competing in the same market-place. By comparing various statistics and ratios, the planner can more easily identify the bank's financial strengths and weaknesses. Some of the data that may be useful include capital structure, return on assets, asset growth rate, loan portfolio mix, fee income as a percentage of total income or assets, occupancy costs, and salaries and benefits as a percentage of total expenses or assets. This information is available from annual reports and from Form 10-K, which is prepared by publicly held banks. In Case F, Consumers National Bank (CNB) did this analysis, but included it within the section on competition.

In addition to the types of data mentioned above, the bank's officers have stored in their minds a great deal of information that should be put down on paper. This information is likely to encompass current competitive strategies and future expectations. For instance, the following questions might be answered:

- What are we doing to get new business? What kind of call program do we have? Have we identified our best prospects? What kind of call program does the competition have?

- What are we doing to cross-market our services to our present customers?

- What new services could negatively affect our market position?

- What will our customers' financial needs be in the future?

- How well do we train our employees in selling? In job performance?

The self-analysis in Case B's marketing plan for a new home equity line of credit lists several factors about the bank's current situation that provide an excellent foundation for offering the new product: prior experience with equity credit, a preponderance of fixed-rate credit in the portfolio, current penetration of the target market, a sales and operating staff that is accustomed to selling and servicing revolving credit products, efficiencies that enable the bank to price very competitively, and the fact that the competition is already offering such a product.

The self-analysis for Consumers National Bank, on the other hand, consists of only a brief overview, since the sections on customers and competitors present a more detailed look at the bank.

Analysis of Macroenvironmental Factors

This step in the situation analysis should address the macroenvironmental factors that are likely to affect the marketing plan. The planner could easily become submerged in the tremendous amount of data available from numerous sources. Therefore, selecting only the categories of information and the specific data that might be relevant is very important. If, for example, a bank wants to know how many families have moved into its market area, the marketing planner would want to get data on the number of home building permits issued. Why? Because a correlation exists between the number of new houses and the number of new families entering the area. Conversely, detailed data describing the existing housing stock—its age and value—would not be pertinent.

As you recall from chapter 2, macroenvironmental factors are economic; demographic; social and cultural; political, legal and regulatory; technological; and natural.

Economic Environment

The business of banking is very much affected by economic conditions in the bank's market area. The level of deposits reflects the cash position of individuals and businesses. New housing construction means more families with banking needs. When business is booming, manufacturers borrow to expand capacity or finance production. If people are confident of their future income, they will borrow to improve their homes or to make major purchases. This list could go on and on, but the point is that, to plan its marketing effort, the bank must have a basic knowledge of the economy in its trade area. This means understanding the economic trends and, to some extent, making projections about the future of the economy.

For a total marketing plan, the analysis of the economic environment should include at least the following types of information:

1. *employment trends*—composition of the area's industry, growth by industry, and wage rates;

2. *retail activity*—evaluation of trends in the retail sector of the economy; and

3. *construction activity*—business and residential.

Some long-range forecasts for the area should also be included in the above information.

Employment Trends

Understanding the wage and salary scales of local employers provides insight into the demographics of employees who might become bank customers.

State departments of labor or employment, chambers of commerce, and public utility research departments may provide valuable sources of information about the labor market, including total workforce, occupational distribution, industrial development, and labor-market projections. Being aware of possible employment trends will enable the bank to project its own labor requirements. The accumulated information may reveal increased activity in a particular industry, which the bank might want to take advantage of by making one of its loan officers a specialist in that field.

Retail Activity

The condition of the retail business in the trade area is important to the bank for two reasons. First, like retailers, the bank serves the consumer market, sharing customers with local retailers. Second, banks lend to retailers, and the financial health of retailers affects the collection of business loans.

Information on the number and types of retail establishments and sales by type of business is available from the *Census of Retail Trade,* published every 5 years (in years ending with 2 and 7) by the Bureau of the Census. Analysis of this information reveals trends in retail sales and helps the planner identify changing patterns of consumer buying.

Construction Activity

Knowing the number of new businesses and houses is relevant to understanding the growth potential for the bank and identifying areas where new branches might be needed.

All of the information mentioned so far is readily available. It is possible to paint a picture of the economic environment in a bank's market with no out-of-pocket cost (except for that of state or government publications, many of which are available at the library). There is a wealth of available information that can be evaluated to get a broad indication of important changes in the market and to call attention to prospective problems and opportunities.

The extent of the information developed will vary with the scope of the plan. Case F, a total marketing plan for a community bank, goes to great lengths to review employment and unemployment rates, retail sales, and construction activity. This information helps the bank understand the forces that are operating in its trade area, which has implications for the bank's marketing strategy.

In contrast, the situation analysis in Case B, a marketing plan for a new home equity credit line, does not call for extensive tabular data. It describes the effect of inflation on the buildup of home equity. It also explains how high interest rates led homeowners to improve their homes rather than take on additional debt in the form of a secondary mortgage. In other words, the situation analysis limits itself to information that is relevant.

Demographic Environment

Demographic data are useful in that they give the banker a picture of the population in the bank's market area and how it is changing in number, income, age, education, and occupation. The size and projected growth of the population are especially important since there is usually some relationship between the number of people in the market and the number of banking services that will be required. The two principal sources for demographic data are the census (conducted every 10 years) and state departments of labor or employment.

Education and occupation are closely related to social class and income, and consumer buying and banking behavior vary among social classes. The rate at which people adopt new products and services is related to age and social class. The marketer who has a good understanding of such relationships and applies it to a study of the market area's demographics will be more likely to succeed in developing marketing strategies that reach the bank's customers and prospects.

In Case F, Consumers National Bank has collected pertinent demographic information, citing the sources. These data show population trends and projections, the aging of the population, and relevant population shifts, all of which have implications for the distribution strategy.

In Case B, Marlton National Bank (MNB) does not use tabular information, but alludes to the demographic foundations for the market for home equity credit lines—that is, the aging of the baby boom generation, the increase in the divorce rate, and the projected growth in the age group that constitutes the target market.

Social and Cultural Environment

As consumers' lifestyles and values change, their need and desire for products and services change. The marketer must be tuned in to these factors. There are countless changes that may pertain to a bank's social and cultural environment, including the aging of the population, the growing diversity of the population, and changes in lifestyle, such as having children later in life and single parents.

While Consumers National Bank's marketing plan does not refer to the social or cultural environment in its trade area, Marlton National Bank's plan mentions the social stigma once associated with second mortgages and notes that this bias is no longer prevalent in society—making the growth in home equity credit possible.

Political, Legal, and Regulatory Environment

Regulatory and legislative factors often influence bank marketing. The marketer should always stay current with changes in banking regulations. Regulation DD, for example, requires detailed disclosures concerning the annual percentage yield (APY) on all advertising that includes interest rates. The marketer should check with the bank's compliance officer to ensure that marketing plans comply with all regulations.

While regulations are not a factor in Case F, they are in Case B. The Tax Reform Act of 1986 affected the deductibility of some types of interest and increased demand for consumer credit secured by a second mortgage.

Technological Environment

Advances in technology are often integral to the development of new techniques for delivering services. The tremendous popularity of personal computers is changing the way many consumers manage their finances at home. PCs have also presented a new distribution vehicle for banks that wish to offer on-line banking services. Technology has enhanced banks' ability to provide the same 24-hour service many nonbank competitors provide. That includes telephone banking, loans by phone, Internet Web sites, and off-site automated loan machines. The surge in technological developments, combined with consumers' increasing acceptance of and use of automation and computers, has expanded the number of distribution avenues available for banks.

The marketing plan for a new home banking service that uses a personal computer with a modem, for instance, would discuss the technology that permits that service as well as projections for increases in the number of households having personal computers.

A marketing plan for a loan-by-phone service would discuss the cost-benefit analysis of a 24-hour call center staff and on-line access to consumer credit information.

Natural Environmental Factors

The natural environment might figure in a bank's planning process in two ways. With the growing concern for the preservation of the environment and the protection of wildlife, every business must consider the effects of its operations and marketing efforts on the natural environment. Supporting environmental causes can benefit a bank's image as well as its community, and a community-oriented image improves the bank's appeal to customers. In addition, the bank must be attuned to the specific environmental concerns of the people and businesses within its trade area because they might play a role in its marketing or public relations program. Issues pertaining to the natural environment did not come into play for either Consumers National Bank or Marlton Nation Bank. However, the advertisement shown in exhibit 4.2 was part of a campaign in which a bank became the dri-

Exhibit 4.2

This checking account helps fight pollution in the Sound.

Open a BanClub® Checking account and we'll make a donation to a Fund that helps fight pollution in Puget Sound waters. In your name. On top of that, we'll also give you all the checks you want for no extra charge. And six other financial services. All in one account. All for just $4.95 a month. BanClub Checking. Clearly, the best value around the Sound.

Puget Sound Bank
Member F.D.I.C.

ving force in an effort to clean up a major waterway within its trade area.

In some parts of the country, the natural environment has a profound effect on the economic environment. Amarillo National Bank in Texas was able to combine support for its agricultural community with a CD promotion that benefited the bank. After seven months of drought, the bank launched a promotion designed to give customers hope as well as the chance for a higher interest rate on a CD. The bank promised to pay an additional one-quarter percent for each one-quarter inch of rain that fell up to two inches. The one-month campaign was a resounding success in three ways. Amarillo got .31 inches of much-needed rain, customers received an additional .31 percent above the 4.75 percent base interest rate on their CDs, and the bank got $7 million in new money.[1]

Analysis of Microenvironmental Factors

The principal microenvironmental factors that bank marketers should consider are customers, markets, competitors, marketing intermediaries, and publics (see chapter 2).

Customers

The bank must understand its own customers—who they are demographically and how they compare with the market at large, how customers of one product differ from those of another, and how many services they purchase from the bank. A bank that recognizes it is in the business of satisfying the needs and wants of its customers will work hard to find out as much as possible about its customers' attitudes about the bank, their needs and preferences in banking matters, and the degree to which they are satisfied with the service they are receiving from bank staff.

By using survey techniques (discussed in chapter 7), the bank can learn a great

By linking product promotions to charitable initiatives, banks can improve their business and show their social responsibility (left).

deal about itself as well as its customers. Ideally, the bank should survey its checking, savings, and loan customers; at the very least, it should survey its checking customers because customers consider checking to be their primary bank account. Such a survey may be done inexpensively by including it with the monthly checking statement or mailing it to a sample of checking account customers.

Consumers National Bank conducted such a survey as part of its planning process and also made use of the information amassed from its ongoing new-account and closed- (or inactive-) account customer surveys. Exhibit 4.3 shows the questionnaire used for the checking customer survey, which was mailed to 1 out of every 12 checking customers, selected at random by computer.

A new-account survey might consist of ongoing or periodic monitoring of the profile of the bank's new customers. Such a survey can be used to determine the source of new business by asking why the customer chose the bank and where the funds for the new account are coming from. (It should be noted that surveying customers in this manner provides only superficial responses. To understand the deeper motivating forces behind consumer decisions requires more sophisticated research techniques, such as focus groups and personal interviews.)

Exhibit 4.4 shows the form used by Consumers National Bank at the new-accounts desk. When customers open a new account of any type, they are given this form to complete while the new-accounts representative is doing the paperwork. Some banks prefer to mail the survey to customers shortly after the account is opened, which provides the banks with feedback on the customer's satisfaction with the service received during the first few visits to the bank.

It is wise for a bank to monitor closed accounts regularly to stay abreast of any unfavorable trends that may be developing. Many banks train their customer service representatives (CSRs) to ask customers why they are closing the account when the

Exhibit 4.3 **Sample Customer Survey Questionnaire**

Instructions: Please circle the appropriate number or write your answer in the space provided. All information will remain anonymous and completely confidential. Thank you for responding to our survey. Your answers will help us improve our services and products.

1. Which office of Consumers National Bank (CNB) do you use most often?
   1___Bridgeboro 2___No. Bridgeboro 3___New Hope 4___Seabrook   (4)
   5___Milltown 6___Libby Plaza 7___Walker Blvd. 8___Plattville
2. How many times do you visit that particular branch during an average month?
   (If "none," please write in "0") _____ times   (5–6)
3. How long have you been a customer of this bank? _____ years   (7–8)
4. Please indicate how satisfied you are with each of the following items:

   V SAT (4) = Very Satisfied   S DIS(2) = Somewhat Dissatisfied
   S SAT (3) = Somewhat Satisfied   V DIS (1) = Very Dissatisfied

		V SAT	S SAT	S DIS	V DIS	
A.	Availability of the Branch Manager	4	3	2	1	(9)
B.	Overall speed of service you receive at the branch	4	3	2	1	(10)
C.	Speed of service you receive from Service Representatives	4	3	2	1	(11)
D.	Friendliness of employees	4	3	2	1	(12)
E.	Employee knowledge of banking	4	3	2	1	(13)
F.	Willingness of employees to solve your problems	4	3	2	1	(14)
G.	Employee familiarity with you	4	3	2	1	(15)
H.	Speed of service you receive from tellers	4	3	2	1	(16)
I.	Hours the branch is open	4	3	2	1	(17)
J.	Courtesy of employees	4	3	2	1	(18)
K.	Accuracy with which your requests for service (such as account transfers, paperwork preparation) are handled	4	3	2	1	(19)
L.	Availability of automated teller machines	4	3	2	1	(20)
M.	Availability of parking at the branch	4	3	2	1	(21)
N.	Adequacy of drive-in facilities	4	3	2	1	(22)
O.	Ability of service representatives to present the products and services that would be most beneficial to you	4	3	2	1	(23)

   (Answer "P" and "Q" only if you have applied for a loan at the bank)

| P. | Speed of response to your loan application | 4 | 3 | 2 | 1 | (24) |
| Q. | Ease of the loan application process | 4 | 3 | 2 | 1 | (25) |

5. Do you consider Consumers National Bank to be your primary or main banking institution?
   1 ___ Yes   2 ___ No   (26)

6. Please indicate which banking services you are currently using with CNB or with other banking institutions. Circle the number in the appropriate column for each service you have.

	CNB	Other Bank	
Regular checking	1	2	(27)
Interest checking	1	2	(28)
Cash reserve (overdraft protection)	1	2	(29)
Statement savings	1	2	(30)
Certificate of Deposit	1	2	(31)
Individual Retirement Account (IRA)	1	2	(32)
Auto loan	1	2	(33)
Personal loan	1	2	(34)
Home equity loan	1	2	(35)
Mortgage	1	2	(36)

7. What are the names of the other banks or financial institutions with which you have accounts?
   _____ (37–38)

8. Have you opened any new bank accounts or loans within the past year?
   1 ___ Yes   2 ___ No **(If no, please go to question 9)** (39)
   8a. What kind of account was it? _____ (40)
   8b. Where did you open the account? _____ (41)
   8c. Why did you select that financial institution? _____ (42)

9. Have you closed any bank accounts in the past year?
   1 ___ Yes   2 ___ No **(If no, please go to question 10)** (43)
   9a. What type of account did you close? _____ (44)
   9b. What financial institution was it with? _____ (45)
   9c. What was your reason for closing the account? _____ (46–47)

10. What is your age? _____ (48–49)

11. What is the highest level of formal education you've completed?
    1___Some High School   4___College degree or higher
    2___High School   5___Technical/Vocational
    3___Some College   (50)

12. Are you... 1___single 2___divorced/widowed/separated 3___married   (51)

13. What was your total household income last year, before taxes?
    1___ Under $15,000   4___ $30,000 to $49,999
    2___ $15,000 to $19,999   5___ $50,000 to $74,999
    3___ $20,000 to $29,299   6___ $75,000 or more   (52)

Thank you for your time and your answers.

Exhibit 4.4   Sample New Account Survey Questionnaire

Thank you for your cooperation! If you would like us to know who you are, feel free to to provide your name. Please use the postage-paid return envelope we have enclosed for you convenience.   (1–3)

Instructions: Please circle the number that corresponds to your answer.

1. How did you first learn of Consumers National Bank?

    1) From a founder/director (Name?) _____
    2) From a friend/relative (Name?) _____
    3) I saw the building/office
    4) From a bank employee   (4)
    5) From the bank's advertising
    6) Other (please explain) _____

2. At which office did you open your account(s)?

    1) Bridgeboro   4) Seabrook   7) Walker Blvd.
    2) No. Bridgeboro   5) Milltown   8) Plattville   (5)
    3) New Yope   6) Libby Plaza

3. Why did you choose Consumers National Bank?
    _____ (6)
    _____

4. Using the scale to the right, please rate the service representative who helped you on the following characteristics:

	Excellent	Good	Fair	Poor	
a. Helpfulness	4	3	2	1	(7)
b. Ability to explain the bank's products	4	3	2	1	(8)
c. Ability to discuss and compare interest rates on various savings options	4	3	2	1	(9)
d. Professionalism	4	3	2	1	(10)

5. Please indicate which banking services you currently have at financial institutions other than Consumers National Bank.

    ___ No-interest checking   (11)   ___ Unsecured credit line   (17)
    ___ Checking with interest (12)   ___ Home equity credit line   (18)
    ___ Money market account   (13)   ___ Residential mortgage   (19)
    ___ Statement savings   (14)   ___ Installment loan   (20)
    ___ Certificate of deposit (15)   ___ Commercial loan   (21)
    ___ IRA   (16)

Exhibit 4.4, *continued*

6. Please circle each number that indicates where you have seen or heard
   advertising for Consumers National Bank.
   1___Cable TV 2___Radio 3___Newspaper 4___Magazine
   5___Other (please specify)_____   (22)

7. How long have you lived at your present address?
   1___ Just moved in   4___ 6–10 years
   2___ Less than 1 year   5___ More than 10 years   (23)
   3___ 1–5 years

8. Do you. . . 1___ Own your home   2___ Rent   (24)

9. What is your age? _____   (25–26)

10. What is the highest level of formal education you've completed?
    1 ___ Some High School   4 ___ College degree or higher
    2 ___ High School   5 ___ Technical/Vocational
    3 ___ Some College   (27)

11. Are you. . . 1___single 2___divorced/widowed/separated 3___married (28)

12. What was your total household income last year, before taxes?   (29)
    1 ___ Under $15,000   3 ___ $20,000 to $29,299 5___ $50,000 to $74,999
    2 ___ $15,000 to $19,999 4 ___ $30,000 to $49,999 6___ $75,000 or more

Thank you for your responses.
(For internal use)_____
Type of account(s) opened_____
Source of deposit (transfer from)_____

customer makes the request. There are some instances in which a CSR can persuade a customer to remain with the bank, such as dissatisfaction with how a request was handled. Apologizing and asking for another chance to serve the customer may keep the customer with the bank. Once the customer has closed the account and left the bank, the opportunity to learn from that customer may be lost.

Some form of follow-up on closed accounts may be required by the bank's auditors as a way of ensuring that the accounts were actually closed by the customer and are not connected to any misbehavior on the part of bank personnel.

For the most part, customers close accounts because they are changing their residence or job and the bank is no longer convenient. Other reasons often cited for closing accounts are related to the quality of service received or, when it comes to savings accounts, the availability of a better rate of interest elsewhere. Exhibit 4.5 shows the closed-account survey form used by Consumers National Bank.

In Case F, Consumers National Bank lists important demographic information about its customers that it collected as part of its research. In Case B, Marlton National Bank's knowledge of its customer base is reflected in the section describing the target market for the new product. It is clear that the bank sufficiently understands its current customer base and recognizes that it closely paral-

---

Exhibit 4.5 **Sample Closed Account Survey Questionnaire**

Dear Ms. Green,

We regret that you recently closed your savings account with our bank. It is important for us to know if you closed your account because you were dissatisfied with our staff, our policies, our products, or our service.

Please take a moment to complete this form. Then simply fold and staple or tape it closed and drop it in the mail. We appreciate your candid responses and hope we can serve you again in the future.

Sincerely,
Jane Doe
President

The savings account was closed for the following reason(s).
____ Transferred the funds to another account within the bank
____ Moved out of area
____ Needed the money for a specific purpose
____ Used the funds for investment purposes
____ Wanted to get more interest
____ Because of the service charge on balances under $100
____ Dissatisfied with service by bank staff
____ Other (please explain)_____
_____
_____

Comments
Please use this space for any other comments you would like to make.

_____
_____
_____

Thank you for your time.

(please fold, seal, and mail)

lels the demographics of the target market for the equity credit line.

Markets

This section of the situation analysis addresses the size, growth, geographic distribution, demographics, and current and potential profitability of the relevant market or markets that might be targeted by the bank.

As a result of its economic, demographic, and customer analyses, Consumers National Bank identified a need to target its marketing efforts toward newcomers to the area and higher-income professional and managerial workers. Marlton National Bank, as already noted, identified the target market and addressed its growth in its situation analysis.

Competition

The purpose of the competition section of the situation analysis is to present data that enable marketers to evaluate the bank's performance in comparison with that of its principal competitors operating in roughly the same economic, demographic, and competitive environment.

When defining who the bank's competition is, the marketer should use a broad definition of the term. A bank's competitors include other commercial banks, savings and loan associations, mutual savings banks, finance companies, credit unions, investment companies, brokerage firms, mutual funds, and money market funds that perform many of the same services as banks.

The types of information that should be gathered are various operating statistics, information on service offerings, and a comparison of advertising materials, physical plants, and quality of personnel. In other words, the objective is to compare the bank's performance with that of the competition and to compare the use of the two marketing mixes. Case Study F contains two exhibits (F.10 and F.11) that show side-by-side comparisons of products, ser-

vices, and locations. Creating charts like these can show quickly and clearly where a bank's strengths and weaknesses lie.

The three broad categories of information that should constitute the analysis of the bank's competitive environment are:

1. *comparative operating statistics* (these data may be included in the self-analysis);
2. *comparative market shares;* and
3. *comparison of marketing strategies* (products, pricing, advertising and promotional activities, service delivery, and selling efforts).

Consumers National Bank's principal competitors are numerous because the bank is in a state that has long permitted statewide branching. The bank principally competes with five other commercial banks, two savings and loans, and a credit union. In addition, each of four other commercial banks has a 2 percent or smaller market share.

Although these institutions are the principal and most direct financial institution competitors, Consumers National should be aware of other nonbank competitors vying in the marketplace for specific services. For example, consumer finance companies compete for home equity loans and other personal loans; money market and mutual funds compete for both checking and savings funds. These competitors must be kept in mind throughout the situation analysis, although the more banklike financial institutions will constitute the bulk of the data in the situation analysis in Case F.

Operating Statistics
Consumers National Bank compares its condition and income statements with those of its principal commercial banking competitors to assess its financial performance in comparison with theirs. Consumers National Bank operates in a county where only two of its competing commercial banks are headquartered. The rest of the competition has numerous offices outside the county. Because these other areas have considerably different economic and demographic characteristics, and because so much of these banks' business is

generated outside the county, it would be meaningless for Consumers National Bank to compare its financial statements with theirs. For this part of the situation analysis, Consumers National Bank compares itself only with the two other county-headquartered banks.

Exhibit F.8, in Case F, shows selected operating statistics and ratios for Consumers National Bank and these two other banks. This type of information may be obtained from call reports and income statements filed with the Federal Deposit Insurance Corporation. These reports are available on request or they may be accessed by computer through a service bureau or via the Internet. Marketers can search for and retrieve earnings reports, shareholder proxy statements, and other corporate information via the Electronic Data Gathering Analysis Retrieval (EDGAR) system.[2] Additionally, at least one firm compiles in a single volume statistics for all the banks in a state.[3] Data are compiled as of year end and are generally available in the middle of the following year.

Market Share

One of the better indicators of a bank's competitive strength is its market share. Market share is one bank's or branch's portion of all the banking business done in a market area. Through analysis of data from various sources, it is possible to calculate a bank's total market share within its market or its market share for such categories as demand deposits, savings and time deposits, public funds, personal loans, mortgages, and so on.

Unfortunately, no secondary data are available to measure a bank's share of the total personal, or individual, checking balances in a market. In financial reports, this information is combined with information about deposits made by partnerships and corporations. However, information on a bank's share of personal demand deposits may be obtained through primary research or through information sharing. Primary data are information generated from original sources for a specific purpose. Market

research surveys that ask questions of target markets—such as consumers or business owners—generate primary data. Information sharing is popular in some parts of the country. To get the information they need to determine their market share, banks cooperatively engage an outside firm to pool selected data provided by the banks and to give each member of the group the group's totals by category. In this way, confidential data about any specific bank are not made available to competitors.

The principal sources of market share data are reports filed with the financial regulators. Each year, as of June 30, all commercial banks and savings and loans report deposit statistics by branch to the FDIC. This information, along with information on credit union deposits, may be obtained in summary form from publishers who organize it by state, county, and municipality.[4] It may also be accessed directly through computer service bureaus on a time-sharing basis, or the tapes may be obtained from various regulators and the data analyzed on the bank's own computer. Although the information is current to June 30, it is usually not available until spring of the following year.

Information on market share of loans can be obtained somewhat less easily from call reports filed with the regulators. These data are consolidated; that is, they are reported for the entire bank, not by branch. Therefore, in states that permit branching, loan information is not available by county or municipality. Because only two of Consumers National Bank's principal competitors operate exclusively in the same trade area as CNB, information on loans for Overland County, where CNB is located, is not available. This information could best be obtained through primary research in which individuals and businesses are surveyed about their current and recent borrowings. CNB's management felt that this expense was not warranted at this time and that existing data could be used to form its objectives with respect to loans.

In discussing the importance of market share, a warning is in order. Having the greatest market share is not in itself an ideal to be sought. A bank that offers free checking for individuals and businesses might experience greater-than-average increases in market share. Its earnings, however, are sure to suffer. Remember that the marketing concept entails both satisfaction for the customer and profit for the bank. Being biggest is not necessarily best. The goal is to increase share of *profitable* markets, but success is difficult to measure except by primary research.

Marketing Strategies

Until now, the marketer (or market researcher) has been sitting at a desk with a calculator or computer and reference material, poring over statistics to put them into meaningful order. Now it is time to go out and see what the competition is doing. The focus is on observing the competition's use of the 4 Ps of the marketing mix—product, pricing, promotion, and place (distribution).

The competition includes not only existing financial institutions, but also those that are planning to enter the market. It is necessary to look at commercial banks, mutual savings banks, savings and loans, and credit unions. The focus should be on the following:

- *Products and pricing*—What products are offered? What are the service or maintenance charges? What interest rates are paid or charged? What price changes have there been? What new services have been offered?
- *Promotional activity*—What advertising and promotional techniques are the competitors using? What markets are they targeting? What do their current strategies appear to be? Are they effective?
- *Physical distribution*—What kind of facilities does the competition have? How do ours compare? How do our locations compare with theirs in terms of convenience and access? How do we compare for drive-up and automated teller service?

How do we compare for hours of service? Do we have adequate off-site ATMs? Should we offer PC banking access?

- *Personal selling*—How effective are their customer-contact people compared with ours? What sales training do we and our competitors provide? What changes have taken place in their key personnel that might affect our market potential? What changes have taken place in their policies, such as credit standards and rate changes, that might affect our ability to attract business?

There are two principal ways to obtain this kind of information: *observation* (including comparative service shopping, or mystery shopping, as it is sometimes called) and *survey research.*

Service shopping is simply a matter of organizing information that is gleaned from published information or obtained by having bank or other personnel actually go around and "shop" the competition, posing as prospective customers and taking notes along the way. Much information can also be gained over the telephone by an employee posing as a prospective customer. Information gained in this way, however, should be verified by placing more than one call to different sources. Unfortunately, it is not unusual for bank employees to give incorrect information to callers. Placing such calls also reveals a great deal about the customer orientation of the bank—whether callers are treated indifferently or as though their call is genuinely important. It also tells something about the level of sales awareness of the competition. Rarely will the person at the bank ask the caller for a name and address so that more-detailed service information may be provided.

A great deal of information about the relative strengths and weaknesses of the competition may be obtained from a survey of trade-area residents. Through such research, a bank can compare the profiles of the customers of each competitor, determine the relative image of each institution in the minds of customers and prospects, and learn the extent to which people are switching banks and the reasons for it.

The results of competitive shopping done by Consumers National Bank appear in Case F. The exhibits present information only for the retail side of the business. Obviously, in conducting a situation analysis for a bank, information about services for businesses should also be developed. This part of the situation analysis might also contain information that the market researcher obtained by talking to the officers of his or her own bank. In Consumers National Bank's case, some of the information obtained in this way was quite useful.

In Case B, Marlton National Bank provides detailed information about the features and pricing of its competitors' equity credit line, including a comparison of basic products, hours, locations, and operating statistics as well as competitive marketing strategies, to the extent that they are observable.

Marketing Intermediaries

As mentioned in chapter 2, marketing intermediaries in the banking business are firms or organizations that enable the bank to offer a service or distribute its products through a third party. The situation analysis in a marketing plan for a credit card or for a service such as automated balance reporting (where business customers call in for balance information to a third party that collects and reports the information) would include a section addressing relevant factors, such as accessibility, timeliness, pricing, and courtesy, concerning the intermediary. This is not the case for either Marlton National Bank or Consumers National Bank.

Publics

In developing its plans, a bank must be sensitive to the internal and external publics that might be interested in or affected by elements of the plan. For example, community action groups can stand in the way of a bank's plan to acquire another financial institution to expand its distribution system. When such groups demonstrate that a bank has not met the borrowing needs of the community it is already serving, regulators will not approve the acquisition plan until the situation is resolved.

An internal public that must be considered in the development of a marketing plan is the bank's employees. Staff at all levels should be kept informed about the bank's plans, and employees who will be involved in any way in implementing the plan must be trained for the task. The training must be part of the plan.

The planners of Case B considered the impact of the new product on their various publics and determined that no special efforts with regard to these audiences were required. The effect of the new product on the bank's principal internal public, the bank's staff, is addressed within the self-analysis. Because the bank is one of the last in its market area to introduce this product, the plan is to rely on modest levels of advertising to make the public aware of its availability. If the bank had been the first in the market to offer the product, the plan would have included a publicity program to attract the attention of the media.

Analysis of Problems and Opportunities

When all of the data have been gathered and analyzed, the final step of the situation analysis is to summarize the relevant information learned. While in fact this is a summary of the bank's strengths and weaknesses, calling it an analysis of problems and opportunities reflects a more action-oriented perspective. The summary should be a set of factual statements, with no attempt being made to provide either sources of the facts or solutions to the problems. It should cover the main opportunities and problems facing the bank. In the course of the situation analysis, many problems and opportunities will be identified, but not all of them can or should be addressed in the plan. This summary will become the foundation for the development of objectives, strategies, and tactics. The strengths can be used in developing strategies for the coming year (or other planning period). Identifying the weaknesses enables the bank to plan ways to correct them.

In Case B, Marlton National Bank has identified two problems, or weaknesses, that bear on introducing an equity credit line: its late entry into the market and its preponderance of fixed-rate assets in the loan portfolio, both of which will be resolved through the new product. In addition, it lists six opportunities or strengths on which it can capitalize with this new product. Consumers National Bank's summary of problems and opportunities lists 11 points, only one of which is positive. The bank clearly has a serious marketing challenge facing it.

Having answered the question "Where are we now?" through the situation analysis, the next step is to ask "Where do we want to go?" That question is answered through the objective-setting process and the selection of the target market(s). The next chapter treats objective setting and discusses the subsequent steps that will answer the question, "How are we going to get there?"

Summary

Four steps are involved in developing a situation analysis, the first step in marketing planning. First, the bank must look hard at itself by evaluating internal secondary data and by amassing feedback from customers and noncustomers through primary research. The bank should evaluate its current marketing strategies-product, pricing, promotion, and place (distribution)-as well as its current market position and market share. This information may be obtained from internal primary and secondary sources, including market research, financial statements, and observations made by the bank's staff.

The second step in the situation analysis is an analysis of the macroenvironmental factors that pertain to the topic covered by the marketing plan. The bank must understand the economic environment in which it competes. Some of the data that should be part of the economic analysis are employment trends, retail trade activity, and construction activity. Some attempt should be made to forecast the economic environment over the period the plan covers.

In this second step the bank should also study the relevant demographic environment because population size, shifts, age, education, and occupation all bear on the selection of marketing strategies. Social and cultural factors affect values and attitudes, which in turn affect consumer purchasing behavior. The political and legal environment is often a factor in bank marketing planning because banking regulation and legislation affect many bank product and distribution strategies. The technological environment most frequently affects the way banking products are serviced and delivered.

The third step in the situation analysis is an analysis of the microenvironmental factors that pertain to the topic of the plan. These factors include information on the bank's customers, much of which may be obtained from survey research. Actual and potential markets that the bank might target with its strategies should be identified and described in as much detail as possible. Information on the competitive environment should include operating statistics, market shares and trends, and a comparison of competitive strategies. Where marketing intermediaries will be used, they should also be treated in the situation analysis, as should the effect of the plan on the bank's various publics.

The final step in the situation analysis-the summary of the bank's problems and opportunities (or strengths and weaknesses)-concisely summarizes what has been learned in the first three steps, without making judgments or offering solutions. That is left for the objective-setting process.

The situation analysis is a necessary first step in any planning project, whether it be for an entire bank or for one particular product. Whatever the planning topic or period, the marketer must be able to answer the question, "Where are we now?" The situation analysis provides that answer.

Points for Review

1. Make three points in response to the following statement by your bank's chief executive officer: "I know what our strengths and weaknesses are. We don't need to do all this situation analysis business. We can develop our objectives without it."

2. What are the four steps in a situation analysis?

3. Compare and contrast primary and secondary data.

4. What are some of the principal sources of information that might be used in a bank's self-analysis?

5. Why is data on employment trends, retail activity, and construction activity important in an economic analysis? What does this tell the bank?

6. Give examples of surveys banks can conduct to assess their microenvironment. What information useful to the situation analysis can be derived from surveys?

7. What is the meaning of the term *market share*? Why is it of interest to bankers?

8. What three characteristics should the statement of problems and opportunities have?

Notes

1. "Amarillo National Bank Will Pay for Rain," Bank Marketing, July 1996, p. 8; "Rainmaker CD Pays Off for Amarillo National Customers," Bank Marketing, August 1996, p. 8.

2. Jim Boucher, "Using Information Services to Sneak a Peak at the Competition," Bank Marketing, March 1996, pp. 32-35.

3. Sheshunoff & Company, Inc., P.O. Box 13203, Capitol Station, Austin, TX 78711. The volume is entitled *Banks of (State name)*.

4. Sheshunoff also publishes branch deposit data.

5

SETTING GOALS AND OBJECTIVES AND IDENTIFYING STRATEGIES AND TACTICS

Learning Objectives

After studying this chapter, you should be able to

- differentiate among the terms *goal, objective, strategy,* and *tactic,*
- provide five reasons why it is important to set goals and objectives,
- describe three levels of objectives set within a business,
- describe five characteristics that marketing objectives should possess,
- define market segmentation, and discuss as an example of segmentation strategy the purpose and content of the product/market expansion matrix, and
- list eight steps that might be followed in developing a bank marketing plan, and apply the eight steps to a bank marketing plan and a product marketing plan.

Introduction

Armed with the results of the situation analysis, the marketing planner is ready to set a goal that answers the question "Where do we want to go?" To achieve that goal, the marketer must first create objectives that answer the question "How do we reach our goal?" This chapter explains how to set goals and objectives and their importance in the planning process, and what characteristics goals and objectives should possess.

Once the objectives have been determined, the planner is ready to select the market or markets that will be targeted and to design the marketing-mix strategies that will attract them. This chapter introduces the concept of *market segmentation,* a way of subdividing markets into unique groups of consumers who will respond similarly to a particular marketing strategy. It also introduces the product/market expansion matrix, one of the tools that describes four strategies open to a marketer.

To relate this process to the real world, the chapter describes an eight-step procedure that a community bank might follow in developing a marketing plan. It then looks at two very different examples of marketing planning: a product marketing plan (Case B) and a total bank marketing plan (Case F). Although the two are very different in scope, each contains the basic elements of a marketing plan: situation analysis, goal and objective setting, target-market identification, marketing strategies, and plans for evaluating results.

Setting Goals and Objectives

Generally speaking, a *goal* is a broad statement of direction (for example, "to become the leading bank in the retail market in our state") that succinctly describes what the bank wants to achieve. A goal can set the tone and the theme for all groups in the bank, but each group contributes to the achievement of a goal by tapping its unique strengths and specialties. It is important to differentiate between the terms *goal* and *objective* and not to use them interchangeably.

Marketing objectives should speak of specific, measurable results that are to be attained in the pursuit of a broader corporate or financial goal (which might be to achieve a return on assets of 1 percent, or to increase core deposits by $50 million). A marketing objective that supports this corporate goal might focus on increasing a particular product line, such as "increase deposits by $10 million through increased sales of certificates of deposit." For marketing planning purposes, it is necessary to develop carefully thought-out objectives that will support and help attain marketing goals.

A goal can be supported by many objectives or by just one. Here are a few examples of goals and their supporting objectives. These examples will illustrate how a goal describes the broad direction for the bank and the objectives break down more specific steps that will lead to achieving those goals.

Goal: To be recognized as a friendly, convenient bank by the greater community by the end of the fiscal year.

Supporting objectives: To increase press coverage of community relations events by sending out timely notices; to sponsor three community groups with contributions of time and money; to improve customer access to the bank by adding ATMs and expanding office hours.

Goal: To achieve a CRA rating of Outstanding.

Supporting objectives: To reevaluate loan programs and reestablish credit criteria; to establish a community liaison program by year end; to launch a new loan sale program by year end.

As part of the process of developing goals and objectives, the marketer must also develop strategies and tactics. *Strategy* describes the route the bank will take to get to its destination. *Tactics* outline the specific actions to be taken, who is to take them, when, and at what cost. Put another way, strategy defines what will be done; tactics define how it will be done. Strategy and tactics make up an action plan (as opposed to goals and objectives, which set the direction). The terms *strategy* and *tactic* are also often used interchangeably, in error. They have quite different meanings—as any military person will explain.

In planning a road trip, for example, the goal is to take a vacation; the objective is to reach Niagara Falls; the strategy is to map out a sequence of specific highways to follow; the tactics define when to leave, which car to take, who will drive, where to stop along the way, and when to arrive. Exhibit 5.1 defines and compares these four terms.

As a marketer develops a marketing plan, it might take shape as follows. Our goal is to establish a widely accepted image that we are the friendlest, most convenient bank in our community. Our main objective is to increase consumers' loyalty to our bank. Our strategy is to create a warm, inviting atmosphere and easy access to the bank for all customers. Our tactics will include additional

Exhibit 5.1	**The Terminology of Marketing Strategy**	
Term	*Meaning*	*Example*
Marketing Goal	A broad statement of direction	To become the leading retail market in our state
Marketing Objective	The specific measurable results to be attained in pursuit of the corporate or financial objective	Increase retail demand, savings, and money market deposits by $15 million by year-end
Strategy	The specific method devised for achieving the objective	Hire a deposit product manager Introduce at least one new deposit product Improve the cross-sales skills of branch staff Provide an incentive for all employees to refer deposit customers to the bank Solicit additional deposit business from existing customers
Tactic	Specific actions to be taken	Instruct human resources to begin recruiting for a product manager immediately Develop and implement a cross-sales training program by January 15 Prepare proposal for incentive program by year end Using central information file, develop list of customers with total balances in excess of $10,000 who have no checking or money market account with the bank.

customer service training for all staff members, a new television and newspaper ad campaign, a new mobile bank, new ATMs in convenient locations, and extended bank hours.

Importance of Setting Goals and Objectives

Armed with the situation analysis, which tells management where the bank stands now and what the conditions in the marketing environment currently are, the bank must determine which problems and opportunities it wants to address and how it will go about doing that. This step is not necessarily easy, but it is critical. There are at least five good reasons for making the effort to establish goals and objectives.

1. *Goals and objectives serve as a guide for planning strategies and tactics.* The question "What do we want to achieve?" or "Where do we want to go?" (which is the goal) must be answered before deciding how to get there. Likewise, in bank marketing planning, management must decide where the bank should go before it can set the marketing strategies and tactics to get it there. As mentioned earlier, "If you don't know where you want to go, any road will take you there."

2. *Objectives form the basis for the marketing budgeting process.* Once the strategies and tactics for accomplishing the bank's objectives are determined, the cost of executing them can be estimated. In the process of doing this, management will be able to compare the projected income and the expenses related to attaining each objective. It is not unusual at this stage for management to decide that reaching an objective is not recommended because it will not bring in enough revenue. When this happens, management must either create less costly strategies and tactics or select another objective.

3. *Objectives form the basis for evaluating performance.* Appraising how well something has been done is impossible

without knowing what was to be accomplished. Bank marketing experts Joselyn and Humphries[1] use an excellent example of two football coaches, one with a 6-win/5-loss record and one with a 5-win/6-loss record. Which coach did the better job? Without additional information, that question cannot be answered. In fact, the coach with the 5–6 record was given a three-year contract while the other coach's contract was not renewed. The reason in each case had to do with performance relative to goals. The objective of the 6–5 team was to win its conference, but it failed to reach its objective. The 5–6 team had not won at all the previous year, so accomplishing its objective of winning five games represented a tremendous success. Likewise, determining how well a bank has done is impossible if the bank has no objectives.

4. *Without objectives the bank would not know whether its strategies and tactics are working.* When objectives are exceeded, or are ahead of schedule or are not met, the bank can reexamine its situation analysis, strategies, and tactics to see why the results are different from those projected. Goals form the basis for refining and adjusting objectives to keep them on track.

5. *Objectives can help build team spirit.* By communicating the bank's goals throughout the bank and then having every level of bank employee participate in setting objectives to achieve those goals, management makes it possible for each member of the staff to see his or her role in the bank's mission. Also, everyone recognizes that all the other employees are working toward the same goals and that all are involved in a cooperative effort. By and large, employees like to see a purpose in what they are doing on the job every day. In fact, conscientious employees frequently set their own unofficial objectives in the absence of clear direction from management. Since these objectives may not be consistent with management's, it is far better to involve all personnel in the overall objective–setting

process to ensure that everybody's efforts (that is, tactics) are being channeled in the right direction.

The Hierarchy of Goals in Business

A hierarchy of goals establishes the identity, financial plan, and marketing vision of the bank: the mission statement, the corporate or financial goals, and the marketing goals. (See exhibit 5.2.)

Governing the overall direction and purpose of the bank is the *mission statement*. All goals and objectives support the mission statement and are designed to help the bank achieve its purpose. A mission statement is "a brief, communicable, high-level statement that defines the institution's reason for being. . . . The mission statement should identify the business(es) the institution wants to be in, its target market(s), and the way(s) it plans to compete."[2] Every bank's board of directors should develop a mission statement. Once completed, the statement changes very little over time. A mission statement lends a bank its unique identity and differentiates it from the competition. It establishes the bank's short-term and long-term goals. The mission statement serves as the guidance for all new business ideas because it clearly states the purpose and direction of the company. All corporate, financial, and marketing goals should support the mission statement. The mission statement can also unite all the employees of a bank, especially a bank with many branches and locations in other states, because of the guidance it provides. A mission statement might consist of goals such as the following:

- Our bank is dedicated to meeting the financial needs of the people and businesses of Overland County.
- Our ultimate goal is to maximize shareholder value.

Corporate goals (also called *financial goals*) are set by the bank's executive management and are based primarily on the bank's financial statements. They tend to be quantitative, and they tend to be long range in their focus. Some examples might be

- to achieve a 1 percent return on average assets,
- to increase by 10 percent the ratio of interest-sensitive assets in the bank's portfolio, and
- to increase fee income by $5 million.

Exhibit 5.2 **Hierarchy of Goals**	
Category	*Example*
Mission Statement	"To provide for the people and businesses of Overland County quality financial products and service that is distinguished by personal attention to customer needs and expectations."
Corporate or Financial Goal	"To increase noninterest income by $20,000 by year end."
Marketing Goal	"To develop and introduce one new fee-income producing product by the second quarter."

These corporate financial goals should be communicated throughout the bank to establish a common purpose and to form the basis for setting marketing goals.

Marketing goals are set by senior and middle management and are based on the bank's financial goals as well as the situation analysis. A marketing goal may sound quite similar to a corporate goal or financial goal. If a financial goal for the bank is to increase consumer credit outstandings by 50 percent, the marketing goal may be phrased the same way. However, the marketing objectives that support that goal are statements of the specific, measurable results that the marketing effort is expected to produce. These marketing objectives may be short term (one year or less) or longer. A marketing objective to support the above marketing goal might be "to increase the proportion of variable rate credit in the consumer loan portfolio to 25 percent."

Some other examples of marketing objectives that support corporate financial goals (which, again, might be phrased in the same way when used as a marketing goal) might be

- to increase the proportion of commercial loans relative to the total loan portfolio from 15 percent to 20 percent, or
- to increase the use of bank services by existing customers from an average of 2.67 services to 2.85 services per customer.

Another marketing objective that might support a corporate goal of strengthening marketing position from third in the market to second could be to create among at least 60 percent of the banking public in our trade area a perception that the bank is a strong hometown bank with a dedicated commitment to supporting the local community.

Each of these objectives involves marketing expertise, including pricing, personal selling, promotion, and possibly product strategy and distribution strategy. Achieving the bank's marketing goals and objectives also will involve many of the operating areas of the bank.

Characteristics of Marketing Objectives

Although the mission statement and the corporate goals define and affect marketing goals (and hence, the marketer's job), the marketer rarely has a role in developing or revising the mission statement or corporate goals. Therefore we will move directly to a discussion of marketing objectives, which will serve as the road map for every marketer's job and which support the marketing goals that reflect the corporate goals and mission statement.

Marketing objectives should possess five characteristics:

1. *They should be measurable.* They should be stated in terms of specific results to be achieved.

2. *They should complement the bank's financial goals.* By achieving its marketing objectives, a bank should also reach its marketing goals and its financial goals. In addition, marketing greatly reinforces its vital role in the bank's success when it produces a clear financial contribution.

3. *They should be appropriate for the level of job.* Every bank employee should have objectives that are realistic within the context of his or her job. Informing a teller that the bank's marketing goal is to increase deposits by 20 percent is a waste of time. A more realistic approach would be to give the teller the marketing objective of cross-selling the bank's products to at least three customers per week. The teller now has something to strive for that is within his or her capability.

4. *They should be flexible.* The bank must have a system for continually monitoring progress toward achieving its marketing objectives. If an objective turns out to be unrealistic, it must be revised. If objectives are realistic but not being met, corrective action can be taken.

5. *They should stretch the bank and each department in it to excellence.* The marketing objective should relate realistically to the market potential, yet it should be challenging.

Developing a Strategy

Once the bank's management has decided "where it wants the bank to go" and has set goals and objectives that will ensure it reaches that "destination," it is time to develop an action plan—a marketing strategy. This part of the planning process answers in greater detail the question "How are we going to get there?"

In developing a marketing strategy, marketers create a specific mix of product, price, promotion, and place (distribution) to meet the needs of a target group of customers or prospects (that is, a market segment). Thus, creating a marketing strategy is a two-step process: first, selecting or segmenting the target market or markets; second, designing the marketing mix to attract them.

Segmentation and Target Market Selection

Market segmentation recognizes the wisdom of specializing to suit the needs of a segment of the market rather than trying to be all things to all people. A company claiming that its product represents both the highest prestige and the lowest price has not identified its target market. Its products are probably being outstripped in the marketplace by competitors' products promoted as being prestigious or low priced, but not both. The problem with trying to be all things to all people is that buyers in the market for the same product (for example, bank services, wristwatches, automobiles) are far from homogeneous in how they want their needs and wants satisfied. Consequently, they differ in how they respond to specific marketing mixes. When it is segmented, a market is subdivided into groups of customers who are very similar in needs, wants, preferences, and responses to specific stimuli.

Banks can very effectively segment their own customer base by using a marketing customer information file (MCIF) system, or, as it is sometimes called, a relationship management system. An MCIF is one giant information file containing customer data. Not only does an MCIF allow a bank to track its customers' account holdings, it also allows the bank to determine the correct audience for cross-sell campaigns. With an MCIF, any of these groups, or market segments, might be selected as a target market to be reached with a distinct marketing mix. The bank can also purchase customer information and merge it with the bank's database to produce an even more targeted market segment.

Throughout the early 1990s, MCIF systems focused only on customer information; therefore, although groundbreaking initially, they are now somewhat limited. Some MCIF companies are working to broaden the technology to include more information that will make the system even more effective. For example, in the mid-1990s, even though some systems could process 2 million records per minute, companies were working to increase processing speed and storage capacity.[3] These advances will help marketers get answers to marketing questions more quickly, "mine" customer information more effectively, and identify the optimal time and way to communicate with profitable prospects.

Many firms have segmented their markets so successfully that they have dramatically influenced their industry. For instance, Timex is famous for having identified a market segment made up of people who desire an inexpensive, stylish, and durable watch. Timex proved that not everyone wants an expensive, elegantly styled watch with a high-prestige brand name. In contrast, the manufacturer of Rolex watches targets an entirely different market segment with its product and marketing mix strategies. The Rolex is priced in four figures, and the images projected by its advertising relate to success and prestige. In contrast with both Timex and Rolex is Swatch. With its bright colors and creative designs, Swatch appeals to a younger, more contemporary market.

In the banking industry, more banks are finding ways to meet the needs of both "upscale" and "downscale" markets. San Francisco–based Union Bank found a way to bring low- and moderate-income families into the bank. These families found checking accounts too expensive and were taking their paychecks to check-cashing stores. Union Bank created a product that would allow noncustomers to carry a special photo identification card and, for a nominal annual fee, cash checks and request free money orders.[4] To meet the needs of customers who have higher balances and investment needs but who do not qualify for the traditional trust services, Citicorp has created upscale CitiGold offices.

Since the object of market segmentation is to identify a specific group and then pursue it with a tailored mix of product, pricing, promotion, and distribution, market segments must have certain qualities that make it possible to tailor the marketing approach. A market segment must be measurable, accessible, and substantial. In other words, it must be possible to measure the size and purchasing power of the market segment. It must be feasible to reach members of that segment through advertising and distribution methods. And it must be substantial or sizable enough to generate a profitable volume.

There are a number of different approaches to market segmentation. The approach a particular bank chooses should enable the bank to make each group of customers and prospects as distinct as possible from the other segmented groups in its needs and wants. The various types of segmentation alternatives that a firm or bank might follow are described in chapter 8.

Marketing Strategy and Tactics

Once the target market or markets have been identified, the marketer must determine which marketing mixes and which tactics should be used. This is a two-stage operation that requires considerable evaluation of alternatives and plenty of imagination. The two stages are discussed below.

Marketing Strategy

The basic elements in the market mix are the bank's products and the target markets at whom those products will be aimed. Once it is determined what will be sold to whom, the pricing, promotion, and distribution strategies will fall into place more easily.

Given any single objective, any of a number of paths can be followed to attain it. For example, to meet the objective of increasing core deposits, a bank might develop and market a new type of certificate of deposit, or pay slightly above-market rates on deposits, or design an incentive program to encourage staff to cross-sell deposit services.

One of the many tools the marketing manager can use to identify alternative product and segmentation strategies is the *product/market expansion matrix.* (See exhibit 5.3.) Basically, this matrix indicates how a bank can grow either by selling more of its current products to current and new customers or by selling new products to current and new customers.

As an example, let us assume that the personal-credit product manager is seeking alternative ways to increase outstanding loans. The first task is to identify where on this matrix the bank is currently concentrating the bulk of its energies. (This information would have been included in the situation analysis.)

Next, the product manager can use the matrix to see what options are available. Basically, four options are possible: increase penetration in the current market, find new markets, develop new products for the current market, and diversify by creating new products for new markets. The product manager can concentrate on one option or use all four options simultaneously.

● *Market penetration* (selling present products to present markets). One marketing strategy would be to cross-sell personal

Exhibit 5.3	**Product/Market Expansion Matrix**	

Markets	*Present Products*	*New Products*
Present	Market Penetration Improve bank's position with present products in present markets	Product Expansion Develop new products for present markets
New	Market Expansion Find new markets to use bank's present products	Diversification or Product/Market Expansion Develop new products for new markets

lines of credit to present installment-loan customers or to sell new loans to present borrowers who have very few payments remaining. Many other examples of this type of strategy could and should be enumerated as part of the strategy-setting process.

- *Market expansion* (selling present products to new markets). One way this might be done is through physical expansion, such as establishing a loan production office in a new territory. It might also involve finding new customers within the bank's present trade area by, for example, selling home equity loans through a direct mail solicitation to homeowners who meet certain income and property value criteria, running ads for a loan sale in the local media to attract a greater-than-average share of new auto and personal loans, or offering an incentive to encourage employees to bring in new loan customers.[5]

- *Product expansion* (developing and selling new products to present markets). Product expansion might be accomplished by designing a new installment-loan product. An example would be the variable-rate loan that enables the borrower to take advantage of reductions in interest rates. In this way, the bank can offer new services

to present customers and very likely attract new ones.

- *Diversification or product/market expansion* (developing and selling new products to new markets). Following this strategy, the bank would develop new products intended to attract specific new markets. For instance, the installment loan product manager might decide to go after the high-net-worth market segment. Since these individuals borrow for investment and other purposes requiring larger-than-average sums of money, the product manager might propose the development of a $50,000 to $250,000 line of credit to be marketed to this group. Case B is an example of a product/market expansion strategy.

The recent history of the U.S. banking industry itself provides a good example of the use of these four strategies for growth. Many banks that had achieved a high rate of penetration of their local areas expanded their markets by branching into new areas. They became regional, rather than local, banks. Some even expanded across multiple state lines. As they grew, their bank holding companies acquired or developed other types of financial service companies, such as discount brokerage companies, mortgage companies, commercial finance companies, automobile and equipment leasing companies, and insurance companies, enabling them to offer new products to both present and new markets. These banking companies have used the strategies of market penetration, market expansion, product expansion, and diversification in their attainment of their long-term financial objectives.

These are but a few examples of the many ways that a bank could answer the question "How are we going to get there?" It is all too easy for bankers and other professionals to fall into the routine of coming up with the same stale approaches year after year, without stretching their sights or their imaginations. The product/market expansion matrix can help stimulate new thoughts.

Marketing Tactics

Often the term *objective* is used to refer to results that are to be achieved by individual employees. However, from a marketing planning perspective, those actions performed by employees are marketing *tactics*—specific actions performed in pursuit of the marketing objective.

Tactics describe what specific actions are to be taken, who will take them, when, and at what cost. For the various elements of the marketing strategy to be implemented, a number of individuals will have to implement a variety of tactics (in line with their job responsibilities) that are oriented toward reaching the bank's objectives. (See Case F.) Ideally, every employee in the bank should have specific, measurable, personal goals and objectives that relate to achieving the bank's objectives. If the marketing objective is to increase the average number of services used per customer by some amount, the teller's personal objective might be to cross-sell a specific service three times per week, while the branch manager's personal objective might be to hold quarterly training sessions for the tellers to increase their understanding of the bank's products and services. The bank might choose to provide incentives to further motivate employees to reach or exceed their objectives. (The use of incentives is a sales promotion strategy and is discussed in chapter 13.)

Strategy Formulation in Action

Because it depends on a number of factors, the planning process varies considerably from bank to bank. The marketing planning process is affected by everything from the size of the institution to the personality of the chief executive officer to the status of marketing in the organization. Nevertheless, it is possible to talk about a model situation and to identify eight steps for establishing objectives, strategies, and tactics within a bank.

The Eight-Step Process

The marketing director's role in formulating strategies may vary from bank to bank. In some banks, the marketing director organizes and coordinates the entire process. In others, that role may be played by the planning director or another member of senior management.

The planning process should be started mid-year, after the presentation of the situation analysis. An early start is necessary so that all the steps, including budgeting, can be completed thoroughly before the budget is finalized, usually in October or November in the banking industry. The eight steps in the planning process are as follows:

Step 1: The bank's corporate objectives should be reviewed by all managers. All banks have corporate objectives; however, they might not have been clearly articulated and communicated. This must be done before going any further.

Step 2: Review both the corporate objectives and the situation analysis with all management personnel together. (The areas of responsibility represented might be the community banking department, the commercial lending department, the trust department, the consumer credit department, and so on. Each of these departments serves a specific market or group of markets.) At this meeting, ask each manager to prepare a set of objectives for his or her area of responsibility. Preparing these objectives will force each manager to review his or her department in light of the bank's overall situation and the corporate objectives. Set a date for turning in these recommendations. If any revision in the situation analysis or corporate objectives is needed, it should be done after studying the objectives submitted by the managers.

Step 3: Have each manager go back to his or her department and, working with the senior staff, further refine the department's objectives and its overall strategy in addressing its markets. These are to be submitted at the time specified during the meeting in step 2.

Step 4: Review each manager's objectives individually to determine if they are realistic and consistent with the bank's mission and corporate objectives. For example, if the population is declining, it may be unrealistic to set an objective calling for a 10 percent increase in retail deposits. After reviewing the objectives, negotiate revisions and set a second date for meeting with all management to develop specific, measurable objectives and general strategies for reaching them. It is important at this point to have some idea of the level of resources required to achieve recommended objectives.

Step 5: Meet with managers to finalize the objectives for each department of the bank. At this meeting, the managers will learn one another's objectives and tactics and root out potential inconsistencies in the marketing plan. For instance, the consumer deposit product manager (or the head of retail banking) may want to increase the account base by promoting overdraft checking, and the credit product manager may want to reduce credit losses by curtailing unsecured personal credit. Some compromise will have to be reached. Also during this meeting, top management can allocate resources for the various programs. By looking at the combined plans and the estimated resources required,

management can view potential gains in light of available resources and avoid inconsistencies.

Step 6: The managers should go back to their departments and work out specific strategies and tactics for accomplishing the objectives. The cost is calculated, the responsibility is assigned, and the methods of measurement and control are determined.

Step 7: The managers submit their budgets, which are then consolidated to come up with a projected net income. In many cases, the results are not acceptable to management the first time around. Therefore, budgets are reviewed with the various managers individually, and revisions are negotiated.

Step 8: Department heads and staff develop the specific tactics or objectives for each staff member's role in executing the strategy. These may be put into a management-by-objectives format so that it is clear what each employee is required to do, when it is to be completed, and how the performance will be measured. This procedure is discussed in more detail in the chapter on performance monitoring and evaluation.

Applying Strategy to a Bank Marketing Plan

At this point, it will be helpful to refer to Case F to study the goals, objectives, strategies, and tactics set forth for the hypothetical Consumers National Bank. This case is presented for illustrative purposes only. It is not intended to be all-inclusive, and it focuses only on some of the retail deposit and commercial loan objectives of a bank. In Section II of Case F, four corporate objectives are presented. Although they are quite general, they clearly set the direction for the bank.

Only 10 marketing objectives are presented. Notice that each objective is specific and quantifiable and can be used to measure performance. Furthermore, the dates by which the objectives are to be achieved have been set and the persons responsible for achieving them have been identified.

Section III shows the beginning of an action plan for the achievement of these objectives. A strategy is set, and the tactics needed to implement it are spelled out. Again, the timing, the resource commitment, and the responsibility are clearly defined.

The next stages in the process—implementation and performance monitoring and evaluation—are dealt with in detail in chapter 15. However, a few words are in order at this point. Chapter 1 states that whether a bank (or any organization) has reached the ultimate phase of marketing enlightenment can be determined by examining whether it has installed systems for market analysis, planning, and control. Chapter 2 explains that the marketing management process involves planning, implementation, and evaluation of results. At the risk of overemphasizing this point, it should be repeated.

Measurement, evaluation, and control are necessary elements in the planning process. Without these elements, a bank will not know when it has arrived at its destination. Without this step, the ongoing process of planning comes to a grinding halt.

It is to be anticipated that, in most marketing planning cases, the plan will not work as expected. Conditions change; people do not respond as expected; something does not work. By instituting an adequate program for monitoring the progress of the plan, the bank can identify problem areas and the reasons for them and make "in-flight" corrections to get the plan back on course. The plan must include a control mechanism—a monitoring system. Reports serve this purpose and are a necessary by-product of the planning process. Their frequency (weekly, monthly, quarterly) will depend on the nature of the task and the management level of the person responsible for them. The more strategic the object of control or the more senior the person responsible, the less frequent the need for reports. Conversely, the more tactical the object of control and the more line-related the function, the more frequent the need for reports.

Applying Strategy to a Product Marketing Plan

The planning process remains essentially the same regardless of the scope of the plan. This is demonstrated in Case B, which presents a marketing plan for a new home-equity credit line for the hypothetical Marlton National Bank. All the elements involved in formulating a marketing strategy are presented in Sections II and III of the plan, which was prepared by the consumer credit product manager.

First, the corporate objectives agreed on by the directors in approving the bank's five-year retail plan specified their desire to increase the ratio of interest-sensitive assets in the bank's portfolio and to achieve a profit margin of at least 2 percent on consumer credit products.

The situation analysis had been conducted, and the summary of problems and opportunities was reviewed. As a result of this analysis, the product manager developed five marketing objectives and identified nine specific goals to be attained in working toward them. These objectives will require activity by the product managers, the advertising department, the marketing research department, the training department, the accounting department, and the consumer loan operations division. In other words, accomplishing the marketing objectives involves many areas within the bank.

The product manager, in this case, presents the detailed marketing strategy and tactics in Section III of the plan. The general marketing strategy being used is product and market expansion—designing a new product to appeal to a specific new target market. Although members of this target market are in the bank's current customer base, the objective is to attract new customers who fit the description of high-income heads of full-nest households.

The detailed marketing strategy spells out the product, pricing, promotion, and distribution strategies and tactics to be used in introducing the new home-equity line of credit, as well as the departments responsible for them. For instance, the marketing tactics to be used in executing the "niche" promotional strategy include specific plans for advertising, point-of-sale promotions, direct mail promotions, and telemarketing. Similarly, the distribution strategy specifies tactics for ensuring that the product is cross-sold by the bank staff who are in a position to do so.

Finally, the plan specifies the ways in which progress toward the nine goals will be measured and reported. It makes clear who is responsible for generating the reports and to whom they are to be provided.

When a plan such as this has been finalized, it is useful for the planning manager to prepare a chart such as the one in exhibit 5.4. This chart shows, at a glance, the

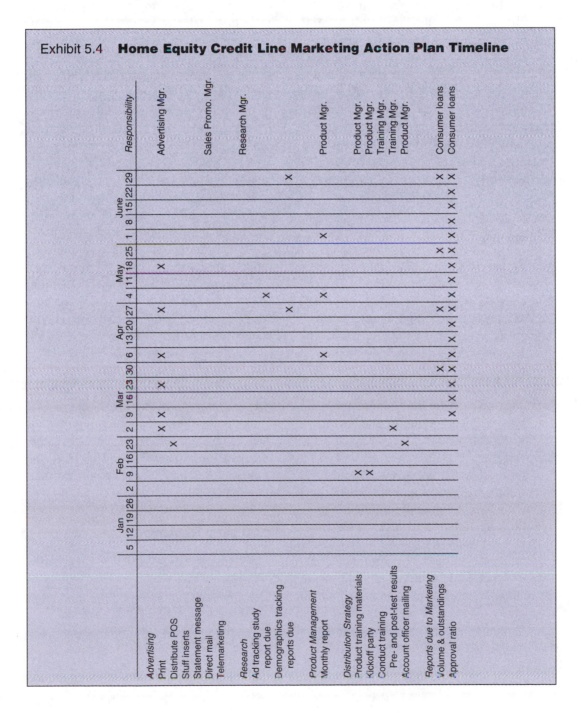

Exhibit 5.4 Home Equity Credit Line Marketing Action Plan Timeline

timetable for implementing the various tactical elements and for measuring the results. It might be posted in the marketing department where it would serve as a reminder both for management and all relevant staff members of the goals of the program and what should be happening at any time. In the ideal situation, the plan for the home equity credit line will be incorporated into the marketing plan for all retail installment loans, and these will become part of the total bank marketing plan.

In a bank that has not yet become planning oriented, such a one-product marketing plan can be completed for one department with great success. Managers who use this management process (which is what planning is) will distinguish themselves as catalysts for planning, and the process may spread to other departments throughout the bank.

Summary

The process of setting goals and objectives answers the questions "Where are we going?" and "What do we want to achieve?" as well as "How are we going to get there?" Marketing objectives are statements of the specific, measurable results to be attained in pursuing a financial objective. Objectives guide the planning of strategies and tactics; they form the basis for the budgeting process, for evaluating performance, and for determining corrective action; they also help build team spirit.

Mission statements express the goals and vision of the bank. Missions are generally set by the directors of an institution and change very little, if at all, over time. They are usually quite brief because they deal only with the general direction of the institution. Corporate, or financial, objectives are long-range objectives that are narrower in scope and are financially oriented. Marketing objectives flow from the corporate objectives and may be long- or short-term in scope.

Marketing objectives should be specific and measurable and should have certain characteristics: they should help the bank achieve its corporate and marketing objectives; they should be capable of being translated into realistic objectives for each individual job; they should be flexible; and they should stretch the bank and everyone in it to excellence.

Through strategy formulation, the bank answers the question "How are we going to get there?" Formulating a strategy requires two steps: selecting target markets and designing the marketing mix to reach them. Markets must first be studied so that they can be segmented into unique groups that will react in the same way to a given marketing mix. Once segmented, the bank can choose the segment or segments that will be targeted with its marketing strategies and tactics. Many possible strategies are available to the marketing planner, and one of the tools that can help the marketer think through them is the product/market expansion matrix. This matrix encompasses four strategies known as market penetration, market expansion, product expansion, and diversification.

Marketing tactics are the specific actions that are to be taken when executing the marketing strategy. Their description should include the identification of who will undertake them and at what cost.

The planning process may vary from bank to bank and situation to situation, but the essential ingredients that should always be included in one way or another are the situation analysis, objectives, target market identification, strategies and tactics, and the procedures for measuring and evaluating results.

Points for Review

1. Define or briefly explain each of the following terms:
   • market segmentation
   • mission statement
   • corporate or financial objective
   • marketing objective
   • strategy
   • tactic

2. What are the five characteristics that marketing objectives should possess?

3. Provide five reasons why objectives should be set.

4. What are three types of objectives that might be set by a bank?

5. Describe the product/expansion matrix and explain its purpose.

6. What is the two-step process in strategy formulation?

7. What are three characteristics that a market segment should possess?

8. What are the eight steps that might be followed in developing a bank marketing plan?

Notes

1. Robert W. Joselyn and D. Keith Humphries, *An Introduction to Bank Marketing Planning* (Washington, D.C.: American Bankers Association, 1974). Much of the information contained in this chapter is based on this publication.

2. George M. Bollenbacher, *The New Business of Banking* (Burr Ridge, Ill.: Irwin Professional, 1995), p. 236.

3. For more information on MCIFs, call leading providers for brochures, information, articles, and updates. Check the resource list in this textbook. Also see Tony Gonchar and David Raab, "MCIFs: An Index of Possibilities," *Bank Marketing*, February 1997, pp. 22–28; David M. Raab, "A Guide to Database Marketing Systems."

4. Michael J. Major, "Check Cashing Services Offer New Profits," *Bank Marketing*, February 1994, p. 55.

5. FDIC regulations govern this type of promotion. For instance, the individuals responsible for approving the loan may not be given an incentive for generating loans since this could possibly result in lowered credit standards. The reader is advised to become familiar with these regulations, or to consult legal counsel, before implementing such an incentive program.

Part III

UNDERSTANDING THE MARKET

Part II consisted of a detailed discussion of the strategic marketing planning process and of the first two steps in that process—the situation analysis and the setting of goals and objectives. Part III deals with the next step, a key element in the development of marketing strategy: selection of the market or markets that will be targeted in the pursuit of the organization's objectives.

Marketers attempt to segment the target market into groups that will respond in a similar way to a given marketing strategy. This task requires the marketer to have some understanding of what causes one group of people to react differently from other groups when exposed to the same strategy. In other words, the marketer must be a student of consumer behavior—with respect to both individuals and organizations.

This part of the book deals with consumer and organizational buying behavior and the various stages in the buying process. It also discusses marketing research—the tool used by marketers to understand and measure potential target markets. It concludes with a discussion of a number of strategies for segmenting markets and for positioning a product offering in order to maximize appeal to the target audience.

6

CONSUMER AND ORGANIZATIONAL BUYING BEHAVIOR

Learning Objectives

After studying this chapter, you should be able to

- describe the process of human motivation,
- define the five elements of the hierarchy of needs,
- explain how selective exposure, selective distortion, and selective retention affect the marketing of bank services,
- describe some of the principal social, cultural, psychological, and personal factors that influence purchase behavior,
- describe the four stages in the consumer buying process for banking services, and
- describe the five stages in the organizational buying process.

Introduction

How do individuals select a bank? When asked this question, people most frequently answer that they chose their bank because it was conveniently located. But in most cities and towns, there are a number of banks with convenient locations—sometimes as many as one on every corner of the main intersection. What motivates one person to choose the bank on the northeast corner, and another person to choose the bank on the southeast corner?

Clearly, there is more at work in the decision to "buy" a bank than the convenience of its location. Some of the other factors that enter into the decision-making process can be determined through skillful questioning of the customer. However, there are other factors at work that no amount of direct questioning will uncover because the customer is not even aware of them. Nevertheless, these factors influence the person's choice of a bank, as well as of other products and services. The following sections focus on the various factors that motivate people and organizations to behave as they do.

This chapter provides some background information based on psychology and other behavioral sciences that will help the bank marketer gain a better understanding of why consumers act in a certain manner. Understanding why, what, and how people buy is the foundation for developing new bank products, advertising, distribution channels, personal selling, and related activities designed to meet customers' needs. Without some understanding of consumer behavior and the consumer buying process, bank marketers implementing a chosen marketing mix strategy are proceeding haphazardly at best.

Motivation and Consumer Behavior

Certain basic psychological concepts are fundamental to an understanding of consumer behavior. A good place to start is with the concept of a motive, which is defined as "an internal, energizing force that orients a person's activities toward satisfying needs or achieving goals."[1]

All behavior is motivated; that is, people have motives, or reasons, for doing the things they do. Psychologists generally agree that all human behavior is goal directed and revolves around the desire to satisfy needs.

The motivation process starts with an unsatisfied need. That need is the spark that initiates the chain of events leading to a certain behavior. A need that is unsatisfied (or not adequately satisfied) causes tension within the individual. The individual responds by engaging in some kind of search behavior—that is, he or she seeks a means to satisfy the need and thus reduce the tension. For example, a thirsty person needs water; this unsatisfied need motivates him or her to search for water or some other liquid to satisfy that need. Motivation, then, is a linear process, beginning with an unsatisfied need and ending with that need being met. Goal-directed search behavior is part of that process.

Needs as Motivators of Behavior

Many different kinds of needs motivate human behavior. Psychologist A.H. Maslow[2] developed a classification scheme known as the hierarchy of needs. His widely adopted theory of motivation stresses two fundamental premises:

- *Humans are a wanting animal whose needs depend on what they already have.* This means that only unsatisfied needs can influence behavior. A satisfied need is not a motivator.

- *Human's needs are arranged in a hierarchy of importance.* Once a lower-level need is satisfied, a higher-level need emerges and demands satisfaction.

Maslow describes five classes of needs in order of importance:
1. physiological needs,
2. the need for security,
3. the need to belong,

4. the need for esteem, and
5. the need for self-actualization.

Exhibit 6.1 illustrates this hierarchy of needs.

Physiological Needs

This category includes the basic physical needs of the human body, such as the need for food, water, and sex. Until these are satisfied, no higher-level need is likely to serve as a basis for motivation. To cite an extreme case, people who are fighting starvation will not be motivated by a need to belong to a status group; they may even engage in behavior that lowers self-esteem (such as stealing) because of the greater need to obtain nourishment.

Need for Security and Safety

This second level of needs consists of the need to be protected from such things as physical harm, ill health, economic disaster, and other crises. Some banking services address these needs, and bank advertise-ments often play up to them: "Going on vacation? Will your valuables be safe while you're away? For only pennies a day, you can rent a safe deposit box."

Need for Belonging and Love

These needs are related to the social nature of human beings and the need for companionship. This level and those above it in the hierarchy are referred to as higher-level needs; failure to satisfy them may affect the mental health, rather than the physical health, of an individual. When banks market credit cards through organizations such as major-league sports teams, university alumni associations, labor unions, and other affinity groups, they are appealing to the need of the target audience to belong.

Need for Esteem

This category encompasses both the awareness of one's own importance to others, or self-esteem, and the esteem demonstrated by others. Satisfaction of the individual's

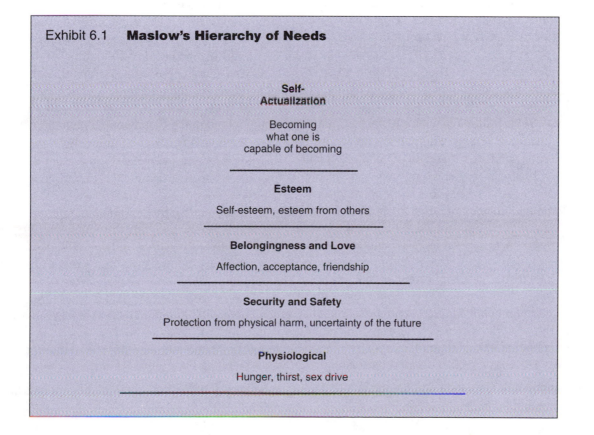

Exhibit 6.1   **Maslow's Hierarchy of Needs**

Self-Actualization

Becoming
what one is
capable of becoming

Esteem

Self-esteem, esteem from others

Belongingness and Love

Affection, acceptance, friendship

Security and Safety

Protection from physical harm, uncertainty of the future

Physiological

Hunger, thirst, sex drive

need for esteem leads to feelings of self-confidence and prestige. Treating bank customers with courtesy and attentiveness and calling them by name enhances their self-esteem and makes them feel good about dealing with the bank. The practice of assigning a personal banker to each customer addresses esteem needs. Personal trust services appeal both to security and esteem needs because they contribute to the self-esteem derived from making provisions for one's heirs.

Need for Self-Actualization

This refers to the need to fully realize one's potential talents and capabilities. Whether someone is a corporate executive, an athlete, a laborer, or a parent, the objective is to be effective and efficient in that role. This drive is usually satisfied only after all other needs in the hierarchy have been met. In our society, where the standard of living is high (relative to that of most other nations), the majority of consumers act at this level. This may help to explain, in part, the tremendous growth in the use of credit cards and personal loans, as people acquire the tools that will help them attain fuller self-actualization. The U.S. Army addresses the need for self-actualization when its advertisements urge young people to "Be all that you can be."

In real life, of course, the need categories are not so segmented. Rather, individuals whose lower-level physiological and security needs are met are usually partially satisfied and dissatisfied in each of the higher-need categories. In other words, at any one time, they are being motivated by needs at several levels. Furthermore, for some individuals, the order of the hierarchy may differ. Esteem needs may take priority over social needs, for example. Nevertheless, the needs hierarchy provides a useful framework for understanding individual behavior and motivation.

If behavior is motivated by unsatisfied needs, why do people with the same needs go about satisfying them in very different

ways? What shapes their behavior? The answer lies in their individual perceptions.

Perception and Consumer Behavior

The following situation occurs daily at banking offices throughout the country: Three individuals approach the bank, which is located at the end of a mini-mall, all needing to deposit a paycheck and obtain some cash. Two park their cars and walk through the front door. The first stops at the automated teller in the vestibule, where no one is waiting in line. The second person waits in a short line in front of a teller station. The third customer pulls up to the drive-in window and waits behind four cars.

What motivates these varying modes of behavior? Why do people continue to buy one brand of soft drink, beer, or cereal even though, when they are blindfolded, they cannot tell the difference between their regular brand and a competing brand? The answer is that each individual brings a unique set of perceptions and attitudes to the process that influences behavior. *Perception* is the process by which people receive information (or stimuli) through the five senses, recognize it, and assign a meaning to it. How people perceive information depends on the nature of the information itself, on its context (that is, what surrounds it), and on conditions within themselves. Furthermore, people's perceptions are limited by three ongoing processes of selectivity: selective exposure, selective distortion, and selective retention.[3]

There are millions of stimuli in our surroundings every day, most of which we do not actually see or respond to. Why is it that some are filtered out and others are perceived? The answer is selective exposure, a process that explains the following:

● *People are more likely to notice stimuli that relate to a current need.* For example, people who are not in the market for a personal loan will not notice ads touting low rates, whereas individuals who are shopping for a loan will notice and even look for these ads. Selective exposure explains the experience that most people have had at one time or another after buying something, such as a particular model car, and then noticing that seemingly half the cars on the road are of that same model.

The advertisement in exhibit 6.2 makes use of several concepts that have been discussed up to this point—specifically, the need for marketers to respond to changes in the environment, recognition of what a powerful motivator safety and security needs can be, and the phenomenon of selective exposure. In late 1992, carjacking emerged as a new way of stealing cars. Thieves were stopping drivers on the road or in parking lots, taking their cars and sometimes abducting and harming the drivers. Publicity about carjacking caused great alarm among drivers and made them worry about their safety. When police authorities suggested ways to avoid carjacking, they included having a car phone. The advertisement in exhibit 6.2 illustrates how one retailer changed its advertising strategy to respond to this situation. Before the carjacking publicity began, the company had been marketing car phones as a holiday gift idea. Counting on the fact that many people, especially women, might want a car phone to feel safe, and looking for a way to satisfy that need, Silo changed its ad to capture safety-conscious consumers' attention.

- *People are more likely to notice stimuli that they expect or anticipate.* This is especially important to bank marketers who are promoting nontraditional bank services, such as mutual funds or travel-related services. Many customers fail to notice the mutual funds desk or the travel agent's desk in a bank because they do not expect those services to be available from a bank. To call attention to these nontraditional services, marketers must use eye-catching promotional techniques.

- *People are more likely to notice stimuli that are large in relation to the normal size of the stimuli.* Banks generally run newspaper advertisements that cover one-quarter or one-third of a page. However, banks that are running a special promotional offer will typically introduce the promotion with full-page ads for a week or two because readers are more likely to notice an ad that is large in relation to the usual bank ad.

Selective distortion, by contrast, is the tendency people have to twist information to make it conform to their existing perceptions. For years, the largest thrift institution in a major metropolitan area paid the highest rates on savings. With the deregulation of interest rates, the institution started to pay rates that were comparable to, or even lower than, rates paid by many commercial banks. Yet, in research surveys, consumers continued to rate this bank as the institution with the highest interest rates. Despite the obvious facts, which could easily be verified by looking in the newspaper and comparing rates, consumers continued to believe that this bank was the best place to save.

Selective retention is the tendency people have to retain only part of what is selectively received, particularly information that supports their existing attitudes and beliefs. Research has shown that consumers are much more likely to recall seeing ads for their own bank than ads for other banks. Their own bank's ads support their choice of that bank.

In light of this inclination, marketers should understand the target audience's perception of the product or service being marketed and play into that perception, not contradict it. A bank should avoid saying something that is inconsistent with the target audience's perception. The bank that ranks third in penetration of the business market but advertises "We're the leading bank for businesses in Overland County" violates this precept. Since the message does not conform to what most business owners or financial officers perceive to be true, these people will either not notice the ad or dismiss it.

Exhibit 6.2

The job of the marketer—especially the advertiser—is to bring about selective exposure that falls within the perception range of the target market. This means selecting the appropriate media (for example, radio stations, newspapers, magazines, TV shows, or sites on the World Wide Web) and presenting a strong message that will be meaningful enough to be retained.

The factors that influence the way people perceive stimuli fall into four categories: social and cultural factors, which influence us from the outside; and psychological and personal factors, which affect us from within.

Social Factors

The way people see things and the way they behave are greatly influenced by the people to whom they relate (social factors). The major social factors influencing buyer behavior are family, reference groups, and roles and status.

Family Influence

Of all the groups that influence consumer behavior, the family is the most fundamental. Many of an individual's basic values and attitudes—for example, one's views of religion, politics, and education, and one's attitudes toward material possessions and thrift—are shaped by the family. In addition to shaping values and attitudes, the family is also a strong reference group whose behavior is imitated, especially by the young. In surveys of a bank's new customers, there is generally a group of respondents who, when asked why they chose this particular bank, reply, "My family has always banked here."

Reference Group Influence

A group that an individual seeks answers from when forming attitudes and opinions is described as a reference group. Most people rely on several reference groups for information on various subjects or relating to different decisions. For example, a person may

This ad targets people who are concerned about security.

consult with one reference group about food-purchasing decisions and another group when seeking financial services or buying a car. An individual need not belong to these reference groups but may aspire to belong to them. Sports stars and other role models may constitute a reference group of one. When it comes to banking, people may look to opinion leaders and other professionals such as attorneys and accountants as guides in choosing a financial institution. Therefore, as part of a bank's marketing strategy, it should identify and reach those reference groups used by personal and corporate clients.

Roles and Status

Every individual belongs to many groups and has a specific position or role within each group. Within a family, a person might function as a wife and mother; in a business organization, that same person may be a sales manager and a supervisor; and in the church, she might be a Sunday school teacher and a choir member. Each role can affect how the individual behaves when purchasing the tools related to that role.

Generally, individuals are anxious to achieve greater status within a given role, and this desire affects their buying behavior. Some products appeal directly to this desire for status. For instance, an ad might imply that good mothers keep a certain brand of children's aspirin handy at all times. Another ad might claim that carrying a certain credit card is a sign of success.

Cultural Factors

Human perceptions and behavior are profoundly influenced, not only by social factors, but by the particular culture in which people live. Cultural influences emanate from the culture at large, from various subcultures, and from social class.

Culture

Culture encompasses the concepts, habits, skills, art, institutions, and values of a given group of people at a particular place and time. Culture significantly affects a person's wants and buying behavior. People the world over have the same basic needs (as described in Maslow's hierarchy), but how those needs are translated into wants and how people go about satisfying those wants vary greatly as a result of their diverse cultures. Some cultural values that prevail in the United States are freedom of expression; a belief in the ability to get ahead through hard work; the importance of education, efficiency, and progress; and the equality of all people.

The influence of culture on banking behavior is reflected in the attitudes of different generations about savings. Emigrants to this country in the late nineteenth and early twentieth centuries scrimped and saved to get here, and then saved even more to buy a house and put down roots. As a result, their children were brought up with a strong savings ethic. Many older firstgeneration Americans remember being taken to the bank when they could not even reach the teller counter to put their small savings into their own account. However, each succeeding generation is further removed from that original culture and is less likely to place as high a value on saving as the prior generation. Combined with that is the cultural importance of material possessions. As a result, the United States now has one of the lowest personal savings rates in the industrialized world.

Subculture

Within the broader culture exist smaller subcultures. These may be based on factors such as national origin (for example, Polish, Irish, Italian, German, or Slavic), race (African American, Asian, Native American), geographic region (New England, the Deep South), or religion (Catholic, Methodist, Jew). Members of a subculture share certain values and attitudes with one another. Marketers who wish to target a subculture must understand its members' needs and wants and develop strategies to meet them.

Social Class

Most societies, including our own, exhibit some kind of stratification that is referred to as *class*. In some societies, the class system is based on religion, kinship, or landed wealth. In this country, social class is determined by education, occupation, and neighborhood of residence-not just the degree of wealth or level of income alone.[4]

Different social classes tend to have varying attitudes and values that are reflected in the consumer behavior of their members. Social scientists have delineated class structures comprising as many as nine classes. Typically, however, class structures include these five groups: the upper class, upper middle class, middle class, working class, and lower class. The middle and working classes combined make up the mass market in this country. Together they account for about 70 percent of the total market. While members of these two groups may have comparable incomes, their source and use patterns (how they earn and how they spend their money) are quite different. Exhibit 6.3 shows some differences between these groups that have been identified by researchers. Obviously these attributes are generalizations and do not apply to every member of a given social class.

Psychological Factors

Society and culture are external factors that influence an individual's buying behavior; psychological and personal factors operate from within. Motivation and perception are psychological factors that are at the foundation of all behavior. However, other psychological factors that come into play in consumer behavior are learning from past experiences, and beliefs and attitudes.

Learning

The learning associated with behavior is not the same as the learning associated with studying something. As applied here, learning means changing one's behavior on the basis of past experiences. When a child gets burned by a stove, he or she learns not to touch it, and the child's mother capitalizes on this learning experience by saying "hot" or "no" when the child approaches an iron or an electrical outlet.

Exhibit 6.3 Differences between the Two Classes That Make Up the Mass Market

Middle Class (32%)	Working Class (38%)
White-collar workers and small-business owners	Blue-collar workers and service workers
Larger, well-cared-for houses in middle-income neighborhoods	Smaller houses in lower-middle-income neighborhoods
Imitate upper classes; spend increasing income on moving up	Spend on larger cars, more kitchen appliances, bigger televisions; spend more on sports
Future oriented; broader horizons	Community oriented; support local teams; buy American; vacation nearby

Source: Adapted from Richard P. Coleman, "The Continuing Significance of Social Class," *Journal of Consumer Research*, December 1983, pp. 270–272.

One popular theory holds that learning is the result of four influences: *drive, cues, response,* and *reinforcement.* This theory, as shall be seen, aligns with the steps in the buying process. Consider a consumer with a drive to improve the interest return on his or her savings. This drive needs to be satisfied, but cues help determine just when and where this will be done. A newspaper advertisement for high-interest certificates of deposit, or a friend's recommendation to open a certificate, might be the cues that stimulate the consumer's response. Reinforcement occurs when the experience involved in making the transaction and the ongoing experience of dealing with the bank is rewarding in terms of interest earned as well as treatment by bank staff. If the response is indeed gratifying, a connection is made between the cue and the response, and a behavior pattern is learned.

Consumers develop brand loyalties when they continually experience rewarding responses. If those rewarding responses become less frequent or cease altogether, the consumer will be open to cues from another bank or from other sources.

Beliefs and Attitudes

A *belief* is a specific, deeply held conviction. A person might believe that savings institutions pay a great deal more interest than commercial banks. This belief will probably influence the person's behavior; that is, he or she will bank at a savings institution. Bank marketers who are well attuned to consumer beliefs are more likely to see when such beliefs are erroneous and, therefore, act to correct them. However, as a result of selective distortion, advertisements that communicate messages that conflict with people's beliefs must be produced in a way that will reduce the likelihood of target audience dismissal.

An *attitude,* unlike a belief, is a positive or negative evaluation, feeling, or tendency toward something. While beliefs are like accepted facts (right or wrong), attitudes are more like feelings (good or bad). People have attitudes toward just about everything, and changing them is quite difficult. Attitudes about thrift ("You should always save a fixed portion of your income") and the use of credit ("It should be used only for emergencies or major purchases") greatly affect banking behavior.

Since attitudes are so hard to change, it is usually preferable to design products and services to coincide with existing attitudes rather than attempt to change them. People selectively retain information that supports their beliefs and attitudes—an important tenet to remember when producing advertising messages.

Personal Factors

Age, stage in the family life cycle, personal economic circumstances, occupation, lifestyle, personality, and self-concept are some of the personal factors that influence consumer behavior.

Age and Family Life Cycle

It should be readily apparent that the kinds of goods and services people buy change over the course of their lifetime. Individuals progress through a series of stages relating to their family situation; these stages have a very important influence on the tastes and consumption patterns of the individual and the family unit.

The family life cycle concept was developed in the 1960s as a tool for segmenting the market for goods and services. It was based on age, marital status, number and age of children, and work status—each of which affects the consumer's needs, wants, and ability to buy.

As originally described, the life cycle began with a young, single, working person living independently, subsequently moving through the various stages of marriage and child-rearing, and ending as a solitary survivor of a marriage, retired and once again living alone.[5] The life cycle concept continues to be relevant, although marketers must recognize that since the 1960s there have been numerous changes in the social factors underlying this framework. Not only are people marrying later in life, but childbearing is often postponed and sometimes foregone entirely. Also, it is no longer unusual for children to be born to unmarried individuals, an increasing proportion of married women are in the workforce, and divorce and separation have become more prevalent. Finally, more people are choosing alternative lifestyles.

Exhibit 6.4 presents several stages in the family life cycle and the banking needs that are most likely to be experienced at each stage. For example, young single or divorced individuals generally need a low-cost checking account and access to credit. Couples with young children are usually interested in purchasing a home, and their liquid assets tend to be low. On the other end of the cycle, older couples with no children at home tend to be more financially secure and are interested in taking more vacations, making home improvements, and enjoying other luxuries.

Economic Circumstances

Because income changes over time, an individual's ability to use financial services will also change. Although it is important to use income as a base for segmentation, net worth figures are benchmarks and do not presume creditworthiness.

Personal economic factors such as income, savings, net worth, and ability to borrow affect people's power to buy all types of goods and services, but they are especially relevant to the purchase of banking services. High-income individuals are good targets for personal or executive banking services. Individuals with a substantial net worth are candidates for investment, insurance, and trust services. Lower-income individuals require banking services that meet their needs without costing much. Basic checking accounts that allow a customer to write a limited number of checks free or at a very low cost are aimed at this market.

Exhibit 6.4   The Family Life Cycle and Banking Needs

Stage	Financial Situation	Banking Needs
Young, single people	Few financial burdens; recreation oriented	Low-cost checking; auto loan; credit card
Full nest: youngest child under six	Home purchasing peak; liquid assets low; many working mothers	Mortgage; credit card; revolving credit line; bill consolidation loan
Full nest: older couples with dependent children	Good financial position; many working mothers	Home improvement loans; equity credit lines; certificates of deposit; money market deposit accounts; IRA; other investment services
Empty nest: older couples, no children at home, one or both retired	Significantly reduced income	Rollover IRA; monthly income checks on CDs; estate planning; direct deposit of Social Security check

Note: Not all possible life cycle stages are included here.

Occupation

Employment patterns also affect the purchase of goods and services. Many jobs require specialized equipment or clothing. In addition, people buy goods and services that will give them greater status in the workplace. For example, unspoken dress codes may inspire an employee to buy a certain style of clothing because of the perception that "this is the way prestigious people in my field dress."

Personality and Self-Concept

Personality can be defined as the aggregation of an individual's traits or characteristics that make him or her unique. Some people are outgoing; others are shy. Some are nonconformists; others are conventional. Some are risk takers; others are cautious, and so on. One study found that ATM users were more self-reliant, impulsive, innovative, curious, and active than nonusers.[7] In short, they were considered to be on a faster track. A television spot for an ATM network, designed to match this psychographic profile of ATM users, consists of fast-paced cuts from one scene to another, showing individuals in various situations that suggest spontaneity, independence, and a high level of activity.

Sometimes marketers look for specific personality traits in a target market and sell into it. For example, Nike came up with the slogan "Just Do It," which it promotes very effectively using a wide range of physically fit people—-from ordinary citizens of all ages to world class athletes. The spokespeople and the slogan both suggest that all anyone needs to do to be in good shape is to "just do it." Nike has identified a broad segment of the population that is longing to be in top physical condition and is very likely to buy athletic footwear to help them achieve their fitness goals.

Self-concept is closely related to personality; it refers to the way we see ourselves and think others see us. People select products, banks, and other services that coincide with their self-concept. If a bank promotes an image of catering to "old money," an individual who sees himself as an up-and-coming professional might be less likely to identify with and select that bank. The bank that uses images of young, energetic people using its PC banking services as they go about their fast-paced lives is likely to attract people who see themselves that way.

Psychographics

Marketing researchers use the term *psychographics* to refer to the combined effect of the many personal and psychological factors that influence buying behavior. Through the use of psychographic principles, consumer markets can be segmented on the basis of lifestyle, personality traits, attitudes, and so on. Psychographics is being used in both bank and consumer product marketing today.

The Consumer Buying Process

The stages involved in the consumer buying process are illustrated in exhibit 6.5, which shows that an unsatisfied need is the starting point in the buying process. The individual then searches for a way to satisfy the need and evaluates alternatives for doing so. This is referred to as *prepurchase activity.*

Finally, a decision is reached and a purchase is made. Then, postpurchase feelings arise, and the process begins again with recognition of the next unsatisfied need. Each step in the consumer buying process poses a significant challenge to the bank marketer, who must understand what happens at each point to develop a marketing program to capitalize on it. While consumers obviously do not go through a carefully executed set of stages each time a purchase is made, effective marketing is based on an understanding of each step in the buying process.

Unsatisfied Needs

The starting point for any type of behavior, including consumer behavior, is an unsatisfied need. The buyer will not be motivated to buy unless there is a perceived need for the product. Thus, identifying customer needs is a prerequisite for successful marketing. If a bank product does not fill a need or is marketed to satisfy a need that customers do not feel, the product will not be marketed successfully.

The bank marketer has the critical task of discovering the needs of the market and those that the bank's products serve. "What is the buyer really seeking when buying my product?" and "What need does my product satisfy?" are questions the marketer must constantly ask. Certain industries

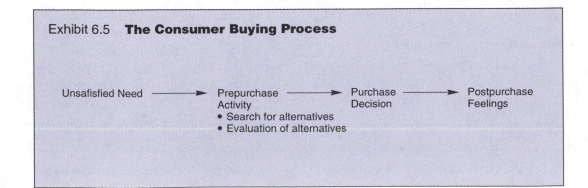

Exhibit 6.5　**The Consumer Buying Process**

Unsafisfied Need ⟶ Prepurchase Activity
• Search for alternatives
• Evaluation of alternatives ⟶ Purchase Decision ⟶ Postpurchase Feelings

have answered these questions very successfully. Consider the cosmetic manufacturer who said: "In the factory we make cosmetics; in the drugstore we sell hope."

Bankers must also continually identify inadequately developed or insufficiently satisfied needs. Apple Computer recognized an unmet need for a user-friendly personal computer, and its Macintosh was the first to successfully meet that need. The cosmetics industry discovered that the need for sophisticated grooming products for men was a market that had not been sufficiently developed, so it began marketing hair coloring, hair spray, cologne, and other cosmetics for male customers.

Insufficiently satisfied needs also might be the result of dissatisfaction with an existing product or service. In the case of banking, customer dissatisfaction with the level of service is the second most often cited reason why people change banks. (The principal cause is the need for convenience—in other words, people change banks because they have moved.)

The need for banking services is closely related to the satisfaction of needs at all levels; satisfying a need frequently involves making a purchase, which requires money—either cash or credit. Checking accounts offer a convenient way of paying for food, clothing, and shelter while ensuring that money is kept in a safe place. Credit cards enable customers to respond quickly to needs that arise unexpectedly. Savings accounts are a form of security and a way to prepare for emergencies. Installment loans give people access to large amounts of money to buy cars and improve their homes now while paying for them over a period of time, and mortgages enable people to buy houses that cost far more than they could save, even over many years.

The customer-contact staff of a bank are in an excellent position to make customers aware of unsatisfied needs. A customer buying a large amount of traveler's checks, for example, is probably going to be away from home for an extended period. This might prompt the bank employee to remind the customer about safe deposit boxes. Someone who is opening a checking account might be unaware that the bank can provide overdraft protection and, being made aware of it, might find it very appealing. This service can help avoid the embarrassment of inadvertently overdrawing the account—an unpleasant event that clashes with an individual's esteem and security needs.

Bank versus Customer Needs

The explosive growth in the development of new technology in banking has enabled banks to handle work more efficiently and to become less reliant on labor (which is becoming more expensive every year). As a result, many new bank services or service delivery mechanisms are introduced because they suit the banking industry's needs, not necessarily the consumer's. Sometimes, considerable time is needed to explain to bank customers how new services, which require a change in banking behavior, meet their needs.

An example is the direct deposit of Social Security checks. When this service was first introduced, most senior citizens declined to use it. It took careful marketing aimed at a group of people who, by virtue of their age, are not innovators and may be slow to adopt something new, to convert so many to direct deposit. Now more than 58 percent of all Social Security payments are sent using direct deposit.[6] This service appeals to senior citizens who fear the theft of their checks from the mailbox or the threat of being mugged on the way home from the bank. Although at first it was true that the majority of senior citizens did not take advantage of this service because they feared a failure of the technology used by the government, the clearinghouse system, or the bank, and that their money might not get into their account, most now see technology as a convenience. There still are those who view the trip to the bank on Social Security check day as a social event, a response to the need for belonging.

This example shows that when a banking service is targeted to a need that is not widely perceived, that requires a substantial change in behavior, or that is aimed at a market that tends to be slow to respond, the bank should recognize that the service is likely to be adopted slowly and may require considerable effort to educate consumers.

Prepurchase Activity

People become sensitive to the cues around them that they believe will bring them closer to satisfying certain needs. A cue can be thought of as a piece of information that starts a thought process. In the context of marketing, cues might take the form of advertisements; conversations with friends, neighbors, and bank personnel; or contacts with business associates.

How long a person deliberates before purchasing will vary with the individual, the urgency and complexity of the need, and the extent of the consumer's knowledge about ways to satisfy that need. For example, most people deliberate for a considerable time before purchasing an automobile or a major appliance because the risk is high both financially and socially, whereas products such as toothpaste and soap are usually purchased with little deliberation. Before making a major purchase an individual will typically engage in prepurchase search behavior that involves evaluating various alternatives. During this period, the consumer is a prime target for communications from marketers; in fact, the buyer may be actively seeking such information. (Recall the discussion of selective exposure.) For this reason, literature explaining the bank's services should be readily available and visible in bank lobbies. This is also why many banks regularly include inserts with customers' checking and savings statements to promote bank services. They are a relatively low-cost way of reaching a large number of customers, and although many people will pay no attention to a particular stuffer, customers who are in the prepurchase stage for the ser-

vice being promoted are likely to notice the message.

Every purchase decision has some degree of risk attached to it. Much of the consumer's behavior in this stage will be directed toward reducing this risk. While consumers can turn to publications such as *Consumer Reports* to help minimize purchase risk, there are no formal sources of information designed to help consumers shop for banking services. Again this underscores the importance of knowledgeable bank personnel and the availability of promotional literature within the banking office. The customer may also turn to informal sources of information such as the advice of friends, relatives, and business associates. For this reason, banks need to establish strong ties with centers of influence in a community.

Purchase Decision

Prepurchase activity generally culminates in a purchase. But the purchase decision itself encompasses a myriad of decisions. It may require selection of a product type, model, size, color, price, means to pay, and dealer, among other factors. For example, to open a checking account, the consumer first has to decide to go to a particular bank; must then choose between different types of checking accounts; must decide whether to take advantage of related services such as automated tellers, overdraft protection, and automatic savings; and must select a style and color of checkbook and checks. The easier the bank and customer service representative make these decisions, the more comfortable the customer will be with the purchase decision.

Postpurchase Feelings

We have discussed the behavior leading up to the point of a "buy" decision and the purchase itself. But what takes place and how the consumer feels after the purchase are also very important elements of the buying process and are, therefore, crucial to the marketer.

Buyers often feel some anxiety after purchasing something that entails a relationship (as in banking) or that involves significant cost. This is understandable, since each of the alternatives from which the selection was made will have had both positive and negative features. The wise marketer helps make the buyer feel good about his or her choice. Some banks send a thank-you note to the new checking customer. They may do this simply as a courtesy, or to check the address given by the customer, but the gesture is grounded in behavioral psychology and helps reduce customers' postpurchase anxiety.

Reducing postpurchase anxiety by providing the customer with excellent service is especially important in the case of products that are bought infrequently, such as automobiles and banking services. If a new car owner's experience with the dealer's service department is unpleasant, the likelihood of repeat business or referrals to friends will be greatly diminished. Conversely, the bank customer who is treated with responsiveness, courtesy, and professionalism will feel that the decision to select that particular bank was justified. Customers who are very satisfied with their bank's service are more likely to look to it when applying for a car loan or other service. The more their choice of bank is positively reinforced, the more likely they are to develop a habit of using that bank's services. In a marketing sense, habitual behavior leads to brand (or bank) loyalty. Such habits, once entrenched, are extremely difficult for the competition to alter.

The growth of the service quality movement in this country reflects an expanding recognition of the importance of ongoing customer satisfaction as a way of building customer loyalty, increasing sales, and ultimately increasing profits. Seen in the context of the consumer buying process, the service quality movement reflects a heightened understanding of the importance to a business of recognizing and addressing consumers' postpurchase feelings.

Organizational Buying Behavior

There are both important differences and many similarities between the buying behavior of individual consumers and of organizations. The most obvious difference is that organizations generally purchase goods and services not for consumption, but for application to the production process. In the case of banking services, for instance, manufacturers purchase money (that is, get loans) to finance production and expand capacity. A second major difference is that in an organization, more people are likely to be involved in making the purchase decision. Each of these individuals has a specific role to play in the process, and each is subject to all the forces that influence an individual consumer's buying behavior—which makes the buying process for an organization much more complicated.

The Organizational Buying Process

As is the case for individuals, the buying process for organizations begins with recognition of a need and involves identifying and evaluating possible purchase alternatives. Organizational behavior experts Webster and Wind have developed a theory of organizational buying behavior that will be reflected throughout this section. They define organizational buying behavior as "the decision-making process by which formal organizations establish the need for purchased products and services, and identify, evaluate, and choose among alternative brands and suppliers."[8] This decision-making process is illustrated in exhibit 6.6.

Need identification may arise from within an organization—for example, when it recognizes a need for working capital. A bank might suggest a need through its advertising ("We can put your overnight money to work for you"). Or a need may be uncovered through skillful probing by a bank officer who has prepared well before calling on a company.

The need that is central to most corporate banking relationships is credit. The need for

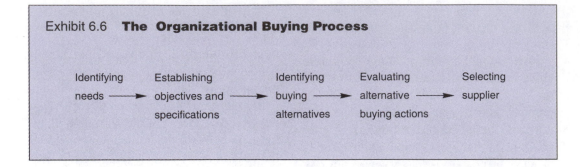

Exhibit 6.6 The Organizational Buying Process

Identifying needs → Establishing objectives and specifications → Identifying buying alternatives → Evaluating alternative buying actions → Selecting supplier

credit services is the leading motivator for organizations when it comes to selecting a bank, and loan approval or rejection is the principal reason that firms establish or end a banking relationship.

Organizations also need noncredit services such as cash management to help them better manage their cash flow. Many banks see the unrecognized need for cash management services as a way to get a "foot in the door" of a company that is not actively seeking a credit provider.

Once the organization's need has been identified, the buyer defines the objectives and specifications that the product must fulfill—that is, what the product or service must be able to do. This step is more often related to the purchase of goods and noncredit banking services than to the purchase of credit services.

When a business wants to buy banking services, the firm will generally begin by consulting the banks with which it is already doing business. In small- to medium-sized businesses, the firm's attorney or independent accountant may be asked to direct business to a specific bank. Since a great deal of bank business can be generated through these channels, it pays banks to work to develop a good reputation among such centers of influence.

In the process of evaluating alternative buying decisions, the firm may study the services offered by several banks (for example, comparing lockbox facilities) and evaluate the differences between them in light of the firm's specific needs.

The process of selecting a supplier (or bank) generally involves several people, and the ultimate decision may reflect the relative power of various members of the purchasing group. Consider, for example, a firm that is considering the purchase of direct deposit of payroll for its employees. The payroll department chief will use the service, yet the firm's president may be the one who makes the final decision. In addition, the treasurer very likely has some influence in the decision. The treasurer may also be the one who is the buyer—that is, the one who notifies the bank of the decision and handles the necessary paperwork. A bank's corporate calling officers must make a point of identifying the individuals who play these various roles within a prospect company.

Because services vary little from one bank to another, individual and interpersonal factors take on great importance in the selling of banking services. Therefore, the caliber and performance of the calling officer is critical. Research has repeatedly shown that financial decision makers expect calling officers to have the ability to effect prompt decisions and to take action. Research has also shown that these decision makers want attention; they like to feel that the bank knows them, wants their business, and cares about their needs. This can only be done through interpersonal contact, and it explains why the most successful corporate banking groups have substantial expense accounts.

The organizational buying process also applies to the sale of goods and services to government agencies. The primary concern of government units, however, is to minimize the cost to the taxpayer. For this reason, sales of products and services are more likely to be subject to open bidding, with the sale going to the bidder with the lowest price or the most favorable rate.[9]

Summary

This chapter began with a study of the theories and techniques that form the basis for an understanding of markets. Marketers must understand why and how people buy to develop ways of meeting their needs with products that are priced, distributed, and communicated effectively to the target market. Unmet or incompletely met needs motivate buyer behavior; the resulting behavior is also influenced by individuals' perceptions of the stimuli surrounding them.

Maslow's hierarchy is a useful framework for understanding the way various levels of needs motivate people. A multitude of factors influence buyer perceptions and buyers' resulting behavior. These are external influences such as social and cultural factors, and internal influences such as psychological and personal factors. The class structure in this country, for example, is a significant cultural factor that affects buyer behavior. An individual's stage in the family life cycle is a personal factor that greatly affects consumer needs and purchase behavior. *Psychographics* is a term used to refer to the combined effect of many personal and psychological factors.

The buying process provides a concrete example of how the process of motivation influences behavior. The four steps in the buying process involve first becoming aware of an unmet or incompletely satisfied need; followed by prepurchase activities, which entail searching for alternative ways to meet the need and then evaluating the alternatives that have been identified;

making the purchase decision; and finally experiencing postpurchase feelings. Marketing techniques can be applied to each step of the process—from making consumers aware of a need, right through to providing them with evidence that they have made the right choice.

The buying behavior of organizations is both similar to and quite different from that of individuals. The five stages in the organizational buying process closely parallel the four-stage consumer buying process. Furthermore, individuals involved in the organization's buying process can assume one of several roles. While the buying process of organizations involves more people and is more complex than that of an individual consumer, unmet or incompletely satisfied needs are still at the core of the process.

The next chapter looks at marketing research techniques, which help marketers identify those needs, motivations, and perceptions that affect consumers' buying decisions.

Points for Review

1. Define or briefly explain the following terms:

- motivation
- hierarchy of needs
- psychographics
- reference group
- life cycle
- selective exposure
- selective distortion
- selective retention

2. How do family and reference groups influence buying behavior?

3. Give a bank-related example to explain how an unsatisfied consumer's need leads ultimately to the use of a bank service, and indicate how the bank might respond to that need.

4. In what ways does the buying behavior of an organization differ from that of an individual consumer?

Notes

1. William M. Pride and O. C. Ferrell, *Marketing* (Boston: Houghton Mifflin, 1997), p. 140.

2. A. H. Maslow, *Motivation and Personality* (New York: Harper and Brothers, 1954), chapter 5.

3. Kotler, *Marketing Management,* pp. 176–177.

4. Richard P. Coleman, "The Continuing Significance of Social Class to Marketing," *Journal of Consumer Research,* December 1983, pp. 270–272.

5. William D. Wells and George Gubar, "The Life Cycle Concept in Marketing Research," *Journal of Marketing Research,* November 1966, pp. 355–363.

6. National Automated Clearinghouse Association Web site, direct deposit/direct payment information (http://www.nacha.com, March 1997).

7. Arthur J. Lucey, "Maximizing Your ATM Network," *American Banker,* February 11, 1981, p. 4.

8. Frederick E. Webster, Jr., and Yoram Wind, *Organizational Buying Behavior* (Englewood Cliffs, N.J.: Prentice-Hall, 1972).

9. *Ibid.,* p. 188.

7

Marketing Research and Marketing Information Systems

Learning Objectives

After studying this chapter, you should be able to

- define and explain the purpose of marketing research,
- describe how different size banks approach the task of marketing research,
- describe three primary types of marketing data that make up situation analysis, and identify sources for this data,
- describe the five steps in the marketing research process,
- compare and contrast personal, telephone, and self-administered surveys,
- list ways to ensure marketing research results are used, and
- describe a marketing information system and contrast it with marketing research.

Introduction

Research is important at every stage in the marketing management process. How does the marketer obtain information about the bank's internal and external macroenvironments for the situation analysis? How does the planner establish measurable objectives when the goal relates to increased market penetration, consumer awareness, or customer satisfaction? How does the marketer determine which market segments are likely to make worthwhile target markets and which needs are not being satisfied? The answer is marketing research.

Marketing research enables the marketer to identify and analyze various target markets. It provides information on how the members of various markets are motivated, how they perceive the world, and how they behave in response to various stimuli (for example, small differences in interest rates paid, or cash bonuses to attract deposits).

Marketing research is invaluable in the design of product mix strategies. New product ideas can come from marketing research; new product concepts and alternative pricing schemes can be tested among the target market. Research on the attitudes and behavior of the target market can help in designing the advertising aimed at attracting that market. Research can also be used to test the market's reactions to the advertising's creative strategy and the effectiveness of the ad copy.

Marketing research can identify the geographical areas into which the bank might expand its distribution network. It can be used to measure the sales effectiveness of its retail and commercial customer-contact staff. Completing the planning loop, research is an integral tool for evaluating and controlling the marketing management process. It can measure the success of the marketing strategy and track its effect over time. Repeating the surveys used in setting benchmarks provides the necessary feedback from the market on how the strategy is working.

This chapter provides an overview of the techniques used in marketing research and presents a five-step process for conducting a research survey. It also discusses the differences between marketing research and marketing information systems.

Definition of Marketing Research

The American Marketing Association's definition of marketing research is as follows:

> Marketing research is the function which links the consumer, customer, and public to the marketer through information—information used to identify and define marketing opportunities and problems; generate, refine, and evaluate marketing actions; monitor marketing performance; and improve understanding of marketing as a process.
>
> Marketing research specifies the information required to address these issues; designs the method for collecting information; manages and implements the data collection process; analyzes the results; and communicates the findings and their implications.[1]

In short, marketing research is the acquisition and use of information that can be beneficial to the marketing management process. How important is marketing research? If the goal of a business is to satisfy consumer needs and wants at a profit, and if research provides the information to help management make informed decisions toward that end, then research might well be seen as the most important function performed by a marketing department.

Marketing Research or Market Research?

Some writers distinguish between *marketing research* and *market research*.[2] A market may be a geographical area in which a firm does business (such as a branch trade area), a group of customers (such as senior citizens), or an environment in which buyers and sellers make their decisions (such as a tight money market). The market, however, is only one of the elements with which marketing information is concerned.

Marketing research is helpful not only in identifying and analyzing markets, but also in planning, problem solving, and control. Marketing research gathers information for the four elements of marketing-mix strategy development: product, pricing, promotion, and distribution. Since the term *marketing research* implies a broader scope than market research, that term is used in this text.

Marketing Research in Banking

Banks' use of marketing research varies greatly. According to one industry analysis, in 1995 banks spent anywhere from 1 percent to 6 percent of their total marketing budget on research.[3] This represents a decline in spending compared with 1991 figures, which showed that banks spent between 2 percent and 8 percent of their total marketing budget on research. (These figures do not include the salaries of banks' internal marketing research staff.)

Exhibit 7.1 indicates how much money banks of various sizes spend on research. It

Exhibit 7.1 **Bank Expenditures for Marketing and Marketing Research**

Asset Size (millions)	Median* Marketing Budget ($000)	Median* Research Expenditure ($000)	Average % of Marketing Budget Spent on Research
Less than $10**	$21.5	$1.0	2
$10–25	23.0	.3	>.5
$25–50	29.5	.2	>.5
$50–100	60.8	2.0	1
$100–250	128.5	5.0	2
$250–500	308.8	7.1	2
$500–1,000	551.9	14.8	2
$1,000–5,000	1,046.6	25.5	2
More than $5,000	6,067.4	230.0	6

*The median, unlike an average, represents the midvalue of the amounts reported by the respondents. In other words, half of the respondents in each asset category reported budgets or expenditures greater than the median, while half reported amounts less than the median.

**This category includes a number of new banks whose marketing expenditures include the cost of startup marketing research and advertising.

Source: *1996 Analysis of Bank Marketing Expenditures* (Bank Marketing Association, 1995), based on information reported by 300 banks.

also shows the proportion of marketing budgets spent on research by banks of various sizes. Many banks are still struggling to justify the cost of marketing research to senior management. From the information presented, the following conclusions may be drawn:

- The majority of banks in the United States have assets of less than $500 million. These banks spend very little on marketing research. Banks with assets of less than $250 million spent only 1 percent to 2 percent of their marketing budgets on research during 1996. For example, among banks with assets between $250 million and $500 million, the average expenditure on research during 1996 was just $6,700.

- Banks with assets greater than $500 million but less than $5 billion spent between 2 percent and 3 percent of their marketing budgets on research. Because these budgets are typically in the hundreds of thousands of dollars (or more), the amount spent on research is substantial. For example, among banks with assets of between $1 billion and $5 billion, the average amount spent on research in 1996 was $39,900. That figure is still slightly less than the 1991 study reported.

- The largest banks (those with more than $5 billion in assets) spend comparatively more of their annual marketing budgets on marketing research than do smaller banks. There are at least two reasons for this. First, these banks are the market leaders, the ones continually striving to develop new products to meet changing consumer needs. They use research to identify unmet needs and to test alternative product ideas. New products introduced by these banks and accepted by consumers are generally imitated by smaller banks, which may introduce the products without any market research or with only a small amount of local market testing of consumer receptivity. Second, the larger the bank, the greater the potential impact (either positive or negative) of alternative marketing decisions and, therefore, the greater the need for information to help reduce the risk of making wrong decisions.

Banks also vary in the way they are staffed to conduct research. A bank with a sizable marketing department may have an in-house staff of professionals who conduct research projects from start to finish, while another bank may contract with research suppliers and consultants to do each project. Most banks use a combination of these two approaches: some research is done entirely by bank staff; other projects are done completely by consultants; and other projects are done partly in-house and partly by suppliers.

With advances in the Internet and technology allowing research on-line, banks may experience additional savings in market research costs.

Using Marketing Research to Understand the Market

Information about the market is an essential starting point in the planning process; it is the foundation on which the marketing effort is built. All banks, regardless of their size, should have readily available and up-to-date information relating to

- the bank's geographical market,
- its customers,
- its competition, and
- its position relative to that of the competition.

Types of Market Data

Collecting basic market information constitutes the situation analysis—the first step in the marketing planning process (see chapter 4). It should incorporate the development of three basic profiles: a customer profile, a market profile, and a competitive profile.

Customer Profile

Successful marketers know their customers. Banks should have the information required to answer questions such as "Who are our customers?" "How do our customers differ from those of competing banks?" "How do our customers differ from other residents of the trade area?" (For example, is the bank attracting a disproportionate share of younger or older customers?) A customer profile should include demographic information about age distribution, occupation, educational level, income, and ethnic composition. Such information may be obtained from internal data, surveys of customers, or information collected at the new-accounts desk.

A customer profile also should be created for commercial customers. Such data would include the number of commercial customers by type of business, balance size, number and types of services used, length of banking relationship, and profitability.

Market Profile

The financial health of a bank is inexorably tied to the economic well-being of the geographic area it serves. A market profile provides management with the information it needs to identify potential problems and opportunities in both the retail and commercial markets. Much of the information is widely available from a variety of sources, but keeping the information current requires special monitoring of economic trends.

A market profile defines the boundaries of a bank's primary trade area (the geographic area from which 75 percent of the bank's business is derived) and the secondary trade area (the broader area from which the balance of its business comes). It also includes the number and value of housing units, population data, and demographic information in those geographical areas.

On the commercial banking side, the market profile should include the number, types, and locations of businesses in the trade area. Ideally, management should also have specific data about every firm or merchant in the area, including information about the nature of the business, its approximate sales volume, the number of employees, and its current banking affiliations. Such information forms the foundation of an effective officer-calling program.

Competitive Profile

In today's banking market, competitors abound, and bank marketing decisions must take into account competitors' marketing strategies (that is, their product offerings, pricing, hours, and services) and their likely reactions to the bank's own marketing activities.

A bank's competitive profile should answer such questions as "Who are our competitors?" "What are their services and how are they priced?" "What is each institution's market share?" "Who is the market leader (if there is one)?" "How do our services, facilities, hours, and staff compare with theirs?"

Profile information is neither difficult nor expensive to collect, and any bank operating without it is putting itself in a highly vulnerable situation. Consider the following scenario:

A bank in an old urban area hired a marketing research expert to analyze its possibilities for expansion. The researcher soon discovered that the bank did not have even the most basic market information with which to begin, so the researcher immediately began compiling the information needed to create profiles of the bank's customers, markets, and competition. In the course of developing the customer profile, the researcher discovered that the bank had customers who were substantially older than the customers of other banking institutions in the city, and a core of high-balance savings accounts, but its customer base was aging and dying and was not being replaced. Without corrective action to appeal to a younger market, the bank was destined to lose even more market share at its present locations and to have limited appeal in the new markets it wanted to enter.

Updating Market Data

Management requires a continual flow of up-to-date information on the customer, the market, and the competition. Since market information describes situations that are constantly changing, it would be naive to think that, having once gathered this basic information, a bank could continue to rely on it over a period of years. Customer bases continually change as residents and businesses move in and out of trade areas. Also, the local economy of the trade area is affected by the state and national economies, both of which are dynamic. Thus the basic market information must be constantly updated.

Most banks use a marketing information system (MIS) to manage and integrate data. An MIS is a tool for managing and structuring internal and external information. It incorporates both software and hardware. An MIS is often called a universal marketing database or datawarehouse because of its ability to sort, collate, analyze, and gather a tremendous amount of information.

A marketing customer information file (MCIF) is an example of a type of software that can be run on an MIS. There are varying degrees of complexity in MCIFs, but they all help continually track vital information on customers, products and services, competitors, demographics, and more. For example, with an MCIF, banks can learn the proportion of customers having one, two, three, or more services with the bank. Banks can monitor the number of accounts and balances in checking, savings, and loan accounts opened and closed and where there is the most traffic, and thereby anticipate changing demands for services.

Market Data Sources

Market data are obtained from two sources—secondary and primary sources. Data from secondary sources were created either within the bank or outside the bank for a purpose other than the market profile. An example would be an accounting report from the bank, or a list of new homes built in a particular district.

Secondary information about the local market can be obtained from external sources such as the Bureau of the Census, local chambers of commerce, and munici-

pal offices. Information on competitors can be obtained from reports published by regulatory agencies. Secondary data regarding competing banks' services and pricing can be obtained by calling or visiting these other banks and posing as a prospective customer.

However, much information (especially regarding customer motivation and needs, opinions, knowledge, attitudes, and behavior) cannot be obtained except by generating it in response to a specific need, and this is known as primary data. Primary data are collected for a specific purpose (such as to answer questions generated by the market profile project). For example, if the bank wishes to find out if it should create a new CD product, it might first examine secondary data such as reports on CD sales at other local banks and overall CD sales statewide or nationwide within the last year. It might also examine internal product profitability reports to determine whether CD products are profitable and in demand. If secondary information is inadequate for deciding whether to go ahead with new products, however, there may be good reason to commission primary research to answer the question "Should we create a new CD product?" Primary research is usually obtained by creating a customer survey asking questions about customers' financial product preferences. Or primary research might include shopping competitive banks for their CD rates and promotions.

The Marketing Research Process

This section discusses the five steps involved in conducting a marketing research study:
- defining the problem,
- planning and designing the research project,
- collecting the information,
- analyzing the data, and
- reporting the research findings.[4]

This process is generally applicable to any research or problem-solving activity.

Step 1: Defining the Problem

Defining the problem is the most important step in the research process. If the problem or question to be studied is not correctly identified and clearly defined, the answer—however scientifically obtained and professionally presented—will be off the mark.

Defining a problem requires management to determine the "nature and boundaries of a negative, or positive, situation or question."[5] Without a clear understanding of why the research is being undertaken and what the research should reveal, all the effort that follows will lead to the wrong conclusion. Taking the time to clearly outline the objectives of the research in a written research proposal will accurately dictate the scope and detail of the information the researchers must find. Writing a marketing research proposal that includes a hypothesis, or informed guess, about the information being sought will help the marketer determine how the research should be carried out. A written proposal also serves as a clear guideline for everyone involved in the project.

Take the case of the State Bank of Wheatville (a hypothetical bank, based on an actual case), a small (under $100 million in assets) and relatively new (17 years old) bank in a two-bank town. The other bank, Western National Bank, had for many years been the only bank in town. State Bank was experiencing moderate growth, and its management was pleased, until a branch of a third bank, Warranty Bank, entered the market and began to show rapid growth. The management of State Bank had believed that the only thing hindering its ability to grow was the community's loyalty to the old, established Western National Bank. However, this belief was shattered by the far-superior performance of the new market entrant, Warranty Bank.

A marketing research firm was hired to find out why the new bank was growing faster than State Bank. The answer could lie in any one or a combination of factors, such as products offered, customer service, hours, pricing, location, staff, image, or advertising. However, in this case, State Bank had already done its homework and it was clear that it was competitive on these issues with both of the other banks in town.

Through exploratory interviews with State Bank's management and a few professionals with offices on the town's main thoroughfare, the researchers formulated the hypothesis that the bank did not have as much contact with the centers of influence in the community as did its older and newer competitors. Further research confirmed this hypothesis, with the result that State Bank made some staffing changes and initiated a formal call program.

In this case, the real problem had nothing to do with the new competitor. The initial question "Why are we not doing as well as our new competitor?" had to be refocused based on the primary data the researchers gathered through their exploratory interviews to ask, "Does our bank have as good a reputation with the town's centers of influence as our competitors do?" Once the nature and boundaries of the question were determined, the research effort could be focused on the relevant market (community opinion leaders, influential business owners, and professionals).

Step 2: Planning and Designing the Project

After the problem to be studied has been clearly defined, the next step is to plan how the information will be found. It is essential to take care and time planning and designing the project, because without a solid foundation the quality of the results will be seriously compromised.

In developing a marketing research plan, the marketer must (1) search secondary sources of data to refine the research as well as answer the research questions; (2) select the right research technique for the job; and (3) design an appropriate sample. To have results that are accurate, the marketer must ensure that the methods used are reliable,

Exhibit 7.2 Selected Secondary Sources Useful to Bankers

I. Information on the Competitive Environment

  A. Individual Bank Data
    1. Bank quarterly and annual reports; 10-K reports
    2. Report of condition and report of income and dividends (available for individual banks from the FDIC)

  B. Banking Data
    1. The 12 regional Federal Reserve banks publish a great deal of banking data. Availability varies by region. In addition, the Federal Reserve Board publishes much useful information. Some examples are:
- Functional cost analysis (annually)
- Assets and liabilities of insured domestically chartered and foreign-related banking institutions (weekly)
- Weekly consolidated condition report of large commercial banks and domestic subsidiaries
- Commercial and industrial loan commitments at selected large commercial banks (monthly)
- Consumer installment credit (monthly)
- Debits and deposit turnover at commercial banks (monthly)
- Loans and securities at all commercial banks (monthly)
- Flow of funds: seasonally adjusted and unadjusted (quarterly)

    2. Federal Deposit Insurance Corporation
- Bank operating statistics (annually)
- Summary of deposits (by branch, annually)

II. Information on the Economic Environment

  A. Population
    1. U.S. Department of Commerce, Bureau of Census
- Census of population (every decade)
- Current population reports (irregularly)
- Statistical Abstract of the United States (annually)
- County and city data book (irregular)

    2. State departments of economic research

  B. Regional Income and Employment
    1. Survey of buying power (published annually by *Sales Management Magazine*)
    2. State departments of labor or employment agencies

  C. Construction Activity
    1. *Construction News* (monthly), F.W. Dodge, a division of McGraw-Hill Information Systems Co.
    2. State departments of economic research
    3. *Housing and Urban Development Trends* (monthly), U.S. Department of Housing and Urban Development

meaning they will produce nearly identical results time after time, and valid, meaning the methods will measure what they are supposed to measure.

Searching Secondary Sources

The marketer should always conduct a thorough search of existing data before embarking on primary research, since the answers to management's questions may be readily available in bank and public documents. However, care must be taken to obtain the most up-to-date information available. Exhibit 7.2 lists a number of secondary sources useful to bankers.

Examples of internal secondary data are reports from other departments (for example, accounting and branch administration) and information gathered at the point of sale (signature cards and new-account information forms). A large volume of external secondary data is available from regulatory agencies, the American Bankers Association/Bank Marketing Association's Center for Banking Information, trade associations, the federal government, state and local governments, and the media.

If the marketing research question cannot be answered using secondary data, it may be necessary to obtain primary data. The collection of primary data can range from simply observing customer behavior at the point of sale to a complex multistage study starting with small group discussions and following up with numerous personal interviews.

Selecting a Tool for Primary Research

The research technique selected depends on the marketer's objectives, budget, and time frame. There are three main methods of gathering primary data: mail surveys, personal interviews, and self-administered questionnaires. More detail on these methods follows.

A marketing research survey (no matter which method is selected) administered to several hundred respondents produces *quantitative* data; that is, it generates percentages, frequency distributions, and other statistical information that identifies similarities and differences among various; groups of respondents. However, at times the researcher needs more *qualitative* data; that is, information about how people think, feel, and talk about a need or a product. Qualitative information often can best be obtained by conducting one-on-one interviews, by conducting in-depth interviews with a small number of individuals, or by holding focus groups. A focus group is a discussion among 10 to 12 people who are representative of the target audience and who are led by an experienced moderator. Intercept interviews, in which a customer is stopped in the bank lobby, are also effective ways to gather information.

Designing a Sample for Primary Research

In survey research the marketer must determine the group of people about whom management wants to know more (for example, all checking account customers, persons 60 and older, or businesses in the $20 million to $125 million sales category). The researcher must select a small proportion of that group to whom the questionnaire will be administered. It is rarely practical to get feedback from the entire group, called a population or universe, so the marketer examines a small part of the group, called a sample.

The sample must be truly representative of the universe so that the researcher can project the findings to the universe with a reasonable degree of certainty. To accomplish this, the sample size and the method of selection must meet scientific standards. For example, if information about checking account customers is being collected, randomly stopping 25 customers during the day at 4 of a bank's 50 branches and interviewing them will result in 100 interviews. However, the results will not be representative of all of the bank's checking customers to the extent that (1) the customers who use these four branches have different economic or social backgrounds, or different attitudes from those who bank at the other 46

branches; and (2) the customers who physically enter the branch differ from those who use the automated teller or drive-in, or who do their banking by mail or on evenings or Saturdays. Because of the many factors that influence consumer behavior, as discussed in chapter 6, it is likely that there will be significant differences between these groups of people, making the sample statistically invalid.

It is also possible to obtain a scientifically valid sample using sophisticated statistical techniques, as is done by the media when they conduct daily surveys of voter sentiment during a presidential campaign. In these "mini-surveys," a small sample of voters is polled on who they would vote for if the elections were held that day. The sample response is extrapolated, with a margin for error, to the population in general.

Sample design requires a solid knowledge of the theory of statistics because minor variations in the size of the sample can have a major impact on the margin of error and thus on the reliability of the survey results. Exhibit 7.4 describes how one bank designed a sample for a customer satisfaction survey and how the sample size affected its conclusions. While it is not possible to go into detail on statistical probability theory, which is the basis for sample design and data analysis, interested students should be able to find a basic statistics text at almost any library.

Step 3: Collecting the Data

There are many elements to collecting data, but the three main parts are selecting a survey technique, designing a questionnaire, and fielding the study.

Selecting a Survey Method

As mentioned earlier, surveys are the principal method used for collecting primary information. When testing customer awareness and comprehension of services, any of the three methods (personal interviews, telephone interviews, and self-administered questionnaires) may be used, so the decision about which method to use must be based on such factors as the complexity of the information presented, the cost, or the time frame within which answers must be obtained.

Each of the three survey methods has strengths and weaknesses. For instance, respondents are likely to be more receptive to a personal, face-to-face interview than to a telephone interview; therefore, the personal interview questionnaire can be longer, thus generating more information. This is also the only feasible way to obtain feedback on an ad or brochure since the interviewer must be able to show the ad to the respondent. Personal interviews also allow interviewers to observe the respondents. (Is the ad language clear? Are the benefits of the investment account understood?) Personal interviews allow the marketer to reach a representative sample quickly because interviews can be conducted in different neighborhoods, branches, or states at the same time. This method can yield results more quickly than a mail survey, but it can be difficult to interview enough people for the survey to be reliable and valid. Further, personal interviews are expensive to conduct and are subject to interviewer bias and cheating (for example, filling out a questionnaire without conducting the interview).

The self-administered questionnaire, whether sent by mail, E-mail, or conducted via on-site computer questionnaire, is the least expensive to administer and the least subject to interviewer bias, but it is also the least likely to be completed and offers the least amount of control over the composition of the sample. For example, if a bank mails a survey form to 1,000 checking account customers, the response might be greater from customers who have been with the bank the longest, or who are most favorably disposed toward the bank, or who have the most free time.

Telephoning customers greatly reduces this selection bias. All customers, regardless of their attitudes or other characteristics, have an equal chance of being called and interviewed. Telephone interviewing is also faster than other interview methods. It might take six weeks or more to get back the completed surveys mailed to checking customers, but it may be possible to complete the same number of telephone interviews in just a few days.

Exhibit 7.3 ranks each type of survey technique on a scale of 1 to 3 with respect to nine variables that should be considered when designing a survey.[6] For example, the first variable is the "amount of information"; the ranking of 1 for personal interviews means that personal interviews yield the most information, while telephone interviews (with a ranking of 3) yield the least information. Similarly, a self-administered questionnaire (with a ranking of 1) is the best method to use if interviewer bias or cheating is a concern.

The exhibit also shows that all three interview techniques have very close total scores. This indicates that no one technique is the most effective in all cases. Therefore, the choice must be made on a case-by-case basis, selecting the method that best suits the particular situation.

Designing the Questionnaire

After determining which survey technique to use, the researcher must develop the questionnaire. As was mentioned earlier, the questionnaire must be reliable and valid, but it must also be relatively easy for respondents to answer. In other words, the questions must be simple, clear, and direct. Using words that are emotionally colored, ambiguous, or loaded with unintended meaning can influence the respondents' answers and thus invalidate them. For example, "How likely would you be to switch banks if another bank were more convenient and had longer hours?" is ambiguous. There is no way of knowing whether a respondent's answer is based on concern about the bank's hours or its location.

Also, the questions should not be embarrassing or annoying, nor should they use

Exhibit 7.3	**Comparison of Survey Techniques**		
Variables	Personal Interview	Telephone Interview	Self-administered Questionnaire
Amount of information	1	3	2
Types of information	1	2	3
Complexity	1	3	2
Completion rate	1	2	3
Interviewer bias or cheating	3	2	1
Respondent bias	3	2	1
Sample composition	2	1	3
Cost	3	2	1
Speed	2	1	3
Total Score	17	18	19

unfamiliar terms without defining them. For example, many people refuse to state their income, especially at the start of a questionnaire. Thus, including this question (especially at the beginning of the questionnaire) may reduce the amount of other information collected, increase costs (more contacts must be made), and raise the possibility of erroneous results.

Another difficulty in the design of questionnaires relates to the extent to which respondents are conscious of the factors underlying their own behavior. Most survey research assumes that people understand the meaning and implications of their answers.[7] Yet often a wide gap exists between what people say they would do in a given situation and what they actually do. This is perhaps the least recognized and most frequently encountered pitfall in bank marketing research—especially in research conducted to aid pricing decisions. For example, a marketing researcher might ask banking customers if they would move their checking account if the monthly service charge increased by one dollar. If 25 percent of the respondents said they would

be very likely to move their accounts, the researcher would be seriously wrong in projecting that 25 percent would actually do so. The researcher should use responses to questions of this type (What would you do if . . .?) only to analyze the variation in responses across different groups of people as a way to predict which groups are more or less price sensitive. (See Case A.)

Questionnaire design requires knowledge of both psychology and statistics, and many potential pitfalls await the unwary and the inexperienced. The design of questionnaires should be left to professionals, or at the very least, a professional should be called on to assist in this task.

Fielding the Study

The next step in the survey process is administering the questionnaire to the selected sample. This step is referred to as fielding the study. As with questionnaire and sample design, a number of potential pitfalls can introduce bias or error into the results.

In surveys that use personal interviews or telephone interviews, interviewers must be carefully selected and trained to avoid interviewer bias. If the interviewer fails to state the question exactly the same way in each interview, places more emphasis on one of the possible responses, or even subtly varies the tone of his or her voice, the respondent's answer could be influenced.

Whether the interview is face-to-face, by telephone, or self-administered, the respondent may be a source of bias to the extent that he or she does not answer accurately (either deliberately or because of ignorance or misunderstanding). Another source of bias is nonresponse error, which was alluded to previously in relation to the self-administered questionnaire. If those people who refuse to answer (or could not be reached) differ in some way from those who did participate, the findings will not truly represent the universe.

Step 4: Analyzing the Data

When the questionnaires have been completed, the challenge of analyzing the collected information begins. Responses to open-ended questions (in which the respondent uses his or her own words to answer, as opposed to being given an answer from which to choose) must be categorized, or coded. By reading through a substantial proportion of the answers to a question, it will be apparent that many respondents have given basically the same answer although each has stated it somewhat differently. Identifying these similar answers is the function of coding. In effect, the researcher is creating closed-ended answer categories after the fact.

Although survey results can be tabulated by hand, using a computer is faster and facilitates cross-tabulation of responses. For example, responses to each question can be broken out by age of respondent, sex, income, job classification, branch used most often, and behavior or psychographic variables. (See exhibits A.3 through A.6 in Case A for examples of cross-tabulation.) Clearly, these various classifications should be determined while the questionnaire is being designed so that the appropriate classification questions will be asked of respondents. The classifications must also be determined in advance to determine the required sample size. The sample must be large enough to result in valid comparisons between the classification groups. (See exhibit 7.4.)

At this point, the researcher must interpret the results of the survey. The questionnaire may have generated answers to dozens of questions, but unless the researcher can put them into the proper context, they may be meaningless. For example, if a survey shows that 15 percent of the bank's customers opened a checking account within the last year, the researcher must place that information in a relevant context. Is 15 percent more or less than the previous 12 months? If the researcher can use benchmarks such as the previous 12 months or a competitor's increase in checking accounts during the same time frame, the information becomes more meaningful.

Step 5: Reporting the Data

After the survey results are analyzed, they must be presented in a way that will be most useful in helping management reach a decision. Research reports that sit on a shelf unread or that are not acted on are not only a waste of money, but are damaging to the credibility of research in general and to the department that generated it. The goal of a research report is to get the results read and used. Therefore, results should be summarized briefly at the beginning of the report, with supporting data in the body of the report.

There are two philosophies with respect to the writing of research reports. One school of thought says that research reports should present results only; the other school of thought says that a report should present both results and recommendations for action. If the research process has been carefully followed, helpful conclusions and recommendations should emanate from the study. While management may choose not

Exhibit 7.4 Survey Sample Design for Great Service National Bank

Great Service National Bank wanted to measure the level of customer satisfaction at each of its three branches. The marketing research manager decided to mail a questionnaire to a sample of the bank's transaction account customers because these customers have the most ongoing contact with the bank and are most likely to consider Great Service to be their main bank.

The bank wanted to compare the level of customer satisfaction between the branches on a number of service issues. The marketing research manager determined that 75 completed interviews for each branch, or 225 total, would be a large enough sample to determine whether differences between branches were statistically significant or merely the result of sampling error (that is, differences due to chance, or random variation, that do not reflect meaningful differences because of the relatively small sample size).

The bank's research manager determined the size of the sample. He estimated (on the basis of previous surveys) that 40 percent of those who received the questionnaire would fill it out and return it. Therefore, it would be necessary to mail out 188 questionnaires per branch (75 divided by .40, the expected response rate, is 187.5), or a total of 564 questionnaires.

The next step was to determine how the sample would be drawn. In its customer information file, in which all accounts are grouped by household, the bank had a total of 3,400 transaction account customers evenly distributed among the three branches. The required total of 564 is roughly one-sixth of 3,400. The research manager, therefore, instructed the data processing manager to select every sixth transaction account customer from the CIF and to print mailing labels for the resulting sample. (This type of sample is called a systematic sample.) This generated 566 labels, and the survey was mailed to this sample.

Only 185 completed questionnaires were returned, a response rate of 33 percent. The data from each returned questionnaire was entered into the computer using special market research software that performs statistical data analysis. Some of the differences found between branches are summarized below. The software identified which differences were statistically significant, and those that were not were disregarded.

Branch:	#1	#2	#3
(Number of respondents)	(62)	(72)	(51)
Service Factor	*Percent Very Satisfied*		
1. Overall speed of service	80	93	82
2. Accuracy with which requests for service are handled	69	85	80
3. Hours the branch is open	50	59	67
4. Speed of response to loan application	65	75	64

Differences between branches on service factors 1 and 2 were found to be significant. (Customers of branch #2 are much better satisfied with overall speed than are customers of the other branches; customers of branch #1 are less satisfied with accuracy than are customers of the other two branches.) Differences between the branches on service factors 3 and 4 were found to be not significant; that is, they could be due simply to chance.

The survey results were based exclusively on the percentage of customers who said they were "very satisfied" on each of the service elements rather than on those who said they were less than very satisfied (that is, "somewhat satisfied," "somewhat dissatisfied," or "very dissatisfied"). The marketing research manager made this decision for two reasons. First, bank customers who are *very* satisfied have been found to behave differently than customers who are less than very satisfied. For instance, they are more likely to be multiple service users and to consider the bank their main bank. Second, the goal of a quality-driven bank is to maximize the percentage of customers who are *very* satisfied.

to act on the recommendations or may take some alternative action, it is the responsibility of marketing management to generate information that can be acted on. Researchers should always be prepared to answer the question "What should we do, or do differently, as a result of this research?"

When and Why Results Are Used

Whether the results of marketing research are used in making bank decisions depends on several factors. One of the jobs of the researcher is to avoid errors that result in research not being used.

When research is not used, the problem is generally the result of one or more fundamental problems: (1) the client's or end-user's lack of receptivity, (2) the researcher's preoccupation with methodology, (3) the absence of interpretive material, or (4) the unreliability of results.

1. *Client's or end-user's lack of receptivity.* Sometimes the end-user has already decided about the answer to the problem being researched. It may be that the president, division head, or other decision maker in the organization has a strong bias and will ignore or undermine results that conflict with this bias. Advertising professionals frequently encounter this problem when a client decides that he or she does not like an advertising campaign even though research results demonstrate its effectiveness.

2. *Researcher's preoccupation with methodology.* Sometimes researchers get carried away with the methodology and lose sight of the stated objectives of the research. They may overanalyze the data or provide countless pieces of information that are not relevant to the problem at hand. The researcher may find details of the research approach fascinating, but this is usually not of interest to the firm's management, which is seeking concise information on which to base marketing decisions.

3. *Absence of interpretive material.* Some research reports contain page after page of tables, but leave it to the reader to draw conclusions from the data. Again, the research report should always answer the question

"What can we do, or do differently, now that we have this information?"

4. *Unreliability of results.* Sometimes results of a survey cannot be projected to the market at large. In some cases, the methodology may be flawed in some way. If the sample of people questioned is too small, if the interviewers were biased, if the questions were loaded—all these flaws will render the results unreliable and, therefore, unusable.

When research does get used, the reasons are generally the inverse of the reasons why it does not. Research results are likely to be used when

- the end-user or client is aware of the problem being studied and receptive to information that will facilitate understanding how to deal with it;

- the researcher has correctly identified the purpose of the study and keeps it in view when writing the results;

- the research makes clear to the end-user how the findings can be interpreted and used; and

- the end-user is confident that the results are reliable and applicable to the market at large.

Marketing Information Systems

Without question, business is experiencing an information explosion. Managers are faced with more information than they can possibly read or absorb. However, computer science is being put to use to reduce information to manageable and usable proportions, thus making it more effective.

For the marketing manager, the marketing information system (MIS) is becoming an increasingly important tool. A marketing information system can be broadly defined as "a framework for the day-to-day management and structuring of information gathered regularly from sources both inside and outside an organization."[8] It is a system that comprises both hardware and software. Because of its broad scope, tremendous capacity, and speedy ability to process great quantities of information, MIS is often called a universal marketing database or dataware-house.

MIS serves as a system of organizing and sorting information, whereas marketing research serves as a method of gathering research. In other words, MIS is a data bank that includes both internally and externally generated information relevant to the marketer. MIS can manage and organize sales, customer service, prospects, and marketing campaigns and more. When a specific marketing question arises, the marketer describes to the MIS manager the problem and the information required. The MIS manager designs the required report and provides it to the marketing manager.

Some examples of internally generated information that might be contained in an MIS are the bank's customer information file, information by branch on number of accounts opened each week and balances in new accounts, number of accounts closed and balances, total deposits by type, and total loans by type. The technology for these systems is evolving very rapidly to expand their capabilities even further. MIS is especially useful because it does not reside on just one computer, but can be tapped from anywhere in the bank. As the technology continues to evolve, banks are using intranets to tap into the bank's MIS.

It is possible to append externally obtained data to internal information. For example, available software can be used to code each customer household according to the census tract and block in which the customer resides. This information can then be used to identify those neighborhoods where the bank has not sufficiently penetrated the market. It can also be used to help select customers who will receive a direct mail solicitation. For instance, the bank might identify the census tracts and blocks containing an especially high proportion of equity credit line customers. It can then order a mailing list that includes only households in tracts and blocks with demographic characteristics that are similar to those where the bank's existing equity credit line customers live. By screening out areas where customers are less likely to have or be interested in this product, the bank hopes to increase its response rate.

Clearly, this kind of information can improve the quality of decisions and reduce the risks associated with them. A marketing information system can be an invaluable tool in the marketing planning process. In fact, it is a requirement for serious strategic planning. The proliferation of marketing information systems has given rise to a new type of targeted marketing that has been called micromarketing (the opposite of mass marketing), target marketing, and one-to-one marketing.

MIS and Marketing Research

Clearly, marketing information systems and marketing research have the same goal: to provide information for marketing decision making. Nevertheless they are quite different information sources. One difference is that an MIS provides a system for managing marketing information. It helps make effective use of many kinds of available information; it can handle internal and external secondary data as well as primary data; and it can store subjective estimates when facts are not available.

A second major difference is that an MIS provides an environment in which learning can take place. It provides the ability to store and process information in a way that makes it easy to recall and evaluate past experiences, thus allowing lessons to be learned and remembered.[9] Therefore, a marketing information system is broader and more flexible than marketing research.

Another difference is that marketing research is typically done on a project-to-project basis, whereas an MIS is an ongoing system. A marketing research department might typically be researching four or five different problems at one time in response to questions involving advertising, product development, pricing, or distribution. It might use the MIS to obtain information concerning one or more of these problems. Later, the results of the marketing research project may be an important source of input to the MIS. The chart in exhibit 7.5 summarizes the contrasting characteristics of marketing research and an MIS.

The use of marketing information systems by banks is sure to grow and spread because of the dramatic expansion of data that confronts managers, the frequency and speed of changes in market conditions within which banks operate, the increasing availability and declining cost of marketing information from external sources, and the recognition by banking executives that information can be a powerful marketing tool.

Summary

This chapter defined marketing research as the major source of information to aid management in making decisions about marketing. The chapter outlined the basic market information that the management of every bank should have at its disposal and then described the steps in the research process, emphasizing the importance of defining the problem precisely. It stressed the fact that research results must be capable of being acted on, and it looked at factors that reduce research effectiveness. Because errors can easily be introduced into research results, the value of using professional researchers (internal or external to the bank) was underscored. Finally, the concept of a marketing information system was discussed, including the differences and similarities between marketing research and marketing information systems.

Having examined the many factors that shape consumer behavior and the research tools that help the marketer identify and understand potential target markets, the discussion will now turn to the process of selecting the markets to be targeted with the marketing strategy, and positioning the

> **Exhibit 7.5 Contrasting Characteristics of Marketing Research and Marketing Information Systems**
>
> *Marketing Research*
>
> 1. Emphasizes the handling of external information
>
> 2. Is concerned with solving problems
>
> 3. Operates in a fragmented, intermittent fashion—on a project-by-project basis
>
> 4. Tends to focus on past information
>
> 5. Is not necessarily a computer-based process
>
> 6. Is one source of information input into a marketing information system
>
> *Marketing Information System*
>
> 1. Handles both internal and external data
>
> 2. Is concerned with preventing as well as solving problems
>
> 3. Operates continuously—is a system
>
> 4. Tends to be future oriented
>
> 5. Is a computer-based process
>
> 6. Includes other subsystems besides marketing research
>
> **Source: William J. Stanton and Charles Futrell,** *Fundamentals of Marketing* **(New York: McGraw-Hill, 1987), p. 64.**

product offering to maximize appeal to the target market.

Points for Review

1. Define or briefly explain the following terms:
   - marketing research
   - marketing information system
   - primary data
   - secondary data
   - sample
   - quantitative data
   - qualitative data
   - research process

2. Why might marketing research be described as the most important function performed by the marketing department?

3. Describe the basic market information that every bank should have available to its management.

4. Describe the relative merits of personal, phone, and self-administered surveys on the basis of speed, cost, accuracy, and amount of information obtained.

5. What are the differences between marketing research and a marketing information system?

Notes

1. "New Marketing Research Definition Approved," *Marketing News,* January 2, 1987, pp. 1, 14.

2. Luther H. Hodges, Jr., and Rollie Tillman, Jr., *Bank Marketing: Text and Cases* (Reading, Mass.: Addison-Wesley, 1968), p. 231.

3. *1996 Analysis of Bank Marketing Expenditures* (Washington, D.C.: Bank Marketing Association, 1996).

4. This section contains information from Pride and Ferrell, *Marketing,* pp. 112–118; Jeffrey L. Pope, *Practical Marketing Research* (New York: American Marketing Association, 1993), pp. 40–44; and Hodges and Tillman, *Bank Marketing: Text and Cases,* p. 7.

5. Pride and Ferrell, *Marketing,* p. 113.

6. Ronald Kurtz, *Strategies in Marketing Research,* revised edition (American Management Association Extension Institute, 1970), p. 114. See also Pride and Ferrell, *Marketing,* p. 116.

7. Patricia J. Labaw, *Advanced Questionnaire Design* (Cambridge, Mass.: Abt Books, 1980), p. 65.

8. Pride and Ferrell, *Marketing,* p. 106.

9. Bertram Schoner and Kenneth P. Uhl, *Marketing Research, Information Systems and Decision Making* (New York: John Wiley & Sons, 1975), pp. 20–21.

8

SEGMENTATION AND POSITIONING STRATEGIES

Learning Objectives

After studying this chapter, you should be able to

- discuss the concept of market segmentation and how MCIF technology can aid segmentation,
- describe and contrast geographic, demographic, psychographic, volume, and benefit segmentation strategies, in general, and specifically in the commercial banking industry,
- compare and contrast differentiated, undifferentiated, and concentrated market segmentation strategies for selecting target markets, and
- explain the concept of positioning.

Introduction

As discussed in previous chapters, many variables affect the behavior of consumers as they select the particular way in which they will satisfy their needs and wants. You have also been introduced to marketing research, which can be used to help identify, measure, and understand market segments. This chapter deals with the many choices facing the marketer who must segment the market and select those segments that will be targeted with marketing mix strategies.

First, this chapter shows how marketing customer information file technology revolutionized banks' ability to analyze and segment their markets. Next, five approaches to market segmentation will be discussed: geographic, demographic, psychographic, volume, and benefit segmentation. The segmentation strategies used in addressing the corporate banking market will also be reviewed. Then, guidelines for selecting target markets, and three alternative approaches to segment selection, will be discussed: undifferentiated marketing, differentiated marketing, and concentrated marketing. In conclusion, the concept of positioning, or carving a niche for the institution or the product, will be addressed.

Segmenting the Market

Market segmentation, as an element of marketing strategy, recognizes the wisdom of specializing to suit the needs of a segment of the market rather than trying to be "all things to all people." The problem with the latter approach is that buyers in the market for a product (whether it be checking services or automobiles) are far from homogeneous in how they go about satisfying their needs and wants for that product. Consequently, they differ in the ways in which they respond to a particular marketing mix strategy. What catches one person's attention or appeals to another person's imagination might leave yet another person cold. Market segmentation subdivides a market into groups of customers who have similar product and service needs. This allows any subset of the market to be targeted with a distinct marketing mix.

A major tool that banks have been using in rapidly increasing numbers since the early 1990s is the marketing customer information file (MCIF) system. An MCIF is a software program that organizes information on households and individuals and sorts or summarizes the information similarities and differences among groups of consumers. Because of this focus on the customer, MCIFs are also referred to as relationship management systems. MCIFs can greatly assist clear, customer-focused marketing efforts.

Banks use the information generated by MCIFs to identify profitable customers and single-service customers as well as markets with potential for cross-sales. More advanced MCIF systems allow bankers to identify the most and least profitable products and branches as well.

The data generated by an MCIF are critical in preparing strategic reports, too, and are used to support strategic marketing initiatives.[1] For example, some MCIF systems offer modeling capabilities that permit bankers to run test scenarios that predict the effect that such changes as new fees, increases in minimum balance requirements, and decreases in delivery costs will have on profitability.

Some firms have done such a good job of selecting and segmenting a target market that they have dramatically influenced an entire industry. Remember the earlier discussion of the wristwatch market. For years, the major watch companies made expensive watches that they sold through jewelry stores. The U.S. Time Company recognized that there were target markets whose needs for a low-cost, durable watch were not being met. The company developed such a watch and marketed it through mass merchandisers. The Timex watch made U.S. Time one of the world's largest watch manufacturers.[2]

The object of market segmentation is to identify a specific user group (or groups) and then pursue it with a tailored product, supported by appropriate pricing, promotion, and distribution strategies. Market segments must have certain qualities that make it possible to specialize the marketing approaches. In particular, market segments must be *measurable, accessible,* and *sizable.* In other words, it must be possible to measure the size and purchasing power of the market segment; it must be feasible to reach the segment through advertising and through the distribution system; and there must be enough members in the segment to generate a profitable volume.

Segmentation Strategies

Markets can be segmented in a number of different ways. A bank should choose an approach that subdivides the market into groups that differ in some distinct fashion from one another with respect to their preferences. Some principal segmentation alternatives are

- geographic segmentation,
- demographic segmentation,
- psychographic segmentation,
- volume segmentation, and
- benefit segmentation.

Geographic segmentation divides the market according to geographic units. A firm might decide to market different products in different areas or to market its products in certain areas and not in others. For example, consider how the range of cornmeal products marketed by the Quaker Oats Company reflects regional cooking preferences. Whereas the company markets only yellow and white cornmeal in the Northeast, the consumer will find two types of cornmeal, corn flour, and a variety of Quaker Oats cornmeal baking mixes in the South. Similarly, a bank practices geographic segmentation when it decides on the location of a new branch. Acquiring or renovating a facility is one of the two "largest, least flexible capital/expense risks

for financial institutions"[3] (the other is computer purchases and conversions). Since a bank clearly cannot have locations everywhere, it must carefully allocate its limited resources to meet its business goals. It does that by locating its new branch offices in the most promising geographic market areas. (For more on location analysis/site selection, see chapter 11.)

Demographic segmentation categorizes the market in terms of population characteristics, such as age, sex, income, occupation, and position in the life cycle. For example, the bank that establishes an executive banking group specifically for attorneys, accountants, and doctors has targeted an occupational segment. A bank that develops an equity credit line aimed at homeowners with incomes in excess of $35,000 is targeting another specific demographic segment.

Psychographic segmentation entails classifying the market in behavioral terms according to lifestyle, social class, or personality profile. For example, a bank might identify the "young professional on the fast track" as a prime market segment for credit card sales. Or a bank might focus on conservative consumers who want to shield their savings by marketing a five-year CD to them.

Volume segmentation refers to the marketer's attempt to distinguish heavy, medium, and light users of a product. In many businesses, a small proportion of the users generate a large proportion of sales. This is called the *Pareto principle,* which says that 80 percent of profits come from 20 percent of customers, and it is just as true for savings accounts as it is for beer. A reasonable marketing strategy is to determine the characteristics that those 20 percent have in common and then to direct the marketing effort toward attracting more people like them.

Benefit segmentation is the process of categorizing the market in terms of the main product-related benefits sought by different groups. The various approaches used in marketing mouthwash illustrates this type of segmentation. Some people simply want their breath to smell fresh and to have a pleasant taste in their mouths. This market is targeted by Scope. Others are primarily concerned with killing germs that might cause gum disease. Listerine appeals to this segment. Still others want to fight the buildup of plaque on their teeth, and Viadent and Plax aim their marketing efforts at this segment.

Exhibit 8.1 illustrates how one company identified eight market segments that can be applied to the financial services market: wealth market, upscale retired, upper affluent, lower affluent, mass market savers, mass market spenders, lower market, and downscale retired.[4] Each of these groups seeks a different principal benefit from their financial services provider. A bank

---

Exhibit 8.1 **Markets Can Be Segmented by Financial Status and Behaviors, as well as Demographics and Neighborhoods**

The Eight P$YCLE Segments

- *Wealth Market:* This group of over 1 million households makes up 1 percent of the U.S. population. They have investable assets of over $1 million and command 18 percent of the total U.S. household income.

- *Upscale Retired:* These are affluent retired persons representing 8 percent of all households. They have more than $25,000 in annual income and less than $1 million in income-producing assets.

- *Upper Affluent Market:* With annual incomes in excess of $75,000 and income-producing assets under $1 million, this market is made up of affluent executive families, representing 11.5 percent of all U.S. households.

- *Lower Affluent Market:* This segment represents 14.8 percent of all households and consists of upscale white-collar families. Annual incomes are above $61,000.

- *Mass Market Savers:* A relatively small segment consisting of 2.1 percent of all U.S. households. Average income is under $50,000 and investable assets are between $100,000 and $1 million.

- *Mass Market Spenders:* This is the largest segment representing 35.9 percent of all U.S. households. This group is solidly middle class with incomes averaging $30,000.

- *The Lower Market:* Incomes of this group, which consists of 13.5 percent of all U.S. households, are below $15,000, and income-producing assets are under $100,000. Many live below the poverty line.

- *Downscale Retired:* These are retirees on fixed incomes, representing 12.3 percent of all U.S. households.

Source: Abbreviated information drawn from Katherine Morrall, "Market Research Helps Home In on High Potential Segments," June 1996, *Bank Marketing*, p. 36. The above market segmentation strategy (P$YCLE) was created by Claritas, a database marketing and strategy company located in Arlington, Virginia.

using benefit segmentation would build its strategy around the delivery of a specific benefit. For example, a bank targeting the upper-income segment might offer after hours appointments with private bankers, seminars on investments, and free safe deposit boxes.

Some banks segment the market for specific bank products. For instance, in any one geographic market at any one time, all commercial banks offer installment loans. One bank might target the rate-sensitive loan customer and prominently feature the bank's current interest rate, inviting consumers to compare it with the rates of other loan providers. Another bank might target the segment that seeks the benefits of speed and convenience. This bank might promote its telephone loan service, promising same-day approval with no mention of the interest rate. In fact, the rate might be 50 or 100 basis points higher than the rate advertised by the competition, but the customer to whom convenience is a high priority will not be highly sensitive to the price differential. A third bank might aim at the segment that wants to borrow to pay off credit card bills. Its advertising might focus on debt consolidation.

Most banks' checking product line reflects some demographic segmentation. For example, a bank might segment the market along income lines by offering a "no-frills" type of checking account for people who maintain low balances and write few checks, a regular checking account for the mass market, and an interestbearing checking account with a high minimum balance requirement for those who maintain a high balance.

The upscale segment (which is defined differently from bank to bank but which can be broadly defined as households earning more than $75,000 with net worth of $500,000 or more, excluding equity in a home) is growing. This growth is prompting many banks to establish private banking groups in market areas where enough people meet this criteria. The multitude of senior citizen package accounts introduced for people over 50 years of age is another example of demographic segmentation.

Many banks engage in limited market segmentation, but in general the banking industry has not exploited this strategy to the extent that consumer product manufacturers have. The principal reason for this is that many bankers have difficulty endorsing a strategy in which some customers are more important than others. Phillip D. White provides a response to this concern:

> It is easy to agree that every customer is important and is entitled to some basic level of service. However, what is missing from that viewpoint is the recognition that certain identifiable segments want different levels of service, different payment alternatives, and different distribution alternatives. Banks that ignore these customer preferences for specific levels of service do so at their own risk.[5]

Segmenting the Commercial Banking Market

Segmentation strategy can be applied to the commercial banking market as well as to the consumer market. The three segmentation strategies most likely to be used by banks in their approach to the commercial banking market are *geographic segmentation, sales volume segmentation,* and *industry segmentation.*

A bank might use all three strategies simultaneously. For example, if a bank were to segment the commercial market by sales volume, it might have a small-business department that addresses the needs of firms with sales of $2 million or less. Another department might target firms with sales between $2 million and $20 million; a third might handle customers with sales from $20 million to $120 million; and a fourth department might concentrate on the few very large firms with sales over $120 million.

Within any one of these target markets, the bank might also practice geographic segmentation. For example, if many firms in the area have sales of $2 million to $20 million, the bank might establish regional loan centers in the downtown area and in the northern, southern, eastern, and western suburbs. The bank might also target a distant geographical market—one that is not within the area served by its existing branches. At that outlying regional office, the commercial banking officers might work to develop business among firms of all sizes, from $2 million on up.

The same bank might also practice industrial segmentation. It would identify specific industries having enough firms in the bank's trade area to be a sizable and potentially profitable target market. Each market segment might have unique financing needs to which the bank could cater. Some examples of specific industries that could be targeted include the health care industry (hospitals, nursing homes); higher education (colleges and universities); insurance companies; commercial real estate developers; and government entities (states, cities, and municipalities).

Whichever approach the bank chooses to take, the targeted segments must meet the criteria of being measurable and accessible and must have enough members to be a potentially profitable target.

Once an organization has identified the market segments that it might address, the next step is to select the target market or markets.

Target Market Selection

Financial services providers should follow these guidelines when selecting target markets.[6]

1. *The target should be consistent, or at least compatible, with the bank's goals and image.* For instance, a bank that is known as a leading wholesale bank cannot suddenly target the market for retail install-ment loans with much success. Recall the importance of perceptions and the need to present a message that will support, rather than contradict, the target market's perceptions.

2. *A firm should seek markets that are consistent with its resources.* If a particular market segment can be reached only through mass media advertising, and if a firm cannot afford the level of expenditure necessary to carry out a media campaign, the project is doomed. Similarly, if the target market requires a high level of knowledge and sales skill at the point of sale, but the bank has not taken steps to provide that level of service, it should not aim at that market. A small, new bank in the heart of a large metropolitan area might be successful in targeting executives with six-figure salaries who require a high level of personal service. The same bank would likely find it prohibitively expensive to take on the major metropolitan banks in the mass market.

3. *A firm should seek markets that will generate not only sufficient volume, but profitable volume.* The bank that targets the cost-conscious checking customer by offering totally free checking might find itself doing a land-office business but losing money on 80 percent of its accounts. In seeking target markets, the basic precept of marketing—customer satisfaction at a profit—should not be forgotten.

4. *A firm should seek a target market for which the number and size of competitors is small.* Aiming at a market saturated with competitors requires winning customers away from the competition. It is much harder to shift customers away from a need-satisfying situation than it is to fill an unmet, or incompletely met, need.

A bank or firm might use one of three strategies in selecting a target market or markets: undifferentiated marketing, differentiated marketing, and concentrated marketing. (See exhibit 8.2.)

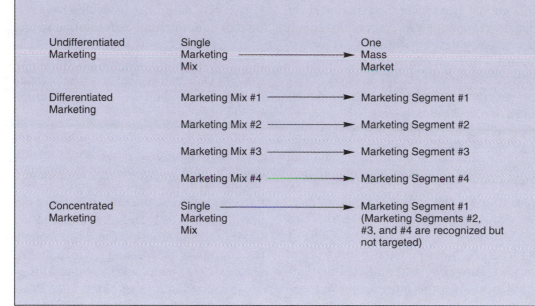

Exhibit 8.2   **Alternative Segment Selection Strategies**

Undifferentiated Marketing	Single Marketing Mix ⟶	One Mass Market
Differentiated Marketing	Marketing Mix #1 ⟶	Marketing Segment #1
	Marketing Mix #2 ⟶	Marketing Segment #2
	Marketing Mix #3 ⟶	Marketing Segment #3
	Marketing Mix #4 ⟶	Marketing Segment #4
Concentrated Marketing	Single Marketing Mix ⟶	Marketing Segment #1 (Marketing Segments #2, #3, and #4 are recognized but not targeted)

Undifferentiated Marketing

Undifferentiated marketing, which is also known as *market aggregation,* avoids segmentation altogether and targets the mass market with a single offer. The firm designs one product, pricing structure, distribution system, and promotional program to appeal to the largest number of people. This strategy is most often found in industries where there is little real difference between competing products. In such cases, a firm may seek to gain a competitive edge by differentiating itself from its competitors by images. For example, table salt is a product that does not admit to any real variation, yet Morton's successfully distinguishes itself from the competition with its slogan, "When it rains, it pours."[7] In many respects, banking is an industry with little product differentiation between institutions. As a result, many banks engage in undifferentiated marketing with mass media image-building campaigns that are primarily designed to set the bank apart from the competition in the minds of customers.

Differentiated Marketing

With *differentiated marketing,* or *multiple segmentation,* a firm selects two or more different segments as its target markets and develops separate offers for each segment. This may be done in one of two ways: a firm might offer different products to each market segment, or it might offer the same product, but vary the offer through the promotional strategy.

The major automobile manufacturers provide an example of differentiated marketing in which a different product is aimed at each market segment. General Motors, Ford, and Chrysler all manufacture a variety of models aimed at different market segments. Banks that offer different types of checking accounts for different demographic segments are also practicing this type of differentiated marketing segmentation strategy.

An example of the second type of differentiated marketing—in which a firm markets the same product to different segments using different promotional strategies—is

Johnson & Johnson, which markets its baby shampoo not only to mothers who need a "no more tears" shampoo for their small children, but also to adults who are seeking a gentle shampoo. Banks practice this strategy when they develop different ads for one product. For example, when promoting an equity credit line, a bank might target different benefit segments. One ad might be aimed at parents of college-bound students who need additional financing, while another ad aims at households who seek a home improvement loan.

Whereas undifferentiated marketing leads to low penetration of the total market, differentiated marketing is likely to result in greater sales volume because it can lead to greater penetration of smaller markets. However, differentiated marketing also tends to be more expensive because of the cost involved in producing and delivering different products and in executing a variety of promotional strategies. Nevertheless, most banks use differentiated marketing as their approach to market segmentation.

Concentrated Marketing

The third strategy for selecting a target market is *concentrated marketing,* or *single-segment marketing.*[8] With this strategy, the marketer selects one target market and develops only one marketing mix strategy to address it.

This strategy enables a firm to make good use of limited resources as a result of the economies that can be realized by having specialized product, distribution, and promotional strategies. It also enables the firm to penetrate one market deeply and to develop a reputation as an expert in that market. However, the risks associated with this strategy are great. If the firm is highly successful, other firms may be attracted to the market, thus increasing competition and possibly reducing sales volume and increasing promotional expenses. The other danger in pursuing only one target market is that if the market's purchasing behavior changes for any reason, the firm could be put out of business.

Two very dissimilar firms that have followed a concentrated segmentation strategy are Hyundai, which entered the U.S. market by targeting the market for small, efficient cars; and Rolls Royce, which targets the upper end of the high-income market.

Positioning

Having identified and selected a target market or markets, the firm must carve out a position for itself and its product in the minds of the members of the target market. The concept of positioning came to prominence in 1972 when Jack Trout and Al Ries wrote a series of articles titled "The Positioning Era" for the trade publication *Advertising Age.* They later wrote a book called *Positioning: The Battle for Your Mind,* in which they cited a number of familiar cases to demonstrate positioning successes and failures.

Trout and Ries define positioning as "not what you do to a product," but rather "what you do to the mind of the prospect. . . . You position the product in the mind of the prospect."[9]

There are several possible positioning strategies, some of which follow:

- *Positioning in relation to a competitor.* A classic example is Avis, which positioned itself against the rental car industry leader, Hertz, by saying, "We're No. 2; we try harder." Case E describes the new logo and image campaign created by LaSalle State Bank to differentiate it from its competitors and to update its image.

- *Positioning in relation to a product class.* When Tylenol initiated the marketing campaign that led to its position as the leading analgesic, it positioned itself against aspirin by pointing out that aspirin was upsetting to the stomach, triggered allergic reactions, and could cause internal bleeding. Then it offered itself as the alternative. In a similar vein, 7-Up has positioned itself as the alternative to cola drinks by calling itself "the uncola."

• *Positioning a product or service as more accessible.* Visa has had an ongoing marketing campaign to position itself as a more useful credit card because it is accepted by more merchants and in more countries. Visa has specifically targeted American Express card, which has long used the slogan "Don't leave home without it" for its card, by showing popular attractions such as the 1996 Olympics in Atlanta as an example of an event where Visa is accepted and American Express is not. The Visa slogan highlighting that card's utility and accessibility is "We're everywhere you want to be."

• *Positioning along price or quality dimensions.* Piaget positions itself as "the most expensive watch in the world," while Maytag positions itself as the highest quality washing machine manufacturer.[10]

The bank can take a number of approaces to positioning. However, careful consideration must go into selecting a positioning strategy. It is not an element of a bank's marketing strategy that should be changed often. Once you select a position, it should be part of every marketing campaign and platform. Here are five rules of positioning as they apply to the banking industry:

1. Position your bank or someone else will.
2. Know your target customer thoroughly.
3. Be only what you can be (the better you define your products and services, the more relevant your positioning will be).
4. Tell your customers why you are special.
5. Be consistent.[11]

Although this list of positioning strategies is not exhaustive, it demonstrates that positioning is a strategy that addresses the way the target market thinks, and then either finds an opening that can be filled or creates one.

Summary

MCIF technology enables banks to define target markets and further segment them to create consumer groups most likely to be interested in the bank's offer.

Market segmentation recognizes the wisdom of specializing to suit the needs of a segment of the market rather than trying to be all things to all people. The object of segmentation is to identify a specific user group and then pursue it with a tailored product that is supported by appropriate pricing, promotion, and distribution strategies.

The market segments that are selected should be measurable, accessible, and sizable. Marketers can segment along a variety of lines: geography, demographics, psychographics, usage volume, and benefits sought. Banks generally segment the market for consumer products using a combination of segmentation strategies. The corporate banking market is usually segmented geographically, by sales size, or by industrial classification.

Some guidelines for selecting a target market are that it should be consistent with the organization's goals, image, and resources; it should be capable of generating profitable volume; and it should be a market that is not already being targeted by a large number of competitors. The three target market selection strategies are undifferentiated marketing, which is basically the absence of targeting; differentiated marketing, in which the marketer selects two or more targets; and concentrated marketing, in which the marketer selects only one target. Having selected a target market, the marketer can use positioning strategy in order to create a special place for the product or the institution in the minds of the targeted segment.

This chapter concludes the discussion of the important planning task of selecting the target market. The theories and the research tools for understanding markets, and the alternative strategies for target market selection, have been addressed.

Finally, the concept of positioning, or making a place for the product or the institution in the mind of the target, has been introduced.

The following chapters focus on the next step in the planning process: designing the marketing mix strategies that will appeal to, and communicate with, the target market.

Points for Review

1. Define or briefly explain the following:
   - market segmentation
   - differentiated marketing
   - undifferentiated marketing
   - concentrated marketing
   - positioning
2. What is the purpose of an MCIF system? Give an example of how it can be used.
3. A bank might use geographic segmentation to market home equity loans to an area with single-family homes and mortgage loan products to rental areas. Give an example of how a bank might apply each of the following segmentation strategies: demographic, psychographic, volume, and benefit.
4. Why would a bank choose to use a differentiated marketing strategy rather than an undifferentiated strategy?
5. Give an example of how a bank could position itself relative to a competitor.

Notes

1. Kotler, *Marketing Management,* p. 273.
2. Scott A. Hansen and Marie Hearn, "MCIF Training for Users and CEOs Improves Marketing Results," *Bank Marketing,* February 1996, pp. 13–18.
3. Paul Seibert, *Facilities Planning and Design for Financial Institutions: A Strategic Management Guide* (Chicago: Irwin Professional, 1996), p. 1.
4. Katherine Morrall, "Market Research Helps Home In on High Potential Segments," *Bank Marketing,* June 1996, p. 39. See also Claritas Financial Services Group, Arlington, Va., 800-284-4868.
5. Phillip D. White, "Market Segmentation: Overcoming the Problems to Capitalize on the Premises," *Bank Marketing,* March 1992, pp. 32–33.
6. Stanton and Futrell, *Fundamentals of Marketing,* p. 40.
7. *Ibid.,* pp. 169–170.
8. *Ibid.,* p. 171.
9. Al Ries and Jack Trout, *Positioning: The Battle for Your Mind* (New York: McGraw-Hill, 1986), p. 2.
10. Doug Stone, "Five Key Rules of Market Positioning," *Bank Marketing,* December 1995, pp. 19–21.
11. For additional positioning strategies, see Kotler, *Marketing Management,* pp. 281–284.

Part IV

MARKETING MIX STRATEGIES

Having learned in part III why consumers behave as they do and how to measure potential markets, we turn in part IV to the next step in marketing planning: the design of product, pricing, place (distribution channels), and promotion strategies (the "four Ps" of marketing). These four elements constitute the *marketing mix*—in other words, the strategies that will ultimately determine whether the target markets are reached and the plan's objectives achieved.

Chapters 9 and 10 deal with product and pricing strategy, while chapters 11 and 12 address distribution strategy. Since the distribution, and especially the sale, of banking services is difficult to separate from the people who are delivering these services, this text views personal selling as part of a bank's distribution strategy. Therefore, chapter 12 is devoted to the important role of personal selling in banking. (General marketing texts treat selling as part of promotion strategy.) Once the marketer has put together the offer—consisting of a product or service aimed at a target market, priced to maximize appeal while providing a profit for the firm—and has put into place a system for distributing it, it is time to communicate that offer to the target market. The final chapter in part IV, therefore, addresses promotion strategy. Here, the marketer brings to bear all that is known about the target market's needs, perceptions, motivations, and behavior to develop an appealing, creatively executed message designed to inspire members of the target market to select this one particular product or service over all the others.

9

PRODUCT STRATEGY AND NEW PRODUCT DEVELOPMENT

Learning Objectives

After studying this chapter, you should be able to

- define the term *product* and explain the five aspects of a product from a marketing point of view,
- differentiate among a product item, product line, and product mix,
- describe the four characteristics that differentiate services from products,
- enumerate the five most common product strategies,
- describe the product life cycle,
- categorize consumers on the basis of how soon they adopt a product that is new to the market,
- explain the concept of systems selling,
- describe four product development categories, and list the stages in the progressive rejection system,
- describe the responsibilities of a product manager, and
- enumerate several reasons for product failure.

Introduction

The formulation of a detailed marketing mix strategy is the fourth key element in the marketing planning process as discussed in chapter 3. Strategy formulation involves determining how the marketing mix will be used. This chapter on product strategy discusses the meaning of the term *product* and the similarities and differences between products and services, presents some alternative product strategies and introduces the concept of the product life cycle, and describes the development process for new banking products. The chapter also discusses the concept of product management and delves into some of the reasons that products fail.

Importance of the Product

The product is the key element in the marketing mix for two fundamental reasons:

1. *The product is the firm's reason for being.* All firms (including banks) are in the business of satisfying customer needs, and they do this through their product. A firm that does not deliver a need-satisfying product has no reason to exist.

2. *All the other elements of the marketing mix revolve around the product.* This does not imply that the other elements of the mix are not vital. Rather, they typically play the role of facilitating market acceptance of the product.

This is illustrated by exhibit 1.1, which shows the elements of the marketing mix as a three-legged stool. *Distribution strategies* make the product available when and where the market wants it. *Pricing strategies* make the product available at a price that is both attractive to the market and profitable to the seller. *Promotion strategies* communicate to the market the potential benefits of the product accruing from its design, distribution, and price attributes.

What Is a Product?

Kotler proposes the following definition: "A product is anything that can be offered to a market for attention, acquisition, use, or consumption that might satisfy a want or need."[1] Within this broad framework, a candidate for public office, the Bahamas, the Army, and the idea that smoking may be harmful to your health might all be considered products to be marketed. In a banking context, all banking services (including checking and savings accounts, certificates of deposit, safekeeping services, lockbox operations, cash management services, and loans) are also products.

From a marketing point of view, a product has five different aspects: (1) the core product (benefit), (2) the generic product, (3) the expected product, (4) the augmented product, and (5) the potential product.[2]

The *core product* (benefit) is the *essential* benefit that the customer is buying (for example, the convenience of being able to pay for goods and services with checks).

The *generic product* provides that benefit (for example, the basic checking product).

The *expected product* includes the product features that customers assume will be part of the product (for example, prompt and accurate clearance of checks, accurate monthly statements, and ability to access the account through ATMs).

The *augmented product* includes all the specific features and benefits that help the marketer differentiate the product from its competitors (for example, package products link accounts and can provide a number of customer benefits such as no-annual-fee credit cards, loan discounts, and bonus rates on CDs). The customer shopping for a disposable razor is confronted with a variety of razors, all having the same expected features: a certain size, disposability, sturdy plastic construction, and a shape that fits the hand. However, each is a different augmented product. Each one bears a unique brand name, has a different color and shape of package, and is associated with a certain quality level in the customer's mind.

Banking products are augmented by the level and quality of service provided to the customer, the reputation of the bank, the decor and physical environment of the bank, the brochures and other printed materials provided to the customer, and any specific brand names given to the products.

The *potential product* includes all the modifications that the product might undergo over time (for example, access through a special display telephone or an ATM that dispenses a snapshot checking statement). Product managers are oriented toward the potential product and thus spend much of their time researching and planning product enhancements.

Exhibit 9.1 looks at Marlton National Bank's Home Equity Credit Line (see Case B) from the perspective of these five aspects of a product.

Product Item, Product Line, and Product Mix

A *product item* is a specific version of a product, such as Honey Nut Cheerios or a one-year CD. A *product line* is a group of closely related products, such as the full line of General Mills ready-to-eat cereals. Savings products are an example of a banking product line. (See exhibit 9.2.)

The *product mix* is the full range of products offered for sale by the bank or firm. General Mills' product mix includes cereals, snacks, beverages, prepared baked goods, baking mixes and frostings, seafood products, potato products, and flour. The product mix of a large bank might easily include more than 100 different bank-related services.

Exhibit 9.1 The Five Aspects of a Product: Marlton National Bank's Home Equity Credit Line

Aspect	Components
Core benefit	The ability to obtain a loan whenever cash is needed, without having to reapply each time; the potential tax deductibility of the interest expense
Generic product	Equity-secured revolving line of credit
Expected product	Variable rate of interest; check-writing capability; approved loan amount related to equity in primary residence and credit analysis
Augmented product	Marlton National's Home Equity Credit Line, priced at prime + 1.75%, adjusted quarterly; accessible by check or automated teller; 120-month repayment period; amounts up to 70 percent of the appraised value of the house, with a minimum approved line of $10,000 and a maximum of $100,000 (see Case B)
Potential product	Access through the bank's VISA card; purchase protection on items bought by writing checks on the credit line

A company's product mix has two characteristics: breadth and depth. Breadth refers to the number of different product lines in the mix. Depth refers to the number of product items within each product line.

Services vs. Products

Before proceeding with the discussion of product strategy, it will be useful to consider the differences between products and services, since this text focuses on marketing in a service industry. Although there are many similarities between the marketing of tangible products and intangible services, there are also some important differences.

First, it is necessary to define the term *service:* "A service is any act or performance that one party can offer to another that is essentially intangible and does not result in the ownership of anything. Its production may or may not be tied to a physical product."[3] Health care, private education, transportation, communication, medical and professional services, and banking are examples of service industries.

Services have certain characteristics that create special challenges for marketers. As a result, the marketing techniques used by banks and other service industries are often very different from those found in product marketing. These characteristics are

- intangibility,
- inseparability,
- variability, and
- perishability.[4]

Intangibility

Since a service cannot be seen, touched, or otherwise experienced by the senses, customers cannot shop for a service as they would for a tangible product—by picking it up, examining it, and evaluating it. Yet, the prepurchase stage is important in that it enables the customer to assess the quality and reliability of a product. Service marketers must compensate for the customer's inability to physically examine the product by providing evidence of the quality of their service and by building a reputation for reliability in delivering the principal benefits of the service.

Many service marketers try to overcome the problems associated with *intangibility* by identifying their service with a tangible symbol. For instance, Travelers Insurance uses an open red umbrella as its symbol;

Nationwide Insurance uses a blanket. Bank marketers are attempting to make tangible their service offerings when they use a mascot or other symbol, or when they give a new customer an attractive envelope full of colorful and informative brochures and other documents as evidence of the intangible accounts that have been opened.

Inseparability

A service cannot be separated from the person who is selling or delivering the service. In banking, the customer's personal contact with a teller or customer service representative is an important channel in the distribution of banking services. In most cases, a customer can open a checking account, the core product in a banking relationship, only by dealing directly with a bank employee. This characteristic, called *inseparability,* results in a bank's consumer banking services being sold only in markets where there is a "retail outlet"—that is, a branch office. Innovative banks have found ways around this limitation and now solicit new business (especially credit business) through mail and telephone marketing, as well as via the Internet and on-line banking, but there is always a person at the other end of the transaction with whom the customer can communicate.

Variability

Although many service outlets (such as branches of a particular bank) may sell and deliver the same services, the augmented products they dispense are not identical from branch to branch. No service business can have precisely the same standard of service in every outlet at every moment. Even McDonald's, which works hard to provide its customers with essentially the same experience regardless of which outlet is visited, cannot achieve the impossible. In contrast, mass-produced products, such as a particular brand of aspirin, are manufactured under rigidly standardized procedures and then inspected for any variation

from the norm before being distributed to the customer. As a result, everyone buying a package of this aspirin gets exactly the same product.

Because of the difficulty of standardizing a banking service from one banking office to another (for example, the way a checking account customer is serviced and the quality of the service he or she receives), it is all the more important for the bank or other service company to set measurable standards for quality service and to pay particular attention to training and motivating its staff to meet and exceed those standards.

Perishability

If you were asked to make a list of perishable items, you would probably think immediately of things like fruits and vegetables, but not banking services. Yet services are highly perishable because they cannot be stored. For example, empty seats from one football game cannot be carried over to provide more seating at the next. Similarly, hours when tellers are idle cannot be used to provide quicker service at noon on Friday when long lines are forming.

Another characteristic of many services is that the demand for them fluctuates considerably by season, by day of the week, and even by the hour of the day. For example, consider long-distance telephone service, for which the busiest day is Thanksgiving; public transportation with its rush hours and holiday traffic; and restaurants with their lunch and dinner peaks. The demand for banking services also fluctuates by day and by hour. The day before a holiday weekend, most Mondays and Fridays, lunch hours, and the third of each month (the day Social Security checks arrive in the mail) are heavier-than-normal banking times.

The combination of *perishability* and fluctuating demand presents challenges for marketers engaged in product planning, pricing, promotion, and distribution in service industries. Telephone companies try to spread out the demand for their services by pricing off-peak hours to make them more attractive to callers. Restaurants offer early-bird specials to off-load some traffic to an earlier dinner hour. Some banks charge a fee for check cashing to encourage customers to use automated tellers and thus reduce lobby traffic. Through advertising, banks highlight the convenience of being able to bank day or night through PC banking services rather than just during banking hours.

Product Strategies

There are any number of product strategies that a bank or business may select, but for the most part they fall into two broad categories: strategies relating to the product mix, and strategies relating to the product life cycle. Product adopter categories relate to the product life cycle and are also discussed. Systems selling—which follows the mature stage in a product's life cycle—is described as well.

Product Mix Strategies

The most common product mix strategies are

- product expansion,
- product contraction,
- product modification,
- product repositioning, and
- trading up or trading down.[5]

Product Expansion

Product expansion can entail adding new products to an existing product line or adding new product lines to an existing product mix. When new items are added, this "deepens" a company's product line; when new product lines are added, the company "broadens" its product mix. (See exhibit 9.2.) For example, when Coca-Cola introduced caffeine-free Coke, it was expanding or deepening its product line of cola drinks. However, when it started marketing sportswear bearing the Coca-Cola logo, it was broadening its product mix.

When a bank adds a basic checking account to its line of checking products, it is deepening the product line. When that bank enters the discount brokerage business, it is broadening its product mix.

Product Contraction

Sometimes firms thin out their product lines by eliminating products, or entire product lines, that may be contributing little to profits. They do this to concentrate their resources on a narrower product mix that will generate more profits. In a major move a number of years ago, General Electric dropped a number of products from its consumer product mix (including blenders, vacuum cleaners, fans, heaters, and humidifiers) in order to concentrate on those products where it had a competitive edge.

Product Modification

New products proliferate as firms engage in product expansion, modification, and repositioning to maintain and increase market share and to take advantage of growth markets. A firm can improve its product, or redesign or repackage it—perhaps even give it a new name—in the hope of increasing sales. Manufacturers of consumer products continually alter their products in an attempt to respond to changing consumer preferences.

During 1996, nearly 24,000 new products hit the shelves of grocery stores and drugstores as companies sought to increase their market share and take advantage of growth markets. Avon Products alone introduced 649 new products. New foods and new health and beauty aids accounted for nearly 80 percent of these new product introductions.[6] (See exhibit 9.3.) As always, most of these "new" products were not entirely new but were new varieties, formulations, sizes, or packages of existing brands.

Banks frequently modify and enhance existing products too. For example, a bank might add new features and benefits to its credit card product by allowing customers to write checks against the credit line, by offering a "buyer protection" program, or by making the credit line available through the bank's automated tellers.

Product Repositioning

As was noted in chapter 8, positioning is not something that is done to a product as much as it is something that is done to the collective minds of the target market. Each marketing firm attempts to set its products apart from the competitions'. The makers of the Snickers candy bar repositioned the product as a wholesome, between-meal snack, thereby setting it apart from its competitors. Orange growers repositioned orange juice when they advertised: "It isn't just for breakfast anymore." Common household vinegar is being repositioned and reintroduced by H. J. Heinz as a cleaning solution. Arm and Hammer promotes multiple uses for its baking soda in its toothpaste, laundry detergent, carpet freshener, and litter box deodorant.[7]

Many banks have repositioned themselves as a result of mergers and acquisitions. Because of the different circumstances for mergers and acquisitions, there are a variety of reasons and ways to reposition the bank. Some banks work to retain their existing customer bank during a merger by positioning themselves as even better able to serve customers' needs. Others need to announce a dramatic change in a manner that eases customers' and employees' transition to the new company. (See Case H for greater detail on repositioning during a merger or acquisition.)

Trading Up or Trading Down

These closely related product expansion strategies are based on the allure of prestige. A manufacturer "trades up" by adding a higher-priced or prestige item to a product line, in the hope that this will attract customers for its lower-priced items as well. "Trading down" involves adding a lower-priced item to a prestige line in the hope that people who are attracted to, but cannot afford, the original will buy the lower-priced item. Mercedes-Benz traded down when it introduced the 190 Series of smaller, lower-priced, sporty cars. Kmart, on the other hand, engages in trading up by offering both discount merchandise and higher-priced, name-brand items in the hope of attracting both the value shopper and the discount shopper. Banks that offer free checking as a means of selling the customer additional services might be said to be trading down.

Product Life Cycle Strategies

Products come and go—some sooner than others. The study of the sales histories of many different types of products has led to the concept of the product life cycle. The typical product life cycle, showing the pattern of sales and profits at each stage in the cycle, is shown in exhibit 9.4. This chart is a useful, albeit simplified, model; it is not meant to imply that all products follow precisely this pattern. Some products enter the market, take off quickly, and die off just as fast. Others revive after they have already entered into the decline phase, so that their life cycle looks more like a double-humped camel. Nevertheless, the life cycle shown in exhibit 9.4 is a useful tool for understanding product strategy and the importance of new products to businesses.

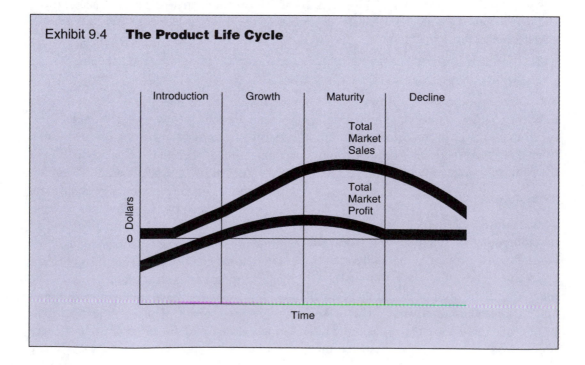

Exhibit 9.4 **The Product Life Cycle**

Exhibit 9.4 depicts the life cycle of a class of products (such as the personal checking account or cellular telephones) rather than a particular firm's product (First National Bank's checking account or Motorola's cellular phone). The vertical axis represents the dollar value of sales and profits, and the horizontal axis represents time. A product typically passes through four stages: *introduction, growth, maturity,* and *decline* (a stage which may lead to product abandonment). For reasons that will soon become apparent, the total market sales curve for a product is quite different from its total market profit curve.

Introduction

The first phase in the life cycle of a product is characterized by slow growth in sales as the product is introduced and the market gradually becomes aware of it. The profit curve shows a loss during this phase because of the heavy expenses incurred in introducing the product. In addition to the research and development costs, there is the cost of putting in place the distribution system to deliver the new product to the market and the substantial advertising expense required to make consumers aware of the new product. In banking, significant costs are involved in developing the computer systems required to deliver a truly new product (that is, one that is not simply a modification of an existing product). These up-front expenses make it impractical for banks to test-market products the way consumer goods manufacturers do.

The length of the introductory stage depends on the rate at which consumers accept the product. Home banking by personal computer has been in the introduction stage of its life cycle since the early 1980s. Because it involved changing customer banking and bill-paying behavior, the initial growth in numbers of customers using the service was slow. However, the numbers are now increasing as more customers (from Generation Xers to senior cit-

izens) grow comfortable with technology and seek ways to save time. Advertising strategy has concentrated on educating the public about the benefits of the service.

The debit card is another banking product that has been in the introduction stage for many years. (See exhibit 9.5.) The marketing challenge for this product is not only to overcome consumers' resistance to the loss of float on their funds, but to persuade merchants to install the necessary equipment and to agree to accept and promote debit cards. With a credit card, consumers retain the use of their funds until the monthly bill is paid. With a debit card, however, the funds are taken from the checking account immediately. When the number of debit card transactions per year increases at a faster rate, more banks will offer debit cards and a period of rapid growth can be expected.

Growth

The growth stage in a product's life cycle is characterized by an acceleration in sales as more people become aware of the product and buy it. The increased sales will also attract competing firms to enter the market. However, until they can do so, the firm that introduced the product has the edge in an increasing market—an ideal situation. The combination of limited competition and accelerating sales allows the product to quickly become profitable. The Sony Walkman is an example of an innovative product that became very successful and was soon copied by many electronics manufacturers. Because of the profit potential of marketing products that are in their growth stage, highly competitive firms such as Sony spend heavily on consumer research and on the development and marketing of a steady stream of new products.

One example of a growth product in banking is the home equity line of credit. This product was available in some banks in the early 1980s. When the tax-deductible status of the interest on installment debt was

Exhibit 9.5   The Debit Card—A New Product Experiencing a Lengthy Introductory Stage

Year	Millions of Transactions	Percent of Growth over Previous Year
1987	96	—
1988	130	35
1989	179	38
1990	261	46
1991	355	36
1996	1106.5	311

Note: The annual growth in number of debit card transactions ranged from 35 percent to 46 percent between 1987 and 1991. Between 1991 and 1996, the number of transactions per year more than tripled. Visa now has more than 32 million debit cards in circulation, called CheckCards; MasterCard has 7.6 million debit cards in circulation, called MasterMoney.

Source: *The Nilson Report*, as presented in "After Series of False Starts, Debit Cards Show Promise" by Jeane Iida, *American Banker*, Aug. 19, 1992, p. 1. 1996 Data from *The 1997 Debit Card and POS Market Book* appeared in *Debit Card News*, October 1996.

eliminated, interest on equity-secured debt continued to be deductible and home equity lines of credit became increasingly attractive. During 1986, outstandings more than tripled over the previous year, and the volume grew even more in 1987. Equity credit line outstandings continue to be a growth market, although the rate of growth has been declining since 1988. (See exhibit 9.6.)

Maturity

The profitability of a product in the growth stage attracts intense competition as the maturity stage approaches. Maturity is characterized by a slowed rate of sales growth, as most of the prospective buyers of the product have already purchased it. This stage is also characterized by aggressive advertising (in an attempt to boost demand), which increases the cost and, thus, reduces profit.

Many traditional banking services are in the maturity stage. In this stage, competing firms often cut prices to increase sales. Checking accounts provide an example of this. In the mid-1970s, some banks moved to free checking in an effort to increase their market share for this product. (Before that time, free checking was a rarity.) The strategy backfired when many banks followed suit, thus reducing revenues for all involved and cutting seriously into bank profits. In 1996 and 1997, however, free checking once again gained popularity as banks raced to capture customers left looking for a new bank after a merger, and to increase market share. Some bankers want to establish customer relationships through checking accounts now because they believe paper checks will become obsolete by the turn of the century.[8] Free checking remains a somewhat volatile issue as banks define free checking as free under certain conditions (with direct deposit, with a minimum balance, with certain fees) while the letter of the law defines free checking as a no-cost

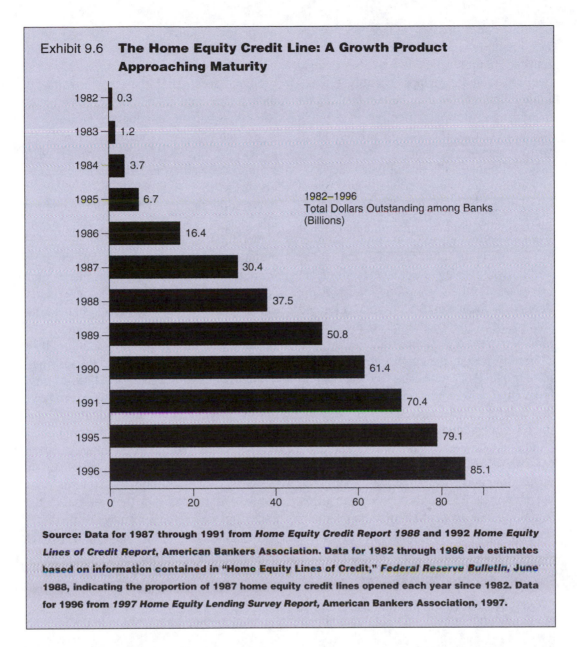

Exhibit 9.6   **The Home Equity Credit Line: A Growth Product Approaching Maturity**

1982–1996
Total Dollars Outstanding among Banks
(Billions)

Year	Value
1982	0.3
1983	1.2
1984	3.7
1985	6.7
1986	16.4
1987	30.4
1988	37.5
1989	50.8
1990	61.4
1991	70.4
1995	79.1
1996	85.1

Source: Data for 1987 through 1991 from *Home Equity Credit Report 1988* and 1992 *Home Equity Lines of Credit Report*, American Bankers Association. Data for 1982 through 1986 are estimates based on information contained in "Home Equity Lines of Credit," *Federal Reserve Bulletin*, June 1988, indicating the proportion of 1987 home equity credit lines opened each year since 1982. Data for 1996 from *1997 Home Equity Lending Survey Report*, American Bankers Association, 1997.

account.[9] However, since the majority of consumers uses some type of checking account, it is a key mature product that needs to be marketed and highlighted to differentiate it from competitors' checking accounts.

Because most consumer products being marketed are mature products, marketers must be creative in extending the life of their products through product modification and improvement. These strategies may be aimed at encouraging existing users to increase their use of the product or to use the product in new ways, or enticing new users to try the product.

Another strategy used when products are in the mature stage is "systems selling." However, before discussing that, let's look at the last stage in the product life cycle—the period of decline.

Decline

When total sales of a product take a marked downturn, the final stage in the product life cycle—decline—has been reached. In the banking industry, regular savings accounts are in this stage of their life cycle.

The decline in sales may be caused by any number of forces, including new products that come along to replace the product. For example, the introduction of money market mutual funds led to the gradual decline of regular savings accounts. Technological innovation may be responsible for triggering a dramatic decline in product sales. For example, the development of word processing software for computers has nearly eliminated the sale of typewriters.

Federal laws and actions of the federal regulatory agencies may also be responsible for pushing a product into decline or even abandonment. For example, tougher environmental standards have led to the withdrawal of many garden pesticides from the market. In the banking industry, the decline of the savings account accelerated as a result of the regulatory creation of the money market deposit account.

Finally, social change may be responsible for a product's decline. The fact that men no longer wear dress hats or that fewer people drive large, fuel-inefficient cars can be traced to social and environmental factors.

The decline phase is characterized by fewer firms offering the product, reduced promotion, and a restricted variety of product offerings. Although one or more firms may continue to profit from the product, total profit drops substantially during the decline stage of a product's life cycle.

Product Adopter Categories

Closely related to the product life cycle is the pattern by which consumers accept and adopt new products. Consumers vary greatly in the rate of their response to a new product offering. Very few people try new products soon after they are introduced; most people wait a while before buying; and still others may never adopt the product.

Researchers have identified five categories of product adopters: *innovators, early adopters,* the *early* and *late majorities,* and *laggards.* (See exhibit 9.7.) People who never adopt the product are not included in this analysis. The category into which a consumer falls is generally related to demographics, social status, and information sources. Innovators are risk-takers and, along with the early adopters and early majority, tend to be younger and better educated and to have higher incomes and social standing than late adopters. In addition, their sources of information tend to be multimedia-based and, thus, more varied. In contrast, the late majority and laggards tend to have limited information sources and often rely on their reference groups to form their opinions.

The amount of elapsed time between adoption of a product by innovators and by the early and late majority depends on a number of factors. On the one hand, the greater the perceived advantage of the innovation, the shorter the time lapse. On the other hand, the more complex the innovation, the longer it will be. Bill-payment by telephone is a service that has been available for a number of years in some markets, but consumer adoption has been slow. Only the

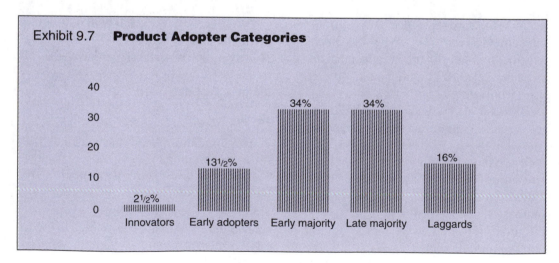

Exhibit 9.7 **Product Adopter Categories**

40

30

20

10

0

2½% Innovators
13½% Early adopters
34% Early majority
34% Late majority
16% Laggards

innovators and very early adopters use this service, probably due to the complexity of the product and the inability of consumers to sample or try out the service.

Systems Selling

The point has been made that many bank products have reached maturity, and that one strategy for marketing products in this phase of their life cycle is systems selling. Systems selling involves the marketing of coordinated solutions to the totality of the customer's problem. This strategy is based on the recognition by marketing-oriented executives that customers do not buy products—they buy solutions to problems or needs.

The careful observer will find systems selling in many industries today. IBM is a good example, with its full range of hardware, software, servicing, and computer-related equipment and supplies. Other examples of systems selling include companies that market total home-protection systems (not just locks) and companies that market total interiors (not just furniture or floor coverings).

In the banking industry, systems selling takes the form of service packaging. Wells Fargo Bank pioneered package accounts with its introduction of the "Wells Fargo Gold Account" in the early 1970s. The forerunner of a number of similar programs across the country, this program in its introductory stage attracted 7,000 new accounts during one month—three times the normal new-account rate at that bank.

Package accounts work this way. For a fixed monthly fee or a specified combined deposit balance, the customer receives a total banking relationship, including unlimited check writing, a money market deposit account, overdraft protection, special rates on installment loans and certificates of deposit, and a combined monthly statement. The package might also include a special rate on a credit card, free safe deposit box, or free traveler's checks and official checks.

Such packages of financial services make sense for customers because they conveniently provide a total solution to the financial problems facing them. They make sense for the bank, because the package concept provides an automatic vehicle for increasing the number of bank services used per bank customer. This is highly desirable because statistics show that the more relationships customers have with a bank, the less likely they are to switch banks.

New Product Development

The realities of the product life cycle underscore the importance of new products to a firm. Since products tend to be most profitable in the growth stage, a firm should ideally have a solid proportion of its product mix in this stage at all times. Conversely, a firm that does not develop new products can expect that eventually it will become totally dependent on the later (and theoretically less profitable) stages of its various products' life cycles.

While a typical bank develops products that are new to it, some banks develop banking products or service delivery systems that are new to the market. These innovators tend to be very large banks with substantial research and development budgets.

Types of New Products

Before discussing the development of new products, let's look first at what is meant by this term. A product may be new to the firm or new to the market. Most new products developed by banks are new to the bank but not to the banking market. This type of "new" product development falls into one of four categories:

1. *Modification of existing products.* The introduction of a "new" certificate of deposit during a period of low interest rates is an example of product modification. For example, a bank might offer a three-year "rising rate" certificate that gives the customer the option of switching to a higher rate if rates increase or of maintaining the original rate if rates fall. (See exhibit 9.8.) This new product

Exhibit 9.8

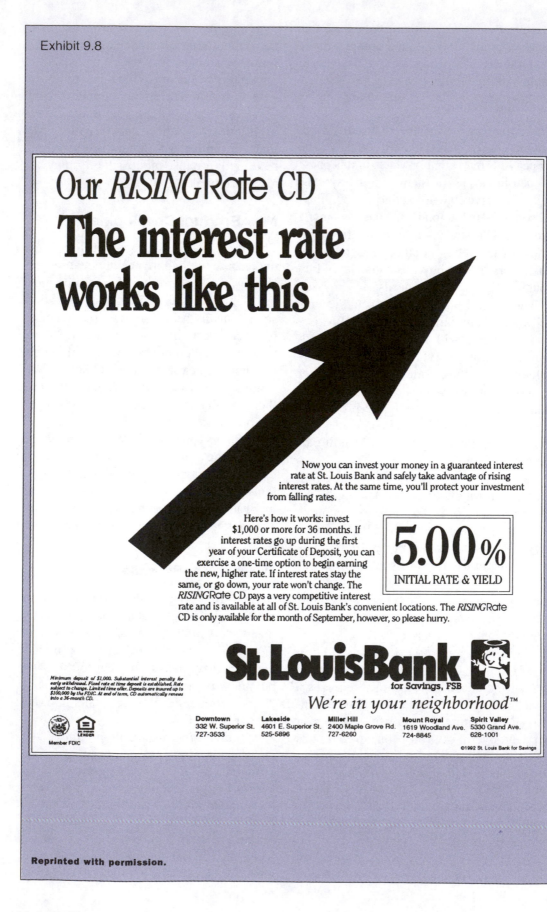

is simply a three-year CD enhanced with a rate- change option to meet a current customer need.

2. *Extension of a product line.* The development of a basic or "lifeline" checking account for low-income customers is an example of a new product being added to a bank's checking product line.

3. *Development of a banking-related product.* Banks that have introduced the sale of annuities or mutual funds have added a new, banking-related product line to their product mix. Such products are clearly new to banks, but not to the financial services market.

4. *Diversification into new product categories.* Some bank holding companies have expanded into nontraditional banking services, such as insurance products. Again, this is a service that is relatively new to the banking industry but not to the market.

How a bank approaches product development generally depends on its size and structure. More than any other area of bank marketing, product development has a considerable operational component. In some banks, the product development department reports to the director of marketing. In others, the responsibility for product development lies within the relevant line function of the bank (retail, commercial, or trust). In still others, a team approach is used with representatives from systems and programming, operations, and the relevant line department coordinated and headed by the product manager or marketing head. Wherever the responsibility lies, the business of developing a product to be marketed involves coordinating the efforts of a number of different departments.

New Product Development Stages

Regardless of whether a product is new to the bank or new to the market, the foremost challenge is to maximize new product

This certificate of deposit was designed to be marketed when interest rates were exceptionally low. It is a five-year CD enhanced to offer a one-time rate increase.

development potential and avoid mistakes. Although there is no magic formula, a firm can go a long way toward generating new ideas and reducing risk by establishing a formal procedure for new product development. The market point of view must be built into such a system from the start. One type of system for developing new products is the eight-stage product development system. (See exhibit 9.9.) A new product idea must survive each phase of development before proceeding.[10]

Exploration and Idea Generation

A company eager for new product ideas can conduct a formal search of the market. In a bank, new product ideas might come from ongoing research to help identify consumer banking needs that are not being met. Or they might come from management or other employees. Some firms offer cash incentives to employees for generating new product ideas. Ideas might also come from customers, banks in other parts of the country, or from competing banks. Also, an idea for a new product occasionally comes from the banking regulators. The money market deposit account arose from this source. The main point of idea generation is to find, in a structured, goal-oriented manner, new ways to serve the bank's customers in a meaningful way.

Product Screening

Ideas for new products must be screened against product objectives, product policy, and company resources. Not every new product idea can or should be pursued. A preliminary judgment must be made as to whether an idea deserves further study. In an aggressive and imaginative bank, an unusual idea that at first appears to be unworkable and not within present regulatory constraints will not be screened out until it has been evaluated in more detail. Each idea for a new product must also be evaluated to ensure that it does not take business away from existing products. The development of the NOW account, the predecessor to interest-bearing personal check-

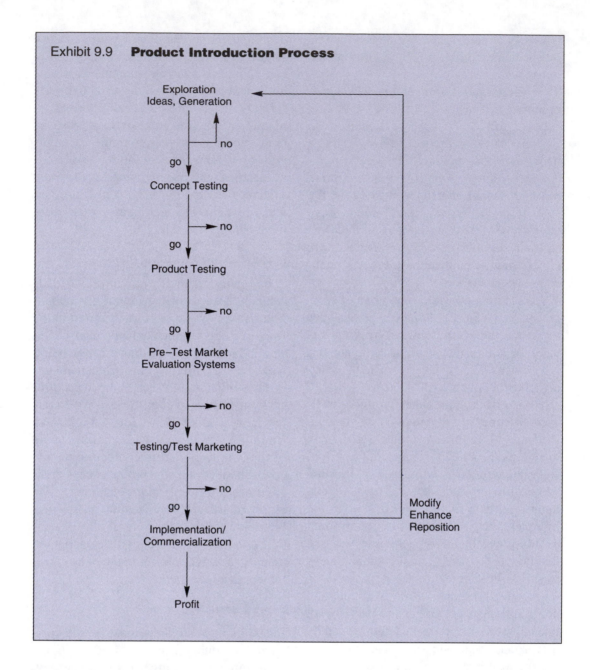

Exhibit 9.9   **Product Introduction Process**

Exploration
Ideas, Generation

no

go

Concept Testing

no

go

Product Testing

no

go

Pre–Test Market
Evaluation Systems

no

go

Testing/Test Marketing

no

go

Modify
Enhance
Reposition

Implementation/
Commercialization

Profit

ing accounts, was spearheaded by a small, persistent bank in Maine. It found an ingenious way to evade a regulation banning the payment of interest on demand deposits by offering negotiable orders of withdrawal (which work like checks) on savings accounts.

Concept Testing

This is a crucial phase in new product development. Concept testing is a function of consumer marketing research, but it does not simply entail asking a large number of consumers what they think of a new product idea. This type of questioning neither elicits the underlying attitudes, beliefs, and concerns that consumers might have about a new product, nor gains insight into how they would actually behave if the product were available. There would be no frozen foods in our grocery stores today if the industry had been guided by preliminary consumer reaction to the concept.

It is best to first assemble small focus groups to explore reaction to a new product concept. This type of research, as noted in chapter 7, is called qualitative research and is more effective at drawing out feelings and motivations that may affect the acceptance of the new product. It can also provide insight into how the product might be positioned or promoted.

On the basis of insight gained through such qualitative research, it is possible to design a meaningful questionnaire for quantitative research among members of the market. This will generate data that are scientifically sound with respect to the probable market response to the product. This type of survey research can also help identify particular market segments to whom the product is most attractive.

Business Analysis

This stage in the development of a new product involves developing a written business case and recommendation based on the results of market analysis, production feasibility analysis, marketing strategy development, and cost and revenue projections. The business analysis includes supporting materials that indicate there is sufficient demand for the product and show that the product fits in with the bank's overall goals and objectives. In short, a situation analysis must be developed for the new product, including preliminary objectives, selection of the target market, and a marketing strategy. If the recommendation is approved by management, the product development coordinator will pull together the group necessary for developing the product. Case B presents just such a business plan for a new home equity credit line.

Product Development

During this stage, the bank determines whether it is feasible to produce or provide the product or service at a cost and quantity that will make the product's retail price attractive to customers. The elements of the product that will be particularly important to consumers must be identified at this point and clearly highlighted as the product is designed. This is also the stage at which

the promotion, distribution, and pricing strategies are developed. The development stage involves production of prototypes or samples of the new product. In banking, the development phase for a new savings product would require modification of the savings computer system by the programming staff, the design of forms and documents to be used in setting up the accounts, and the writing of procedures for the branch staff to follow in completing the forms and processing them.

Test Marketing

Consumer goods manufacturers usually test-market new products. It is not unusual for a company to try out a new product in one or two geographic markets, perhaps using a different promotional approach in each market to test their relative effectiveness. It is said that in the packaged goods business, only about half of the products rolled out for test marketing ever make it to the commercial distribution stage.

Test marketing is increasing in banking, too. For example, Deposit Guaranty National Bank has piloted five automated loan machines (ALMs)—two in malls, one in a large grocery store, one in a large appliance store, and the last in a large furniture showroom.[11] The benefits of test marketing are that the bank can assess customer response as well as familiarize employees with the planned new products.

Test marketing can be expensive and time-consuming, however, and can offer competitors an opportunity to quickly copy the bank's new product or service. Therefore, it is beneficial to move quickly from the test marketing stage to a full-scale implementation or roll-out of the product.

Implementation, or Commercialization

This is the stage at which a company commits its resources to a full-scale introduction of the product to the market. Introducing a new banking product requires heavy involvement by the marketing department. A great deal of money is invested in advertising and sales promotions. Ideally, the training director has undertaken programs to ensure that each customer-contact employee thoroughly understands the service and how to sell it (that is, knows its benefits as well as its features). It is also critical to inform all staff members of the advertising campaign that has been launched so they can be fully prepared for customer inquiries. The launching of a new product is often tied to an employee incentive campaign to boost initial sales. At the same time the bank might offer a premium to the customer for purchasing the new product.

One of the problems that banks face when introducing new deposit services is the resulting drain on deposits in existing products—an effect called *cannibalization.* For example, when the money market deposit account was introduced, dollars were drained out of lower-cost regular savings and checking accounts, increasing the cost of these already deposited funds to the bank. Because of this effect, banks must attempt to enter the market early with product innovations that are likely to be offered by many competitors. This lead in entering the market serves to offset the cannibalizing of their existing deposits by attracting new customers and deposits from outside the bank. Naturally, the first banks into the market with a good new product stand to gain. But it does not usually take long for the market followers to offer the same product, thus diluting the competitive advantage and moving the product along to that part of the life cycle where profits start to flatten out.

Evaluation

The final stage in developing a new product involves the use of primary and secondary research to monitor the progress of the new product in relation to the company's goals. No product development plan is complete if it fails to include a system for monitoring the results of the plan. Effective monitoring enables the bank to take corrective action where needed, as well as to gain additional knowledge that will facilitate the introduction of the next new product. In other words, the purpose of the evaluation stage is to learn from experience.

Product Management

Once a product has been launched and is part of the bank's overall service offering, who is responsible for what happens to it? Some banks have adopted the product management concept, in which one person is assigned overall responsibility for a specific product or group of products.

Procter & Gamble "invented" the product management concept in 1927. When the firm's newly introduced Camay soap failed to sell well, one person was assigned the task of developing and promoting the product. This proved such a successful strategy that this concept has since been adopted by many other firms, including banks.

The amount of responsibility and authority held by product managers varies greatly from bank to bank, depending on the size and organizational structure of the bank. Generally the product manager is responsible for developing annual marketing plans and strategies, seeing that they are carried out, tracking the product's performance, and taking corrective action as needed.[12] In many cases, the product manager is a staff person in the marketing department with no responsibility for the profitability of the product. This puts him or her in a position of having to manage by persuasion and of having to negotiate the cooperation of individuals who have the ability to make or break the product— namely the sales, service, and operations staffs.

In other situations, however, product management is a line function, with the manager assuming profit and loss responsibility for the product. For example, managers from the retail banking department might manage consumer deposit products, while the head of the consumer credit department might assign managers to oversee installment loans, revolving credit lines, and credit cards. In this type of organization, the product manager not only has responsibility for creating a marketing plan, but is accountable for the plan's success and has the authority to get the plan executed.

As profit margins continue to be squeezed by the increasing cost of funds and the rising cost of doing business, the product management concept is becoming more popular in banking circles as a way of maximizing the performance of every item in the product line.

Product Failures

Many statistics are cited about the high failure rate for all types of new products. The statistics vary widely, but the underlying truth is that many new products never make it beyond the introduction phase. New product failure is a common occurrence in industry, and banking products are no exception. Some product failures reflect a weakness in one or more of the elements of the marketing mix—such as pricing, promotion, or sales strategy. In addition, there are four underlying reasons for product failure that are directly related to the product itself.

1. *Failure to look at the new product from the market point of view.* One common error that contributes to new product failure, especially in smaller institutions, is the temptation for bankers to depend on their intuition as a basis for new product development. The problem is that the intuitive process tends to be disproportionately biased in favor of one's own experiences, values, and needs. As a result, benefits that the banker sees as real and important may seem unimportant or nonexistent to prospective customers. To avoid this, a marketer must do everything possible to view the new product idea from the buyer's viewpoint. This means conducting valid research.

2. *Failure to research the needs of the market segments creatively.* Conducting extensive interviews in which respondents are asked to indicate what new products they want from a bank is a useless exercise. Not only do consumers not know what services are feasible (they lack knowledge), in many cases they are not truly in touch with their unmet needs (they lack conscious awareness). A better research strategy is to hold periodic, informal dialogue sessions with small groups of respondents who can be asked to discuss issues such as what they like and dislike about dealing with a bank; what they would do if they were running the bank; and how, when, and why they use certain banking products. The purpose of such focus group sessions is not to ask the participants to design a new bank product, but rather to get them to focus on their own financial management weaknesses so that their unfulfilled needs might surface. Although consumers of banking services may not be able to articulate precisely what they need from a bank, their comments may enable the creative and innovative banker to see new product opportunities for the bank.

3. *Failure to consider the degree of behavioral change required of the prospective customer.* If a new product requires a change in the banking behavior of the customer, the marketing effort must recognize this and must aim at minimizing the customer's psychological discomfort. An example of a service that has required a leap of faith on the part of the customer is the direct deposit of Social Security checks. This service was first offered in 1975, but initially most senior citizens chose not to take advantage of it. Despite the safety and convenience of direct deposit, most users did not wish to alter established patterns of banking and rely on automation. For a generation that matured before the proliferation of computers, entrusting one's income to the workings of an automated system is threatening. However, by 1995, 58 percent of Social Security checks were direct deposited, and the Social Security Administration reports that it receives eight times as many calls concerning checks that were mailed than checks that were direct deposited. Ironically,

by 1995, only 42 percent of the general population was taking advantage of direct deposit of paychecks.[13]

4. *Failure to communicate a new product's benefits clearly.* Another factor that sometimes contributes to a new product's demise is a failure to make clear its benefit to the customer. Ultimately, the customer wants to know, "What's in it for me?" An underlying reason for this problem is that bankers tend to talk like bankers instead of using language with which customers are familiar. Consider the difference between "overdraft checking" and "no-bounce checking," or "Super NOW account" and "interest checking." A communication problem may also result when a bank tries to find too clever a name for a promotion.

Product Elimination

What happens when a product dies? What happens to products when banks merge? What does one do with a product when its profitability declines steadily and cannot be revived? Obviously, the product should be eliminated. Yet most companies, including banks, do not have a well-planned procedure for handling products that are in decline. American industry has traditionally paid less attention to establishing formal procedures for eliminating products than to establishing procedures for developing new products.

Benefits of Product Elimination

Perhaps the most obvious benefit to be derived from a formalized product elimination plan is the potential effect on profitability. This is perhaps most often true during a merger or acquisition when there is generally a great deal of product redundancy. Reducing the number of products offered streamlines the new bank's product line and can improve efficiency as well as profitability.

Often a large percentage of a firm's product mix accounts for a small percentage of its total sales and profits. This suggests that at least some of these products are unprofitable or have an unacceptably low return on investment. For example, one firm with annual sales of $40 million eliminated 16 products that accounted for only 8 percent of its sales volume. Within three years, the firm's profits increased 20-fold: aggressive product abandonment was cited by management as the prime reason.[14]

Since weak products can consume important company resources, eliminating them can spur overall sales by freeing up resources for more promising uses. Also, marginal products tie up sales personnel, warehouse space, advertising budgets, equipment, raw materials, and other resources to the same extent as strong products. Weak products also tend to require a disproportionate amount of management time.[15] Finally, failure to dump weak products may delay an aggressive search for more profitable products.

Establishing procedures for determining under what circumstances a product should be eliminated offers other benefits as well. It may cause a firm to analyze for the first time why certain products need to be dropped. As a result, past mistakes are more likely to be identified and practices instituted to prevent a recurrence of the same problems.

Coupon-book holiday clubs are an example of a deposit product that many banks have eliminated because the cost of administering them was too great in relation to the relatively small average deposits they generated. Some banks have replaced them with totally automated "clubs," debiting the customer's checking account for each monthly payment and then crediting the account with the payout at the end of the term. Other banks have reduced the cost of the service by eliminating the payment of interest.

Regulatory changes in recent years are another factor that have led banks to eliminate some products. Not so long ago, most banks offered two types of consumer checking accounts: one for persons who wrote few checks (with a low monthly maintenance charge and an item charge) and one for heavier-volume check writers (generally with no charge provided a certain balance was maintained). Then, interest-bearing NOW accounts were allowed, and several years later, money market–rate Super NOW accounts were allowed. Banks found themselves with four or more types of interest- and noninterest-bearing retail demand accounts. With the elimination of all rate ceilings in 1986, many banks restructured their product line by reducing the number of transaction accounts to only two, one with and one without interest. A similar pattern developed in the certificate of deposit product line as the number of allowable maturities increased over the years.

Having too many product offerings is difficult and time-consuming for the staff that helps customers open accounts, as well as being confusing to the customer. The elimination of rate ceilings spurred a much-needed exercise of product elimination and refinement of the retail deposit product lines for banks.

Industry Resistance to Product Elimination

Firms tend to resist product abandonment for a variety of reasons:

- Dropping a product may be disruptive because employees may have to be shifted or laid off.
- Dropping a product might alienate certain key customers who depend on the product, thereby adversely affecting other business with them.
- To "save face," there is a tendency to take less drastic action (such as changing the advertising or modifying the pricing), even when eliminating the product is clearly warranted.

Banks are probably no more or no less adroit at eliminating products than other industries are. But certainly with the increasing competition and pressure on their profit margins, banks should see the importance of periodic and rigorous review of their product mix. Banks might do well to look anew at that proud list of "over 100 services" they offer and determine which ones they might do just as well, or better, without.

Summary

This chapter began a detailed study of marketing strategy. It started with product strategy because the product is the organization's reason for being, and as such is the pivotal element in the marketing mix. *Product* was defined in such a way as to make it clear that the term, in marketers' parlance, means much more than the tangible or intangible thing being sold. Inherent in the product is the core benefit being sold; the basic, generic product; the expected product; the augmented product, which is the sum total of all the related features that go along with it; and the potential product, which includes all the modifications the product might undergo over time.

Services represent a special class of products having the following characteristics: intangibility, inseparability, variability, and perishability. Each of these poses specific marketing challenges that are not faced by marketers of tangible goods.

Various strategies relate to the product mix and to the product life cycle. Product mix strategies include product expansion and contraction, product modification, repositioning, and trading up or trading down. Other product strategies relate to where the product is in its life cycle: introduction, growth, maturity, or decline. For example, one strategy for a mature product is systems selling, which entails marketing coordinated solutions to the totality of the customer's need. Packaging of multiple bank services provides a good example of this concept.

The development of new products is important if a bank is to stay profitable. This means every bank should have a system for introducing new products while minimizing the chance of product failure.

Product management is a concept that originated in consumer goods firms but is now widely used by banks as well. It entails giving individuals within the bank varying degrees of responsibility and authority over specific products or product lines.

There are four major reasons why some bank products fail—all relating to a lack of understanding of customers and their needs. When products have served their purpose and constitute a drain on company resources, they should be eliminated. But there is generally great reluctance within a bank or other firm to actually remove a product from the market.

As a product is developed and introduced, and as it progresses through its life cycle, decisions must be made about the pricing of the product. Because of the close link between the product and its price, pricing strategy is the subject of the next chapter.

Points for Review

1. Explain the five aspects of a product from a marketing point of view. Give a bank-related example of each.
2. What is the difference between a product and a service?
3. Define and contrast these terms:
   - product item
   - product line
   - product mix
4. How does the fact that services are intangible, inseparable, and perishable affect the following?
   - the promotion of services
   - the physical distribution of services
   - the personal selling of services
5. Explain each of the five most common product mix strategies.
6. Why is it important for a firm to have a good proportion of its products in the growth stage of the product life cycle?

7. How are consumers categorized with regard to the rate at which they adopt a new product?
8. Describe the eight stages in the new product process.
9. What are the responsibilities of a product manager?
10. What are some reasons that a new banking product might fail?

Notes

1. Kotler, *Marketing Management*, p. 529.
2. *Ibid.*, pp. 429–431.
3. Kotler, *Marketing Management*, p. 455.
4. *Ibid.*, pp. 456–459.
5. *Ibid.*, pp. 220–222.
6. Marketing Intelligence Service Ltd., Naples, New York. (800) 836–5710 or http://ourworld.compuserve.com/home-pages/marktngintelsvc.
7. "Everything Old Can Be New Again," *Advertising Age,* October 5, 1992, p. 12.
8. "Free Checking Saturates Market," *Bank Advertising News,* July 15, 1996, p. 4.
9. "Free Checking a Common Practice, Survey Finds," *Bank Advertising News,* September 9, 1996, p. 4.
10. See William M. Pride and O. C. Ferrell, *Marketing* (Boston: Houghton Mifflin, 1997), chapter 10, for a detailed description of developing and managing products. See also *Effective Bank Product Management: How to Be Profitable in a Competitive Environment* (Rolling Meadows, Ill.: Bank Administration Institute, 1988), chapter 5.
11. D. Blair Bingham, Jr., "Deposit Guaranty Pioneers ALMs," *Journal of Retail Banking Services,* Spring 1996, pp. 36–40.
12. Information from the National Automated Clearinghouse Association home page: www.nacha.com., April 1997.

13. For more information on the product management concept and why it is effective, see *Effective Bank Product Management* (BAI, 1988); William J. Wichman, "Product Management: Lessons from the Package Goods Industry," *Journal of Retail Banking,* Winter 1984, pp. 27–34; and "What Institutions Should Expect from Their Product Managers," *American Banker,* February 7, 1986, pp. 4ff.

14. Charles H. Kline, "The Strategy of Product Policy," *Harvard Business Review,* July-August 1955, p. 100.

15. R. S. Alexander, "The Death and Burial of 'Sick' Products," *Journal of Marketing,* April 1964, pp. 1–2.

10

PRICING STRATEGY

Learning Objectives

After studying this chapter, you should be able to

- define the term *price* and explain how a bank's pricing contributes to its profitability,
- describe how price elasticity of demand affects a firm and a market,
- discuss strategies for pricing a new product and changing the price of an existing product,
- differentiate between incremental cost and fully allocated cost,
- name three audiences whose reactions must be taken into consideration when making bank pricing decisions, and
- discuss regulatory and compliance issues that affect pricing.

Introduction

As discussed previously, the objective of marketing is customer satisfaction at a profit. In chapter 9, the product was pinpointed as the instrument for attaining customer satisfaction. This chapter shows that the way the product is priced is a key factor in attaining a profit.

Making the product conveniently available (through distribution) and communicating its need-satisfying capacities (through promotion) facilitate the product's acceptance. But however good the product, its distribution, and its promotion, an unacceptable price will impede product acceptance. Therefore, pricing strategy is an extremely important element in the marketing mix. When handled unwisely, it can result in product failure.

The Definition and Role of Price

The element in the marketing mix that marketers call *price* has many names: fare, fee, charge, toll, tuition, rent, fine, and assessment, to mention a few. Stated most simply, price is whatever must be exchanged in return for receiving a good or service. In banking, prices include the interest rate charged on loans and paid on deposits, monthly maintenance charges, transaction or item charges, minimum balance requirements, compensating balance requirements, commissions, and service fees. With the exception of interest paid on deposits, which is an expense to the bank, these prices show up on the bank's financial statements as income, specifically interest income and noninterest (or operating) income. While the interest rates that banks pay on deposits are an expense, they are an element of pricing that directly affects demand (that is, the volume of new business)—especially the demand for certificates of deposit.

Pricing is the only element in the marketing mix that generates income. The other elements—producing, selling, delivering, and promoting the product—are costs. *All*

the elements of the marketing mix affect the volume of sales, but *only* price directly contributes to profit.

Price serves at least two purposes.[1] First, it helps buyers decide how to allocate their buying power among various goods and services. They compare products and prices and determine how much they will spend to meet each of their needs. (See exhibit 10.1.) Second, price provides information to consumers. A higher price may suggest higher quality, especially when the brand is unfamiliar or the product is intangible, making it difficult to measure the benefits objectively.

In setting the price of a product, eight objectives should be considered:

1. Survival: adjust price levels so that the firm can increase sales volume to match expenses.
2. Profit: identify price and cost levels that allow the firm to maximize profit.
3. Return on investment (ROI): identify price levels that enable the firm to yield targeted ROI.
4. Market share: adjust price levels so that the firm can maintain or increase sales relative to competitors' sales.
5. Cash flow: set price levels to encourage rapid sales.
6. Status quo: identify price levels that help stabilize demand and sales.
7. Product quality: set prices to recover research and development expenditures and establish high-quality image.
8. Communicate an image.[2]

Generally, the price affects how much of the product will be sold. The mental pictures created by the phrases "rock-bottom prices" and "the most expensive wristwatch in the world" corroborate the assertion that price contributes to the image of a product or service. The person who said "There ain't no brand loyalty that two-cents-off can't overcome" must have been selling products for which sales volume was exceptionally responsive to price. In the pricing of bank services, the relationship between pricing and sales volume is not that simple a matter, as this chapter demonstrates. The income generated by the volume of sales is an element in the calculation of the firm's profit. How this works in banking is the subject of the following section.

Pricing and the Bank's Profitability

The pricing of bank products and services directly affects the bank's profitability because (1) prices paid by customers generate income and (2) price influences the volume of sales. This section discusses how a bank generates a profit—that is, how it earns a net income—and the relationship between the price of a product and the demand for it.

How a Bank Earns a Profit

Reduced to the simplest terms, a bank makes money (earns a profit) by taking in deposits and putting them out as loans or investments (after setting aside a portion of the deposits for reserves). In this process, the bank incurs an expense in the interest it pays on these deposits, and it earns income

from the interest charged or earned on the loans and investments it makes. The difference between *interest income* and *interest expense* is *net interest income,* or *spread,* and the object is for the spread to be a positive number. In other words, interest income should exceed interest expense by some margin.

That is a basic explanation of how a bank makes money, but it is not the only way. Banks are now generating income through fee income from nontraditional products as well. Investment management services and sales of insurance and mutual funds are additional sources of income for a growing number of banks.

In taking in deposits, making loans and investments, and managing such third-party business as selling insurance, a bank incurs many *operating expenses*—including salaries, benefits, rents, taxes, advertising costs, and the cost of deposit insurance. Besides charging interest on loans, a bank creates *operating income* from service charges, maintenance charges, trust department income, fees, and commissions. The bank's objective is to have income from all sources (interest and operating income) exceed expenses from all sources (interest and operating expenses). The difference between these two figures is *net operating income*. When adjusted for income taxes, dividends on preferred stock, and extraordinary items, this amount becomes *net income,* or *profit*. All businesses try to maximize their profit, the so-called bottom line.

The four basic elements in the profit equation provide management with four areas on which to concentrate in order to maximize profit: interest income, interest expense, noninterest income, and noninterest expense.

+ interest income (from the pricing of bank loans)

− interest expense (from the pricing of bank deposits)

= net interest income

+ noninterest income (from fees, service charges, etc.)

− noninterest expense (salaries, rent, taxes, etc.)

= income before taxes, preferred stock dividends, and extraordinary items (also called net operating income). (Income after these items is net income, or profit.)

Since the deregulation of interest rates, the rates that banks pay on deposits is dictated largely by market conditions, making interest expense difficult to control. Operating expenses are more easily controlled. Banks can hold the line on salary increases and watch carefully over such highly controllable expenses as travel, entertainment, and advertising. In other words, expenses can be manipulated to some extent to improve earnings. This was seen in the early 1990s when many large banks, in an effort to improve their profit margins, restructured and consolidated operations, laying off numerous employees. Although reducing expenses does improve the bottom line, there is a limit to the amount of operating expenses that can be cut.

Finding ways to increase income is even more challenging. The interest a bank can charge on loans is heavily influenced by market conditions and to some extent by

regulation. A bank can concentrate its efforts on generating more of the kind of loan business that provides the greatest potential return (such as variable-rate commercial loans, which are tied to the prime rate). But the greatest opportunity in most banks for increasing income is in the area of other operating income: fees and service charges. However, this can trigger strong reactions from consumers, as the ATM user fee did in the mid-1990s. Changing a bank's fee structure and service charges is a matter that requires careful thought and planning.

Price Elasticity of Demand

Although pricing can immediately improve profit, it does not take place in a vacuum. The major challenge to the marketer trying to determine the pricing strategy for a particular product is the uncertainty about how the market will react in response to the price change. The theory of price elasticity of demand addresses this question.

Generally speaking, as the price of any product increases, the demand for it diminishes. But demand might diminish very quickly or very slowly in response to the increase. When the response is quick, demand is said to be elastic; when the response is slow, demand is said to be *inelastic*. Exhibit 10.2 illustrates this concept.

In theory, a firm can maximize its total revenue by increasing the price of inelastic products (since this would result in more revenue without much loss of business) while reducing the price of elastic products (in order to gain new customers). (See exhibit 10.3.) Of course, this is a gross oversimplification. There is more to consider in making pricing decisions than total revenue.

In the case of a price cut, the cost of providing the extra products sold or servicing the new accounts brought in by the price reduction may more than offset the increase in revenues. For instance, offering free checking may bring in many new

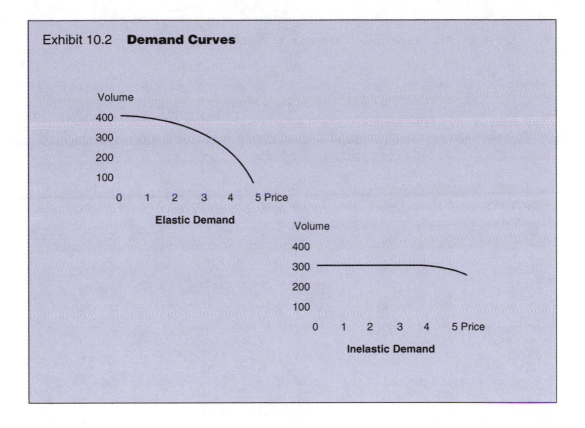

Exhibit 10.2   **Demand Curves**

Elastic Demand

Inelastic Demand

accounts, but they may be low in balances and high in activity—and thus very costly to the bank. In the case of a price increase, the firm might find that its cost of operating does not decline as the number of products made and sold declines, so while total revenue increases, profit may not increase proportionately.

Factors Affecting Elasticity

Why is the demand for some products very sensitive to price and the demand for others relatively insensitive? A number of factors affect *price sensitivity:*

- existence of close substitutes,
- consumer awareness of price differences,
- length of time a price difference persists,
- range of use,
- significance and frequency of purchase, and
- nonprice benefits.[3]

Existence of Close Substitutes

If a less expensive (that is, more favorably priced) alternative of similar quality is available, customers tend to respond quickly to a price change. This underscores the importance of positioning a product or service and finding ways to differentiate it from the competition so that customers do not see competitors' products as close substitutes. The packaging of bank services—tying a group of services together as one offering—is a good way of differentiating a bank's products and reducing price elasticity.

The decline in savings interest rates and the resultant shifting of funds to uninsured stock mutual funds in the early 1990s is an example of elastic market demand. As the pricing of bank certificates of deposit became less favorable to savers (that is, as deposit interest rates fell), many savers began to look at more favorably priced alternatives and were willing to give up the benefit of FDIC insurance on their

Exhibit 10.3 The Economics of Price Elasticity of Demand

Following are two simplified examples to illustrate the effect of price elasticity of demand on sales and profits from two different products. Demand for the first product is *inelastic,* while demand for the second is *elastic.* In each of these hypothetical cases, the unit price of the product is increased from $36 to $41. The manufacturer's cost remains constant at $18 per unit.

Case 1: Inelastic Demand. Sales volume declines 5 percent in response to the 14 percent price increase. Because the drop in sales is smaller than the increase in price, total revenue and net profit increase:

	Before	*After*	
Price	$ 36	$41	(14.0 percent price increase)
Units sold	**1,000**	**950**	**(5.0 percent drop in volume)**
Revenue	$36,000	$38,950	(8.2 percent revenue increase)
Cost	$18,000	$17,100	
Profit	$18,000	$21,850	(21.4 percent profit increase)

Case 2: Elastic Demand. Sales volume declines 22 percent in response to the 14 percent price increase. Because the drop in sales is so large relative to the increase in price, both total revenue and net profit decrease:

	Before	*After*	
Price	$ 36	$41	(14.0 percent price increase)
Units sold	**1,000**	**780**	**(22.0 percent drop in volume)**
Revenue	$36,000	$31,980	(11.2 percent drop in revenue)
Cost	$18,000	$14,040	
Profit	$18,000	$17,940	(0.3 percent profit decrease)

investment in exchange for a significantly higher return.

Awareness of Price Differences

Buyers must be able to perceive meaningful differences in price before they will make the effort to switch brands or switch banks. Banking customers are often unaware of the prices of services at other banks. This is especially true for unadvertised prices such as charges for checks, fees, late charges, returned-item charges, and check-cashing fees. As a result, increases in these fees have little effect on customer behavior.

Duration of Price Difference

The longer a price differential exists between two brands or two banks, the greater the chance that customers will switch. If the customers of a bank that has recently raised its minimum balance requirement and service charges on checking expect that other banks will eventually raise their prices too, the customers may not make the effort to get the lower price in the short run.

Range of Use

Products that have more than one use tend to be more elastic. If something can be used in more than one way, lower prices may encourage heavier use for secondary purposes. For example, totally free checking encourages people to write checks for small items that normally would be paid for in cash.

Significance and Frequency of Purchase

If the cost of a product is relatively small, price responsiveness is not likely to be great. This is especially true if the product is purchased only infrequently. Banking services do not involve repeat purchases. On the contrary, bank customers change banks on the average only once every five years, usually because they move. While they may add an individual service more frequently than this, the decision to buy a banking service is clearly made infrequently. Therefore, price responsiveness is generally less of an issue in banking than in some other industries.

Nonprice Benefits

Banks differ in terms of community standing, convenience, reputation, and quality of service. These side benefits are not measurable, but they do have a value to the customer and can help a bank maintain customer loyalty.

Price Elasticity of Demand at the Market and Firm Levels

The concept of price elasticity of demand may be applied to the whole market for a product, such as the market for personal computers, or to one company's product, such as Macintosh personal computers. If the total market demand for a generic product is elastic, a price reduction will increase the total number of products sold. Again, personal computers provide a good example. When they were first introduced, PCs were very expensive and demand for them was limited to those who had a need for them and could afford them. However, as more manufacturers entered the market and the price dropped, demand for personal computers soared. Customers who had been kept out of the market by the high initial price now raced to purchase them.

If market demand is inelastic, total sales volume will not be affected very much no matter how much the price of a product drops. (See exhibit 10.2.) The reason is that the current supply of the product is adequate to meet the needs of everyone who wants it. Lowering the price will not generate any additional demand because no potential customers are being kept out of the market by price considerations.

In some cases, market demand for a given product, such as personal checking, may be inelastic while the demand for a specific bank's checking product is elastic. Consider a hypothetical market where all banks require customers to maintain minimum balances to avoid service charges. If one bank were to begin offering totally free checking, it would very likely experience an increase in demand as price-sensitive customers changed banks. However, the total number of checking accounts in the market would remain unchanged. In this situation the bank's demand curve is elastic, but the market demand curve is inelastic. This results in a situation that has been seen all too often in banking: one bank lowers its price, the others follow suit, and everyone ends up with the same market share as before the price change, but with reduced income.

Since so many banking services are in the mature stage of their product life cycle, the market demand for them is largely inelastic. If more than 90 percent of the households in the United States already possess a checking account, no amount of price adjustment is going to expand that market. In contrast, the demand for certificates of deposit is responsive to price. Most consumers will not shift funds from one bank to another for a quarter of a percent or less, but a rate differential of one-half percent or more can cause deposit inflows or outflows. Of course, some customers will always take their maturing CDs to whichever bank is paying the highest rate.

While the elasticity theory helps explain the relationship between price and demand for a product, predicting how customers will respond to a price change is not easy. The following section deals with trying to estimate customer response to price changes.

Estimating Customer Response to Price Changes

One of the challenges inherent in formulating a pricing strategy is that marketers generally do not have precise information about the shape of the demand curve for a product, so they cannot precisely predict the outcome of a proposed price change. This absence of information can be overcome to some degree through the acquisition of primary and secondary data—that is, through marketing research.

Primary Data and Pricing

Using primary research as a basis for making pricing decisions must be done very carefully and professionally. Asking people outright how they will react to a price change, or what price they would be willing to pay, is practically useless. On the one hand, consumers are unwilling to reveal their sensitivity to price because they do not want to appear to be "cheap." On the other hand, they cannot be expected to identify and isolate the influence that pricing has on their decision to make a purchase or obtain a service. Remembering the concept of the augmented product (chapter 9), one can understand that many features and characteristics contribute to a customer's value judgment concerning a particular product or service.

Furthermore, research on banking services has repeatedly shown that "free" (in terms of price or service charge) and "more" (in terms of interest received) are always better in the mind of the customer. Respondents will almost always respond negatively to questions about price increases, although in practice their response to price increases is not always negative.

Quantitative primary research (surveys) can be useful in measuring the relative appeal of alternative pricing schemes to various market segments. An example of this is in Case A, in which several methods of pricing a basic checking account are evaluated. Respondents were asked to indicate a preference among five pairs of pricing schemes that included a flat monthly fee, an item charge, a combination of fee and item charge, and an item charge alone. Exhibit A.6 shows the results of this trade-off analysis broken down by various demographics.

Qualitative research in the form of focus groups can be very useful in identifying the value that customers attach to banking services, their willingness to pay, their willingness to shift to a competing bank, and their preferences for different types of fee structures.[4]

Because of the limitations of primary research in providing pricing information, banks need to get as much information as possible from secondary data sources regarding price elasticity of demand for banking services.

Secondary Data and Pricing

In setting prices for banking services, banks should tap three sources of secondary data regarding customer reaction to price changes: (1) the bank's own records, (2) the experience of other banks and other markets, and (3) the pricing of the competition.

Records of how customers have reacted to price changes in the past can help a bank estimate the response to a proposed price change. The more banks review and revise their pricing, the more information they will have for each subsequent decision.

Frequently, one region of the country will adopt a new pricing policy ahead of the rest of the nation. This may give banks in other regions an opportunity to get information about the reaction to the new pricing in the lead market. Although one cannot assume that the reaction to a price increase in one region will be precisely the same as in another region, such information can be useful in evaluating alternative pricing strategies or in comparing the results of primary research with actual experience. For instance, if 20 percent of the customers interviewed in the Rocky Mountain region indicated that they would switch banks in response to a price increase, but only 5 percent actually did so, the 4:1 ratio of proposed to actual switchers might hold true in the Northeast as well.

Finally, before making any pricing decisions, the bank should chart the prices of all its major competitors. This information should not, however, be used as an indicator of what the prices should be. Relatively few banks have done a thorough job of evaluating their costs and pricing, and many prefer to be price followers—changing only after a price leader does so.

Pricing Decisions

Pricing decisions may relate to pricing new products or changing prices of existing products. A bank should consider changing the price of an established product when (1) there is a sudden change in the bank's costs; (2) the competition initiates a price change; and (3) the establishment of a new price becomes permissible as a result of a change in regulation. While all of these situations demand that the bank take a fresh look at its pricing, it does not mean that a price change should necessarily result.

Pricing Strategies for New Products

When pricing a new product (whether it is new to the firm, new to the market, or both), bank management will have at least three general objectives in mind: (1) getting the product accepted, (2) maintaining strength in the market in the face of competition, and (3) creating profits.[5] Two of the most important strategies for pricing new products are skimming pricing and penetration pricing.

Skimming Pricing

Skimming pricing is a strategy that involves setting a high initial price for the product so as to "skim the cream" of demand for the product. This strategy is especially suitable for products that are new to the market for the following reasons:

- The amount of the product that can be sold is less likely to be affected by price when the product is new than it will be later, when competition has more of an influence.
- A skimming price strategy allows the marketer to attract customers who are less price-sensitive before lowering prices to attract those who are more price-sensitive.
- A high initial price may help the new product achieve an image of quality and prestige.
- A skimming price can be used to test the demand for a product. It is preferable to begin with a high price and then reduce it, rather than to begin with a low price and then have to raise it to cover unforeseen costs or to capitalize fully on the popularity of the product.

When cellular telephone service was first introduced, monthly charges were so high that the market was limited to business users and the wealthy. Although the cost per minute of use remains high, now that cellular telephone service costs about the same as home telephone service, use of this service has skyrocketed. Similarly, when PC banking was introduced, the cost was very high—consumers had to own a PC, and the monthly cost of the service could easily be $19.95. Now many banks are providing software and PC banking services at no or low cost.

Penetration Pricing

Penetration pricing is the opposite of skimming. It uses a low initial price as a means of capturing a large share of the market as early as possible. This strategy warrants serious consideration when one or more of the following conditions exist:

- The quantity of product sold is highly sensitive to price, even in the introductory stage of the product life cycle.

• Substantial economies in production or distribution costs can be achieved with a large volume of sales.

• The product will face the threat of strong competition soon after introduction, or at the time of introduction.

• There is not an elite market for the product—that is, no group of potential customers is likely to be willing to pay a premium price to obtain the product early.

Penetration pricing was seen on a large scale when money market deposit accounts were introduced. Because all banks were introducing the new product on the same date, competition was expected to be stiff. Some aggressive banks reasoned that a higher-than-market interest rate would attract a greater share of this new market. They further reasoned that when rates stabilized, customers who had been attracted by the high rate would remain with the bank as long as its rates were competitive with those of other banks. For many banks, this turned out to be a successful strategy.

Other Pricing Strategies

The strategies of skimming and penetration pricing are relevant to the introduction of a new product. Three other pricing strategies may be used either in pricing new products or repricing existing ones: *perceived value pricing, relationship pricing,* and *behavior modification pricing.*

Perceived Value Pricing

This strategy is based not on the question "What does it cost us to deliver this product?" but rather on the question "What is the perceived value of this product to the customer?" The more tangible and intangible features (including such things as excellence of service and the perception of prestige) that are added to a product, the higher the perceived value to the customer and, consequently, the higher the price that can be charged. To use perceived value pricing effectively, a firm must reduce the customer's price sensitivity or the price elasticity of demand by differentiating the product, tying other products to it, or adding nonprice benefits.

For example, Maytag washing machines have a reputation for being reliable, a reputation that is maintained through a consistent advertising message. As a result, Maytag prices its washers above the other leading-brand washers, and many consumers are willing to pay the premium because they believe that, over time, it will save them money and avoid inconvenience.

Consumers pressed for time have been wooed by banks with the enticement that they can do their banking from the comfort of home and at any time. Many ads feature slippers, bathrobes, coffee cups, and dogs to emphasize the relaxing, easy way to bank from home. The perceived value for many busy consumers is that the bank eliminates the hassle of seeking out a branch during the day and reconciling their accounts only when they receive or request a statement. They also receive many benefits, such as being able to transfer funds, pay bills, and reconcile their account all at once. Banks price this service according to their markets—some offer the service for free to establish relationships and open opportunities for cross-sales, others believe the consumer is willing to pay for the convenience the bank offers and charge per transaction or monthly fees for PC banking service.[6]

Consumers' willingness to pay for perceived value helps justify a bank's expenditure to develop an image or position in the market and to make the necessary investment to provide a high level of customer service. The bank with a reputation for quality products and a high level of personalized service, and whose overall image among the target market is highly favorable, will be able to charge slightly higher fees (or pay slightly lower interest rates) than its competitors. Customers who feel that the employees at their bank know them, treat them personably and professionally, and are eager to help them are not likely to shop around to save a few dollars on a checking account or to get a slightly higher interest rate on a certificate of deposit.

Relationship Pricing

Relationship pricing strategies encourage customers to have multiple accounts and services with the bank. This encouragement is provided in the form of lower fees, higher savings interest rates, or lower loan interest rates for customers with multiple accounts. Some examples are

- allowing combined balances in all accounts to offset balance requirements for no-charge checking;
- paying higher rates on deposits and charging lower rates on loans, or reducing loan application fees for customers who have both checking and savings with the bank and maintain a specified combined monthly balance;
- charging a lower rate on personal loans to a customer who agrees to have the monthly payment automatically deducted from his or her checking account;
- charging a lower annual fee, or lower interest rate, to credit card customers who also have a checking or savings account; and
- paying a higher interest rate on larger savings or certificate of deposit balances.

To use relationship pricing effectively, a bank must have either an integrated system that enables the various computer applications for checking, savings, and loans to communicate with one another, or a monthly updated central information file linking all relationships for each account holder.

Three benefits accrue to the bank that uses relationship pricing. The first is economic. Assuming accounts can be consolidated on one statement for customer reporting purposes, it is less labor-intensive and paper-intensive to service one customer with five accounts than five customers with one account each. The second benefit relates to customer retention. As mentioned earlier, the more services a customer uses, the more likely a bank is to retain the customer's business. The third benefit is, or should be, increased profitability. When packaging products, a bank should determine that providing the package of products will be at least as profitable as providing the same products separately.[7]

Colorado Springs Savings & Loan is an example of a firm that used a new pricing strategy to increase customer relationships. The S&L introduced a CD with a preferred interest rate that was only available to customers who already had another relationship with the firm. The CD was available for either 9 months or 18 months—the latter offered a one-time bump up opportunity, which allowed customers to take advantage of a higher interest rate if rates went up during the term of their CD. In six months the new CD brought in $3.5 million.[8]

Behavior Modification Pricing

This strategy uses pricing to get customers to take certain actions that will lower costs for the bank. For example, a bank in an automated teller network must pay an interchange fee when the customer uses another bank's ATM. To discourage its customers from using ATMs of other banks and thus causing it to pay the interchange fee, a bank often charges customers more for using other banks' ATMs than for using its own. This pricing strategy will work only to the extent that demand (in this case, demand for the use of a bank's ATMs) is elastic—that is, that customers will choose the lower-priced alternative rather than pay the higher fee. In addition, the bank's ATMs must be conveniently located. If they are not, customers who use ATMs frequently may decide to move their accounts to a bank with more convenient ATM locations.

In April 1996, Plus and Cirrus, the national ATM networks, permitted member banks to charge their customers fees for using ATMs the customers' bank did not own. Within just six months, 25 percent of all the ATMs in the Plus network charged these fees. At this writing, of the 10 banks that own the most ATMs, only two have refrained from imposing the surcharge. The other eight charge between 50 cents and $2.00 for using another bank's ATM. Clearly, the behavior modification sought by these banks is to have their customers use only proprietary ATMs.[9]

The banks implementing the ATM surcharge exemplify several concepts discussed above. They are attempting to modify behavior by encouraging some customers to avoid using other banks' ATMs, thereby saving themselves the interbank fee for that service. The surcharge also increases fee income and encourages customers to do more of their banking with their own bank.

Changing the Price of Existing Products

Pricing strategy must be considered when repricing existing products as well as when pricing new products. Banks may change the price of existing products either on their own initiative or in response to a competitive or regulated price change.

Initiating Price Changes

Firms initiate price changes for many reasons. Often a price reduction is used to increase the demand for a product, while a price increase is used to pass along increased costs. See exhibit 10.4 for a list of reasons that may cause banks to change the price of an existing product.

Many factors must be considered as part of a bank's pricing strategy. For instance, management must determine the timing of the price change—when it should be announced and when it should take effect. The bank must also decide whether to reprice only one product, an entire product line (such as all checking accounts), or a broad spectrum of products (for example, all miscellaneous fees and charges on consumer deposit accounts). Management must also consider how repricing one product will affect other products. For example, if a bank that offers two or three personal checking services increases the price of only one, many customers may shift to the account with the most favorable pricing. This creates

Exhibit 10.4   **Why Banks Change Prices**

1. The number of accounts or market share has declined.
2. Prices are too high relative to the competition and relative to the benefits of the product.
3. Prices are too low, given cost increases or heavy demand.
4. The bank, or banks in general, are being criticized for not offering pricing that meets the needs of low-income customers.
5. The price differentials among items in a product line are objectionable or unintelligible.
6. The bank is offering its customers too many price choices and is confusing them.
7. The bank's prices seem higher to customers than they really are.
8. The bank's pricing behavior makes customers unduly price sensitive and unappreciative of quality differences.
9. The product has been enhanced, adding cost to the bank or value to the customer.

work for branch staff and eats into income anticipated from the price increase. Therefore, the prices for related bank services must be consistent with one another.

Price changes are often most effective when combined with other marketing actions—such as the repackaging of a product, a new advertising campaign, or an upgrading in product quality. Further, prices might be changed in some markets but not in others. A bank or bank holding company that operates in several different markets should consider local market conditions before implementing company-wide repricing.

Changing the price of a product is a more complex problem than one might imagine. It affects customers, employees, prospective customers, and competitors. The success of the price change depends on the response of each affected group. The difficulty in correctly anticipating these responses adds to the complexity of effective pricing strategy.

Despite the complexity and challenge involved, properly timed, well-conceived price changes can produce results that make the effort and risk worthwhile. For example, consider the case of a bank near a major university. The bank noticed that many students—both customers and non-customers—were cashing checks from home. This was creating considerable work for the branch staff, taking time away from servicing the sizable base of nonstudent customers and increasing bad check loss—without providing any offsetting profit. In response to this situation, the bank im-posed a service charge of $.50 to $2.00 per check for cashing out-of-town checks or checks on other banks for noncustomers. Long-distance calls to confirm the availability of funds were also charged at cost. There were some complaints and a few students closed their accounts as a result of the bank's new pricing policy. However, many more students opened accounts at the bank to have the convenience of check

cashing.[10] All in all, the service charge was projected to result in a $25,000 increase in revenue by year end.

Reacting to Competitive Price Changes

Sometimes firms are forced to reprice goods or services because of price changes by competitors. Where there is little difference among competing products, the pressure to respond to a competitor's price reduction may be acute. Fare wars among airlines are an example of this.

When competing products are *not* essentially alike (for example, different makes of automobiles), a firm has more flexibility in responding to a competitor's price cut because buyers tend to select a product on the basis of multiple considerations, not just price. When there are differences in quality of service or convenience, for example, a competitor's price drop may cause only a slight shift in buying patterns. In other words, a firm's reaction to a competitor's price change should depend on the expected price elasticity of demand for the product in question.

Whether and to what extent a firm chooses to meet a competitor's price cut (or counter it by modifying other elements of its marketing mix) should depend on considerations such as the following:[11]

• *Why did the competitor change its price?* Is it trying to increase its market share, respond to an improvement in productivity that lowered costs, or lead a market-wide price change? In the early 1990s, many ailing thrift institutions raised interest rates on certificates of deposit above market levels in desperate attempts to remain liquid. Healthier institutions wisely allowed their especially rate-sensitive customers to move their deposits rather than increase their own costs and imperil their earnings.

• *Will the price change be temporary or permanent?* If a competitor's price cut is merely a promotional offer, the best course of action may be to wait it out and provide customer-contact staff with techniques for selling against the lower price temporarily available from the competitor.

- *What will happen to the bank's market share and profits if it ignores a competitive price cut?* The answer depends on the price elasticity of the bank's customers. Building added value through high-quality products and service helps reduce such elasticity.

- *How will other banks respond?* Are they likely to "wait and see," as often happens when one large bank drops the prime rate? If the rate reduction does not appear to be called for by market conditions, other banks may not follow suit and the price leader will ultimately have to get back in line with the rest of the industry.

- *As other banks react to the price leader's price change, what is likely to happen next?* The bank that initiated the price change might drop prices again in response to copycat pricing, or it might offer additional product features. In some situations, such as local gasoline markets, price wars break out, hurting everyone except the consumer.

Similar questions should be asked when a competitor raises, rather than lowers, its price.

Responding to Regulations Affecting Pricing

The threat of regulation is another impetus for price changes in the banking industry. In the early 1990s, when interest rates were plummeting to the lowest level in decades, many banks left their credit card interest rates unchanged. Some banks were charging nearly 20 percent on credit card debt while the prime rate was less than 10 percent. As soon as Congress began investigating the matter, banks rushed to reprice their credit cards in order to halt the threat of impending regulation. The result was much more rational pricing. Many banks established different pricing tiers for customers who paid their balance in full each month (so they rarely or never pay interest) and for those who carried low, moderate, and high balances. Other banks offered different cards for these different market segments.

How Pricing Decisions Are Made

Up to this point, the discussion has concentrated on *when* pricing decisions are made. This section explores *how* pricing decisions are made, particularly the fundamental element on which pricing decisions are based: the cost of producing and delivering the product. While large banks go through the process described here when pricing a new product or reviewing prices of existing products, community banks generally do not have the staff and resources to do so. Instead, they are more likely to simply follow the actions of a price leader.

Costs

Unless a firm intentionally decides to sell a product at a loss, the cost of providing the goods or the service serves as the floor under which the price must not go. There are basically two categories of costs to be considered: variable costs and fixed costs.

Variable costs vary with the volume of sales (or accounts). In banking, variable costs include postage, supplies, materials, part-time help, and the like.

Fixed costs are incurred regardless of sales volume. In banking, fixed costs are generally categorized as (1) direct costs and (2) general and administrative (G&A) expenses. Direct costs are the principal resources the bank has in place to provide its services, including its buildings, land, equipment, full-time staff, and data processing equipment. As a rule, these costs do not vary with volume over a short period of time, but they can vary with volume over a longer period of time. For example, the volume of business at a branch may grow to the point that the office requires expansion.

G&A expenses are incurred to support and administer the organization. Examples of these are advertising, interest on the corporate debt, administrative salaries and expenses, and insurance.

Ideally, the price of a product should cover its fair share of fixed costs, its variable cost, and a reasonable margin of profit. However, pricing based on a determination of costs is not a simple matter.[12] To begin with, there is considerable disagreement over which costs should be taken into consideration when pricing bank services. Two alternative approaches hold sway: (1) pricing based on incremental cost only, and (2) pricing based on fully allocated cost.

Incremental versus Fully Allocated Cost

Incremental cost is the amount by which the total cost of producing a good or providing a service (that is, variable costs plus fixed costs) increases when the volume of products sold increases or when a new product is added.[13] For example, if a 10 percent increase in the number of checking accounts requires that additional branch or operations staff be hired, the cost of the new staff plus the additional postage expense (for mailing out the statements) is the incremental cost of those new accounts. *Fully allocated cost,* by contrast, includes not only the incremental costs of each service but also that service's "fair share" of indirect expenses and other fixed costs.

Imagine that a bank is planning to increase its service charges on checking accounts. The fixed cost of servicing the current level of 1,000 checking accounts is $150,000 per year. If the product manager decides to base the new pricing on fully allocated cost, each checking account must cover $150 of fixed cost, plus variable costs (such as postage). Assume that the product manager raises the price of checking accounts to cover this substantial cost, and 250 customers respond by closing their accounts. The bank still has $150,000 of fixed cost, but now it is spread over only 750 accounts ($200 per account). Taken to

its extreme, one can imagine the product manager continually readjusting the price upward in response to these "increased costs" until the bank has no checking accounts at all, but still has $150,000 in fixed costs. This exaggerated scenario illustrates the possible pitfalls of pricing products and services based on fully allocated costs.

Advocates of pricing on the basis of incremental costs argue that they more accurately reflect future, as distinct from present, cost levels.[14] In pricing, the concern is to estimate the changes in total revenue and total cost so that only incremental costs are relevant. This does not mean that the bank should not assign a share of fixed costs to each service. Rather, it means that for pricing purposes, fixed costs for each service must be allocated on a per-unit basis. Incremental costs should include both variable costs and "semivariable" costs that may change due to higher volume levels.

Both fully allocated and incremental costing may be appropriate methods of pricing, but in different situations. Generally speaking, incremental costing is preferable when pricing a new service (that is, a service that will not simply cannibalize or replace an existing service). When setting prices on basic services and on services for which volume is reasonably predictable, a bank is more likely to use fully allocated costing. However, a bank must have up-to-date cost data to use this approach effectively.

Who Makes Pricing Decisions?

Because pricing is critical to the profitability of a bank, executive management should establish the policy that directs the bank's pricing strategies. The pricing policy—which should be in writing (and included in the annual marketing plan)—might state, for example, that

- the bank will be a price leader; or
- the bank's prices will consistently

rank among the upper third of its competitors' prices; or

- the bank's prices will consistently rank in the middle of its competitors' prices.

How a bank establishes its pricing strategies will depend on its size and structure. Many banks rely on a pricing committee or task force approach. For example, one bank reported having two pricing committees, one for pricing retail services and one for pricing business services.[15] The committees meet regularly and, on a quarterly basis, recommend pricing revisions to management. Both committees include representatives from marketing, operations, the branch system, managerial accounting, planning, and data processing. In addition, the retail pricing group includes a representative from installment lending, and the business pricing group includes representatives from national accounts, international accounts, and corporate lending. In a community bank, fewer individuals would be involved in the pricing process, but the planning and decision-making process remain the same.

Reactions to Pricing

A well-thought-out pricing strategy will include plans for dealing with reactions to the new pricing structure from customers, employees, and the competition.

Customers' Reaction

Earlier in this chapter, customer reaction was discussed in terms of demand elasticity. We saw that the demand curve for traditional banking services is somewhat inelastic. This means that customers do not switch banks in large numbers or very quickly in response to moderate price changes. However, switching banks is not the only reaction about which a bank should be concerned. One researcher found that bank customers are more concerned with how they learn about a price increase than with the increase itself.[16]

In most cases, banking regulations set out minimum requirements for how and when retail customers are notified of price changes. These standards may range from simple posting of a notice in a conspicuous place in the bank to a 30-day advance notice mailed to each customer. However, a bank that announces a price change (for example, raising the fee for a returned item) by simply posting notices in the branches is asking for negative customer reaction. In some locations, a majority of the bank's customers never set foot inside the branch and would therefore not be informed of the new pricing policy. Most banks insert a printed fee schedule in all statements the month before a price change goes into effect.

When a bank raises interest rates on revolving credit, increases minimum-balance requirements on checking, or imposes a service charge, this should be communicated to customers in a straight-forward manner. The bank should not make excuses or couch the increase in the guise of a sales pitch. Customers do not want to hear that a price increase is required "in order to help us serve you better."

In addition to considering how best to communicate price changes to customers, a bank must also anticipate the reaction of its employees to a price increase.

Employees' Reaction

The reaction of bank employees to a price increase may be more pronounced than that of most customers. The smaller the bank, the more difficult the problem because employees are likely to feel more closely connected with their customers. For this reason, any price change must be explained fully and clearly to employees in an attempt to gain their support through the transition phase.

Competitors' Reactions

If a bank *reduces* its price on a product for which demand is elastic, the competition will generally follow suit. If both market and bank demand are elastic, the total revenue of all banks will increase. But this is rarely the case in banking. Typically bank demand is elastic while market demand is inelastic, so all competitors suffer reduced profits when they cut prices to hold onto their market share.

If a bank *increases* its price on a product, competing firms will generally follow suit only if they believe that their demand curve is inelastic. If so, there is no point in maintaining a lower price since the price leader's customers are unlikely to switch banks. If, however, the bank's competitors believe that demand is elastic, they might advertise their lower prices. A number of years ago, when bank regulators first permitted banks to impose an annual fee on credit card holders, a few smaller New York banks that were competing with money center banks chose not to impose such a fee—a fact they promoted heavily. One of the banks later reported that it had not only acquired a large volume of new credit card customers, but related deposit business as well. This was a case of taking advantage of elastic demand for bank credit cards.

Regulation and the Pricing of Bank Services

Since the deregulation of interest rates, few federal controls directly affect the pricing of bank services. (States still impose usury ceilings that limit the interest rates banks can charge on consumer loans.) Since deregulation, consumer watchdog groups have taken on a more visible role in monitoring the pricing of bank services. The rush to reprice credit cards in the early 1990s, noted previously, occurred after consumer groups began protesting that credit card interest rates had not responded to greatly decreased market rates. Bank service charges and maintenance fees are also subject to scrutiny, if not to explicit regulation. In the wake of the introduction of the ATM surcharge, legislation was introduced to require financial institutions to disclose that a surcharge would be added and to provide consumers the opportunity to cancel the transaction before incurring the charge. In some cases, class action suits have been filed against banks for their pricing practices. To defend and justify their price changes, banks must know the true costs of providing each service.

Banking is under the same antitrust regulations as other industries with respect to practices that might reduce or eliminate competition between businesses. For example, it is illegal for competing banks to get together to set prices. Such collusion in price setting is considered to be a "conspiracy in restraint of trade." While it is highly unlikely that competing banks would meet to discuss their plans for pricing a new product, it is not unusual for one or two price leaders to announce their proposed pricing well in advance of the date a new bank product is to be introduced. When NOW (interest-paying checking) accounts first became legal in New York, Chemical Bank announced its pricing early. When NOW accounts were about to be introduced nationwide, Bank of America announced its pricing first. These price leaders apparently wanted to communicate to other banks that they were going to price this product high so as to minimize losses. This kind of price signaling is legal because it does not involve any explicit or implicit agreement between competitors regarding price.

Banks still struggle with the burden of regulatory compliance, the cost of which is passed on at least indirectly to customers. Consider the effect of the 1991 Banking Act, known as FDICIA (the Federal Deposit Insurance Corporation Improvement Act). This law essentially provided for recapitalization of the bank insurance fund, a necessary step. However, the Federal Reserve Board has estimated that the paperwork required to comply with all the new rules could add $4 billion to the $11 billion already spent by banks each year on compliance. At that rate, the total amount spent on compliance would have equaled 83 percent of the banking industry's 1991 profits.[17]

FDICIA was followed up in 1993 by Regulation DD, which implements the *Truth-in-Savings Act*. This 267-page regulation includes rules for advertising consumer deposit interest rates and service charges. It specifies the conditions under which an account may be advertised as "free" and requires that, in newspaper advertisements, deposit interest rates be stated in terms of the "annual percentage yield" so that consumers may compare rates. It also spells out guidelines for the disclosures that banks must provide their customers.

Another way that regulation affects bank pricing is through the fee charged to banks by the Federal Deposit Insurance Corporation. FDIC premiums tripled between 1989 and 1992. Banks passed the added costs on to their customers in various ways. Some implemented a flat monthly fee on checking and savings accounts, which shows up as a line item on the monthly statement. Others added the cost of their FDIC premiums into their total cost calculations and revised their deposit prices accordingly. Under the Truth-in-Savings Act and Regulation DD, banks are prohibited from recouping this expense by paying interest only on a customer's investable balance—in other words, the balance after deducting the amount of the deposit that must be set aside in reserve.[18] In recent years, however, FDIC premiums have actually decreased.

Now that the product and its pricing have been discussed, the next two chapters will focus on distribution strategy, the element of the market mix having to do with getting the product to the customer. In chapter 11, we will look at the physical distribution of banking services; then, in chapter 12, we will look at personal sales and service, a critically important element in the distribution of bank services.

Summary

Pricing is the only element of the marketing mix that directly generates income. Price affects the volume of goods and services sold to a greater or lesser degree, depending on the price elasticity of demand for the product. Through intelligent pricing of services, banks can substantially increase their earnings because demand for most traditional bank services is relatively inelastic. Yet while market demand for such services is inelastic, individual bank demand may be elastic. This opens the door to price cutting, which frequently leads to diminished earnings for all competitors.

Banks can use both primary and secondary sources to obtain information on which to base pricing decisions. Qualitative research often proves more useful than quantitative research because most people cannot isolate the potential effect of pricing on their decision to buy or to switch banks.

Pricing decisions are made when a new product is being introduced or when existing products are being repriced. Typically, repricing occurs when costs increase, the competition changes a price, or regulation allows or requires a price change. Two of the most important strategies for pricing new products are skimming and penetration pricing. Other pricing strategies are relationship pricing, perceived value pricing, and behavior modification pricing. Pricing decisions must be based on a number of factors, but the cost of providing a service is the floor below which a price should not be set. Bankers continue to debate whether prices should be based on incremental cost or fully allocated costs, or some combination of the two.

Price changes must be carefully communicated, not only to the bank's customers, but to its employees as well. If a price increase is explained to them, bank employees are more likely to support the bank's objectives and be better prepared to handle customers' objections to price increases.

Finally, in all their pricing decisions, banks must be aware of regulatory restrictions and the possibility of drawing adverse reaction from either consumer groups or regulators.

Points for Review

1. Briefly explain the following key terms or concepts:
    - price
    - price elasticity of demand
    - incremental cost
    - fully allocated cost
2. How does the pricing of a bank's products affect its bottom-line profit?
3. What factors can affect the price elasticity of demand for a product?
4. Why is it necessary to differentiate between price elasticity of demand for a generic product and for a specific firm's product?
5. Compare the strategies of skimming and penetration pricing and give examples of each.
6. Explain perceived value pricing and the rationale behind it.
7. What are some things a bank can do to make its customers less responsive to competitors' price reductions (or to their more favorable interest rates on deposits)?
8. Explain why the reactions of customers, employees, and the competition must be considered when making a pricing decision.
9. What are the principal ways in which banking regulation affects the pricing of bank products?

Notes

1. Gary Erickson and Johny Johansson, "The Role of Price in Multi-Attribute Product Evaluations," *Journal of Consumer Research,* September 1985, pp. 195–199.
2. Pride and Ferrell, *Marketing,* p. 475.
3. Based on Joseph P. Guiltinan, *Pricing Bank Services: A Planning Approach* (Washington, D.C.: American Bankers Association, 1980), p. 12.
4. *Ibid.,* p. 72.
5. This and the discussion of skimming and penetration pricing are based on Joel Dean, "Pricing a New Product," *The Controller,* April 1955, pp. 163–164.
6. Jennifer Kingson Bloom, "Pricing Home Banking Services a Puzzle for Vacillating Bankers," *American Banker,* February 7, 1997, p. 1.
7. G. Michael Moebs and Eva Moebs, *Pricing Financial Services* (Homewood, Ill.: Dow Jones–Irwin, 1986), pp. 179–182.
8. "Relationship-Based CD Grows to $3.5 Million in 6 Months," *Deposit Growth Strategies,* May 1996, p. 4.
9. "New ATM Fees Have Spread Fast," *Money,* December 1996, p. 56.
10. Neil M. Ford, "Pricing Bank Services," a paper presented at the Seventh Annual Marketing Research Conference of the Bank Marketing Association, May 1974. This paper also appears in the conference proceedings titled *Research as a Management Tool,* published by the Bank Marketing Association.
11. Kotler, *Marketing Management,* p. 500.
12. For a thorough treatment of this subject, see Guiltinan, *Pricing Bank Services,* and Moebs and Moebs, *Pricing Financial Services.*
13. Guiltinan, *Pricing Bank Services,* p. 39.
14. *Ibid.,* p. 40.
15. "Pricing Bank Services: Theory and Practice," *ABA Banking Journal,* October 1980, p. 134.
16. Jack W. Whittle, "Fundamental Truths about Pricing Financial Services," *Financial Marketing,* March 1979, p. 32.
17. Robert M. Garsson, "For Bankers, '91 Law Was 'Red Tape Act,'" *American Banker,* November 30, 1992, pp. 1ff.
18. Information derived from *Marketing Update,* a monthly newsletter published by the Bank Marketing Association, March 1992.

11

DISTRIBUTION STRATEGY: PHYSICAL DISTRIBUTION

Learning Objectives

After studying this chapter, you should be able to

- explain the concept of a channel of distribution and how it applies to the banking business,
- explain some ways in which the intangibility, inseparability, variability, and perishability of banking services affect their distribution,
- discuss seven physical channels of distribution for banking services,
- describe the kinds of information that should be obtained in evaluating a prospective site for a new branch, and
- provide examples of intermediaries in the distribution of banking services.

Introduction

The preceding chapters explored the marketing mix decisions involved in offering the right product, at the right price, to the right market. But there is more to marketing than that. The product must be available at the right place and time, and its benefits must be communicated effectively to the target audience. This chapter focuses on distribution strategy—making the product available in the right place at the right time. Then chapter 12 and chapter 13 focus on promotion strategy.

The important differences between the marketing of goods and the marketing of services have already been noted. These differences are perhaps most clearly seen, however, in the area of distribution strategy. The unique characteristics of services (as described in chapter 9) impose severe restrictions on their delivery. Because of the intangibility and inseparability of services, service industries cannot normally use intermediaries in the delivery process the way product manufacturers do. Instead, most services are distributed using direct sales and direct personal contact.

Although banks are beginning to find alternatives for the traditional intermediaries (discussed later in this chapter), most banks continue to rely heavily on personal involvement in the distribution of their services. However, personal selling as the chief method of distributing bank services is the subject of chapter 12; this chapter focuses on the physical channels of distribution: the bank's physical location and the techniques and devices that make the bank's services more convenient and accessible to the user.

Marketing Channels

"A marketing channel (also called a channel of distribution or distribution channel) is a group of individuals and organizations that directs the flow of products from producers to consumers."[1] A channel of distribution for consumer goods is easy to follow: most manufacturers of consumer goods sell their products to wholesalers, which in turn sell the product to retailers, which in turn sell them to consumers. (See exhibit 11.1.) As shown in the exhibit, some manufacturers (but very few) sell directly to the ultimate consumer. W. Atlee Burpee, the mail-order seed company, for example, uses this type of distribution system. More typically, a manufacturer sells to retailers either directly or indirectly through such intermediaries as wholesalers or agents. For example, a cold-remedy manufacturer will sell to drug wholesalers who, in turn, sell a vast array of drug products to various retail outlets. Small manufacturers often use independent sales agents since they may not have sufficient capital to support their own sales force. Whatever the specific distribution channel, most manufacturers depend on intermediaries to get the product to the ultimate user.

Distribution in a Service Industry

The use of intermediaries is not generally possible in a service industry. Banks do sometimes use automobile, mobile home, and boat dealers as intermediaries for the distribution of secured consumer loans, but the use of intermediaries is not typical in a service industry. Therefore, bankers must think of a channel of distribution for services somewhat differently than one for tangible goods. A distribution channel for services can be defined as any means of increasing the availability or accessibility of a service that also increases its use or the revenues from its use. The distribution channel may help to maintain existing users, increase use among existing users, or attract new users.

An Example from the Communications Industry

AT&T has defined itself as being in the business of communications—not just "the telephone business." It is continually seeking ways to increase the availability and convenience of its communications products and services. As early as the 1950s,

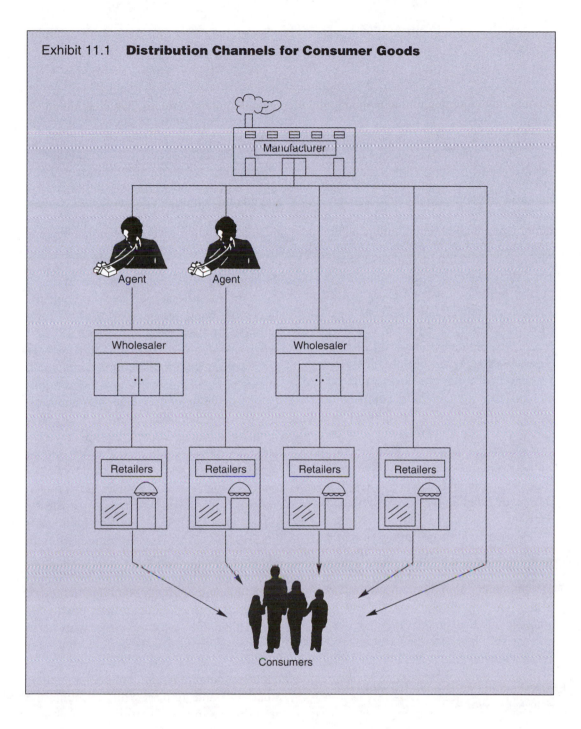

Exhibit 11.1   **Distribution Channels for Consumer Goods**

Manufacturer

Agent   Agent

Wholesaler   Wholesaler

Retailers   Retailers   Retailers   Retailers

Consumers

AT&T found that 85 percent of U.S. households already had a telephone and concluded that there was little possibility of increasing revenues from increased penetration of households. Instead the company decided that it could best expand by increasing the availability, convenience, and attractiveness of the services it had to offer, both within and outside the home. AT&T began this new focus by designing phones for various rooms of the house; it has since enhanced home phones with such added features as message-taking and automatic dialing of stored numbers, mobility (cordless phones), and picture-phones that allow a person to see the person with whom he or she is talking. AT&T also developed the technology that makes phone installations as simple as plugging the phone line into a wall receptacle—so that adding phones and changing phone styles is now a simple matter.

Meanwhile, AT&T was busy expanding its service outside the home by placing public coin-operated telephones at roadsides, making phone service conveniently available to travelers. It then developed a telephone calling card to enable customers to make calls without a pocketful of change and designed public telephones that could read the magnetic stripe on calling cards. AT&T has also unveiled plans to enhance cellular phone technology to enable callers "to make and receive phone calls wherever a radio signal can reach—not just in a car or on the street, . . . but also inside buildings and on mountaintops in remote sections of the country."[2] The company is also developing a new wireless network that, by the end of the century, will enable customers to make and receive phone calls using notebook-sized computers that will also transmit and receive fax messages. These are all examples of distribution innovations.

These distribution strategies are clearly different from charging lower rates for long-distance calls during periods of idle telephone capacity (late nights and weekends). The latter is a pricing strategy to help manage line loads more efficiently, increase the use of otherwise idle capacity, and promote a service that is already available.

Challenges to the Distribution of Bank Services

In making decisions about the distribution of banking services, banks have the same objective as manufacturers of consumer goods and communications firms—that is, to select distribution channels that will maximize the bank's profit over the long run. For a bank, this means providing optimum service and market coverage at a minimum cost. However, unique and complex problems surround the distribution of bank services.

Again, the *intangibility, inseparability,* and *variability* of banking services mean that the traditional channels of distribution for consumer products do not apply. The next section looks at these three characteristics again, this time from the standpoint of how they affect the distribution of bank services. One more characteristic that was not discussed earlier—the *client relationship* aspect of banking—is also discussed.

Intangibility

Most of the problems as well as many of the opportunities encountered in the distribution of bank services are due to their intangibility. Because many bank services (such as deposit accounts) are simply pieces of information stored in a computer, advances in electronics and telecommunications have helped extend their availability. (This is discussed in more detail later in this chapter.) However, the fact that bank services cannot appeal to the senses places a burden on the sales staff. Since the bank is usually selling an idea, not a physical product, the salesperson must tell the buyer what the service will do for him or her because it is usually impossible to demonstrate or display the service in use.

For example, a bank employee cannot show a home equity loan to a prospective customer. Instead, sales efforts must concentrate on telling the customer what he or she can accomplish with the loan—for example, add a room to the house, take a vacation, send a child to college, or consolidate outstanding debt while reducing the monthly payment. In selling this service, its intangibility heightens the need for a direct channel of distribution—namely, personal contact between the buyer and the seller.

Inseparability

In many cases, bank services cannot be separated from the person of the seller or deliverer. For example, a customer cannot get a home equity loan without, at some point, interacting with somebody at the bank. It may be done over the phone or through the mail, but a customer cannot simply pick up a home equity loan without the involvement of bank staff who must take the application, review the credit, arrange the necessary searches, and so on. Thus, inseparability often means that direct sale is the only feasible channel of distribution.

Again, however, because many bank services are computer-based, banks have begun to work around the characteristics of intangibility and inseparability that have traditionally limited the marketing of bank services to personal sales efforts. For example, banks have installed PC banking systems that enable customers to communicate, directly or through a third party, with their accounts on the bank's computer; telephone banking systems that enable customers to transfer funds between accounts; ATMs that enable customers to make deposits and withdrawals without entering a branch; and credit cards that allow approved customers to obtain credit repeatedly without interacting with a bank employee. These are all ways in which banks are using technology to overcome the complications associated with the marketing of services characterized by intangibility and inseparability.

Variability

Most consumer goods are stamped out on a production line, one after the other, all identical. Such products are homogeneous. For example, Dixon Ticonderoga No. 2 pencils are all the same size, shape, color, and composition. In contrast, while all personal checking accounts within a bank may be the same operationally, they are different in terms of the way customers experience them. The ambiance of the particular branch used by the customer, the personality of the teller who takes the deposit, the length of time the customer has to wait in line—all these and more contribute to the variability of bank services and add to the difficulty of standardizing the level and quality of service delivered in a bank.

Again, such variability is inherent in the personal distribution of bank services. An advantage of electronic channels of distribution, such as automated tellers, is that the distribution of the service is homogeneous and standardized. The machine may occasionally be "down," but when it is working, it provides the same service in the same way to each customer.

Perishability

Because bank services are not tangible and therefore cannot be inventoried, they are considered to be perishable. Unlike manufacturers of goods, bankers need not be concerned with storage, transportation, and inventory control. Moreover, since bank services cannot be inventoried, they cannot be distributed through traditional intermediaries.

This inability to inventory means that banks are limited in the amount of business they can handle, which can cause difficulties in times of unusually high demand. For example, a lockbox operation can process only a limited number of items in a day. During a very busy day in a peak period, some of the work may not get processed within the usual time frame. Banks have responded by turning to electronic means of handling excess capacity. For example, most banks now provide a telephone customer-service center to answer many of the questions that tie up branch staff and keep them from performing other duties, such as selling.

Client Relationship

In many bank transactions, a client rather than a customer relationship exists between the buyer and seller. This is especially true in the case of many corporate, private banking, and trust accounts. In client transactions, buyers place themselves in the hands of sellers and rely on their suggestions or advice. Obviously, a client relationship requires close personal contact between the service provider and the client.

Physical Channels of Distribution for Bank Services

As stated previously, a channel of distribution for a service is any means used to increase the availability or convenience of the service that also helps maintain existing users or increases use by existing or new users. In banking, both physical channels of distribution and personal channels of distribution come into play.

Seven physical channels exist for distributing bank services. The first and most obvious one is the banking office. The others are the array of techniques and systems that extend the delivery of banking services beyond the "brick and mortar" locations of the bank: the automated teller machine, the automated loan machine, the telephone, the personal computer, the plastic card, and the virtual bank.

The Branch Network

Because most bank services are delivered to the customer through personal selling by a bank employee, the location of the bank's offices is an important consideration for marketers of consumer banking services. The technical aspects of analyzing possible locations are not discussed in depth here, but the basic decisions that must be made and the types of data necessary in doing a feasibility study are reviewed.[3]

Consumer goods manufacturers find that the more willing an individual is to shop around for a particular product, the less effort the manufacturer needs to exert in finding convenient outlets. For example, shoppers are more careful and discriminating in the selection of a designer garment than a soft drink. Thus soft drinks are available at numerous locations, whereas a high-priced line of designer clothes may be available at only a handful of stores in very select locations.

Banking is fundamentally a convenience business. Consumers will make exceptions and go out of their way when there is a higher interest rate on a consumer deposit product or a lower interest rate on a consumer credit product. But for daily services, location is key. That is, most people do not shop around for day-to-day banking services, but simply select the most convenient location. If several alternatives are convenient, prospective customers might shop around among them; however, in choosing between a bank that has a branch several blocks from a person's home and another bank that has a branch four miles away, most people will open an account at the closer bank. Therefore, location decisions are an extremely important element to the success of the marketing mix for most banks.

Site Location Decisions

The laws of each state govern the ability of a local or out-of-state commercial bank or bank holding company to expand its service delivery system through branching or acquiring other banks. However, legislation permitting interstate banking took effect in 1994, and legislation allowing interstate branching in most states took effect in June 1997, which enhanced banks' ability to locate in regions with high potential as well as high profitability.

Regardless of the branching and banking laws, a bank seeking to expand to a new location faces a number of important decisions. The same considerations apply to the establishment of a new bank or branch by a bank or holding company. First, decisions must be made about expansion within the bank's present trading area; then, decisions must be made regarding expansion to new trading areas.

As a city grows and expands, a bank may have to expand or move its base of operations in order to maintain its existing customers and attract new ones. This may reflect population shifts within the city, as well as an influx of new residents moving into the city. If a city is growing, other banks will likely be attracted to it, in which case establishing additional branches may be a necessary defensive move. If its competitor's location is more convenient to a segment of the trade area population, a bank stands to lose customers from that area.

Or the move may be an offensive one, designed either to forestall the entry of new competitors or to attract customers from competing banks or from a newly developing part of the city. In either case, the bank will have to decide not only where, but what type of branch, to open—a full-service office, a drive-in auxiliary, a mini-branch, a platform-free branch, a reconfigured or downscaled branch, an in-store branch, a mobile branch, a virtual branch, or a fully automated branch. The decision should reflect the bank's objectives and the needs of the local market, and it will depend, in part, on whether the best expansion in the local market is another location or added electronic services.

If state regulations allow a bank some flexibility in the location of branch sites, the bank must first decide which new trade area to enter. Once the new area has been identified, the bank must decide whether to enter the market by acquiring an existing bank or by adding a new branch (often referred to as *de novo* expansion). If the decision is to open a new branch, then the bank must select both the specific trade area and also a specific site within that trade area.

Factors in Location Selection

Two levels of decisions are required when selecting a location for delivering a bank's services: (1) the general location or area, and (2) the specific site within the selected area. (See exhibit 11.2.)

General Area Analysis
The general area selected for locating a bank may be either an entire community or a section of that community. In a large city, the area may be less than one city block, or even one building. In an industrial area, the defined area may be a particular industrial park. For each proposed general location, the bank must obtain and evaluate basic information regarding the area's resident and daytime working population, business, industry, and banking situation.

Much of this information is readily available from published sources.[5] Other information must be obtained through on-site investigation and questioning of knowledgeable individuals. Many larger banks have developed computerized models for evaluating site feasibility, and they make this service available to smaller institutions. Also, private consultants may be called on to perform this task. A bank that has had limited experience in branching would be well advised to obtain professional outside assistance.

The following information is required for a general area analysis of a proposed bank location:

1. *Population characteristics.* Information such as the current and projected residential population, median household income, distribution of household income, size and income of the daytime working population, and employment characteristics of the resident population is needed. Area employment data by occupation category and by location should be collected, as well as information on residential housing, present and planned. The housing information should include the condition and value of residences, proportion of owner- versus renter-occupied units, and occupant turnover. All this information is used to estimate the potential amount of retail or personal deposits and loans that would be generated by a branch in the general area under consideration.

2. *Commercial structure.* An expanding bank should also collect such information as the number of commercial establishments by classification, retail establishments, service establishments, and whole-salers, as well as the location of major shopping areas in the area being investigated. The bank should also get estimates of the annual sales volume for each type of business classification.

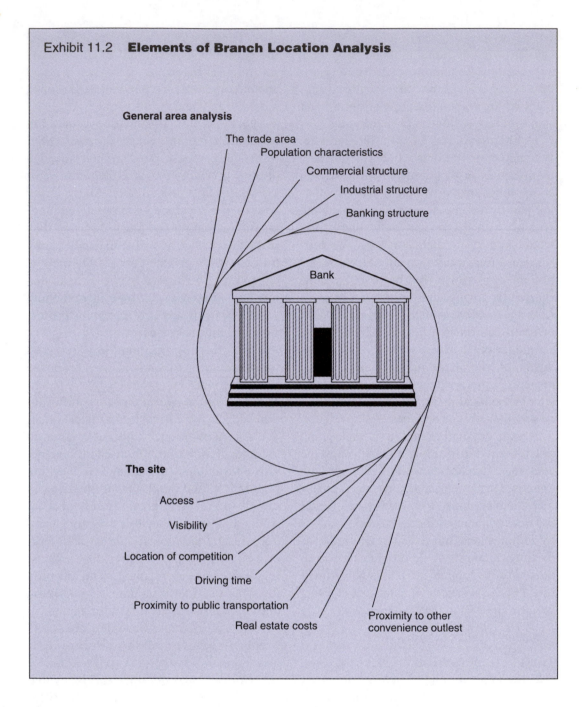

Exhibit 11.2   **Elements of Branch Location Analysis**

General area analysis

- The trade area
- Population characteristics
- Commercial structure
- Industrial structure
- Banking structure

Bank

The site

- Access
- Visibility
- Location of competition
- Driving time
- Proximity to public transportation
- Real estate costs
- Proximity to other convenience outlest

3. *Industrial structure.* A general area analysis should also include the number of major industrial firms (and annual sales volume), the working population by industrial categories, and working hours. The information on the commercial and industrial structure of the area is needed to estimate the potential for commercial and industrial deposits and loans for the area.

4. *Banking structure.* Finally, an expanding bank must determine the number, location, and deposits of all the offices of existing financial institutions (commercial banks, savings banks, and savings and loan associations, as well as credit unions, finance companies, and any other organizations providing financial services). Information regarding banking hours, services

offered, size and type of offices, parking facilities, and whether there are drive-in, walk-up, or automated banking facilities is also needed.

This is by no means an exhaustive list of the data needed for a trade area analysis, but it provides a general idea of the kinds of information needed for this decision-making process. After analyzing the data, the expanding bank must estimate the level of deposits that a branch in the area might generate in its first few years of operation. (This information must also be included in the branch application.) Earnings on these deposits, compared with the costs of operation, will determine the profitability of the branch.

Estimating deposit potential for a trade area has been greatly simplified by the annual publication of deposit information for every branch of every bank, savings and loan association, and credit union in the nation.[6] By compiling these data and looking at deposit trends among the area's financial institution offices, it will be apparent whether, and to what extent, area deposits have been increasing. Although not all the deposits of the residents, businesses, and workers in the trade area will be maintained in local offices, these data are a good indicator of the volume of deposits available in the area the bank seeks to penetrate.

Specific Site Analysis

After the above information has been gathered and evaluated and the general area for expansion has been selected, several possible sites within that area might be available for consideration. In selecting the specific site, such factors as the following should be considered:

1. *Access.* Is it convenient to enter and leave the site? Will traffic in front of the site make it difficult to enter and leave quickly and safely? Is there room in the drive-in lane for waiting cars? Is it on the right side of the street to fit into the predominant traffic pattern of the area? Is there room to provide adequate parking, or is there an adjacent business with whom some parking spaces may be shared?

2. *Visibility.* Will the office and its signs be visible to passing foot and vehicular traffic? Are there any obstacles, present or planned, that would obscure visibility?

3. *Location of competition.* Where are the nearest competitors? The existence of a branch of another bank within several hundred feet of a potential location should not necessarily be a deterrent. It makes more sense to locate next door to the competition if a site is very convenient to the bulk of trade area residents than to locate in a less convenient site away from the competition. It is no accident that in many towns the major intersection has a bank on each of the four corners.

4. *Driving time.* Is the bank within a reasonable distance of residential areas, business districts, or industrial plants?

5. *Proximity to public transportation.* Locating a branch at an end-point of a travel pattern is generally a good strategy. Locating a branch at an interchange point is generally not a good strategy. Traffic-in-transit may not result in banking activity.

6. *Real estate costs.* Financial considerations might weigh heavily in the decision of where to locate a new branch. However, a bank must be careful that, in being economical, it is not being "penny wise and pound foolish." A more costly site may, in the long run, generate a greater return on the investment than a less expensive but less convenient or accessible alternative. Outside professional advice can be valuable in weighing the cost of alternative sites. One bank, on the basis of professional advice, bought a branch site in a developing community when the site looked more like a pasture than a commercial location. The bank held onto the site, although it could have doubled its money by selling it after three years. Now the branch sits right in the center of the new development, and it became profitable in its first year of operation.

7. *Proximity to other convenience outlets.* Since banking is a "convenience good," it is advantageous to locate branches near destination points such as food and other convenience-type stores.

These factors (and others that may be relevant to a particular situation) should be examined in light of their influence on the future deposit potential of the proposed site. The site that is chosen should be the one that offers the most advantages and the fewest drawbacks.

Once a proposed site has been selected, the bank must apply to its regulatory agencies for permission to establish the bank or branch. In most cases, the approval of two agencies is required. State banks that are members of the Federal Reserve System apply to the state Department of Banking and to the Federal Reserve. State banks that are not Federal Reserve members apply to the state Department of Banking and the FDIC. National banks apply to the Comptroller of the Currency and the Federal Reserve. Although each agency has slightly different requirements, they all require that the proposed location meet three criteria: (1) that the office has a reasonable promise of successful operation; (2) that the convenience and needs of the banking public are served; and (3) that no harm will result to existing offices of financial institutions.

The length of time required to obtain approval for an office varies from state to state and from regulator to regulator. Normally, however, unless the application is contested (in which case written and oral arguments must be conducted), the approval process takes from three to six months.

Merging as an Expansion Strategy

During the 1970s, most U.S. banks expanded into new geographical markets through branching. During that decade, the number of offices of commercial and savings banks grew from 37,166 to 57,232, a 54 percent increase.[7] Since then the practice of acquiring and merging existing banks has become the dominant form of expansion. And although branches are clearly the most costly capital investment a bank can make, the banking industry has been reluctant to give up the branch as a delivery channel. Despite significant evidence that increases in electronic delivery channels have taken large numbers of consumers out of the branch, the number of branches operated by FDIC-insured commercial banks did not change significantly between 1991 and 1996.[8] Many large banks have shifted their marketing strategy from market extension to market concentration.[9] That is, they are focusing on increasing their share of an existing market.

During the 1980s, many banks acquired other banks as a defensive maneuver: to establish a market presence and to become large enough to prevent another bank from merging them out of existence. Mergers in the 1990s are driven more by economies of scale. As banks get larger, the ratio of overhead and other noninterest expenses to asset size decreases. One large bank can be run more cost-effectively than several smaller banks. (See Case H, which traces the merger history of a bank holding company and how it addressed merger-related marketing issues.) Since interstate branching legislation took effect in June 1997 (except in Texas), the banking industry has been able to take advantage of the economies of scale that can result from larger bank operations. A holding company can now merge all its banks into one structure, resulting in substantial economies and improved earnings.

The Decision to Close a Branch

For any number of reasons, a bank's management may be faced with the difficult decision to eliminate a branch. This decision must be handled carefully since it has social as well as economic implications. Managers generally must face this decision eventually when a branch is losing money—that is, not earning enough to cover its costs. For example, an older branch may be located in an area that was once economically healthy but has deteriorated. A newer branch may have been projected to break even in its second or third year of operation, but is still losing money after five years or more. In these types of situations, the bank must be concerned about its public image, but the negative consequences of the branch closing can be minimized if there is another office of the bank nearby to which customers may be referred.

Making Banking Services Accessible to the Disabled

The Americans with Disabilities Act of 1990 (ADA) was passed to ensure that persons with disabilities have access to employment, public transportation, public accommodations, government services, and telecommunications.[10] Banks fall into the category of public accommodations. The law requires not only that banks make it easy for disabled customers to enter a bank and conduct business, but also that they make it possible for disabled customers to access the banks' various channels of communication and distribution—such as ATMs—through auxiliary aids and services. Consequently, in addition to removing physical barriers to banking locations, banks are retrofitting ATMs for the disabled, in some cases upgrading them to offer such options as voice-response systems, high-contrast large-print displays, Braille keyboards, and telephone assistance. Banks are also redesigning their signage to include high-contrast colors, easy-to-read typefaces, and visible signals for the visually impaired.[11] Many banks have also installed teletypewriter equipment that enables their telephone customer-service representatives to communicate directly with the hearing impaired.

Beyond Brick and Mortar

Beyond the bank office itself are the electronic and telecommunication-based channels of distribution for banking services: the telephone, the automated teller, the automated loan machine, the personal computer, the virtual branch, and plastic cards. (See exhibit 11.3.) Since these are tools that

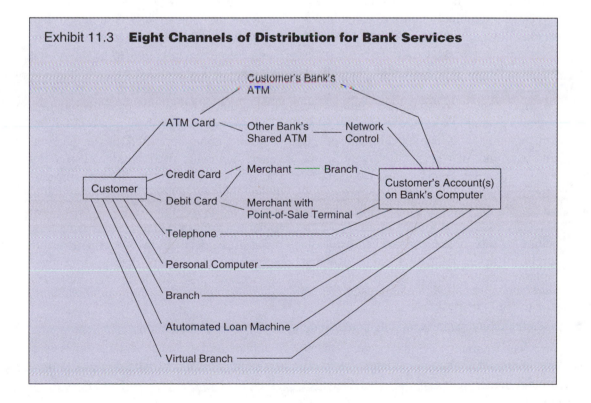

Exhibit 11.3 Eight Channels of Distribution for Bank Services

help make banking services available to users, they clearly may be thought of as distribution channels.

Telephones and Call Centers

The telephone is increasingly being used by banks as a way to extend transaction capability, account information, and customer assistance to any location where a customer can reach a phone. This is accomplished through call centers and through services such as telephone banking and telephone bill payment.

Call centers allow banks to have experienced representatives available to customers during extended hours. Some banks offer 24-hour services, such as loan approval and credit card applications, that are handled by call centers. With telephone banking, the customer may access account information to learn his current balance or whether a specific check has cleared as well as make transfers between accounts. Telephone bill-paying permits the customer to instruct the bank to pay specific bills either in response to the called-in instruction or on a pre-arranged basis. Both of these services are typically available 24 hours a day, 7 days a week, allowing customers unlimited access to the bank's services from their home, office, car, or anywhere else a phone is located.

Many banks also make personal credit services available over the telephone. Customers apply for a loan by calling a special number, and in many cases receive an answer the same day-some banks even offer an answer before the customer hangs up the phone. Customers who use this service pay a slightly higher interest rate in return for the convenience of being able to apply for credit from their home or work and receive such a prompt response.

Automated Teller Machines

ATMs are another way banks are making their services more accessible and convenient for customers. Again, because of their around-the-clock availability, customers can conduct their banking on their own schedule. A bank's participation in regional or national networks enables customers to get cash elsewhere in the country and around the world, wherever the network logo is seen.

Technological advances are expanding the capabilities of ATMs to make more services and information available to customers. Some experimental ATMs now scan and show pictures of deposited checks. Others offer two-way video communications or touch-sensitive displays, while still others dispense coins, stamps, coupons, and tickets. Some banks now also provide bank statements through their ATMs and allow customers to buy, sell, or exchange their money market funds through a touch screen.

Automated Loan Machines

The first automated loan machine (ALM) was unveiled in 1994, and it offered banks another way of extending credit to consumers outside of banking hours and at locations convenient to the consumer. The ALMs being piloted at this writing are located in malls and stores as well as in the external lobby of bank branches. Consumers can access these ALMs whenever the stores or malls are open and apply for an unsecured loan up to $10,000. If the loan is approved, the check and loan documents are printed out right at the ALM, within about 15 minutes. The customer also has the option of having the loan amount deposited into an account. When the loan is approved, the customer's photograph is taken by the ALM and the customer writes his or her signature on a "digital signature capture" device. The systems save banks hundreds of dollars in processing fees, and most banks offer the same interest rate as conventional loans or slightly lower interest rates because of the lower processing costs.[12]

The Personal Computer

The increased use of personal computers in the home and the office has opened up a tremendous service delivery opportunity to banks. At this writing, the 100 million U.S. households contained 85 million personal computers, which suggests PCs have already become integral to most American's lives in some fashion. It also illustrates how banks and consumers can interact much more readily than through the 200,000 brick and mortar banking outlets that currently exist.[13]

Since bank products are primarily bits of information stored in the bank's computer, and since computers can communicate with one another over standard phone lines, personal and business customers now can access their accounts and conduct transactions from their own PCs. Individual customers can obtain balance and transaction information, pay bills, consider investment opportunities, and move funds between accounts without ever going to the bank. Business customers can do all that and more. Many banks offer firms the capability to initiate wire transfers and letters of credit, invest excess balances, and pay down loans—all by PCs in their own offices.

Banks are also capitalizing on the widespread use of PCs to launch Internet banking. October 1995 saw the opening of the first exclusively on-line bank-Security First Network Bank (http://www.sfnb.com). Within the first year, 6,000 checking accounts were opened.[14] Many other banks have created home pages and offer on-line loan applications, product information, account access, and e-mail question-and-answer forums. PC banking opportunities stand to increase dramatically as technology is perfected and security issues are eliminated.

Plastic Cards

Bank credit and debit cards are also innovations in the distribution of a bank's credit and deposit services. Like AT&T's walk-up telephones, their purpose is to increase the bank's capacity to provide credit and deposit services by increasing the number of locations where those services can be obtained.

Credit cards have helped overcome the marketing characteristic of inseparability—that is, the inability to separate a bank's services from the person who sells or delivers the service. Credit cards allow credit services to be applied for, and received, through the mail, enabling many banks to maintain credit customers far outside their immediate trading area.

The credit card has also enabled bankers to use the retail merchant as an intermediary in the distribution of credit. In the marketing of credit cards, banks rely heavily on retail merchants to encourage their customers to apply for the cards. When retail merchants accept a bank's credit card, they in effect become an intermediary in the distribution channel for this bank service.

The debit card may be either a national brand (Visa or MasterCard) or a private brand (the bank's own card). A debit card looks like a credit card and is accepted in payment of purchases wherever that brand is accepted. The difference is that with a debit card the amount of the purchase is deducted directly from the customer's checking account rather than being billed. The effect is the same as if the customer wrote a check, except the transaction is much simpler, requiring only that the clerk pass the card through a card reader and that the customer enter his or her personal identification number and sign the receipt.

A third plastic card, the "smart card," has been around since the 1980s but still has not gained sufficient popularity to be a major payment tool. All smart cards have embedded in them a microchip that can store information. Some smart cards are used specifically to hold monetary value. After the value on a smart card has been spent, it can be "reloaded" with additional monetary value and used again. The cards offer security and privacy, as well as convenience and speed.[15] As technology continues to develop, the smart card will allow consumers to make a withdrawal from their bank accounts via PC by downloading the value into a smart card.

Visa and three banks, First Union Corp., Wachovia, and NationsBank, piloted the smart card during the 1996 Summer Olympics in Atlanta, Georgia. Consumers used smart cards to ride the public transportation system, buy gas, use pay phones, and purchase meals in restaurants. The Smart Card Forum (an industry group with 225 members) predicts that 25 percent of American homes will have smart cards by the year 2000.[16]

Part of the challenge of smart cards is persuading merchants to purchase smart card technology so they can accept the cards. Smart cards also cost much more than a magnetic stripe debit or credit card—3 to 6 dollars versus 10 cents. Another part of the challenge is to educate consumers about smart cards and their benefits. For the most part, financial experts believe smart cards will be used for small dollar purchases.

Virtual Branches and Automated Video Banking

Technology now allows banks to create what looks like a branch in a business building's lobby or shopping mall without having to hire any staff. Virtual branches have been created by several banks, including Huntington Bancshares in Ohio and PNC Bank in Pennsylvania. These branches have ATMs, phones, and interactive two-way video monitors and communication systems that allow customers to buy and sell CDs and mutual funds, open accounts, apply for credit cards, and even buy stamps.[17]

Intermediaries in the Banking Industry

Banks and other service firms do not use intermediaries in the way producers of consumer goods use them. However, an increasing number of bank services are provided by persons or companies that are external to the bank itself. These may legitimately be thought of as intermediaries if an intermediary is defined as a distribution channel that

- increases the availability or convenience of a service,
- increases its use or the revenues from its use, or
- helps maintain existing users, increase use among existing users, or attract new users.

Two types of firms have been mentioned as acting as intermediaries for banks: the car dealer who sells the bank's auto loans to customers; and the retail merchant who, by accepting a credit or debit card transaction, makes the bank's services available to the cardholder. In addition, regional and national ATM networks act as banking intermediaries by making customers' funds available in any city or town where there is an ATM that is part of the network. The Federal Reserve Wire Network (Fedwire) is another intermediary used by banks to move customers' funds quickly and conveniently around the world. This list is not exhaustive, but it illustrates some of the ways in which intermediaries serve the banking industry.

Summary

In a consumer goods industry, marketing channels are the intermediaries (wholesalers and retailers) that move the product from the producer to the ultimate user. In a service industry, the marketing channels are any means of increasing the availability or convenience of the service that also increases its use or the revenues from its use.

The fact that banking services are inseparable from the person of the seller means that the sales force—the customer-contact people—is a primary channel of distribution. As a result, the way banking services are delivered can vary greatly from customer to customer and location to location. It is difficult for a bank to standardize its products and deliver a homogeneous service that is the same at all times and all places. Moreover, since services are perishable (not capable of being stored), intermediaries in the traditional sense cannot be used to distribute them. However, banks have been innovative in finding ways to increase the availability of their services beyond the branch offices.

The most obvious marketing channel for a bank's services is the bank office, which may range from a full-service branch to a self-contained automated teller. Locating a site for expansion requires research to first identify general areas that are promising and then to identify specific sites for the new location. Considerable information must be gathered about the economic and demographic characteristics of an area, not only for the bank's use in selecting an appropriate site, but to present to the relevant bank regulatory agencies in defense of the branch or bank application. While expansion through branching was popular in the 1970s, more recently banks have been expanding primarily through merger and acquisition activity.

Other ways a bank delivers its services are through the automated teller machine, automated loan machine, telephones and call centers, personal computer, plastic card, and virtual bank. These methods have helped banks overcome some of the limitations of intangibility, inseparability, and perishability that make the marketing of services such a challenge.

Regardless of these innovations, personal contact will remain important in the delivery of banking services for sales and service. In the next chapter, personal selling, which is still the primary means of delivering most bank services, will be discussed.

Points for Review

1. Define or briefly explain the following terms and concepts:
   - marketing channel in a consumer goods industry
   - marketing channel in a service industry
   - direct channel
   - intermediary

2. How do the following characteristics of banking services affect the way in which these services are distributed?
   - intangibility
   - inseparability
   - variability
   - perishability

3. Describe the kinds of information that a bank should obtain in evaluating a prospective site for a new branch.

4. How has technology allowed banks to expand their marketing channels beyond branches? Describe six other distribution channels for banking services.

5. What are some examples of intermediaries to the banking industry?

Notes

1. Any basic marketing book will have a complete discussion of the concept of a channel of distribution. This example is from Pride and Ferrell, *Marketing* (1997), section IV, chapter 13.

2. Anthony Ramirez, "A Telephone Visionary Who Is Cutting the Cords for Consumers," *The New York Times,* November 15, 1992, p. 5.

3. For those interested, here are four excellent publications devoted entirely to selecting bank locations: Paul Seibert, CMC, *Facilities Planning and Design for Financial Institutions: A Strategic Management Guide* (Chicago, Irwin Professional, 1996); *A Guide to Selecting Bank Locations* (Washington, D.C.: American Bankers Association, 1968); James E. Littlefield, G. Jackson Burney, and William V. White, *Bank Branch Location: A Handbook of Effective Technique and Practice* (Chicago: Bank Marketing Association, 1973); and Rex O. Bennett, *Bank Location Analysis: Techniques and Methodology* (Washington, D.C.: American Bankers Association, 1975).

4. See Seibert, *Facilities Planning and Design for Financial Institutions.*

5. *Ibid.*

6. For example, Sheshunoff Information Services, Inc., of Austin, Texas, can provide deposit information for every bank, savings and loan, savings bank, and credit union either in print (published under the title *Branches of [State name]*) or through its Bancpen Branch PC Program. Call 1-800-456-2340 for information.

7. *Statistical Abstract of the United States,* 1991.

8. Wendy S. Mead, "Alternative Delivery Is Nearer," *American Banker,* March 12, 1997, p. 1.

9. James J. McDermott, Jr., "The Changing Landscape of Banking," *The Stonier Forum,* Fall 1991, p. 2.

10. Nessa Feddis, "Americans with Disabilities Act," *Bank Marketing,* July 1995, pp. 118–119.

11. "Information Center Issues," *Bank Marketing,* January 1992, pp. 38ff.

12. Patrick J. Maio, "Selling People on Borrowing from Machines," *Bank Marketing,* September 1996, p. 53.

13. D'Anne Hotchkiss, "Brickless Banking," *Bank Marketing,* January 1997, p. 36.

14. "Convenience Attracts 6,000 Checking Accounts to Internet Bank," *Deposit Growth Strategies,* October 1996, p. 1.

15. Katherine Morrall, "IQ Tests for Smart Cards," *Bank Marketing,* March 1997, p. 19.

16. *Ibid.,* p. 20

17. Maio, "Selling People on Borrowing from Machines," p. 53.

12

PROMOTION STRATEGY: PERSONAL SELLING

Learning Objectives

After studying this chapter, you should be able to

- describe how selling is interwoven with the concept of customer service and satisfaction,
- discuss the difference between selling and marketing,
- explain why everyone in the bank is responsible for selling and how selling affects the bank's profitability,
- explain why personal selling is critical for acquiring and retaining customers, improving productivity, and maximizing return on advertising dollars,
- describe the personal attributes and selling skills characteristic of successful salespeople,
- discuss the six elements of the sales management process, and
- discuss how to design and execute a successful sales training program and describe effective training program content.

Introduction

Personal selling, along with advertising, sales promotion, and public relations/communications, falls under the broader topic of promotional strategy.[1]

Much of marketing theory applies to both consumer goods and services, but there are some important differences. Some of these differences—relating to product strategy, pricing strategy, and physical distribution strategy—have already been discussed. But when it comes to the role of personal selling, the differences between consumer goods and banking services are even greater. The main reason personal selling is so important in banking is because there is no product for the consumer to see, hear, feel, taste, or touch. Therefore, the seller must earn the confidence of the consumer by clearly explaining the product or service and how it will benefit the customer. Because the intangibility of banking services makes it difficult for consumers to distinguish them from services offered by other financial institutions, many banks now rely heavily on superior customer service to help differentiate them from their competition.

Differences between Selling and Marketing

Many people fail to distinguish between selling and marketing. They do not understand that marketing is a very broad field and that selling is only one part of it. Peter Drucker said that "marketing is so basic that it cannot be considered as a separate function. It is the whole business seen from the point of view of its final result, that is, from the customer's point of view."[2] Professor Theodore Levitt made the distinction between marketing and selling clear in one short sentence: "Selling is finding customers for what you have; marketing is making sure you have what customers want."[3] The American Marketing Association (AMA) defines selling in more depth and emphasizes that the customer will be satisfied in the selling process. Selling is "the personal or impersonal process whereby the salesperson ascertains, activates, and satisfies the needs of the buyer to the mutual, continuous benefit of both buyer and seller."[4] (The AMA's definition of marketing, discussed in chapter 1, clearly incorporates the concept of selling.)

To further clarify the concept of selling, look at two definitions given by *Webster's Ninth New Collegiate Dictionary.* One is "to persuade or influence to a course of action or to the acceptance of something." This definition clearly describes the activities of people aggressively involved in direct selling. They are helping to influence a course of action by the customer or prospect. Examples of this type of selling situation in a bank include

- officer call programs directed at businesses and correspondent banks,
- calls on consumers by bank personnel or branch bank neighborhood representatives,
- deliberate selling efforts by members of advisory committees and the board of directors, and
- employee efforts to sell additional financial services to new or established customers (cross-selling).

The other definition in *Webster's* states that to sell is "to develop a belief in the truth, value, or desirability of something."

A marketing-oriented organization or a market-driven bank will offer products that fit the needs of its target markets. The sales force—including the commercial calling officers, the customer service representatives, and the branch managers—works at getting customers for those products by finding prospects with unmet needs, not by forcing products on customers who do not need or want them.

Selling as an Element of Customer Service

Many people have negative images of selling and salespeople and believe that salespeople are out to take advantage of the consumer. However, the best and most successful salespeople are usually totally customer focused:

- they question and listen to the customer to understand waht the customer really needs or wants;
- they suggest the specific product that will best meet those needs and wants;
- they answer customers' questions and help them undersand the product being sold; and
- they make it easy for the customer to purchase and use the product.

When done in this way, selling is truly an element of customer service because the salesperson is helping the customer solve a problem or fill a need. A salesperson who focuses exclusively on selling "the product of the day" without regard for the customer's needs reinforces the negative image of selling as pushing product.

The selling of bank services is no longer limited to certain employees; rather, everyone in the bank sells either directly or indirectly. In a service industry, there are those who are clearly charged with selling responsibilities; however, continually and consistently providing good service is a form of indirect selling. How a phone is answered, how a teller handles a complaint, how quickly a payment is processed—all of these activities and more are part of the ongoing selling of a bank's services. Back office staff are also "salespeople" since their work, no matter which department they work in, in some way supports the activities involved in selling and in servicing customers.

In a marketing-oriented bank, everyone sees his or her job as being involved in selling the bank and its services because every job in a bank can be traced ultimately to some point of contact with the customer.

The Importance of Selling in Banking

Personal selling is more important for some products than for others. Some products are "presold." For example, national-brand convenience goods, such as grocery products and cosmetics, are purchased by consumers with little assistance from store personnel.

Other products (such as industrial goods, automobiles, and bank services) are seldom presold, and personal selling plays an important role in finalizing the sale. In the case of many banking products, consumers have too-limited knowledge of them to compare them. Consequently, personal selling becomes important because customers tend to associate the quality of their banking services with the reliability and trustworthiness of their customer service representative.

The basic purpose of any business is customer satisfaction at a profit. Selling directly affects both customer satisfaction and the attainment of profit. It affects the income of the bank through customer acquisition and retention and, less directly, by helping to improve staff productivity and by maximizing the return on the bank's advertising expenditures.

Customer Acquisition

Acquiring new customers and keeping them is very important in retail banking. If a bank's services are priced correctly, each new account contributes to the income of the bank. New accounts generally result from a selling process. The extent of the selling effort depends on what is being sold. Bank employees in all types of positions within the bank can be effective salespeople using either of two distinct levels of selling: low-level selling and high-level selling. (Bank employees can also be the source of valuable referrals because they can be very effective in convincing their friends, neighbors, acquaintances, and relatives to do business with the bank.)

1. *Low-level selling* entails consummating a sale with a customer who already has a clear notion of what he or she wants. Basically, the salesperson performs a service function and may even be sought out by the buyer. This type of selling is frequently involved in providing retail banking services—for example, helping a customer open a personal savings or checking account. Even so, the bank employee

should not see his or her role as one of simply taking orders from customers. With the high level of competition from other banks and nonbank financial sources and the increased sophistication of banking consumers with regard to investment alternatives, branch sales staff must be knowledgeable and able to recognize opportunities to inform customers of other services that might be useful.

2. *High-level selling* involves generating demand for new products or influencing a change in patronage from one seller to another. The salesperson attempts to convert a prospective customer's neutral or negative attitudes into positive wants or demands, since the prospect often does not recognize his or her own need for the product. Products such as mutual funds and trust and private banking services require the extensive selling efforts typical of high-level selling. Cross-selling by the bank's customer-contact personnel and much of the selling activity by the bank's loan officers would also be considered high-level selling.

Customer Retention

Opening and closing accounts is expensive in terms of staff time and processing costs. Studies have shown that it costs six times more to acquire a customer than to keep one. What's more, generally speaking, the longer a customer stays with the bank, the more of a bank's products that customer will use and the more profitable that customer will become to the bank. Therefore, a bank that keeps its customers will operate more efficiently and more profitably than one with high customer turnover.

These facts reinforce the need for high-quality service. If a customer who is frustrated about a bank error (such as a misposted item) receives impersonal, inattentive, or slow service in getting the error corrected, that customer is much more likely to close the account—especially if that is the only account he or she has with the bank. However, if the bank provides quality customer service by addressing the problem quickly and

courteously, the customer will have positive "postpurchase feelings" about having selected that bank. These positive feelings in the customer pave the way for additional business relationships and help build long-term loyalty for the bank.

Cross-selling—the selling of additional services to prospective or existing customers—can significantly improve the bank's profitability by helping the bank retain its customers. It is generally agreed that customers with only one or two accounts are more likely to switch banks, and that the greater the number of bank services a customer uses, the less likely that customer will be to switch banks. Still, the best time to sell a customer an additional service is when an account is being opened. The customer has come to the bank with an unfulfilled need and is ready to buy. This should be seen as an ideal opportunity to acquaint the customer with the range of products and services the bank offers, but not as a chance to load up the customer with unwanted products. For example, a customer who has come to the bank to open a checking account may be interested in an ATM card, a line of credit for protection against bounced checks, and a savings account that can receive automatic deposits from the checking account. The customer may even be interested in a credit card or debit card. But it may not be appropriate to do more than mention that the bank has a home equity loan sale in progress, and that the trust department is available should the customer need its services. Good listening and questioning skills will help bankers decide which products are appropriate to discuss.

What happens in those first few minutes of contact with the bank is critical. Case C provides dialogues that illustrate effective and ineffective techniques for handling the sale of a checking account. One scenario results in the sale of an interest-bearing checking account, savings account with bimonthly automatic transfers, and automated teller access cards to a man who came into the bank to open only a checking account; the other scenario results in a disgruntled customer leaving with only a checking account. The key in both cases is the way the customer is treated during those few precious minutes.

Taking advantage of this first opportunity to cross-sell is extremely important since as many as half of a bank's customers do not walk into the branch again after they become customers. They use the drive-in or automated teller, PC banking, or bank by mail, so the personal sales contact opportunity is often lost.

Improved Productivity

Increasing the average number of services used by each customer also increases the productivity of the bank's staff. It is less expensive and more efficient for a bank to service 1,000 customers who have two accounts each than to service 2,000 customers who have one account each, which in turn affects the profitability of the bank. If expenses are kept to a minimum by having fewer customers who cost less to maintain but who generate more income by having multiple accounts, the improved productivity leads to greater profitability. The amount of time and volume of paperwork required to service accounts is more a function of the number of individuals served than the number of accounts.

Surveys show that most people deal with more than one bank or financial institution, and some do business with several. Therefore, a sales-oriented (which also should mean a customer-oriented) staff will find opportunities to cross-sell additional services to both new and existing customers.

Maximized Return on Advertising Expenditures

Advertising typically accounts for 50 percent or more of a bank's total marketing expenditures.[5] Banks spend millions of dollars on advertising every year in an effort to get prospective customers to walk in the door. If an employee acts only as an order-taker and opens just the account the customer came in for, the advertising dollars are not as fruitful as if the customer had been cross-sold appropriate additional services. If instead the sale is lost, the advertising dollars are wasted.

To prevent that, employees need to be trained to sell to and deal effectively with potential customers who come into the bank. Employees must also be thoroughly briefed on the bank's advertising campaigns and goals so they know which ads their customers are referring to. A well-trained, informed customer service representative is far more likely than an untrained employee to sell one or more services to prospective customers.

Similarly, the purpose of advertising directed at the corporate banking market is to create an image and to predispose the prospective customer to receive and listen to the calling officer. (See exhibit 12.1.) If the calling officer is making calls without proper preparation simply to meet a quota, the money spent on the corporate advertising program is also wasted. Experts on calling programs say that the majority of the work is in preparing for the calls.[6] That means researching what the customer has and most likely will need and arriving with information to show that the calling officer has the customer's best interests at heart. Not making these preparations is like a branch manager calling on a merchant who is clearly a good prospect for a credit-card depository relationship but failing to bring the forms necessary to enroll the merchant.

You may wonder whether adequate sales training to support advertising goals is really a problem for most banks. According to published statistics, an average of just 2 percent of the marketing budget is spent on sales and customer relations training.[7] Only at the very largest banks ($5 billion or more) is 6 percent of the marketing budget spent on training. While some sales training expenses might be included in the budgets of personnel departments rather than marketing departments, it is clear that many banks still have not fully grasped the importance of selling in making their marketing efforts effective. Too many banks fail to see personal selling as either a marketing or customer service tool, and too many employees resist selling because of the misconceptions stated earlier. Training can help educate employees and help them feel comfortable incorporating selling into their jobs.

Characteristics of a Successful Salesperson

To be successful in sales anywhere requires certain personality attributes, but some selling skills, such as listening carefully to a customer and asking engaging questions to elicit additional information, can be learned through training and practice. In general,

Exhibit 12.1

"I don't know who you are.
I don't know your company.
I don't know your company's product.
I don't know what your company stands for.
I don't know your company's customers.
I don't know your company's record.
I don't know your company's reputation.
Now—what was it you wanted to sell me?"

MORAL: Sales start **before** your salesman calls—with **business** publication advertising.

McGRAW-HILL MAGAZINES
BUSINESS • PROFESSIONAL • TECHNICAL

however, a person's sales ability reflects at least two things: (1) personal attributes, and (2) selling skills.

Personal Attributes

Many attributes might be listed as desirable qualities for a salesperson, and there is some general agreement as to what these attributes are.[8] Ten of these traits are self-confidence, planning ability, industriousness, persuasiveness, intelligence, technical knowledge, job interest, ambition, health, and social development. (See exhibit 12.2.) If a person has strong planning ability and ambition, for example, it might be easy to assume that he or she would be an accomplished salesperson-contacting numerous customers in a short amount of time to be the most successful salesperson on the team. However, singling out specific personality traits can be misleading because it suggests that if an individual is ambitious, confident, and persuasive, he or she will automatically be a good salesperson. Clearly, matching a set of characteristics to an employee profile cannot by itself ensure the hiring of successful salespeople; moreover, this approach ignores the role and needs of the customer. Other attributes that are equally important are in-depth product knowledge; business expertise; trustworthiness; reliability; responsiveness; and a proven performance record, particularly in trust and private banking.

Each selling job is characterized by a unique set of duties and challenges. Each salesperson serves different customers with individual needs and expectations. That is why a sales force can be made up of different kinds of salespeople with different jobs and goals.

Selling Skills

Most experts believe that, given appropriate training, the majority of individuals can become salespeople and that both the few "born" salespersons and the many "made" ones can improve with continued training. It takes a variety of personalities to make a successful sales team—so you will most likely find a variety of people involved in sales, ranging from loan officers to direct mail copy writers. Nevertheless, certain sales techniques apply to most types of selling activities. (See exhibit 12.3.) Most sales executives recognize that formal sales training programs significantly improve selling performance. Because this issue is so important in banking, sales training will be discussed in greater detail later in this chapter.

Personal selling should be seen as social interaction, which requires behaving correctly toward the customer. The buyer should not be seen as playing a very limited, passive role in the sales transaction; to the contrary, the buyer should be seen as having an active, involved role. After all, the interplay between the salesperson's characteristics and actions and the buyer's characteristics and actions determines whether a sale is consummated.

The personal selling process has three major stages: the greeting and impression formation stage (when the customer service representative initially meets and greets the customer and begins to establish a rapport); matching customer needs (when the CSR asks appropriate questions to determine which products and services best meet the customer's needs); and closing the sale (which means asking for the business—a step often overlooked—after seeing that the customer has accepted the idea of the suggested product and seems ready to buy).[9] Case C offers three examples of the three stages of personal selling and how they may be effectively (or ineffectively) implemented. Effective sales training programs emphasize these steps and that selling entails understanding and meeting customers' needs, not just selling products whether or not they benefit the customer. Training programs incorporate effective sales techniques that can be used during each of the three

The purpose of this ad is to capture a corporate customer's attention and to convey a strong, positive image of the publishers.

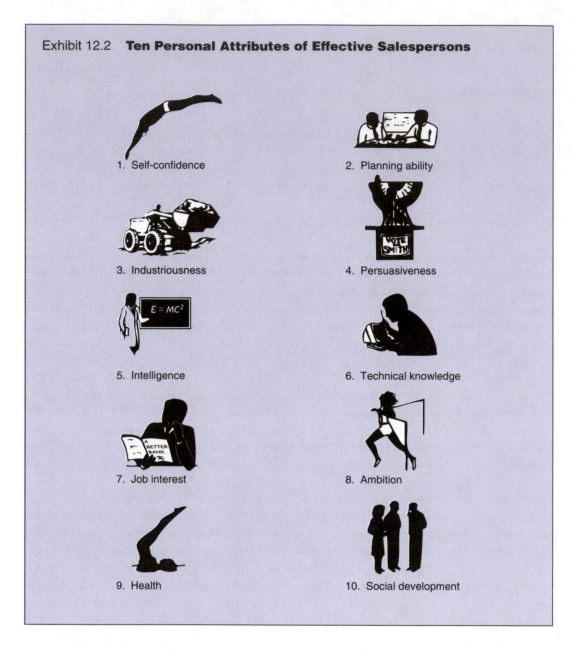

Exhibit 12.2 **Ten Personal Attributes of Effective Salespersons**

1. Self-confidence

2. Planning ability

3. Industriousness

4. Persuasiveness

5. Intelligence

6. Technical knowledge

7. Job interest

8. Ambition

9. Health

10. Social development

stages of the personal selling process so bank employees can be confident in their product knowledge as well as their selling and presentation skills.

Every salesperson should know how to:

1. Ask probing, usually open-ended questions to determine the customer's needs, qualify a customer for a particular service, or clarify the true source of an objection.

2. Suggest a service, especially in terms of the benefits to the customer.

3. Make an incremental close by testing the customer's understanding and accep-

tance of the product and answering any additional questions.

4. Handle objections by making sure the customer's questions are understood and answered and stating the benefits of the product that solve the objection or question.

5. Close the sale, generally by summarizing the benefits of the product or service, reaching an agreement with the customer on which products he or she would like to purchase, and asking the customer for the business.[10]

Exhibit 12.3   The AIDAS Formula

Describing the actual process of selling is difficult because it involves so many variables that are difficult to measure and control. There are many "how-to" formulas for selling, but they usually describe only *what* a salesperson should do, without explaining "why." Nevertheless, one such formula that lists the steps leading to a successful sale and a satisfied customer is know as the AIDAS formula. It is also frequently cited as a tool for direct mail letters.

1. Gain the prospect's **A**ttention.
2. Arouse his or her **I**nterest.
3. Stimulate **D**esire for the product.
4. Get buying **A**ction.
5. Build **S**atisfaction into the transaction.

This approach to selling is overly simplistic because it assumes that, to a large extent, the salesperson can control the behavior of the prospective buyer if this process is managed skillfully. But the major limitation of the AIDAS formula is that it emphasizes the "how to" and ignores the "why." That is why most sales training and techniques, while they may follow this sequence, also build in the important skills necessary for effective interpersonal interaction. They also develop an understanding and empathy in salespeople that help them meet customers' needs, rather than just putting them through the steps of a formula to achieve a sale.

AIDAS is an effective framework for direct mail letters, however, because it lends a structure to the information and tone that work best in capturing a prospect's attention.

Begin a direct mail letter by capturing the reader's *attention* with a strong phrase or question. Arouse *interest* by explaining what's ion it for the reader. Stimulate *desire* for the product or service by explaining benefits to the reader. Include a call to *action,* such as "Call now!" with a toll-free number, or "Send in your reply today!" Build *satisfaction* into the transaction by offering a guarantee, or by providing a secondary reward for accepting your offer.

This is a simplified explanation of how AIDAS works for direct mail, but it is a useful tool that can help you pack the most punch into your letters to prospects and customers.

Within the sales culture and the sales training programs, there must be a continuing emphasis on customer communication. With a priority on customer satisfaction, salespeople should be trained to use the following seven simple steps to good communication. Although they may seem obvious, they are essential to establishing a good rapport with the customer:

- Make eye contact.
- Smile.
- Greet the customer.
- Use the customer's name.
- Avoid overuse of the bank's jargon.

- Respond in a positive fashion (meaning providing a positive solution, even if you don't know the answer or are not the right person to handle the customer's request).
- Say thank you.

As mentioned earlier, an important part of customer communication, and also part of asking probing questions, is effective listening. Without this skill, salespeople cannot determine what a customer's true needs are and cannot suggest the best products and services to meet the customer's needs. The seven elements of effective listening are

1. taking time to listen,
2. ignoring distractions,
3. concentrating on the customer's main ideas,
4. reinforcing the customer with positive feedback,
5. asking questions and restating the main ideas,
6. tuning out personal prejudice, and
7. observing voice inflections and body language.

Effective questioning goes hand in hand with listening because it helps elicit more information from the customer, which helps the salesperson make the correct product and service recommendation to the customer. Open-ended questions, such as "How do you prefer to pay your bills?" can provide the banker with more information than asking "Would you like to order checks?" With an open-ended question, the banker may learn that the customer pays most bills by telephone or personal computer, and uses checks only occasionally. With the closed-ended question, the customer might just say "Yes," and the opportunity to sell telephone banking services or PC banking services would be lost.

A related element to effective customer communication is appropriate personal appearance. Many banks are allowing more casual business attire in the office, but it is important for salespeople to maintain a professional appearance.

Managing the Selling Process

The six essential elements in managing the selling process are recruiting, training, motivating, monitoring results, evaluating, and rewarding.[11]

Recruiting

With the tremendous increase in competition for bank customers, more banks have come to believe that selling is fundamental to the future of the banking industry. They have begun rewriting job descriptions to include sales responsibilities, and they have reoriented employee recruitment efforts toward finding the most energetic, goal-oriented sales teams possible. They are also investing in training that supports both corporate and marketing goals and the sales culture banks are striving to adopt. In more and more banks, the human resources department finds and screens applicants, but the sales manager and director of marketing are involved in the final selection process.

Training

The success of a sales training program depends on a number of factors, including the extent to which selling is valued by bank management. (See exhibit 12.4.) An employee's motivation to learn about selling will be influenced by his or her perception of management's views on selling and marketing in general. If the bank's management appears less than enthusiastic about the sales culture, the sales training program is not likely to be effective. The commitment of management to both the sales culture and an effective training program is vital.

No matter which department handles sales training, a successful program provides ways for trainers to interact with every level of the marketing staff. Marketing professionals are in the best position to understand the product from the con-

Exhibit 12.4   Sales Training in Banks

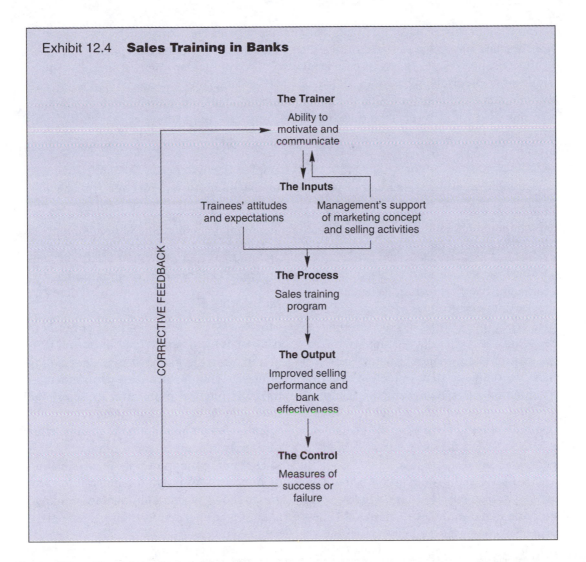

The Trainer

Ability to
motivate and
communicate

The Inputs

Trainees' attitudes
and expectations

Management's support
of marketing concept
and selling activities

The Process

Sales training
program

The Output

Improved selling
performance and
bank
effectiveness

The Control

Measures of
success or
failure

CORRECTIVE FEEDBACK

sumer's viewpoint and already will have developed a strategy for selling each product as part of the total marketing effort. Sales training and product knowledge training are, after all, part of implementing the marketing mix, and interaction between sales and marketing is essential for optimal efficiency and effectiveness in achieving the bank's overall goals. In addition, since training is an ongoing process, not a one-time event, current staff as well as new recruits can benefit from periodic training and follow-up.

Motivating

Motivation is critical to a successful sales program. There must be a sense of purpose to the program, an underlying customer service mission, and an understanding that there is a reward for the successful salesperson. It is important to encourage salespeople to make good sales, always keeping in mind their customer-service orientation. Again, the goal is not only to meet a dollar goal (although that often eclipses the more important customer-oriented goals) but to create satisfied customers.

There are many ways to create an atmosphere that encourages salespeople to make profitable sales to customers. One important ingredient in motivating a sales team and in creating an effective sales program is goals. Setting achievable yet challenging goals serves several purposes.

First, sales goals give the sales staff direction and something to strive for. This is useful because people function best when they know precisely what is expected of them. When they know they need to achieve a certain goal within a specified time frame, salespeople are more motivated than if they are simply told to "go out and sell" without specific parameters or goals to meet.

Second, by setting a standard of performance, management has a basis on which to measure performance. This, in turn, allows management to set up a reward system or to evaluate a salesperson's annual performance.

Third, goals can also be used to set or change the bank's direction. When management wants to shift its priorities (for example, from promoting a new product to deepening account relationships with existing customers) a change in sales goals will help accomplish that objective. Having established goals also gives salespeople a stepping-off point from which to evaluate and set further goals: "Were the goals unrealistic?"; "Were they too easy?"; "Are new goals warranted?"

An individual's sales goals should be arrived at through negotiation between the individual and the sales manager or supervisor. This helps ensure that the salesperson is motivated and committed to attaining the goals. And, as with any job in the bank, the salesperson's goals should be SMART—"specific (including results statements), measurable (quantity, quality, time and cost), acceptable (understood and agreed to), realistic (challenging but doable), and tied to the business (promote overall business goals)."[12]

Finally, it is important to mention the variety of incentive programs that have been successfully used in banks across the country. In the early 1990s, many incentive plans did not work well because they were based solely on quantity—number of accounts opened, number of dollars in new deposits, number of loans made, and so on. Salespeople who were eager to achieve the target amounts set for each sales campaign often overlooked the customer's true needs in their effort to win the cash prize.

Today, a wider range of incentive plans is available, and customer service and customer needs are clearly part of the sales campaign. Banks have successfully motivated employees through rewards ranging from a monthly award posted in the bank's employee newsletter or a plaque on the wall in the lobby, to special recognition luncheons and parties, to a night out on the town or a day off with pay. Fewer banks operate strictly on a cash incentive basis, and that has had a positive effect on sales programs and incentive programs alike.

Monitoring Results

Monitoring results is essential not only in bank sales management and in overall marketing strategy, but also in sales training programs.. Both sales programs and sales training must be monitored to determine their effectiveness. The following paragraphs describe monitoring techniques that can apply to both a sales program and a sales training program. The feedback from monitoring sales programs and training programs shows where additional training and attention are needed to improve effectiveness and efficiency.

As with marketing planning, the bank must know where it wants to go (set the sales and training goals) and be able to determine when it gets there (monitor results). This step, unfortunately, is often overlooked—either because the sales goals or training aims were never clearly defined or because of the difficulty of measuring the training's effectiveness.

Techniques are available to measure the effectiveness of both sales campaigns and training programs. For example, a shopper study can be used to identify sales training needs and to set goals before initiating the training program and then used again at the conclusion of the training program to measure the difference in behavior. Likewise, employee surveys can be used to compare product knowledge before and after training.

Another way to track the effectiveness of a sales training program is to set up or purchase a system for keeping track of cross-sales activity. Under this type of system, the new-accounts personnel maintain records on every customer who comes in to open an account, noting not only what products were sold but also each product the employee attempted to sell. This data can then be computer analyzed, and reports can be generated by branch and by employee. Although this type of sales monitoring may be helpful, putting too much focus on the number of products sold rather than on meeting customer needs is dangerous.

One bank that kept track of its cross-sales statistics reported that, before it instituted a sales training and motivation system, 7 out of every 100 customers opening a new account were sold a second service. Thus the average number of accounts opened per new-account customer was 1.07. One year after starting its training program, the cross-sales ratio had risen to 2.84; the average new-account customer was being sold nearly three services—and in many cases, five and six services were being cross-sold. However, further analysis revealed that in an effort to get cross-sales ratios up, some customer service representatives were encouraging customers to open (with a small minimum balance) savings accounts that they didn't need and to take the bank's ATM card, even though they had no intention of using it. In other words, some of the bank's employees were not practicing customer-focused selling, but were persuading customers to take unwanted products.

Measuring the number of products sold can help keep sales staff aware of their responsibility to sell. However, it is also important for management to stress customer satisfaction and customer profitability and to measure the success of each branch in this area. A program to measure customer satisfaction will remind staff that the focus should always be on the customer, not on sales volume alone.

Evaluating the Sales Effort

After the sales training program is completed, unless there is regular follow-up and reinforcement of sales training, many trainees will fail to use and improve on the skills they have learned. Recognizing this, many banks have created the position of sales manager or added sales management to the responsibilities of branch managers. The sales manager is responsible for setting sales goals, monitoring the performance of the staff, holding sales meetings to reinforce the training, coaching individuals who need additional help with specific skills, and keeping the sales staff motivated.

Rewarding Results of the Sales Effort

Sales training programs are more likely to have lasting results if the bank's trainees are rewarded for putting what they have learned into practice. There are many ways in which this can be done: through the annual performance evaluation, through increased responsibilities and promotions, through recognition, and through an incentive or bonus program.

Annual Performance Evaluation

If the bank has recognized the need for a sales orientation program, employee job descriptions should be rewritten to include the responsibility for selling. If the employee meets the selling goals, the annual performance evaluation should rate his or her sales effectiveness, as well as the other elements of the job. (This, of course, requires that some tracking or measuring system be in place.) Salary increases should also be based in part on the employee's success in meeting his or her sales goals. The knowledge that any pay increase will be related to one's sales and service efforts is an effective motivator, but again, should not be the sole motivator.

Increased Responsibilities and Promotions

Another way to reward employees that is related to the annual review is giving the employee additional responsibilities or authority or promoting the employee to a higher-level job as recognition for his or her accomplishments.

Management and Peer Recognition

Another way to reward results is through recognition. The bank whose sales tracking system was previously described also established a structured program for recognizing employees who performed well in the cross-sales program. The recognition took various forms, including having the employee highlighted in the monthly program newsletter, receiving a note of congratulations from the bank president, being presented with a "winner's cup" mug, having the employee's name added to a wall-mounted plaque along with the names of previous honorees, and being invited to attend a semiannual awards banquet. The program manager concluded that the peer and management recognition was a greater incentive than the sales commissions, which averaged about $40 per employee per month.

Incentives

In banking as in other businesses, an incentive or bonus program can be an effective way to motivate employees to sell and deliver quality service. However, for an incentive plan to work, there must already be high morale throughout the bank.[13] Implementing an incentive plan in an environment where job satisfaction and morale are poor will neither improve morale nor motivate people to sell.

Incentive programs may be long-term or short-term. Short-term programs are often used in conjunction with an advertising campaign to spur sales of a new product. For example, one bank created a nine-week-long baseball theme incentive program to generate new deposits. The program divided employees into four teams, each with its own sales strategy. Each week was counted as an "inning."

There was a midcampaign rally with a prize drawing, and the grand prize for the winning team was to be a night at a baseball game. The program was so successful that the results exceeded the goal by over $1 million, and the bank took *everyone* to the ballgame.[14]

The truism underlying incentive programs is that people will do what they are rewarded for doing. Ironically, this can also be the undoing of an incentive program. To avoid having staff pass off customers who seem to have low potential or leaving out staff members (such as tellers and operations staff) from incentive programs, banks can reward only the desired end result and put team results before individual ones.[15]

Designing a Training Program

For a sales training program to be effective, the following elements should be present:

- *In-depth product descriptions.* There is no substitute for comprehensive, confident product knowledge.
- *Samples of products and services whenever possible.* These can be either brochures or a grid format illustrating which services are most likely to be needed by particular age groups.
- *Related marketing and advertising efforts.* It is key for sales staff to know what the marketing goals are and what the current advertising campaigns are; salespeople can also offer helpful feedback on products and services.
- *Information about target markets.* Learning the characteristics and key needs and desires of different markets is essential to successful sales; however, it is also important not to lose sight of the customer as an individual.
- *Cross-selling opportunities.* Product and target market knowledge will help salespeople quickly and effectively identify important cross-selling opportunities, from opening the first account to selling additional services to a valued customer.

• *Responses to customer objections.* This is often a delicate area and one in which role playing and carefully considered suggested responses can help salespeople defuse volatile situations, or redirect customers to the benefits of the product or service.

• *Approaches to selling specific products or services.* Mutual funds, insurance, and trust and private banking products are all examples of products whose details are important to explain to consumers. These areas require special knowledge and skills on the part of the salesperson. Often customers will not purchase these products until they know they can trust and rely on the salesperson—which is part of the customer communication process detailed below.

• *Employee participation, such as discussion, exercises, case studies, or role play.* All bank employees will learn more if they "try out" and discuss the ideas in a sales training program.

• *Take-away information for future reference.* Core services grids and information on the bank's target markets, marketing goals, and sales objectives are all examples of valuable handouts.

• *Follow-up and reinforcement.* Without these, the information the salesperson learns on the job will quickly fade, and the effectiveness of the training will be seriously diminished.[16]

Training Program Content

The complexity of the selling task will dictate the amount and kind of training needed. For example, an officer calling on corporate accounts needs different training than does a safe deposit attendant. However, most sales trainers would agree that effective salespeople need to be familiar with the following:

• *the customer*—his or her specific situation, needs, and concerns;

• *the bank*—its position, growth, marketing policies, and goals, and reasons why customers should choose it over the competition;

• *the product*—the bank's full product mix, including the advantages, disadvantages, features, and benefits of each product;

• *the competition*—other banks' products and their strengths and weaknesses compared with one's own; and

• *selling skills*—effective techniques for presenting sales messages, principles of communication, listening, handling objections, behavioral skills, and self-development.

Considering this list of requirements, it is apparent that most employees of a bank could benefit from some kind of sales training. The point is that every bank employee whose job includes any selling element should receive appropriate sales training, especially training in product knowledge and sales techniques.

Product Knowledge

The first element, and the foundation of a successful selling program, is *product knowledge.* Individuals involved in direct selling should thoroughly understand all their bank's products and services their customers might need. Product training sessions must go beyond explaining what the service is and how it works operationally to encompass the benefits it provides to the customer and its comparative advantages and disadvantages, as well as an understanding of target markets. They should also touch on competitors' products and services.

Studies have found that when employees are very confident that they know their products, they are much more likely to suggest them to customers. Employees who are less confident in their product knowledge don't want to risk being embarrassed by having to say to the customer "I wasn't aware of that product," or "I don't know how that product works."

The following elements of product knowledge are key for both the employee and the customer:

- *How the product benefits the customer.* Consider the difference between a benefit statement and a features statement. "You can earn monthly income from this certificate, and to save you time, we can put it directly into your checking or money market account each month" is a benefit statement. In contrast, a features statement tells only how the service works without involving the prospective customer: "This certificate comes with automatic crediting of monthly interest."

- *Its advantages compared with other services of the bank and its competitors.* For example, "Our Money Market Checking Account pays interest on checking balances for those who can afford to keep the required balances, but many people who write few checks and prefer to keep a small balance in checking prefer our regular checking account."

- *Its disadvantages compared with competitors' offerings.* For example, "Yes, it's true they require a lower minimum balance on money-market checking accounts; but if you have $1,000 in a regular savings account, that balance can count toward your minimum balance requirement and give you the benefit of a money-market checking account with no service charge. Furthermore, with our account you can pay your bills by phone or have us pay them automatically every month, so you don't have to worry about forgetting to make a loan or mortgage payment."

Many banks develop a product manual or guide listing all the bank's services. Such manuals are usually distributed in looseleaf format so that, as changes are made, the manual can be easily updated. For example, a manual might include the following information for each service it offers:

1. a brief description of the product,
2. a listing of the product's features and how they benefit the customer,
3. the audience for whom the product is intended,
4. the special requirements for purchasing or using this product, such as a minimum deposit or the approval of an officer,
5. other products and services that are natural complements to this product (for cross-selling purposes),
6. who or what area of the bank handles the product, and
7. the location and telephone extension of the person to call for answers to questions about the product.

This does not mean that the new-accounts person needs to be an expert in trust services. He or she should, however, have a basic understanding of the variety of trust services available, be able to recognize a prospective trust customer, and know to whom the customer should be referred for further information.

Executing a Sales Training Program

After determining the training aims and content for each group of trainees, the instructional method that will most effectively and economically achieve the aims of the program must be selected. Training methods can be categorized as (1) group instructional methods—including lectures, seminars, role playing, simulation of banking situations, and games; and (2) individual training—including on-the-job training, personal conferences, correspondence courses, and programmed instruction manuals.[17]

Each of these methods has been widely used in sales training programs. Other methods that have gained popularity because of their flexibility and interactive qualities are on-line classes via the Internet, CD-ROM courses, and intranet training. The approach chosen should depend on the needs of the trainees, the training task, and the number of people to be trained.

Executing the sales training program requires selecting the trainees, finding a location for the instruction (unless on-line training is chosen), developing or purchasing instructional materials and training aids, and answering the all-important question of who will do the training. It may be particularly difficult to schedule training sessions for platform personnel since the absence of even one such employee for a couple of days may impose a hardship on the remaining employees. Training can be conducted either on-site (if sufficient space is available) or off-site. Correspondence courses and automated courses (such as intranet, on-line, and CD-ROM courses) allow employees to take the courses at their convenience—at home, on the road, late at night, early in the morning. In either case, the trainees must be comfortable and free from distractions, such as telephones.

Summary

Personal selling is an important element of the overall marketing of banking services. Because of the intangibility and inseparability of bank services, personal selling is often the only means for selling and delivering them.

Many bank employees have negative images of selling and salespeople. This image can be dispelled if management wholeheartedly supports a sales culture and the selling of bank services is viewed as a form of customer service. That is, it consists of discovering unmet customer needs and meeting them with the appropriate product offerings.

Effective selling helps the bank's profit picture by attracting new and profitable relationships with new and existing customers. It also helps increase productivity and helps maximize the return on the advertising dollars spent to bring customers to the bank or make them aware of the bank and its services.

Selling is becoming more critical as banks face increased competition from all sides. Now banks are implementing sales cultures, hiring sales-oriented staff, and focusing on tying sales goals to customer service for optimum profitability.

There are many important characteristics of successful salespeople-two essential ones are in-depth product knowledge and good listening skills. These, combined with effective selling skills, help the salesperson identify the best products and services for the customer and ask for the customer's business to close the sale while demonstrating sincere interest in meeting the customer's needs.

Sales training must encompass knowledge of the customer, the bank, its products, and the competition, as well as selling skills. Sales training programs should include information on product descriptions, related marketing and advertising efforts, target markets, cross-selling opportunities, responses to customer objections, and approaches to selling specific products or services. Sales training programs should also include samples, take-away information for future reference, employee participation, and follow-up and reinforcement.

In addition, a successful training program must include the setting of sales goals for employees who have been trained, as well as a system for measuring and rewarding results.

In the next chapter, advertising and sales promotion (two additional elements of the promotion strategy) will be discussed. Armed with competitive, need-satisfying services that are profitably priced, professionally sold, and conveniently delivered, the bank must communicate to the target market what it has to offer. That is the goal of a promotion strategy.

Points for Review

1. Describe how the selling of bank services relates to customer service and customer satisfaction.
2. How would you answer someone who claims to know all about marketing because he or she has taken a course in selling?
3. Describe four ways in which selling can directly or indirectly affect a bank's profitability.
4. Explain why personal selling is critical for acquiring and retaining customers, improving productivity, and maximizing return on advertising dollars.

5. Describe at least two traits that are characteristic of many very successful salespeople.

6. What are the five broad topics with which a good salesperson should be familiar?

7. Discuss some advantages and disadvantages of sales incentive programs.

8. Discuss the six elements that contribute to managing the selling process.

Notes

1. *Effective Bank Product Management* (Rolling Meadows, Ill.: BAI, 1988), p. 153.

2. Patrick Kennedy, *Building a Financial Services Marketing Plan* (BMA/Financial Source Books, 1989), p. 3.

3. "Bank Marketing Roundtable," *Banking,* September 1971, p. 21.

4. Peter D. Bennett, editor, *Dictionary of Marketing Terms,* 2nd edition, definition by Barton Weitz (Chicago: American Marketing Association, 1995).

5. *1996 Analysis of Bank Marketing Expenditures* (Washington, D.C.: Bank Marketing Association, 1996).

6. "Sales Strategies from Successful Calling Officers," *Cross Sales Report,* April 10, 1995, pp. 1–2.

7. *1996 Analysis of Bank Marketing Expenditures* (Washington, D.C.: Bank Marketing Association, 1996).

8. For detailed descriptions and explanations of bank selling skills and processes, see *Understanding and Selling Bank Products* (Washington, D.C.: American Bankers Association, 1992); and *Branch Sales: Creating a Plan for the 90s* (Washington, D.C.: American Bankers Association, 1994). This training program deals with the responsibilities and skills needed by a sales manager: running effective sales meetings, coaching the individual salesperson, motivating the sales team, and developing an action plan to accomplish these tasks.

9. *Effective Bank Product Management,* p. 169.

10. See *Branch Sales.* Sales training programs are available in numerous forms. Off-the-shelf programs can be bought from training firms or consultants, consultants can tailor a program specifically for the particular needs of the bank, or the bank's own training department may want to design the program. Similarly, the actual training might be conducted by a consultant, an in-bank trainer, or some combination of the two. The American Bankers Association, through its American Institute of Banking, offers training products and classroom-based instruction in personal selling, and the Bank Marketing Association offers workshops in selling.

11. *Effective Bank Product Management,* p. 169.

12. "High Performance Banking," March 1997, pp. 3–4.

13. Dale A. Arahood, "Are You Ready for A Bonus Plan?" *Bank Marketing,* December 1992, pp. 22–23.

14. "Baseball Contest Adds $6 Million in New Deposits," *Cross Sales Report,* April 1997, pp. 1–2.

15. For a treatment of the components that have contributed to the success of 10 banks that have built effective sales programs, see Leonard L. Berry, Charles M. Futrell, and Michael R. Bowers, *Bankers Who Sell* (Homewood, Ill.: Dow Jones–Irwin, 1985).

16. See *Branch Sales: Creating a Plan for the 90s.*

17. See *Understanding and Selling Bank Products.*

13

PROMOTION STRATEGY: ADVERTISING AND SALES PROMOTION

Learning Objectives

After studying this chapter, you should be able to

- describe the six steps in the communication process and explain where the process most often fails,
- list and describe the four elements of the promotion mix,
- discuss the four factors a marketing manager should consider when determining the optimum promotion mix,
- discuss four methods of setting advertising budgets within the overall marketing budget and note how those resources may be allocated among various media outlets,
- list the four goals of advertising and discuss how specific advertising objectives support those goals,
- describe various ways to execute the advertising message and to measure its effectiveness, and
- discuss various sales promotion options and list the steps involved in developing a promotional campaign.

Introduction

This chapter deals with the last, and arguably the most interesting, element of the marketing mix. It is certainly the most visible element and one to which consumers are exposed every time they pick up a newspaper or magazine, turn on the television or radio, drive along a highway, or enter a store or bank. One company, in its annual report on television, radio, magazine, and newspaper advertisements, estimates the average consumer could be exposed to as many as 254 of these ads each day, of which he or she might notice as many as 146. The company estimates as many as 15 ads a day from any or all of these four sources might capture the consumer's full attention.[1]

Once a bank has developed its product, priced it competitively, and arranged for its distribution to prospective customers, it must inform the target market about its product offering. It must communicate the need-satisfying benefits of the service in order to generate sales and profits. This communication is accomplished through *advertising, sales promotion, public relations,* and *personal selling*—the four elements that constitute the *promotion mix.* This chapter focuses on two of these elements: advertising and sales promotion. Public relations is addressed in chapter 14. Personal selling as an element in the promotion strategy has already been discussed. (See chapter 12.)

The Communication Process

Since communication is the foundation of promotion, it is important to first define communication and look at what takes place during the process of communication before moving on to each of the elements of the promotion mix.

The word *communication* is derived from a Latin word that means "to share," and more fundamentally from the root word *communis,* which means "common."

Communication involves sharing a specific message with a target audience.

Webster's Ninth New Collegiate Dictionary defines communication as a process by which information is exchanged between individuals through a common system of symbols, signs, or behavior. More simply put, communication may also be summarized as "Who . . . says what . . . in what way . . . to whom . . . with what effect."[2] The "who" is the communicator, the "what" is the message, "in what way" refers to the medium, "to whom" is the audience, and "with what effect" refers to the feedback. Effective communication results when there is a common understanding between the communicator and the audience—that is, when what the speaker says and means is precisely what the listener hears and understands.

There are six steps in the communication process (as shown in exhibit 13.1.).[3]

1. The communicator (the source)—for example, the bank doing the advertising—wishes to impart a message.

2. Encoding the message, the idea, or the fact to be communicated to the target audience (receivers) is the next step. Encoding involves changing the message into a format for delivery; that is, an advertisement, a radio spot, or a sales presentation.

3. The message is then transmitted, which can be, for example, via press release, television advertisement, or sales meeting.

4. Decoding the message is the next step, during which the receiver translates behavior, words, symbols, and illustrations into ideas.

5. Receiving the message, or interpreting it in light of his or her own experience and frame of reference, is followed by

6. Feedback, or the response of the audience (or receiver) to the message, which is the last step.

During the process of communication, any number of things may go wrong. Communication experts agree that when communication breaks down, the problem is generally due to lack of commonality be-

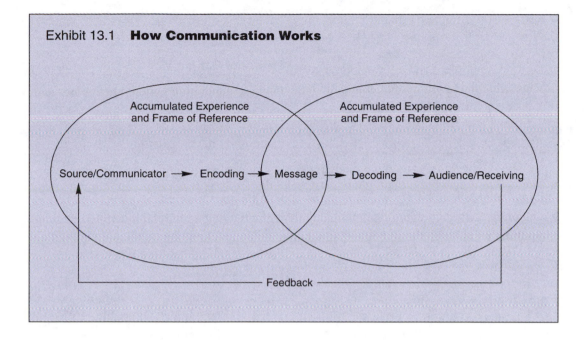

Exhibit 13.1 How Communication Works

Accumulated Experience and Frame of Reference

Accumulated Experience and Frame of Reference

Source/Communicator → Encoding → Message → Decoding → Audience/Receiving

Feedback

tween the communicator's encoding and the audience's decoding. As a result, what the communicator means is not what the audience understands. This problem is depicted in exhibit 13.1 by the overlapping fields of experience of the communicator (the source) and audience (the receiver). If the circles share a large area in common, communication is facilitated. If the circles do not share any area in common, communication becomes impossible or at least highly distorted. Sometimes communication can be clarified by the feedback the communicator receives from the audience. Feedback is an important element in communication. It may take the form of a change in attitude, an increased level of awareness or understanding, the mailing in of a coupon, or the opening of an account. Research can be used to measure feedback.

The Promotion Mix

This section describes each of the four elements (advertising, sales promotion, public relations, and personal selling) in the *promotion mix* and explains the marketing situation in which each element would be particularly useful.

Advertising

The American Marketing Association defines *advertising* as "the placement of announcements and persuasive messages in time or space purchased in any of the mass media by business firms, nonprofit organizations, government agencies and individuals who seek to inform and/or persuade members of a particular target market or audience about their products, services, organizations or ideas."[4]

In other words, the goal of advertising is to inform, influence, and persuade the target market. Advertising messages are created to change awareness levels of target audiences. The word *purchased* differentiates advertising from other forms of mass communication, particularly from public relations, which is obtained free of charge. Paid advertising takes place through a variety of media: print media (magazines and newspapers), broadcast media (radio and television), outdoor and transit advertising, direct marketing, and on-line through the World Wide Web.

Product advertising focuses on selling a specific product or service, such as the Plymouth Voyager or a bank's loan-by-phone service. Institutional advertising focuses on the image of the company or bank. A bank spot showing attractive scenes of places served by a regional bank holding company and featuring the bank's slogan is an institutional ad. Some ads combine product and institutional advertising. An example of this is the television advertising done by GE ("We bring good things to life"), featuring GE's musical jingle and showing multiple cuts of scenes that include GE products.

Sales Promotion

Sales promotion refers to selling activities that cannot be classified in any of the other promotion categories. The American Marketing Association defines it as "the media and nonmedia marketing pressure applied for a predetermined, limited period of time at the level of consumer, retailer, or wholesaler, in order to stimulate trial [encourage consumers to try the product or service], increase consumer demand, or improve product availability."

Some examples of sales promotion activities in banking are point-of-purchase displays, posters, statement inserts or "stuffers," literature racks, premium promotions, employee incentive programs, World Wide Web pages, and seminars for specific customer markets, such as trust, investment, or corporate clients.

Public Relations

Public relations is defined by the Public Relations Society of America (PRSA) as follows: "Public relations helps an organization and its publics adapt mutually to each other."[5] One element of public relations is stimulating demand for a product or awareness of an organization by obtaining favorable commentary about it on radio, television, or some other medium not paid for by the sponsor. In other words, it is free space in the press, which is achieved by packaging the message in a way that is newsworthy so that the media will pick it up. This type of promotion has a relatively high degree of credibility because it is not paid for by the bank. More will be said about public relations in chapter 14.

Personal Selling

Personal selling is a form of communication that takes place face-to-face. To achieve optimum results, the efforts of the sales force must be coordinated with the rest of the bank's communications—its advertising, sales promotion, and publicity. (See chapter 12 for a detailed discussion of personal selling.)

Relative Use of the Promotion Mix Elements

The elements of the promotion mix are, to some extent, interchangeable with one another, yet each promotion tool has advantages in certain situations. One of the questions that bank marketers face (especially at budgeting time) is "Would we increase profits by concentrating more of our efforts and dollars on personal selling and less on advertising? Or should we focus more on internal promotion efforts, or more on public relations?" While there are no hard and fast rules for determining the optimum mix, the marketing manager should consider at least four factors: the communication goal, the type of product or service, the nature of the market, and the product's life cycle stage.

The Communication Goal

All of a bank's communications should be geared toward creating in prospective customers a state of mind conducive to making a purchase. When making a buying decision, the customer passes through successive levels of "the communications spectrum."[6] At the lowest level of this spectrum, a customer becomes aware of the bank or the specific product being sold. An axiom about the importance of *awareness* states, "Share of mind precedes share of market." In other words, before a bank can expect to make a sale, the customer must be aware of what the bank is offering.

Awareness is followed by *comprehension*, when the customer understands something about the bank or the product. The next stage is *conviction,* when the customer thinks, "The next time I switch banks, I'm going there," or "That service would help me save money on a regular basis, and I need that." The final stage is *action,* when the customer actually visits or contacts the bank with the intention of making a purchase. Exhibit 13.2 compares the stages in the buying process and the stages in the communications spectrum and provides examples of some typical promotion messages for each of these stages.

Generally speaking, personal selling becomes more effective and advertising becomes less effective as the consumer passes through the spectrum from awareness to action. Looking specifically at the market for retail banking services, exhibit 13.3 illustrates the relative importance of the different promotion elements. Personal selling increases in importance and advertising diminishes in importance as the customer approaches the buying decision. Public relations is more effective at the time a new product is introduced, when awareness is the communication goal. Sales promotion—point-of-sale posters, brochures, statement inserts—has a relatively constant level of importance.

These four stages closely mirror the four stages discussed in hapter 6 on consumer and organizational buying behavior. Those four stages, as you will recall, are identifying a need, prepurchase activity, purchase decision, and postpurchase feelings.

Exhibit 13.2 **Relating Advertising's Objective to the Consumer Buying Process**

Stage in Buying Process	General Advertising Objectives	Examples
Unsatisfied need	Awareness	"Now open all day Saturday." "Introducing Commonwealth's new rising rate CD." "Got a car loan? Refinance for a lower rate and make it tax deductible."
Prepurchase behavior	Comprehension	"What to do with your money when you don't know what to do with your money." "Here are the benefits you get with our package account."
Purchase decision	Conviction/ action	"Our loan rate is the lowest in town." "Buy a CD. Get a bonus gift." "Applying for a loan anywhere else is just a waste of time."
Postpurchase feelings	Reassurance	"M&T Bank lends more than money." "You can count on us."

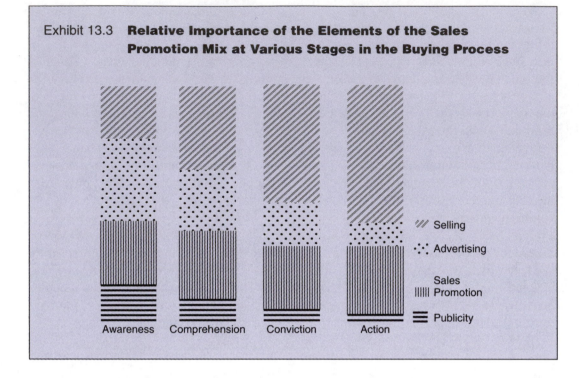

Exhibit 13.3 **Relative Importance of the Elements of the Sales Promotion Mix at Various Stages in the Buying Process**

Awareness Comprehension Conviction Action

Selling
Advertising
Sales Promotion
Publicity

Type of Product or Service

Some bank services require a particular promotion mix because of their specific characteristics. For example, because they are tailored to the needs of the individual customer, trust services call for a greater personal selling effort than most other banking services. The promotion mix for a campaign offering a special high interest rate on a certificate of deposit might include more media advertising and in-branch sales promotion and less public relations and personal selling.

Nature of the Market

Most banks operate in several distinct markets—for example, the consumer banking market, the commercial banking market, the trust market, and the small business market. Each of these markets requires a somewhat different promotion mix. For example, larger corporate customers typically require more personal selling than do small businesses or retail customers.

However, even among retail customers, the level of personal selling will vary depending on the customer and the product being sold. For example, trust services can sometimes take a year or more to sell, while a personal checking account can take less than half an hour. When new retail banking products are introduced, customers generally go to their own bank first to see if the product is being offered. Therefore, internal sales promotion techniques that announce new services to existing customers are very important in capturing and retaining this market.

Product Life Cycle Stage

The effectiveness of the various promotional tools also depends on what life cycle stage the product is in. Advertising, sales promotion, and public relations are especially important in the introduction stage when the principal communication task is to build awareness and comprehension. During the growth stage when sales are increasing, advertising and sales promotion are used to help differentiate the bank's product from its competitors in an effort to attract a larger share of the market.

When a consumer good reaches the maturity stage and sales have leveled off, advertising is generally increased. In retail banking, however, advertising generally stops, and sales promotion and personal selling take over the promotion task. For example, very few banks promote regular personal checking, although information on this service must be available at the point of sale and the customer contact staff should attempt to cross-sell personal checking to new loan and savings customers.

In the decline stage, promotional efforts should be diverted to new growth products or to enhancements in the old product that might help stimulate sales. For example, holiday and vacation savings clubs are in the decline stage, and most banks choose not to spend promotional dollars to generate sales of these noncompetitive products in the face of higher-yielding savings alternatives.

Advertising Expenditures

Billions of dollars are spent on advertising every year in this country, yet a nagging question often lurks in the minds of business executives: "What am I really getting for all those dollars?" Retailer John Wanamaker reputedly expressed this doubt when he said, "I know that about half of my advertising is wasted, but I don't know which half." As a result of this deep-seated doubt, advertising is usually the first to suffer cutbacks when expenses must be curtailed.

Advertising on the World Wide Web can make this doubt even greater. Since the Web is still in its infancy and there is little published information on the success of advertising on the Web or on Web sites as a means of attracting customers, banks must also grapple with deciding whether to spend money on this unproven medium.

Some people praise advertising for being a major contributor to the high standard of living in this country. Others criticize it on the grounds that it creates false aspirations and stimulates demand for unnecessary products and services. In any case, advertising is unquestionably the most widely used promotion tool in the banking industry and is the largest component (half to two-thirds) of most banks' marketing budgets. Therefore, this discussion of advertising starts from the budget perspective.

The Size of the Marketing Budget

The marketing budget for a bank generally includes expenditures for five activities:
1. advertising,
2. sales promotion,
3. marketing research,
4. sales/customer service training, and
5. public relations.

How much should a bank spend on marketing? is a recurring question among both marketers and senior bank management, especially at budgeting time. While there are no rules of thumb, some data indicate that larger banks (banks with assets between $1 billion and $5 billion) spend about $574 per million dollars of assets on marketing. The same report indicates that smaller banks (banks with between $250 million and $500 million in assets) typically spend about $811 per million dollars in assets.[8] These figures are averages, of course, and should not be used to determine what a specific bank should spend in carrying out its marketing objectives. That amount will vary by geographic region, degree of competition, and the aggressiveness of the bank's marketing objectives. They do show, however, that in general larger banks spend a smaller percentage of assets but a greater dollar amount on marketing than do smaller banks.

Advertising's Share of the Marketing Budget

How a bank allocates its total marketing budget among various marketing activities depends largely on bank size. As exhibit 13.4 shows, the largest banks spend more of their total marketing dollars on advertising (60 percent) than do the smallest banks (51 percent). This does not imply that larger banks are less concerned with other marketing activities, such as sales promotion, public relations, or sales training. Rather, it reflects the economies of scale that the larger banks enjoy in buying promotion other than advertising. If a very small community bank allocated only 20 percent of its marketing budget to public relations (as the largest banks do), it probably would not be supporting its community relations activities as much as it should. In contrast, a major money center bank can spend a smaller percentage of its marketing budget on public relations and still meet its community service and public relations goals.

Clearly, advertising is the largest component of the marketing budget for banks of all sizes. Public relations runs a distant second, and sales promotion ranks third.

As seen in exhibit 13.4, banks typically spend between 50 percent and 60 percent of their total marketing budgets on advertising. But how does a bank determine how much it should spend for advertising? Banks use at least four methods to determine what they will spend on marketing in general and on advertising in particular: the percentage method, the competitive parity method, the incremental method, and the objective-and-task method.[9]

Percentage Method

Some banks base their advertising expenditures on the size of their assets or deposits. For example, a bank may decide to spend 1/10th of 1 percent of its total assets, or some percentage of its deposits, on advertising. This percentage method has several flaws. First, it is based on the bank's past performance rather than on objectives for the future. Second, it views assets or deposits as the cause of advertising rather than recognizing that increases in these variables might be, to some extent, the effect of advertising. Third, it discourages aggressive advertising and reduces advertising expenditures in periods of economic slowdown. As mentioned earlier, research indicates that firms that maintain or increase their advertising during periods of recession do better after the recession.

Exhibit 13.4 **How Banks of Various Sizes Allocate Total Marketing Dollars**

Asset size in millions	$100–$250	$500–$1,000	$1,000–$5,000
Advertising	51%	66%	59%
Public relations	26	19	21
Sales promotion	16	8	13
Sales/customer service training	3	2	4
Marketing research	2	2	2
All other	1	2	1

Source: *1996 Analysis of Bank Marketing Expenditures* (Washington, D.C.: Bank Marketing Association, 1996).

Competitive Parity Method

This method might also be called "follow the leader." A bank determines what its competitors are spending on advertising and simply follows their lead. This method is based on the erroneous assumption that the market responds in the same way to the same volume of dollars spent by different banks. It fails to take into account the effects of variations in creativity, different uses of media, the timing of campaigns, and a bank's image and recognition level in its market area. Furthermore, a bank's competitors probably use no more rational a system for determining their advertising expenditures than does the bank that is following their lead.

In another variation of the parity method, some banks base their advertising expenditures on the results of the Bank Marketing Association's annual survey of marketing expenditures by banks throughout the country, which includes breakdowns by size of bank. In addition to the previously cited criticisms, this method disregards the fact that no two markets are identical and that average expenditures may mask wide variations in actual expenditures for banks in a particular size group.

Incremental Method

Using this method, a bank simply increases its advertising budget by a certain percentage each year. The percentage may take into account the rate of inflation or the growth rate of the bank, or it may be dictated by a planner or budgeter whose primary objective is to make the bottom line show a targeted return on assets.

Whatever the percentage increase, this method does not take into account the desired objectives of advertising and the most cost-effective ways to attain them. If the increase is based on the rate of inflation, the bank is making the implicit assumption that achieving its goals will require the same effort year after year. This does not encourage the marketer to question the techniques being used or to take a fresh look at the bank's objectives.

Objective-and-Task Method

Using this method, the bank bases its advertising budget on what it will cost to meet the marketing objectives it has defined. The bank then weighs this cost against the expected net benefit of the new business to ensure that the cost of advertising will not reduce the profit margin on the newly acquired deposits or loans beyond acceptable limits.

For example, assume that a bank's goal is to increase its one-year certificate of deposit volume by $5 million over its expected normal growth during a promotion period. It calculates that the profit margin on those funds will be 2 percent (or $100,000). The bank must then decide how much it is willing to invest in advertising in order to generate an extra $100,000 of income. The selected amount will vary from bank to bank, but it will certainly be less than $100,000.

This method also has its drawbacks. While it works for specific promotions that have immediately measurable results, such as increased deposit or loan volume, it cannot be used to determine the level of advertising necessary to build awareness of the bank and to develop and maintain an image for it. A bank that advertises only when it has a specific promotion to communicate may be out of the media for considerable periods of time. Most marketers agree that some maintenance level of advertising, either product or institutional, is a necessary investment, simply to keep the bank's name in front of its publics.

Despite its drawbacks, the objective-and-task method is the most professional and rational method for arriving at an advertising budget. It may involve more effort than the other methods, but like any planning effort, it helps set the direction and increase the value of the bank's advertising expenditures.

In practice, many banks use a combination of the incremental method and the task method to determine advertising expenditures. The bank determines its advertising budget in the fall using the incremental method. Then, as marketing plans evolve quarter by quarter in response to the bank's changing financial objectives, advertising plans and budgets are developed on a project-by-project basis. If, during the year, it appears that the amount budgeted for advertising is inadequate, management can either approve an overrun or lower its goals.

How Advertising Dollars Are Spent

The major forms of media that carry bank advertising messages are newspapers, radio, television, magazines, direct marketing, and outdoor and transit advertising. Exhibit 13.5 shows the relative advantages and disadvantages of each. Now, as the use of the Internet continues to grow rapidly, banks are creating Web sites that contain everything from the

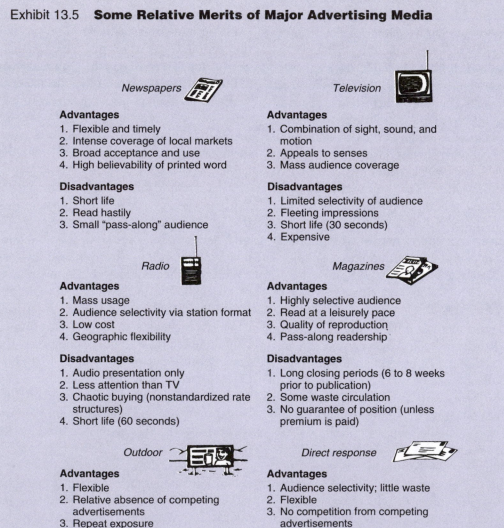

Exhibit 13.5 **Some Relative Merits of Major Advertising Media**

Newspapers

Advantages
1. Flexible and timely
2. Intense coverage of local markets
3. Broad acceptance and use
4. High believability of printed word

Disadvantages
1. Short life
2. Read hastily
3. Small "pass-along" audience

Radio

Advantages
1. Mass usage
2. Audience selectivity via station format
3. Low cost
4. Geographic flexibility

Disadvantages
1. Audio presentation only
2. Less attention than TV
3. Chaotic buying (nonstandardized rate structures)
4. Short life (60 seconds)

Outdoor

Advantages
1. Flexible
2. Relative absence of competing advertisements
3. Repeat exposure
4. Relatively inexpensive
5. Supports other media

Disadvantages
1. Creative limitations
2. Many distractions for viewer
3. Public attack (ecological implications)
4. No selectivty of audience

Television

Advantages
1. Combination of sight, sound, and motion
2. Appeals to senses
3. Mass audience coverage

Disadvantages
1. Limited selectivity of audience
2. Fleeting impressions
3. Short life (30 seconds)
4. Expensive

Magazines

Advantages
1. Highly selective audience
2. Read at a leisurely pace
3. Quality of reproduction
4. Pass-along readership

Disadvantages
1. Long closing periods (6 to 8 weeks prior to publication)
2. Some waste circulation
3. No guarantee of position (unless premium is paid)

Direct response

Advantages
1. Audience selectivity; little waste
2. Flexible
3. No competition from competing advertisements
4. Personalized

Disadvantages
1. Relatively high cost
2. Consumers often pay little attention since they are subject to a great deal of direct mail and telemarketing

history of the bank and a list of employees to interactive credit calculators and direct access to bank accounts. Web sites are now another type of advertising vehicle combined with a distribution vehicle. As a way of reaching out to additional markets and drawing them to the bank's Web site, banks are placing banners with hyperlinks on sites that target markets are most likely to visit. In this way, the bank does not always need to wait for the customer to come to the bank—the bank can include its message in other locations that the customer will visit.

The relative use of these various advertising media varies by bank size and geographic market. Exhibit 13.6 shows how advertising dollars are allocated among the media by banks of various sizes. Community banks spend most heavily for newspaper advertising, followed by radio advertising. Large banks spend proportionately more on television, the most expensive advertising medium. However, cable TV has enabled many community banks to gain access to this important medium as well. Radio is a much less expensive medium than television, and the cost of producing radio commercials is also significantly less than that of producing television spots. Indeed, there is no production cost at all when a radio spot is simply read by an

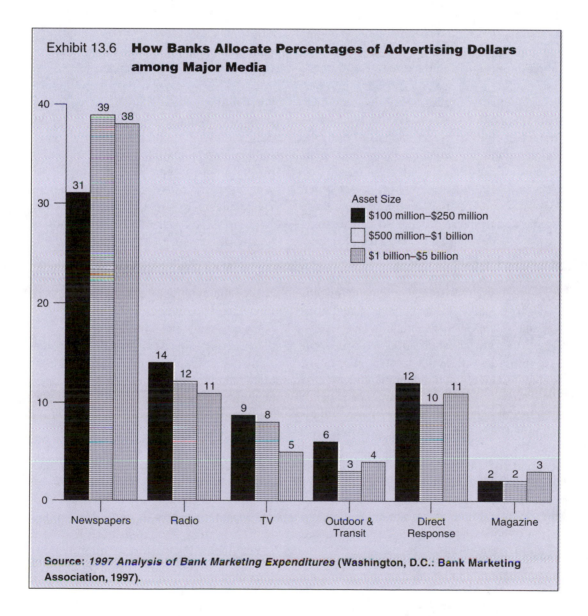

Exhibit 13.6 How Banks Allocate Percentages of Advertising Dollars among Major Media

Asset Size
- $100 million–$250 million
- $500 million–$1 billion
- $1 billion–$5 billion

Media	$100M–$250M	$500M–$1B	$1B–$5B
Newspapers	31	39	38
Radio	14	12	11
TV	9	8	5
Outdoor & Transit	6	3	4
Direct Response	12	10	11
Magazine	2	2	3

Source: *1997 Analysis of Bank Marketing Expenditures* (Washington, D.C.: Bank Marketing Association, 1997).

announcer. This may not be the most effective way to communicate the bank's message, however.

Magazines are of about equal importance in the promotional mix of large and small banks. Since different magazines have very different audiences, magazine advertising can be used to target specific market segments. A bank can buy space in such national magazines as *Time, Newsweek,* and *Sports Illustrated* on a regional basis, enabling it to reach its own trade area.

Direct response marketing is used heavily because it is a very efficient way to reach specific target markets. Direct response consists primarily of direct mail and telemarketing. A bank can purchase or develop lists of residents in targeted income areas, persons who are likely to have the same economic and demographic characteristics as the target market for a specific product, persons who have automobiles or houses more than two years old, and so on. The bank may also obtain from its own records lists of borrowers with only a few payments remaining on a loan, or lists of customers with only one account who might be prospects for other bank services. By combining outside sources with internal database information, banks can develop highly targeted prospects for particular bank promotions.

Through direct mail and telephone contact, used either separately or in combination, banks can market to such prospects and even extend beyond their geographic trade area to market services that do not require physical proximity to the bank. For example, many banks use direct mail advertising to expand their credit card business beyond state lines.

Outdoor and transit advertising can be an effective medium, especially when used in support of advertising in other media. Because of the speed at which people pass billboards and the confined space available, the message must be brief and clear. A rule of thumb is that an outdoor message should contain no more than 11 words, including the name of the bank.

Another very important element of the advertising budget that is not shown in exhibit 13.6 are the fees and commissions paid in connection with the design and development of advertising. These expenses can account for about 13 percent of the advertising budget for smaller banks and up to 20 percent of the advertising budget for larger banks. This includes fees paid to advertising agencies, artists, photographers, typesetters, talent, sound mixers, film and tape editors, production staff, and others involved in the process of producing print, radio, television, and other types of advertising.

The Goals of Advertising

There are four general advertising goals for all financial institutions:[10]

1. to stimulate increased awareness and use of profitable products and services;
2. to achieve a diversified financial base by attracting a steady influx of new customers, including small businesses, corporations of all sizes, and individuals;
3. to promote special events (such as the opening of a new branch); and
4. to promote a favorable public reaction to the bank and to issues affecting the bank.

Specific goals must be set when initiating any advertising campaign, especially when large amounts are to be spent. These goals should support the overall marketing goals of the bank. A specific goal might be to increase deposits or loan sales.

Advertising alone cannot take full credit for increasing sales. If customer service representatives are not prepared for a surge in customers, for example, the advertising campaign will not be as effective. Without CSRs standing ready to answer questions and quickly fill out forms, many sales stand to be lost.

The number of customers opening accounts of various types is very much affected by other elements of the marketing mix and the promotion mix. The product itself, the pricing, the distribution system, the personal selling effort, public relations, the sales promotion devices, and the advertising—all contribute to closing a sale.

Advertising goals should relate to factors that are affected only by advertising. For example, a broad bank-wide marketing goal might be to achieve a 15 percent increase in commercial loan volume. The related advertising goal might be to increase awareness of the bank's commercial loan program among financial executives of corporations located in the bank's trade area. A supporting objective might be to increase advertising in publications targeted to chief executives. The tactics used might be to create a series of full-page, four-color ads that are placed four months in a row.

Advertising goals should relate to one or more of the stages in the buying process. They should be stated in terms of increasing the proportion of the target market

- who are *aware* of the bank, its product, or the idea the bank seeks to communicate;
- who understand (that is, *comprehend*) the message or the benefit to them of using the bank or the service;
- who say they would consider (that is, have formed a *conviction* about) using the bank or the service; or
- who take some *action* related to the bank or the service (for example, watch a demonstration of an automated teller, come into the bank for a free piece of informative literature, or send back a coupon from an ad).

Since bank advertising is most effective in the awareness and comprehension stages, most bank ads fall into those two categories. For instance, the Bank of Boston ad (see exhibit 13.7) is aimed at making readers aware that the bank is offering a six-month no-penalty CD and having them conclude that this is a good investment alternative in an uncertain rate environment. Note that this and most other effective ads include a call to action, such as "stop by your local branch" or "call this number now."

The Key Bank home equity credit ad (see exhibit 2.5) is aimed at both comprehension and action. It provides a clip-out coupon and a toll-free telephone number to make it easy for people to request more information and to generate leads. This is an example of direct response advertising. The Florida First Federal ad (see exhibit 13.8) is designed to build conviction—that is, to convince people that its Club 50 package is better than its competitors' packages.

Executing the Advertising Message

An infinite variety of methods can be used to creatively execute any one advertising message. The task of an advertising agency's creative staff is to develop the style, tone, wording, and format that will produce the maximum effect.[11] However, the ad should not get in the way of the message—which is to communicate to the intended audience the benefit provided by the product or service.

Style

Some of the methods commonly used to communicate a message through advertising follow:

1. *Slice-of-life* or *case history*. This approach shows people enjoying the benefits of the service in a normal setting. Exhibit 13.9 highlights a financial goal that many families have.

2. *Lifestyle*. This type of advertising illustrates how the service fits in with a particular lifestyle. For example, a businessperson on a business trip can log in via her laptop computer to check her accounts and investments.

3. *Fantasy*. This type of ad creates a fantasy about what might happen in connection with the use of the bank's service. Fragrance marketers are notorious for using fantasy in their television advertising. Ralph Lauren's Safari offers "A world without boundaries. A personal adventure and a way of life." Bankers use fantasy when they show people dreaming about what they will buy with the proceeds of their home equity loan.

4. *Mood or image*. This ad style builds an evocative mood or image around the product or the bank—for example, happiness, security, tradition, leadership, or accep-

Exhibit 13.7

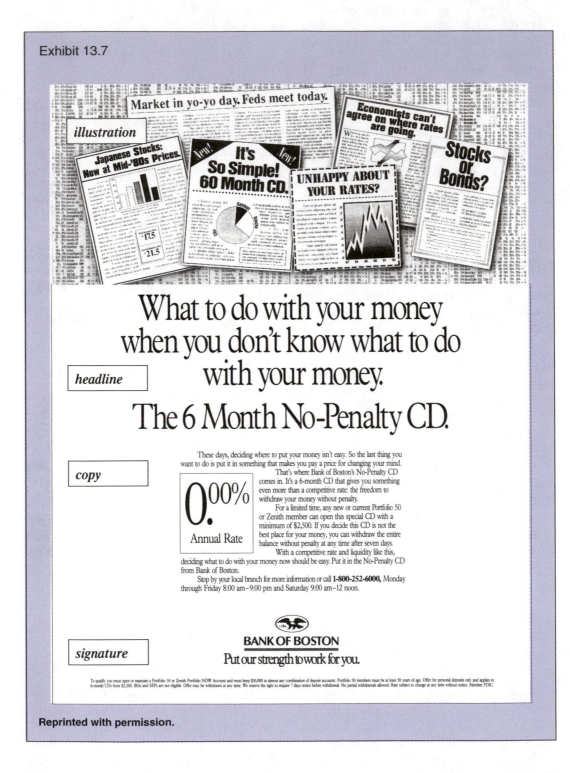

illustration

Market in yo-yo day. Feds meet today.

Economists can't agree on where rates are going.

Japanese Stocks: Now at Mid-'80s Prices.

It's So Simple! 60 Month CD.

UNHAPPY ABOUT YOUR RATES?

Stocks or Bonds?

What to do with your money when you don't know what to do with your money.
The 6 Month No-Penalty CD.

headline

copy

These days, deciding where to put your money isn't easy. So the last thing you want to do is put it in something that makes you pay a price for changing your mind.

That's where Bank of Boston's No-Penalty CD comes in. It's a 6-month CD that gives you something even more than a competitive rate: the freedom to withdraw your money without penalty.

For a limited time, any new or current Portfolio 50 or Zenith member can open this special CD with a minimum of $2,500. If you decide this CD is not the best place for your money, you can withdraw the entire balance without penalty at any time after seven days.

With a competitive rate and liquidity like this, deciding what to do with your money now should be easy. Put it in the No-Penalty CD from Bank of Boston.

Stop by your local branch for more information or call **1-800-252-6000,** Monday through Friday 8:00 am–9:00 pm and Saturday 9:00 am–12 noon.

0.⁰⁰% Annual Rate

BANK OF BOSTON
Put our strength to work for you.

signature

To qualify you must open or maintain a Portfolio 50 or Zenith Portfolio NOW Account and must keep $10,000 in almost any combination of deposit accounts. Portfolio 50 members must be at least 50 years of age. Offer for personal deposits only and applies to 6-month CDs from $2,500. IRAs and SEPs are not eligible. Offer may be withdrawn at any time. We reserve the right to require 7 days notice before withdrawal. No partial withdrawals allowed. Rate subject to change at any time without notice. Member FDIC.

Reprinted with permission.

This advertisement illustrates the four elements of a print advertisement: illustration, headline, copy, and signature. There is also a call to action in the copy.

tance. Much institutional (that is, nonproduct) advertising by banks uses this style.

5. *Musical.* This type of ad is used in radio or television advertising and involves one or more persons singing a jingle about the bank. Some consumer products, such as Dr. Pepper, use television commercials that are full-scale song-and-dance productions.

Exhibit 13.8

The Do-It-Yourself 50 And Over Bank Package Comparison Chart

Theirs	Ours
1.	1. Free Checking With Interest with a rate that increases as your balance increases.
2.	2. Free personalized Club 50 checks. All cancelled checks are returned to you.
3.	3. Free $100,000 common carrier coverage and $5,000 accidental death insurance.
4.	4. A discount of 25% on all safe deposit boxes (subject to availability).
5.	5. No service fee on travelers checks.
6.	6. Free notary service.
7.	7. Free cash advances at over 10,000 locations nationwide.
8.	8. Free direct deposit of government checks.
	9. Free overdraft protection.
	10. Free automated teller machine card.
	11. Savings on eyewear.
	12. Savings on prescriptions and other pharmacy needs.
	13. Cash bonuses on lodging, airline tickets, rental cars and more.
	14. 90-day purchase replacement on merchandise.
	15. Extended warranties on merchandise.

Most seniors packages offered by banks are pretty much the same. But at Florida First Federal we've always tried to offer our customers financial services that were better than the competition's. So when we were putting together our package, we looked at what the others were doing and figured out how we could offer one that was a whole lot better.

We think our Club 50 package is so good that we invite you to compare it with that of any other bank around.

And we even have an enhanced version of our package that we call Club 50 Plus. With Club 50 Plus you get all of the benefits listed above PLUS discounts on automobile maintenance and repairs nationwide PLUS cash rebates on meals at restaurants all over the country. (With Club 50 Plus there is a $5 monthly fee, but you'll save far more than that with the savings.)

If you're 50 or older and don't have a seniors account, or if you have one with another bank, take a few minutes to find out more about Club 50 and Club 50 Plus. It will be time very well spent.

FLORIDA FIRST FEDERAL SAVINGS BANK

Spring Hill Office–Mariner Square
Corner of State Route 50 and Mariner Boulevard, 596-9401. Member FDIC.

Reprinted with permission.

---

6. *Personality symbol.* This type of ad creates a character that represents or personifies the advertiser. For instance, Tony the Tiger has long been the symbol for Kellogg's Frosted Flakes.

7. *Technical expertise.* This approach features the care that the bank exercises and the experience of its personnel. For example, an ad showing the bank's president and international banking officer getting off a plane in the Orient is aimed at creating an impression of expertise.

This comparison chart helps build the conviction that this bank's club is better than its competitors'.

Exhibit 13.9

Get The "Home Field" Advantage

With An Affordable Neighborhood Advantage® Home Loan From BofA.

If you think the dream of owning your own home is out of reach, think again.

Bank of America brings you Neighborhood Advantage home loans, a program designed to make homeownership more affordable in every city and county throughout California.*

You can qualify with <u>30% less income</u> than you normally need with standard home loans. Or, choose to make a down payment as low as 5%. We also offer more flexible refinancing options.

To get more information about the affordable advantage, contact your real estate professional or visit your local Bank of America branch.

BANKING ON AMERICA.

Bank of America

Reprinted with permission.

8. *Scientific evidence.* This style presents survey or scientific evidence that the bank or its services perform better than the competition. For example, an ad could show that a bank's earnings on its trust assets outperformed the Dow Jones Industrial Average over a period of years.

9. *Testimonial evidence.* This style of ad features a highly credible or likable source endorsing the bank or the service. For example, a sports or entertainment star could be used as the spokesperson for the bank, or a locally recognized businessperson could be shown stating how the bank has helped his or her firm.

Tone

The tone of an ad must also contribute to the effective communication of the message. Humor can be very effective. The bank in exhibit 13.10 used humor to let its market know that individuals can borrow money to make their wildest dreams come true. However, humor, especially on radio and television, can be so effective that it detracts from the message. Some banks use a consistently positive, upbeat tone; others use a defiant tone; some are very conservative; others portray themselves as playful and fun loving. Other banks have adopted a helpful tone using a consumer-oriented approach.

Format

Format and layout elements, such as ad size, shape, color, and illustration, also affect the ad's impact. Generally speaking, the larger the ad, the more attention it receives, although the increase in attention may not be proportional to the increase in production and media space costs. Similarly, the use of color, especially in a black-and-white medium (for example, a newspaper), increases an ad's chances of being seen and read. Again, the use of color also substantially increases the cost of producing and placing a print ad.

This slice-of-life ad promotes a special affordable mortgage loan.

Occasional departures from the usual ad size and shape can be very effective, especially when promoting a parity product (that is, a service that every other bank is promoting). The ad might be long and narrow or four inches high, running across the bottom of a one-page or a two-page spread.

Print advertisements have four basic elements: headline, illustration, copy (that is, wording), and signature (the firm's logo). They are highlighted in exhibit 13.7.

Headlines

There are seven basic types of headlines:

1. *News.* "The cost of managing your money is about to go up." "Now your money can work even longer hours than you do." "Introducing First Interstate Bank."

2. *Question.* "Need a home improvement loan?" "What would you say if somebody asked how your bank performs?" "Are you living on a gold mine?" "Is your bank holding you up?"

3. *Narrative.* "Back in 1952, my biggest savings problem was keeping my piggy bank hidden from my brother." "I may never need it. But I sleep better knowing I have a line of credit."

4. *Command.* "If you have a certificate maturing, read this message." "Keep your money where it belongs."

5. *1-2-3 Ways.* "Two ways to earn the highest yield in town on short-term certificates." "135 ways to pay your bills without leaving home."

6. *How-What-Where-When-Why.* "How to start a car" (automobile loan ad). "Where to go when you run out of cash before you run out of holiday." "Why Morgan is a good bank for art and antique dealers." "What to do with your money when you don't know what to do with your money."

7. *Statement.* The majority of headlines for bank ads fall loosely into this category in that they consist of a statement about the bank that cannot properly be called news and that does not fit in any of the other categories either. Many bank ads of this type are not very interesting or very effective.

Exhibit 13.10

If you want it, odds are we'll lend the money.

Who says you can only borrow money for necessities?

Not Magnolia. The way we see it, if something will make your life more enjoyable, we'll do all we can to help you get it. So if you have your heart set on something, give us a call.

Because making your life better is what we do best.

MAGNOLIA FEDERAL BANK FOR SAVINGS

An Equal Opportunity Lender/FDIC Insured

Reprinted with permission.

Illustration

The second major component of a print advertisement is the illustration, or more broadly, the ad's graphic design. A single bold illustration can be very compelling, even when printed in black and white. Consider, for example, exhibit 13.11. A striking image (exhibit 13.12) or a photo taken from an unusual perspective may also be an effective attention-getter.

Exhibit 13.11

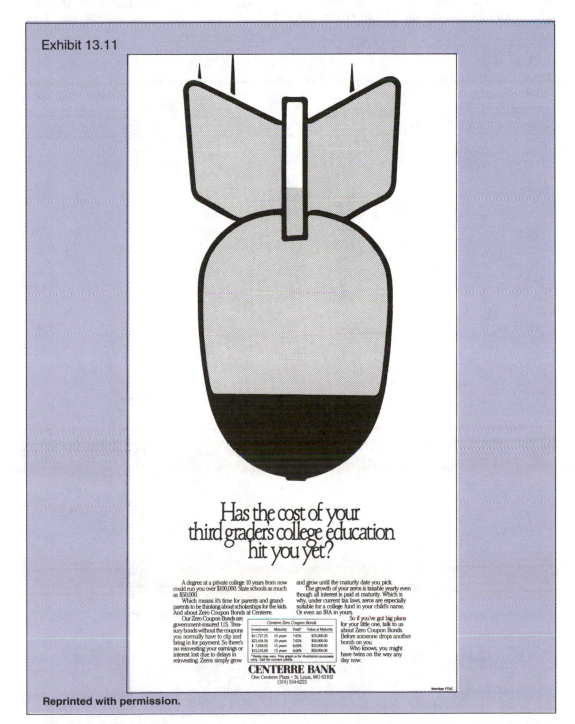

Reprinted with permission.

The single bold illustration in this ad is an attention getter and leads the reader's eye directly to the headline question. (above)

This ad uses humor to make its point. (left)

Exhibit 13.12

THE HUMAN TOUCH

Take your sky-high home-secured loan payment in a different direction.

With the prime rate at its lowest in decades, you're being taken for a ride if you still haven't refinanced the high-interest home-secured loan you took out several years ago.

At Chemical, it costs virtually nothing to refinance. In fact, with some of our home-secured loans, you won't pay a cent in closing costs or refinancing fees.*

Chemical's low-cost, easy refinancing.

Best of all, we make it so easy. Just apply by phone and, in most cases, you'll get a credit decision within 72 hours. Chemical even helps you make the arrangements with your current lender.

So refinance with Chemical right now, and get your payments down to earth. To apply today, just drop by your nearest Chemical Bank, or call our Refinancing Specialists at:

1-800-CHEMBANK, ext. 5500.

CHEMICAL

THE FINANCIAL EDGE

All loans are subject to credit and property approval and are secured by a mortgage on your home. *Some rate options and loan amounts will incur closing costs or refinancing fees. ©1992 Chemical Bank. Member FDIC.

EQUAL HOUSING LENDER

Reprinted with permission.

Copy

An advertisement's copy must be attention-getting and memorable. Headlines especially must compel the reader to read further. The benefit to the customer should be clear from the headline. Too many bank ads leave the reader feeling "So what?" For example, an ad that states, "Bank XYZ announces Flexi-fund," gives no clue that there is any benefit to be derived from the product or service, and gives the reader no reason to pause and decide to read further.

There is no hard and fast rule about how much information or content to put in an ad. Ads that are mostly white space can be very arresting, but ads containing a great deal of information may be called for when the bank's goal is to increase comprehension of a difficult or misunderstood subject. (See exhibit 2.5.)

Signature

The ad's signature identifies the advertiser. Very often, it includes a graphically designed logo, which is a trademarked symbol of the institution, and the tag line or slogan used by the advertiser. (See exhibit 13.7.)

Measuring Advertising's Effectiveness

One reason that bank advertising expenses are so vulnerable in times of economic uncertainty is that bank marketers seldom do a good job of measuring the effectiveness of their advertising efforts. Ideally, an evaluation of the effectiveness of the bank's advertising should be an ongoing process, with research being done in waves over time (that is, doing the same basic study every few months). This kind of research, called *advertising tracking,* is necessary because bringing about a change in consumer attitudes or opinions is a slow process, and it takes time to see substantial results. If marketers cannot make a strong argument for the value of their

A strong image in an ad helps it stand out from the clutter on a newspaper page and sets up the ad's messages.

advertising, they have difficulty justifying the expense. Banks often claim to be conducting advertising research studies, but unless they are tracking the communication effect against predetermined goals, they are not doing a thorough job.

The effectiveness of advertising must be measured against the bank's communication goals, such as the following:

- Increase unaided awareness of the bank's name from 10 percent to 25 percent among individuals 25 and older who live in the three-county area.
- Increase the proportion of the target market who link our bank with the slogan "One day we'll be your bank."
- Among presidents and chief financial officers of firms with less than $10 million in sales, increase the proportion who name our bank as a provider of cash management services.
- Increase the proportion of the target market who name our bank as the bank they would go to if they had to change banks.

Case E presents a study of a bank holding company's positioning campaign. The campaign's goal was to communicate to consumers and financial decision makers in middle market firms specific messages about the bank. The bank conducted research among both these target markets before the campaign began and after its kickoff. The follow-up tests showed a marked increase in awareness of the bank and of those points that were specifically addressed by the advertising. If this campaign's effectiveness in its first four months had been judged on the basis of increased volume of commercial loans, it might have been deemed a failure. But the purpose of the campaign was to create an awareness and an image so that the commercial target market would be more receptive to the sales efforts of the calling officers. As the McGraw-Hill ad in chapter 12 (exhibit 12.1) demonstrates so well, a great deal of communication with prospective customers is often necessary before the salesperson will be well received.

Advertising Research

Not all advertising research concerns itself with setting objectives and measuring the progress toward meeting these objectives. In addition to advertising tracking, there are three other types of advertising research: ad pretesting, audience research (also called ad posttesting), and media research. These tools help the advertiser design advertising and select media to maximize audience attention, interest, impact, and retention.[12]

In *pretesting,* the interviewer shows the proposed ad to members of the target audience before the campaign is run in order to evaluate audience reaction. Ads representing alternative ways of executing the same basic message may be compared with one another. For example, one bank wanted to convey itself as the bank that gives truly personalized service. One of the ads proposed by the agency showed a mass of heads without faces with the headline, "The end of faceless banking." This ad was the favorite of the bank's management, but pretesting revealed that a significant proportion of the people who saw the ad were repulsed by it; they found it eerie and unpleasant.

Audience research surveys people who were exposed to the media (radio, TV, newspaper, or magazine) at the time the ad was running to measure their recollection of the ad without being prompted. In recognition testing (also called posttesting), the bank surveys readers or viewers, showing or describing to them various ads run in a specific magazine or during a specific time segment on television, and asks them to identify what they recognize seeing or reading and to what extent they paid attention to it.

Advertising pretesting and posttesting are useful for measuring whether an ad is understood and for determining its attention-getting quality, but they do not address the extent to which the ad might affect consumer attitudes or behavior, which is the ultimate goal of advertising.

Media research analyzes the size and characteristics of the audience reached by a particular medium. Advertising agencies provide this information to help clients select the most efficient and cost-effective ways to reach a particular target market.

The Advertising Agency

An *advertising agency* specializes in creating marketing and advertising strategies and tactics. Advertising agencies provide creative talent in the form of artists and copywriters to help the bank put its message into words, pictures, or music. They also conduct advertising and media research, select media, place ads in the media, and provide other services, such as the development of promotional materials.

The term *advertising agency* is really a misnomer because a good agency helps the bank with its entire marketing program. During marketing planning and strategy sessions, agency staff can help the bank look at itself more objectively and generate creative approaches to solving old and new problems. A good agency will also want to help the bank set measurable objectives. The agency/client relationship is sometimes likened to a marriage; it is a highly privileged, confidential relationship. For the relationship to be effective, the agency must be considered a partner and must be given access to privileged information, such as the bank's performance figures.

The major source of income for an advertising agency is generally the commission paid to it by advertising media. A newspaper, for example, may quote a price of $1,000 gross, or $850 net of agency commission. The agency will pay the newspaper $850, but will charge the bank the full $1,000. Thus, the agency will have earned a 15 percent commission. Agencies also can earn a percentage of the cost of printing. An alternative arrangement is for the bank to pay the agency a fixed fee (or retainer) that covers both the creative talent used and the services of agency staff (for example, the account supervisor, the account executive, and secretarial help). Or the bank and the agency can agree to some combination of fees and commissions.

Whatever the method of compensation, the advertiser is paying for the time the agency spends on the account. To reap the most value for its dollars, the bank must set clear, measurable objectives for each ad and for each campaign. The bank should identify its target audience, indicate what communication goal it wants the ad to accomplish, and set an expenditure cap. Without such guidelines, an agency can waste a great deal of time.

Bank Advertising Regulation

Over the years, federal and state banking regulators have issued rules that make false, misleading, or deceptive advertising by banks illegal. In addition, the banking industry has itself established advertising guidelines. The Bank Marketing Association publishes the Federal Advertising and Law Guide, which is updated whenever changes occur or new legislation or regulations take effect. The American Bankers Association's Statement of Principles on Financial Advertising includes the following guidelines for ethical advertising:

> An advertisement is ethical: (1) when it is truthful; and (2) when the intended audience can reasonably be expected to understand the message. Because of media physical limitations, it is not necessary for an advertisement to contain all the details about a service. However, any feature, any terms (including prices), or any purchaser benefits should be presented in a manner that does not mislead. The purchaser should not be misled by what is stated nor have false impressions created by what is omitted.

Because a number of banks failed to follow these guidelines, consumer interest groups pushed for and obtained new legislation that would mandate truthful and understandable advertising. Congress passed the Truth-in-Savings Act, and Regulation DD was handed down by the Federal Reserve Board to implement the act in 1993. Among other things, this regulation states when and how the word *free* may be used as it pertains to accounts. It requires that if any deposit rate or yield is stated, it must be stated as the *annual percentage yield* (APY), using that term. The term *interest rate* may also be used, but this rate may not appear more prominently than the APY. The objective of this regulation, which consists of hundreds of pages, is to provide uniform disclosures to enable consumers to compare accounts.

The Federal Reserve's Regulation Z governs the advertising of credit services. Under this regulation, if certain terms are used in a loan ad, the advertiser must provide further explanation. For example, if the ad says, "20 percent down payment," then it must also state the repayment terms and the annual percentage rate. If the loan being advertised relates in any way to housing (for example, mortgages or home equity loans), the ad must include the equal housing lender logo. Exhibit 2.5 is an example of an ad that complies with Regulation Z by including this logo and multiple disclosures in footnotes.

The Community Reinvestment Act (CRA) is another federal law with implications for bank advertising. It requires banks to identify the financial service needs of low- and moderate-income members of the community, to design programs for them, and to inform the target market of their availability. Advertising is an important way of communicating the availability of such programs. During CRA examinations, bank examiners look for documentation that the bank has aimed product-specific advertising at the low- to moderate-income segment.

Bank marketers must keep current on regulations affecting bank advertising since failure to comply can result in the imposition of fines. Moreover, failure to comply with the CRA can result in a bank or bank holding company being denied the right to merge or acquire banks or open new branches.

Sales Promotion

Another important element in a bank's promotion mix is sales promotion. It includes any communications that do not fit into the categories of advertising, public relations, and personal selling. Some examples of sales promotion devices from consumer goods industries are cents-off coupons and offers of merchandise at low cost with a proof-of-purchase. Some of the more frequently used sales promotion tools in banking are point-of-purchase merchandising, incentives, seminars, specialties, contests, and premiums.

Point-of-Purchase Merchandising

A bank's primary audience for new and existing services is its existing customers. The bank has a chance to communicate with this group every time customers come in to conduct a transaction. Furthermore, if the competition is advertising a new or different service, most interested customers will inquire whether their bank offers the same service before going to the competition.

Banks can communicate effectively with their existing customers through posters, counter cards, teller handouts, and literature attractively displayed in the lobby of the bank. This type of promotional material (called *collateral material*) is also useful when communicating with prospective new customers who come into the bank looking for information. Many people feel more comfortable picking up information about the bank's services before approaching a bank employee sitting at a desk.

A number of large banks have developed catalogs to promote their services. This enables people to shop for bank services from home and to bank by phone. For example, one New England banking company put together a 49-page catalog that includes details on all its products and services, any of which may be ordered by calling a toll-free number. The catalogs were mailed to current and prospective customers and were promoted through television and print advertising.

Another way banks are making it possible for customers to shop at home for bank products and services is through their Web sites. A well-planned and creatively executed Web site can be an engaging and informative vehicle for consumers to gather information on the bank and its services.

Web sites also allow customers to search for information at their convenience and in the privacy of their own homes.

Within the branch, effectively worded signs, displays, and other merchandising techniques can be used to support media advertising and to increase sales. Some banks that have tested the effectiveness of coordinated point-of-purchase displays have reported sales at the test branches to be 15 percent to 20 percent higher than at their other branches.

When a customer or prospective customer is in the stage of the buying process in which he or she is comparing various offerings and looking for information, promotional materials and literature can play an important role.

Incentives

Some banks use incentives to motivate employees to cross-sell the bank's products or to bring in business for the bank (see chapter 12). If properly planned and conducted, and if backed by a commitment from senior management, incentive programs can be highly successful.

Seminars

Seminars are an excellent way to target a specific market. For example, some banks sponsor fraud prevention seminars for merchants, economic forecasting seminars for larger businesses, estate planning seminars for senior citizens, and trust seminars for attorneys and accountants (who are excellent sources of referral business). By using seminars as a promotional tool, the bank communicates its expertise to a specific audience and, through follow-up contact, can generate new business.

Specialties

Specialties are the giveaways that banks and other merchants provide to their customers—for example, key rings, pens, calendars, and paperweights that bear the bank's name or logo. These mementos serve as an ongoing reminder of the bank and its services.

Contests

Contests and sweepstakes are used as traffic builders to get people into the bank. They are especially effective when an automated teller is being installed or a new product is being introduced. A bank might, for example, offer a sweepstakes in which everyone who participates in a demonstration of the ATM or comes in and picks up an informative brochure with an entry blank becomes eligible to enter the drawing for a monetary prize or a trip. Building traffic is not an end in itself, however. The bank *staff* must be trained to treat each individual who comes into the bank in response to the contest as a prospective customer.

Premiums

A *premium* is cash or merchandise that the bank gives or sells at a discount to a customer in return for a deposit or loan. A deposit premium, for example, may be given either in addition to or in place of the payment of interest. For years, banks and thrift institutions were leading users of premiums because premiums were a way of providing the customer with added value while financial institutions were forced to compete in a tightly regulated environment. Now that interest rates are deregulated and banks can compete on the basis of rate, premiums have become much less popular. Nevertheless, banks still use cash bonuses and premiums from time to time. (See exhibit 13.13.)

The Promotional Campaign

When a bank has a challenging product-marketing objective, it may use a promotional campaign to do the job. A *campaign* is a coordinated series of promotional tactics, all having a central theme and designed to reach a specific goal. The theme of the campaign should permeate all the bank's internal and external communications.

Six steps are involved in developing a promotional campaign:

1. *Setting objectives.* Every campaign should have a goal that is stated in measur-able terms (for example, to generate $5 million in retail savings and time deposits).

2. *Selecting the media.* Once the target audience has been identified, published media research can help determine the most effective ways to reach this market, whether through television, selected newspapers, magazines, radio, or outdoor advertising.

3. *Creating the advertising.* The next challenge is to develop the theme of the campaign and a method of executing the theme that will break through the clutter of competing advertising.

4. *Developing the sales promotion materials.* Media advertising alone cannot do the entire communication job. Literature explaining the offer must be available, and point-of-sale posters or counter cards should be used to arouse customer awareness and curiosity.

5. *Marketing to the staff.* The most important element in the success of any promotional campaign is the support of the bank's staff. They must understand what is being done, why it is being done, and what their role is in helping the bank reach its goals. The enthusiasm of the bank's employees can help ensure the success of a promotion; conversely, their lack of cooperation may diminish its effectiveness.

6. *Measuring results.* One of the surest ways to negate the possibility of future promotions is to fail to demonstrate the effectiveness of a sales promotion campaign. If the goals are clear and measurable, and if procedures are in place for collecting the necessary data, this very critical step can be relatively simple.

Summary

The purpose of a bank's promotion strategy is to communicate to the target market the bank's need-satisfying services. That communication takes place through the four elements of the promotion mix: advertising, sales promotion, public relations, and personal selling.

A simple way to sum up the communication process is "Who . . . says what . . . in

Exhibit 13.13

Reprinted with permission, American National Corporation, Omaha, Nebraska.

This ad highlights the premiums the bank is offering as a sales promotion.

what way . . . to whom . . . with what effect." Communication is most effective when the communicator (the bank) encodes its message in symbols that are interpreted by the receiver (the target audience) in precisely the way the sender meant them to be understood.

The goal of a bank's communication efforts is to move the target audience through the communication spectrum from unawareness (of the bank or its products) to awareness, to comprehension, to conviction, and, ultimately, to the desired action (for example, the opening of a new account). The various elements of the promotion mix have varying degrees of effectiveness at each stage in the communication spectrum. For example, advertising is most effective for building awareness and comprehension (during need identification), while personal selling is more effective during the prepurchase and purchase phases for developing conviction and obtaining action. Which element of the promotion mix will be most effective also depends on the type of product being promoted, the nature of the market, and the life cycle stage of the product.

Advertising is paid mass communication that takes place through print, broadcast, and other media. The largest proportion of a bank's marketing dollars is spent on advertising, with newspapers the medium most frequently used by banks. Radio, television, newspaper, magazine, direct mail, and outdoor advertising all have strengths and weaknesses. An advertising agency can help a bank determine the best media mix for reaching its target audience in a cost-effective way.

A bank should set specific, measurable goals for its advertising program that correspond to and support, but are different from, its marketing goals. The goals for bank advertising should relate to a specific communication goal, such as "to increase awareness by 30 percent." This type of goal setting requires the use of marketing research before, during, and after the advertising program.

Media research and advertising pretesting enable banks to design and place advertising in a way that will maximize attention, interest, and retention by the target audience. Audience research measures audience recall and recognition of an advertisement.

Banks use a number of methods to arrive at an annual advertising budget. The most rational method is the objective-and-task method, whereby the bank determines its advertising objectives, the most cost-effective strategies and tactics for accomplishing these objectives, and the cost involved in carrying out the strategies and tactics.

Some banks have their own internal advertising department while others use an independent agency. In either case, the advertising professional should be seen as an arm of the marketing department, providing ideas to assist not just in promotion strategy, but in the other elements of the marketing mix as well. In all their advertising, banks must comply with the various regulations that are designed to prevent false or misleading advertising.

Sales promotion includes any communications efforts that do not fit into the categories of advertising, publicity, or personal selling. These include point-of-purchase merchandising, incentives, seminars, specialties, contests, and premium promotions. Any of these methods can help a bank attain its communication goals.

A promotional campaign involves the coordinated use of several promotional techniques by the bank to communicate an important message. The development of a promotional campaign involves setting specific measurable objectives, selecting the media to be used, creating the advertising, developing the sales promotion materials, training the bank's staff, and measuring the results.

The next chapter addresses public relations and communications, the fourth element of the promotion mix.

Points for Review

1. What is meant by the statement "when communication breaks down, the problem is generally due to a lack of commonality between the communicator's encoding and the audience's decoding"? Give a banking-related example to demonstrate this point.

2. List the four elements of the promotion mix and describe when each would be useful.

3. What is the importance of each of the following factors in determining the optimum promotion mix?
   - the communication goal
   - the type of product or service
   - the nature of the market
   - the product's life cycle stage

4. How would you respond to the following statement by a bank president: "Next

year's advertising budget should be 8 percent more than this year's, or the same as the rate of inflation, whichever is lower."

5. How would you respond to a bank executive who says that the purpose of advertising aimed at corporate financial executives is exclusively to sell commercial loans, cash management, and other corporate banking services?

6. Give examples of each of the following types of advertising from commonly seen television ads. Then propose how the technique might be used for a bank product or service.

- slice of life
- fantasy
- musical
- testimonial evidence

7. List the six steps involved in implementing a promotional campaign.

Notes

1. Ed Papazian, editor, *TV Dimensions '97* (New York: Media Dynamics, 1997).

2. These five questions were first suggested by H. D. Lasswell, *Power and Personality* (New York: W. W. Norton, 1948), pp. 37–51.

3. *Effective Bank Product Management,* p. 153.

4. Peter D. Bennett, editor, *Dictionary of Marketing Terms,* 2nd edition, definition by John Eighmey (Chicago: American Marketing Association, 1995).

5. *Ibid.,* definition by Don E. Schultz and Beth E. Barnes.

6. Colley, *Defining Advertising Goals,* pp. 43–54.

7. American Bankers Association/Gallup Poll results, October 1995.

8. *1997 Analysis of Bank Marketing Expenditures* (Washington, D.C.: Bank Marketing Association, 1997).

9. Adapted from Kotler, *Marketing Management,* pp. 581–583.

10. Thomas J. Burns, *Effective Communications and Advertising for Financial Institutions* (Englewood Cliffs, N.J.: Prentice-Hall, 1986), pp. 133–134.

11. Kotler, *Marketing Management,* pp. 604–606.

12. Colley, *Defining Advertising Goals,* p. 35.

14

PUBLIC RELATIONS AND COMMUNICATIONS

Learning Objectives

After studying this chapter, you should be able to

- define the term *public relations* and explain the critical role it plays for the bank,
- distinguish public relations from activities associated with sales and marketing,
- discuss how different size banks could position the public relations function within their organizations,
- describe the various "publics" encountered by the public relations staff and explain the tasks the public relations staff performs,
- list four elements essential to public relations damage control in a crisis situation, and
- explain how a bank benefits when it takes a leadership role in community activities.

Introduction

Although an emphasis on marketing is a relatively recent phenomenon in banking, public relations has been a recognized function in banks for several decades. Public relations entails a great deal more than fielding phone calls from the press. In fact, the role of public relations has grown tremendously over the last few decades. Now, staff members who work in public relations handle everything from press releases and press conferences to disaster management and market research.

The history of the Bank Marketing Association illustrates this shift in focus and the interplay between public relations and marketing. Founded as the Financial Public Relations Association, the organization changed its name to the Bank Public Relations and Marketing Association in 1965, and to the Bank Marketing Association in 1970. Although no longer reflected in its name, the organization continues to be concerned with bank public relations—recognizing that public relations is or can be part of marketing. The relationship between public relations and marketing should be close; the two functions are closely related, and the practitioners of each must work together if either function is to be carried out effectively.

Public relations has long been an important function in banks since banks have traditionally been community institutions, almost totally dependent on the economic well-being and trust of the communities they serve. Therefore, bankers have long recognized the wisdom of being good corporate citizens by doing things for the welfare and growth of their communities.

Public relations and marketing functions overlap to some degree, as exhibit 14.1 illustrates. Each bank has its own organizational structure and philosophy of how public relations should be handled and where the function falls in the reporting structure, yet many banks see the difference between public relations and marketing as follows:

marketing focuses only on revenue-generating activities; public relations focuses on non-revenue-generating activities.

Publicity (in the form of press releases or press conferences, for example) is one of the tools in the promotion mix, yet it is generally provided by the bank's public relations department. Any press coverage that results from press releases was gained both without paying for the exposure and without goals for generating revenue. However, if a public relations campaign requires the development and placing of image, advocacy, or institutional advertising (which require paying for the placement of material), this service is provided by the advertising area of the marketing department.

To understand how public relations and communications are related to marketing, consider again the definition of the marketing concept given in chapter 1: "The objective of marketing is customer satisfaction, at a profit, carried out in an orderly and efficient framework, and in a socially responsible manner." Public relations focuses all year round on enhancing the institution's corporate citizenship and taking action to demonstrate its social responsibility. The marketing department may focus on the bank's image in response to a project headed by the public relations department, through carefully planned advertising campaigns at certain times during the year, or in response to certain events, such as a merger, acquisition, or a competitor's campaign. Again, where responsibility for a particular project falls will depend entirely on an individual bank's structure and marketing philosophy.

In an era of consumerism, environmentalism, conservation, and equal rights, however, banks need more than ever to be socially responsible—and the internal watchdog is the public relations function. For these reasons, no marketing text would be complete without addressing this important function.

This chapter begins with a discussion of what public relations is and does. Then, it looks at public relations activities from the

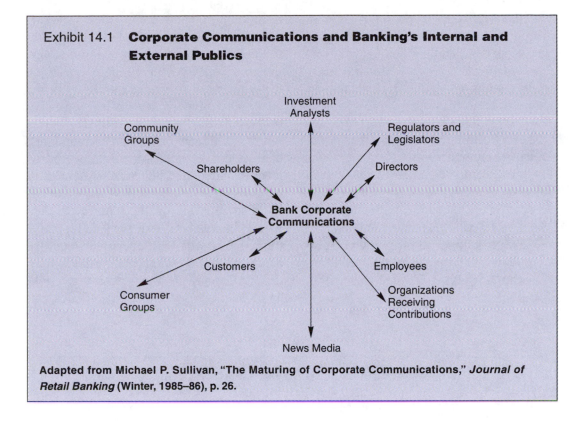

Exhibit 14.1 Corporate Communications and Banking's Internal and External Publics

Investment Analysts

Community Groups

Regulators and Legislators

Shareholders

Directors

Bank Corporate Communications

Customers

Employees

Consumer Groups

Organizations Receiving Contributions

News Media

Adapted from Michael P. Sullivan, "The Maturing of Corporate Communications," *Journal of Retail Banking* (Winter, 1985–86), p. 26.

broader perspective of community involvement and social responsibility.

What Public Relations Is

As mentioned in chapter 13, the Public Relations Society of America (PRSA) developed this definition of what public relations is today: "Public relations helps an organization and its publics adapt mutually to each other."[1] This definition was crafted to encompass the essential functions in public relations: research, planning, communications dialogue, and evaluation. PRSA also deliberately chose the word *organization,* so as not to limit the scope of the definition to companies or businesses, and the word *publics,* to acknowledge that all organizations must earn respect, support, and consent from numerous publics.

In addition, PRSA has identified 15 elements of public relations, to illustrate the tremendous diversity and responsibility this area manages:

- *counseling*—advising management;
- *research*—determining attitudes and behaviors of publics;
- *media relations*—seeking publicity with or responding to communications media;
- *publicity*—disseminating unpaid, planned messages;
- *employee/member relations*—responding to and informing employees and their families;
- *community relations*;
- *public affairs*—developing effective involvement in public policy;
- *government affairs*—relating directly to legislatures and regulatory agencies;
- *issues management*—identifying and addressing issues of public concern in which an organization is, or should be, concerned;
- *financial relations*—creating and maintaining investor confidence;
- *industry relations*—relating with other firms in the industry;

- *development/fundraising*—demonstrating the need for and encouraging support for an organization;

- *minority relations/multicultural affairs*—relating with individuals and groups in minorities;

- *special events and public participation*—stimulating interest by means of a focused event or activity;

- *marketing communications*—combination of activities designed to sell a product, service, or idea, including advertising, collateral materials, publicity, promotion, packaging, point-of-sale display, trade shows, and special events.[2]

Because of all these added responsibilities, a title that is used by many financial institutions in lieu of public relations is *corporate communications*. (See exhibit 14.2.)

Public relations is a communications-intensive activity with special emphasis on the securing of favorable publicity for the bank. This kind of activity is significant because banks operate in a climate of opinion. If the climate of opinion surrounding a bank is unfavorable, a bank may find its plans thwarted, its achievements stunted, its costs distorted, its operations hampered, and its customers taking their business elsewhere. In recent history, bank failures, the thrift industry bailout, questions about the health of the FDIC, escalating bank fees, and the Community Reinvestment Act policy of publicly disclosing banks' CRA rat-

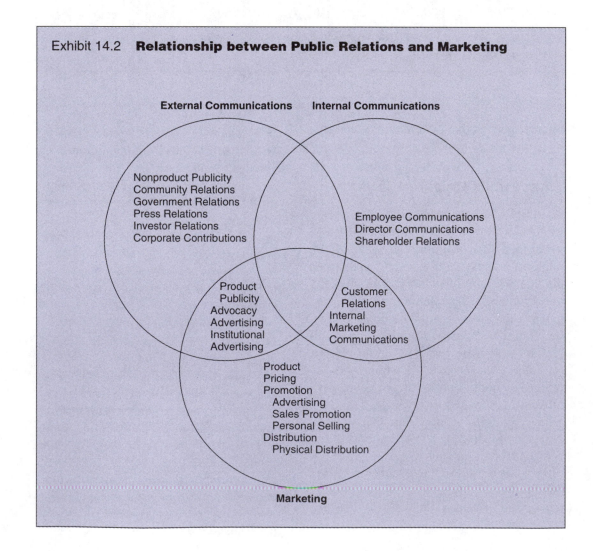

Exhibit 14.2   **Relationship between Public Relations and Marketing**

External Communications   Internal Communications

Nonproduct Publicity
Community Relations
Government Relations
Press Relations
Investor Relations
Corporate Contributions

Employee Communications
Director Communications
Shareholder Relations

Product
Publicity
Advocacy
Advertising
Institutional
Advertising

Customer
Relations
Internal
Marketing
Communications

Product
Pricing
Promotion
   Advertising
   Sales Promotion
   Personal Selling
Distribution
   Physical Distribution

Marketing

ings have hurt the image of the banking industry. More than ever, then, banks need to rebuild their credibility and reputation for financial strength through public relations activities.[3]

Besides communications, the task of public relations is to conduct activities that will create a favorable image for the bank in the community it serves. Depending on the specific needs of its community, a bank might become involved in education, community development, conservation, assistance to small businesses, charitable causes, or any number of other projects that demonstrate social consciousness. A number of examples of bank community relations activities are presented throughout this chapter and in Case G at the end of the book.

What Public Relations Is Not

By now it should be clear that public relations has an identity of its own, but since considerable misunderstanding clouds what public relations really is, it may be helpful to look specifically at what it is not.

Public Relations Is Not Advertising

Although advertising may well be part of a given public relations program, or public relations may be used to support an advertising campaign, advertising and public relations are not the same thing. Advertising entails buying space or time in the media and then using it to convey messages.

With publicity, coverage is not paid for and is never assured, and neither is content. The public relations officer uses press releases, press conferences, and other tools in attempts to elicit a certain type of coverage; but, in the final analysis, the news media determine what is covered, how much emphasis it is given, and what the content of the communication is.

Because of banking's role as a keystone of any community, the news media usually provide a fair amount of attention to banking news. The challenge to the public relations officer is to develop a relationship with news media personnel that enhances the likelihood that the bank will receive positive coverage. In summary, advertising is directly paid for by the bank, which therefore controls its content; public relations materials are disseminated by the bank, but publication is controlled by the news media.

Public Relations Is Not Oriented to Specific Products

Public relations is generally concerned with the image of the bank as a whole. Public relations activity attempts to create a high level of esteem and visibility for the bank as an institution; it does not attempt to generate demand for specific bank products.

This does not mean, however, that demand for the bank's services will not be boosted by public relations activities. For example, a Florida bank that used advertising to make residents conscious of the dangers faced by local wildlife (including the bald eagle, sea turtle, and manatee—see exhibit 14.3) credits that campaign with helping the bank increase its market share for consumer loans and deposits. The eye-catching ads raised awareness of the bank's name and, as a result, increased sales.[4]

Sometimes, however, the public relations staff does become involved in promotional activities.[5] For example, if a bank plans to launch a mobile banking program for which it has developed a high-tech mobile bank that will benefit (among many others) senior citizens who cannot travel easily to the bank, the public relations department will be responsible for writing and disseminating interest-generating, fact-filled press releases. The goal of these press releases will be to gain as much publicity as possible in print and on radio and television. The public relations staff may further be involved in setting up opportunities for the press and select customers to visit the mobile bank at a "grand opening," or introductory event, or they may be responsible for finding and securing a location for the mobile bank near the annual town parade or

Exhibit 14.3

Each winter, the manatee comes here seeking refuge in our warm waters. Many find death instead.

Surely there are more beautiful creatures in the sea. With its small eyes, drooping bristled muzzle and blimpish body, the manatee is short on looks. And yet few animals can match this giant's gentleness and appeal.

In spite of its massive size and peaceful manner, the manatee is faced with extinction. This winter, as in thousands of winters before, the endangered manatee will take refuge in South Florida's warm waters. But in its efforts to escape the cold northern waters, it must confront man-made dangers that threaten the existence of its species.

By understanding the habits and plight of the manatee, and by practicing a few precautions, we can help the manatee make a comeback.

The manatee, also known as the "sea cow," once thrived along the southeastern coastline. But by the late 1800s, the manatee population was threatened after centuries of being hunted for its hide, meat, oil, and bones. As early as 1893, Florida sought to save this creature from extinction by banning its slaughter.

Florida's manatee, the West Indian manatee, is one of four surviving species from the order of Sirenia. "Sirenia" comes from Greek myths about sirens who would lure sailors to their doom with seductive songs and the report of early explorers about mermaids in the seas of the New World. How could any sailor mistake the unattractive seal-shaped manatee for a mermaid? Perhaps he caught a glimpse of a mother manatee nursing a young calf or other manatees embracing one another in a human-like fashion.

The West Indian manatee once ranged the coastal waters from North Carolina to Southern Texas. Today, its home is almost entirely restricted to Florida, with only an estimated 1,000 manatees now inhabiting our waters.

Warm-blooded mammals, manatees cannot survive in water below 46 degrees Fahrenheit, so when northern waters become too cold they migrate to South Florida. Often, they can be found taking advantage of warm-water outlets of power plants.

But this migration exposes the manatee to danger and possible death. Air-breathing mammals, they stay near the surface as they travel via inlets and intracoastal waterways, risking collision with boats or deadly encounters with propeller blades, which can shred the manatee's two-inch skin into ribbons. Often they are trapped or crushed by barges. Floodgates and locks have also caused manatee deaths.

Manatees rest up to 12 hours a day and, while resting near the surface, are vulnerable to collisions with boats. If the boat is traveling at a low speed or if the water is deep enough to submerge, the manatee can sometimes avoid these collisions. Although they can stay submerged for up to 16 minutes, manatees are not fast swimmers and often cannot clear the path of a speeding boat. Most manatees bear scars from run-ins with boats and propellers.

Florida's warm waters also are a food source for the vegetarian manatee, which performs a valuable service by eating unwanted aquatic plants that clog waterways.

Spending six to eight hours a day eating, a manatee will reach lengths of up to 15 feet and weights as much as 2,000 pounds.

Unfortunately, water pollution and the introduction of pesticides and herbicides into freshwater and marine grassbeds have eliminated many manatee feeding areas.

Compounding the man-related dangers is the slow reproductive cycle of the manatee. The average gestation for the manatee is 13 months, which is longer than even that of the elephant. Females birth only one calf every two to three years. Born underwater, calves weigh as much as 50 pounds at birth.

Almost immediately after birth the mother places the baby on her back and surfaces for approximately 45 minutes. She will submerge and surface repeatedly for up to two hours until the baby free swims. This vital lesson, however, often leaves mother and baby at the mercy of passing boats.

Persons who live along Treasure Coast waterways, where manatees live year-round, may have heard them "talk" in bleeps, squeaks, squeals, and chirps. These are actual communications, not merely sounds used for navigation or echo location.

These animals are completely nonaggressive and will not fight back, even when their mates or babies are being attacked. Their only defense is swimming away.

Today, the killing, injuring or harassing of a manatee is punishable by fines up to $20,000 and/or one year imprisonment, under both state and federal laws, and the manatee is protected by the Endangered Species Act. The 1978 Florida Manatee Sanctuary Act declared the entire state "a refuge and sanctuary for the manatee."

Early efforts to protect manatees from collisions with boats included the creation of 21 manatee sanctuary areas, of which seven were located in Treasure Coast waters. More recently, Treasure Coast counties have begun to adopt comprehensive manatee speed limit zones for boats. Boaters will find signs posted which, for example, call for 25-mile-per-hour limits in the Intracoastal Waterway, or main channel, and slow speed outside the channel.

"Slow speed" means operating a boat at a speed slow enough that the hull line stays parallel to the water's surface, and, consequently, a boat is exceeding slow speed when the bow of the boat lifts out of the water or planes. Some signs may indicate "idle speed" or "no wake," in either case the boat should not be operated at a faster speed than is necessary for steerage, or the ability to maneuver the boat.

It is in these areas that boat speeds are regulated from November 15 through March 31, the period when there are concentrated populations of manatees in these waterways.

As residents of the Treasure Coast, we must do our part in the preservation of these helpless mammals by following these guidelines:

- When operating a motorboat, give manatees the right of way.
- Operate boats at "idle" or no wake speed when entering manatee waters and, when possible, in deep water as well.
  - Watch for signs indicating manatee habitats.
  - Do not pass over submerged manatees.
  - When diving, do not touch manatees. Photograph them only when they approach you.
  - Do not pursue manatees while boating or diving.
  - Do not discard monofilament line into the water; manatees can become injured or killed by swallowing or becoming entangled in line.
  - Ask visitors, newcomers and friends along the Treasure Coast to follow these guidelines. If you should accidentally hit a manatee with your boat or discover an injured or stranded manatee, report it as soon as possible to the Florida Marine Patrol so that help may be sent quickly. Call toll-free 24 hours a day: 1-800-342-1821. Also report dead manatees or any individual or boat that you see deliberately harming a manatee, so the authorities can reduce the malicious mistreatment of these mammals.

First National Bank, the area's largest and oldest independent bank, has been a part of the Treasure Coast for more than 50 years. We believe we have a responsibility to assist in preserving the beauty and the unique wildlife of the Treasure Coast.

If you would like to show your support for manatee preservation, you can order the special Florida manatee license plate. Since March of 1990, over 125,000 Florida families have paid an extra $17 for these plates, which picture the manatee. The money raised by this program goes to support research as well as operating expenses for state manatee preservation efforts. There are also several organizations you can contact to make donations. Among these are Save the Manatee located at 500 N. Maitland Ave., Maitland, Florida 32751, and The Nature Conservancy, 2699 Lee Road, Suite 500, Winter Park, Florida 32789.

With this message, First National Bank hopes to encourage Treasure Coast area residents to show their determination to help preserve a vital link in the life cycle of the rare and gentle manatee.

MANATEE ZONE 25 MPH IN ICW SLOW SPEED OUT OF ICW

Posted Manatee Sanctuary Areas on the Treasure Coast.

We're banking on the Treasure Coast.℠

First National
BANK AND TRUST COMPANY

Offices throughout the Treasure Coast

287-4000   569-4000   465-4000

Member FDIC   ©1991 First National Bank and Trust Company of the Treasure Coast the county fair. A public relations effort may increase business for the bank, but the sale of specific products is not its primary goal.

This is where the line between marketing and public relations sometimes blurs. Placing the mobile bank at the fair could be seen as handling the publicity for a new product being offered by the bank. And since product promotion is generally considered a marketing function it is not, strictly speaking, public relations. Again, public relations normally focuses on improving the climate of opinion surrounding the bank, not on promoting specific products.

The Position of Public Relations in the Organization

The position of public relations on the company organization chart will depend largely on the size of the financial services organization. In smaller community banks, everyone may be responsible for marketing and public relations to some degree. For example, one midsize bank in Illinois doesn't differentiate between public relations and marketing. The media are encouraged to contact board members and senior managers in the bank for comments on industry issues instead of going through a public relations department. Press releases (as well as other elements of the promotional campaign) announcing a new virtual bank program are developed in a collaboration between the executive vice president of retail banking (the product center for the virtual bank) and her staff and the marketing staff.

In larger banks, the separation between public relations functions and marketing functions tends to be more distinct. One way some banks separate the responsibilities is by designating public relations to handle all communications that do not directly generate revenue and marketing to handle communications that will or could

This ad, one of three in a series of ads to raise awareness of the dangers faced by local wildlife, also helped the bank to increase market share.

generate revenue. Each bank has its own philosophy, however. A larger bank also tends to have a larger staff, which may partially explain why public relations is a separate unit in that bank.

In some banks, especially large banks with substantial staff, the communication of major events such as a merger or acquisition is a job handled by both marketing and public relations. The public relations staff is responsible for writing and disseminating press releases to the media and also to the acquiring bank's staff. The letters to the acquired bank's customers, however, even though they are not a paid, placed communication, are often written and sent by the marketing department. Because this communication with the acquired bank's customers is essentially a letter to a potential customer, that can be seen as potentially revenue generating and falls to the marketing department to write.

Another bank, however, might find that all communications concerning a merger or acquisition should be handled by the public relations department alone. The qualifier, in many cases, is potential for income. Marketing handles income-generating communications. Public relations does not. A midsize bank in Pennsylvania and a large bank in California each have separate public relations departments. These banks use their public relations departments specifically for non-revenue-generating publicity.

The annual report is a communication to customers—very important customers, the shareholders, and the annual report "sells" the bank to these customers. Nevertheless, in a large bank, the task of creating an appealing annual report falls to a division of public relations called investor relations, not the marketing department. In a community bank, which might have a marketing director who also serves as the public relations director, the annual report would most likely be created by the marketing department.

As you can see, the reporting structure of public relations within the bank varies tremendously. It is difficult to generalize and to offer a typical organizational chart. Community banks, which generally do not have the pressure of numerous branches or banks in other states, often have a senior marketing staff member who handles public relations and who reports directly to the CEO. In the very smallest community banks, the CEO himself or herself may be responsible for public relations. In midsize and large banks, the responsibilities of public relations become more complex due to the greater number of branches, subsidiaries, employees, communities, and issues, and therefore are handled by a separate department.

Whether or not there is a separate public relations function on the organizational chart, the individual who handles those responsibilities should report to senior management, if not the CEO himself or herself. To be most effective, the person who handles public relations must have direct access to the chief executive. For example, when the press is seeking the bank's response to a major turn of events or is seeking verification of a rumor heard in the market, the public relations person must be able to get to the top fast. Also, the public relations director who meets regularly with the chief executive will be better informed on internal matters and should be in a better position to carry out senior management's strategies or respond intelligently to questions from the press. If the public relations person is a professional and the bank is serious about being socially responsible, he or she should be involved in the decision-making process and have a chance to affect bank policy.

The Role of Public Relations

Most of the activities conducted by the public relations department involve communicating with the bank's various publics.

The Bank's Publics

The bank's publics fall into two groups: internal and external. A bank's publics are considered to be internal if the bank has some control over the reception of its communications to them (that is, the bank can control who gets the message, what the message will be, and when it is to be received). The bank does not have control over the reception of communications to its external publics. It sends out its message but cannot control who will receive it, when it will be received, or even, in many cases, what the final content of the message is.

Traditionally, the press release has been the major vehicle for conveying this communication, and traditionally it has been printed. However, with the rapid growth of the Internet as a communication tool, many companies now post their press releases on their Web sites, and some pay an electronic service to distribute their press releases via e-mail. By posting press releases on their own Web sites and on news sites that contain business and industry releases, companies may increase the number of people who read their messages as they were originally written—not in the format a media source decides to use.

The bank's *internal publics* are its employees, directors, customers, and shareholders. The bank's *external publics* are the investment community, the community served by the bank, consumer groups, community action groups, organizations receiving corporate contributions, and government officials and agencies. Public relations tasks revolve around communicating with these publics. Because the news media constitute an important intermediary through which many of the bank's communications are funneled, the press is treated here as yet another public-one with which the public relations person must establish and maintain a good relationship (See exhibit 14.2).

Public Relations Tasks

The primary tasks of the public relations department are media relations and publicity, investor relations (with shareholders and the investment community), government relations, employee relations, customer relations, and community relations.

Media Relations and Publicity

The news media (newspapers, magazines, radio, and public and commercial television) are the most important vehicles for the bank's communication efforts. Through the media, the bank can speak to each of its publics; therefore, one of the most important duties of the public relations practitioner is media relations. The members of the news media determine whether a bank story is newsworthy. Since the media are likely to have a more favorable attitude toward a story offered by someone they know, like, and trust, it is important for public relations officers, or anyone in the bank with authority to speak on behalf of the bank, to establish a good relationship with reporters. If the bank spokesperson treats the media as adversaries, either telling them as little as possible or "stonewalling" on sensitive issues, the bank will soon find itself more vulnerable to adverse publicity. A reporter who is repeatedly turned away with little or no information will begin to rely on information from unofficial and less-reliable sources within the bank. Most banks prefer to give reporters an official statement from a reliable, senior-level source in the bank.

Reporters also frequently need background information, and they appreciate being able to visit a bank's Web site or to consult with a bank public relations officer or other spokesperson to get it. Furthermore, when the news from the bank or from the banking industry is unfavorable (for example, a robbery or an embezzlement), a reporter is likely to listen more favorably to someone he or she knows and trusts and to seek the full, accurate story behind the potentially damaging news.

Again, each bank has its own philosophy about how public relations should be handled. Some have a written policy that the bank's officers notify the public relations director any time they become aware that an important story with implications for the bank or banking in general is about to break. Some also have a stated policy that the public relations director is to be the only point of contact between the news media and the bank. Others set the standard that any senior manager or member of the board may not answer questions from the press without checking first with a central public relations source in the bank. Regardless of its policy, however, a bank should communicate it clearly to every employee, and it should be included as part of the new-employee orientation package. Exhibit 14.4 provides an example of one bank's publicity policy.

Effective media relations is a prerequisite for the public relations task of getting publicity. Publicity entails dissemination to the news media of information with news or human interest value in an effort to promote a product, service, event, idea, or impression that will advance the cause of the bank. To capture the attention of the media, the press release must be exceptionally well written and must contain something of interest to the reader (that is, the editor of the publication or the producer of the show).[6] It must answer the question, "What makes this story newsworthy?" Many events that banks seek to publicize do not pass this test, and it takes considerable talent to write press releases about them in such a way that they will be used by the media.

The two principal ways that a bank provides news to the media are the press conference and the press release.

- *The press conference.* When a bank has a major announcement to make, say, a merger to reveal or an important personality to introduce, it may be appropriate to schedule a press conference. The public relations person should make certain that the press conference does not conflict with the deadlines of the various media. If the local paper's deadline for news is 4 p.m., the press conference should be early in the day. A written statement should be prepared in advance by the public relations office and

Exhibit 14.4 Sample Publicity Policy

Bank Publicity Policy

In order that all statements made to television, radio, magazine, or newspaper reporters are presented in the most accurate and authoritative manner possible, it is necessary that all inquiries be coordinated through the public relations office.

When any officer or other employee is contacted by the news media for a statement regarding bank policies or procedures, the following procedures should be followed:

- No immediate statement should be given. Rather, explain that you may not be the appropriate individual to respond to that inquiry and that the public relations office must make the determination.
- State that you will have the appropriate officer return the call immediately.
- Obtain the reporter's name, company, phone number, and deadline.
- Call the public relations office and convey the nature of the question, the reporter's name, phone number, etc.

The public relations office will refer this information either to the appropriate department or division head, or the bank's public relation's counsel, for immediate oral or written response.

In the case of a robbery, fire, or other emergency where numerous inquiries are received in a short period, public relations, working with the appropriate department head, will formulate a single written statement to be read or delivered to reporters.

Although the above procedures are necessary safeguards, they should not be used to delay unreasonably the transmission of information. When we tell a reporter or other inquirer that we will call back, it is important that the call-back be made by the responsible bank officer within a reasonable time.

The only allowable exception to the above procedure will be prearranged periodic information inquiries made to department heads.

The switchboard and after-hours guards are all provided with the public relations director's home phone number in the event of inquiries made during nonbanking hours.

Source: This policy appeared in "PR as a Marketing Tool," by Arthur J.L. Lucey, in *American Banker,* February 7, 1977; reprinted in *American Banker's Marketing Management,* volume 1, August 1976–April 1977.

presented at the press conference by a spokesperson who can answer questions from reporters. A kit containing a well-written press release and pertinent supplemental information helps ensure that the media get the basic facts of the story.

- *The press release.* A press release calls for a very different writing style from that which is used for other bank communications. A standard format is used for most press releases. The lead sentence is crucial for two reasons: (1) it must catch the reader's attention and cause him or her to want to read further; and (2) it must contain the highlights of the message so that if the reader stops there, the major elements of who, what, where, when, why, and how will have been communicated. A sample press release used by a bank to launch a premium promotion is shown as exhibit 14.5.

In general, press releases are printed on specially designed stationery that features the bank's name and logo and a bold heading, such as "News from . . ." or simply, "Press Release." This serves as an identifying mark that all editors recognize. Innovative and creative methods of preparing press releases, particularly if there is a very important message to be conveyed, should be seriously considered. The media receive many press releases each day that closely resemble each other in format. That is why the writing must be exceptional, and a distinctive flair (if appropriate) is warranted.

News releases may also be prepared and sent to television or radio stations electronically. Many banks use a news service to transmit news releases instantaneously to many news media outlets. News services, such as PR Newswire or Business Wire, can be used to convey an institution's message

---

Exhibit 14.5 Sample Press Release

For Immediate Release   Contact: Jane Mason 201-555-6013

United City Bank to Sponsor Pottery Demonstrations
If you'd like to see how pottery is made, United City Bank has arranged for members of the New England Potter's Guild to demonstrate their craft at some of its branches on November 21 and 28.

According to William L. Lamson, chairman of United City, pottery making demonstrations will be given from 9 a.m. until 2 p.m. on November 21 at the Main Bank branch, 15 West Blackwell Street, Dover; the Panther Valley branch, Route 517, Allamuchy; and at the 144 Main Street branch, Hackettstown. On November 28 the demonstrations will be held at the Roxbury Plaza branch, Route 10, Ledgewood; the Flanders branch, Route 206 and Deerfield Place; and at the Jefferson branch, Route 15 and Bowling Green Parkway, Lake Hopatcong.

The demonstrations, notes Lamson, have been arranged to highlight the bank's one-of-a-kind handcrafted pottery offer, which began November 15. "As an inducement for new deposits," he says, "we're offering customers an opportunity to save on a selection of original pottery handcrafted by members of the New England Potter's Guild." The selection includes vases, pitchers, candleholders, and hurricane lamps.

Customers depositing $250 or more in a new or existing savings account or in a new checking account can obtain a piece of pottery free or at a discount, depending on the amount of the deposit and the piece chosen. "The bigger the deposit," Lamson points out, "the bigger the gift or discount."

A collection of pottery, together with complete details on the offer, is on display at all branches of United City Bank.

quickly and accurately. These messages rely solely on clear, dynamic writing because often no letterhead or logo is conveyed with the message.

Crisis Management

Bank management and public relations staff have had to cope with crises more frequently in the past few years. How a crisis situation is handled can either cause serious damage to a bank's reputation or strengthen its image. A crisis may be a one-time event—such as a fire, flood, earthquake, bomb scare, or robbery—or it may be a long-running problem—such as ongoing publicity about a large volume of bad loans to be worked out. In either case, how the situation is handled by the bank's management affects the public's perception and judgment of both the immediate situation and the bank in general.

To illustrate this point, consider two very different, now classic, responses to crisis situations from the world of consumer products: Tylenol and Audi. When several people died from cyanide-laced Tylenol capsules, one advertising expert predicted that Tylenol would never recover its number one position among nonaspirin analgesics. He was proved wrong by Johnson & Johnson's (J&J) highly effective crisis management program. J&J management took responsibility for the problem even though the poisonings were caused by someone's tampering with the product after it was already on store shelves. It immediately recalled all Tylenol capsules from store shelves, maintained liaison with the press, presented management in paid television "infomercials" to update the public on J&J's activities, terminated the capsule form of pill and replaced it with a gel-cap that would be more difficult to tamper with, and redesigned the packaging so that it would be obvious when a package had been opened. In short, the company spared no expense or effort to assure the public of its concern for safety, and it regained its position as market leader.

In contrast, when a number of reports were published several years ago indicating that a particular model of Audi automobile was subject to accelerating by itself while in the parking gear, the management of Audi refused to acknowledge that the car had any engineering flaw. The sales of that model fell off and the resale value plummeted. Audi eventually replaced the car with another model, but because of the way it handled the situation, the name of the company still evokes negative reactions among many car buyers.

Experts in issues management describe four essential elements that the media expect from a bank in dealing with a crisis:[7]

1. *Describe the risk accurately.* The bank should make clear precisely what the risks are for each customer group that might be affected by the particular event. It is better to overstate risk than to understate it. If the risk turns out to be less than originally described, the bank will get credit for managing the situation well.

2. *Describe what actions the bank will take to mitigate the risk.* For example, the bank may decide to seek a merger partner, call in the appropriate officials, relocate to a temporary facility, have back-office work conducted by another bank, and so on.

3. *Identify the cause of the risk.* This demonstrates to the public that the bank knows what the problem is and will fix it.

4. *Demonstrate responsible management action.* The bank must always appear to be in control of the event while carrying out its plan of action.

Banks should be prepared for crisis situations. Planning for crisis management should go hand-in-hand with development of a disaster recovery plan that would enable a bank to continue in business despite an unforeseen emergency.

Investor Relations

Investor relations entails communications with the bank's shareholders and with those who have the ability to affect the activity in, and price of, the bank's stock. These include institutional investors, brokers, and security analysts who specialize in the study of bank stocks. The principal investor relations efforts for most banks center around producing the annual report and quarterly earnings reports and holding the annual shareholders' meeting. The annual report is an important communications tool that can be used to sell the bank's services as well as the bank itself.

The annual meeting of a bank's shareholders is a brief event that requires a great deal of planning and preparation. In general, it falls to the public relations department to arrange the time and place of the meeting, prepare the speeches to be given by the chairman and others who will address the group, and work with the bank's senior management in preparing answers to questions that are likely to be asked from the floor. The public relations director must also be prepared to deal with the occasional gadfly who buys stock in a company just to attend the annual meeting in order to ask irritating or potentially embarrassing questions.

The public relations officer may also be called on to hold meetings to update stock analysts on the bank's financial situation. Such meetings give analysts an opportunity to ask questions of the bank's senior management, so they can do a better job of projecting the future performance of the bank. This can be a very sensitive undertaking because, while it is desirable to present the bank and its management and performance in a positive light, there can be serious ramifications if a company's problems or weaknesses are concealed. (The Securities and Exchange Commission has strict rules governing financial disclosure.)

Government Relations

The laws and regulations that govern the banking industry and affect its operating environment can, to some extent, be influenced by developing relationships with those who make and enforce those laws. The legislative and regulatory arena ranges from local traffic and zoning ordinances affecting the physical operation of the bank to federal regulation of credit and deposit services.

At the state level, bankers should make a point of knowing and communicating with their state senators and representatives. These individuals frequently know very little about the business of banking, such as how a bank makes money or how market rates of interest are determined. Yet they are in a position to vote on matters that can affect the limits within which banks can operate. Thus it behooves bankers to educate their state legislators concerning the implications of proposed banking legislation, something that is best done on a one-to-one basis. Individual bankers can have considerable influence and can provide needed support to the lobbying efforts of state banking associations.

State and local governments can also be important customers for a bank. Often they are not only a source of large deposit balances, but also major users of bank services (such as payroll services). As such, they should be the object of a bank's calling and sales efforts.

To be effective at the national level, bankers must combine forces in a unified effort. The American Bankers Association (ABA) provides the structure to accomplish this. It has a professional staff that represents banking interests before legislative bodies and regulatory agencies, and it has specialized committees of bankers who serve as a liaison between the banking community and the association. Other national banking associations have a similar, if more limited, role and scope in national lobbying efforts.

Employee Relations

One of a bank's most important publics is its own staff. The attitude and performance of the employees both on the front lines and behind the scenes make the difference between a customer- and quality-oriented, smoothly operated, productive, and personable bank, and its opposite. Of course, no amount of communication can overcome the effects of poor management. But assuming that supervisors and managers are at least trying to follow good management practices, and management has credibility among the staff, an internal employee communications program is a useful tool for building morale and team spirit.

Some examples of internal communications are (1) a regularly published in-house newsletter (printed or put on the local area network [LAN] or intranet) that includes news about the company and its employees and lists job openings within the bank and (2) periodically published communications informing the staff about new programs. The first type of publication generally attempts to communicate management's philosophy and goals and acquaint the staff with the various people and departments within the bank in order to help them understand the bigger picture beyond their individual jobs. In addition, the posting of job openings allows employees to be among the first to apply for vacant positions.

The objective of the second type of communication about new products, services, or marketing programs is to enlist the staff's support and cooperation. It is very damaging to the teller's morale and to the bank's marketing efforts when a customer comes in brandishing an ad about a new service that the teller has not yet heard about. The larger the bank, the more difficult it is to spread the word of new programs quickly, but it is important that a way be found to do it. Some banking organizations use videotapes produced in-house to communicate with employees. Others have found that posting information on the company's LAN or intranet helps employees keep up to date.

Customer Relations

Most of the time, communicating with the bank's customers takes place at the point of sale (that is, at the main office, branch, or at the ATM or ALM) and through the mail. Personal contact is largely the province of the branch administration and marketing depart-

ments. Mailings, which are the province of the marketing department, include letters informing customers about new services or changes in pricing. Customers who use on-line banking can tap into the bank's Web site for new information and will receive notices through their PC banking connection.

Many banks send newsletters to their customers on a regular basis, covering matters of general and financial interest. This type of communication is frequently handled by the marketing department, especially if it has a sales orientation, but it might also be considered a public relations function.

One of the most important areas of customer relations is how the bank handles complaints, which can make the difference between keeping or losing customers. Someone within the bank, whether in the public relations department or customer service center, should see that every complaint is addressed in a helpful and responsive way. In some banks, the public relations department handles all consumer grievances.

In short, there should be either a public relations officer or written, circulated standards governing all nonadvertising communications from the bank to its customers to ensure that they are well written, customer oriented, and comply with management's overall communication goals.

Community Relations

Developing and maintaining a favorable relationship with the community have always been important in banking. However, good community relations has taken on increased importance in recent years because of increased competition from nonbank financial services companies, widespread mergers and acquisitions, and the perception that banks are not consumer oriented (due to rising fees). Now more than ever, banks need to be visible in their commitment to their local communities in order to counteract negative images and publicity about the industry over which the bank has no control.

The majority of banks in this country are

community-based institutions. Those that are not (such as holding companies) are trying very hard to look and act like community-based institutions. Communities are, to some degree, dependent on the banks that serve them (for example, for financing local businesses and providing mortgages and loans to consumers). But banks are almost totally dependent on the communities they serve. Very few banks can get along without the support of their community. Therefore, it is not just for altruistic reasons that banks should play the role of good corporate citizens, intent on working for the welfare and growth of their communities and striving to keep their communities dynamic. If the community suffers an economic setback, the bank should be seen working hard to bring about a rehabilitation.

Community relations activities often include both community development and educational programs. A bank can be a positive influence in a community by providing mortgage loans to first-time home buyers in less advantaged neighborhoods or by providing home-owner seminars in different languages throughout its community.[8] Case Study G gives three examples of banks' community efforts and their effects.

A community relations program might also be aimed at a specific target market, such as the youth market. Fleet National Bank instituted the Fleet Youth Initiative (FYI), a comprehensive program including youth activities and a commitment to issue-oriented programs for children and teens. Under the FYI umbrella, the bank sponsored an American history competition, a hockey championship, a child safety day, and a youth philharmonic concert. The unusual outdoor posters (see exhibit 14.6) and newspaper advertisements not only made the community aware of this particular program, but communicated the bank's commitment to young people.

Banks have traditionally supported their local communities by helping support local nonprofit groups, the arts, and local charities. While these efforts have often been effective in winning the esteem of the public, banks are increasingly engaging in more powerful and more innovative programs that are responsive to changes in society and its values. Banks must continue to be involved in and committed to solutions to important problems faced by the communities they serve. Although a donation to the local Boy Scout troop or the sponsorship of a concert is nice, such singular and unsystematic actions as these are likely to have much less impact on the welfare of a community (and the welfare of the bank) than would a well-planned, ongoing commitment to a particular local problem or cause.

Benefits of a Broader Perspective for Public Relations

The profit-minded reader might ask what a bank stands to gain from involving itself with the problems of the community. Banks that adopt a broader view of public relations and community involvement will reap many benefits—including better market results, stronger employee recruitment and morale, favorable image of the bank, and beneficial community impact. The examples in Case G demonstrate this principle.

- *Market results.* It is just as difficult to attribute precise market results to a public relations program as it is to attribute specific sales results to a promotional campaign. Nonetheless, there is every reason to believe that well-executed, community-oriented public relations programs result in appreciable economic gain for the bank, particularly if long-term as well as short-term results are considered.

- *Employee recruitment and morale.* One of the most overlooked benefits of community-oriented programs is the positive effect it has on present and prospective bank employees. When a bank takes a stand on an issue and does something positive for the community, its employees feel proud to be involved. Programs that demonstrate the bank's social concern attract the attention of people within the

Exhibit 14.6

community and foster an image of being "the kind of place where I'd like to work."

• *Image and credibility.* Banks that adopt a broader perspective of public, or community, relations typically find that this results in enhanced credibility and a greater sense of trust on the part of community members. This kind of response, of course, can be a measurable objective of such a program.

• *Community impact.* A well-planned, cohesive program can have a significant effect on the community to which it is directed, and can also be in the bank's own self-interest. In addition to benefiting the individuals and businesses in the community, a bank's own financial well-being may improve since it is inexorably related to the economic health of the community it serves.

Summary

Public relations concerns all the efforts of the bank to win the esteem of its various publics: the news media, stockholders, securities analysts, legislators and regulators, directors, employees, customers, and the community. Public relation functions and responsibilities continue to evolve and broaden.

Although public relations and marketing overlap, especially in the area of product publicity, most public relations activities can be considered marketing only from the broad perspective of the marketing concept—namely, that all the bank's activities are aimed at customer satisfaction, at a profit, carried out in an organized and efficient framework, and conducted in a socially responsible manner. The public relations function should be the social conscience of the bank.

Many tasks constitute the public relations function. One of them is the development of good relations with the news media and the writing and placing of press releases. Effec-
tive media relations is especially important in crisis situations, since the way in which such situations are handled can affect the bank's reputation and ability to do business. The investor relations function includes the preparation and publication of the annual and quarterly reports, arrangements for the annual meeting of stockholders, and presentations aimed at investors and the investment community. The goal of these activities is to increase demand for, and ultimately the price of, the bank's stock. Government relations includes getting to know, and communicating with, legislators representing the bank's trade area, and working with state and national banking associations to obtain a favorable regulatory climate for banking.

Other public relations functions include internal communications with the bank's staff to improve employee morale and to enlist staff support of the bank's marketing and other programs. In addition, the public relations officer monitors or develops customer communications to ensure that they are customer oriented and in tune with the bank's overall communications goals. A bank's community relations programs are also under the direction of the public relations function. Since banks are so dependent on the vitality of the communities they serve, banks should take an active role in helping their communities solve their most pressing problems as well as provide support to local nonprofit organizations. Increasingly, the public relations function is taking on a broader perspective: one that emphasizes continuing programs of community action and leadership rather than isolated events or contributions. The bank that does this can expect to realize benefits in the areas of market performance, employee recruitment, employee morale, enhanced credibility and image, and the improved economic health of its community.

This outdoor board makes it clear that the bank is targeting a specific market segment: young people with diverse interests.

Points for Review

1. How would a bank's relationship with its community, and its profits, be affected if it did not have a public relations function?

2. How is public relations different from marketing? Give an example of a marketing effort for an education savings account and a public relations effort for the same product.

3. What options does a small to medium size bank have for positioning the public relations function in the bank?

4. Write a lead sentence for a press release announcing the education savings account from question 2.

5. You are the public relations representative from your bank. A reporter is on the phone wanting to know your bank's response to the news that one of your directors has been accused of embezzling funds. Using the four essential elements for damage control described in the chapter, come up with a response.

6. What are some potential benefits to a bank of engaging in programs that address issues of concern to the local community?

Notes

1. *Public Relations: An Overview* (New York: The PRSA Foundation, 1991), p. 2.

2. *Ibid.,* pp. 5–6.

3. George C. Morvis, "Public Relations: New Priority for Banks Today," *Bank Marketing,* September 1991, pp. 44–45.

4. "Wildlife Ads of Florida Bank Trigger Big Boost in Market Share," *101 Marketing Ideas,* volume IV, Bank Marketing Association, 1990, pp. 77–78.

5. Much of the information in the following two sections was gathered through interviews in June 1997 with bankers, including Susan Little Abbott, executive vice president, retail banking, Busey Bank, Illinois; Lance Kessler, senior vice president and director of marketing, Keystone Financial Corp., Pennsylvania; and Lori McCarney, director of brand and merchandising management, Bank of America, California.

6. Kevin Sheridan, "Depressing Releases," *Bank Marketing,* April 1997, pp. 51–56.

7. Samuel D. Ostrow, "It Will Happen Here," *Bank Marketing,* July 1991, pp. 24–26.

8. Susan J. Blexrud, "Barnett's Workshops Teach Home Ownership," *Bank Marketing,* March 1996, pp. 13–16.

Part V
OTHER TOPICS IN BANK MARKETING

Parts II through IV of this text have covered the four planning stages in the strategic marketing management process: conducting the situation analysis, setting marketing objectives, selecting the target market, and designing the marketing strategy. Part V completes the discussion of that process by focusing on the final two stages: the implementation and evaluation of the marketing plan. This is the subject of chapter 15.

This book has focused largely on the marketing of retail banking products because the retail market requires more products, more people, and more promotional activity per million dollars of deposits or loans than does the commercial side of the business. However, a bank's commercial demand deposits and loan volume generally outweigh its retail demand deposit and loan volume. The wholesale side of banking is addressed in chapter 16. Finally, this study of bank marketing concludes in chapter 17 with a discussion of a number of developments that are on the horizon in the world of banking and explores how they might affect the future of bank marketing.

15

ORGANIZATION, IMPLEMENTATION, AND EVALUATION

Learning Objectives

After studying this chapter, you should be able to

- explain how the position of the marketing department on a bank's organization chart can indicate the degree to which the bank is customer oriented and marketing oriented,
- describe ways in which marketing interacts with line and staff departments,
- explain how focusing on the customer influences the implementation and evaluation of a marketing plan,
- discuss five factors affecting the implementation stage of a marketing plan,
- explain why performance monitoring is essential to the planning process,
- list several reasons why results may deviate from the marketing plan, and
- discuss the reasons for implementing a reporting process, and explain how the frequency, distribution, and content are determined.

Introduction

The marketing management process is circular and consists of planning, implementation, and evaluation. Up to this point in the book, the emphasis has been on the planning process; but the best-laid plan is of no use unless it is put into action. Implementation of a marketing plan is affected by organizational issues as well as by the method of execution. Therefore, this chapter looks first at the organizational aspects of bank marketing and at issues pertaining to the interrelationship of marketing with other line and staff departments.

A marketing plan is not just a document that a bank develops and then puts away on a shelf. The planning process is not completed until the plan is executed and the objectives are achieved. This will happen only if all the areas of the bank that are involved in executing the plan have both (1) their own specific objectives and (2) a system for measuring how they are performing in relation to these objectives. Therefore, this chapter revisits the setting of goals and objectives and the measuring of performance in order to evaluate whether a plan is proceeding on track. These steps once again reinforce that marketing planning is an ongoing process, not an event. The chapter also discusses how the service quality movement has affected banking and how it relates to the implementation and evaluation of marketing plans.

Since conditions can change after a marketing plan has been written and set into effect, a plan needs to be adjusted from time to time. Performance evaluation and monitoring enable the marketer to identify precisely which strategies or tactics must be adjusted. (See exhibit 15.1.)

Organizing the Bank for Marketing

The way a bank is organized can affect the implementation of its marketing strategies and tactics. Besides being an organizational philosophy and a management process, marketing involves numerous functions that should show up on the bank's organization chart. Some of these functions are marketing research, product development and management, advertising and sales promotion, and publicity, to name just four. This section considers the organizational aspects of marketing and how marketing activities relate to other departments of a bank.

The location of the marketing department, or various marketing functions, within a bank's organization chart will vary depending largely on two factors: (1) the degree to which the bank is customer focused and (2) the size and structure of the bank. In a very small bank, one individual—such as the retail banking head—may be responsible for most marketing tasks and have other responsibilities as well. Slightly larger banks may have a marketing director whose sole responsibility is to develop advertising and sales promotional programs, obtain publicity for the bank, plan and carry out community relations activities, arrange for the necessary marketing research, and so on. Many community and larger banks have marketing departments consisting of a marketing director and staff who handle advertising, sales promotion, community relations, publicity, marketing research, and, in some cases, product development.

The trend for midsize to large banks is toward decentralized marketing functions.[1] While the marketing strategy and brand management may be centralized, the majority of the marketing tasks are decentralized and handled by each line manager. Today, large banks especially are much less likely to have a single marketing head than ever before. Individual product line managers are now responsible for their own marketing, as long as it follows the marketing strategy set forth by the holding company. A central department may exist to carry out production needs. In some banks, the line managers are expected to work in teams and to break down any barriers that exist between departments (which can cause turf battles)

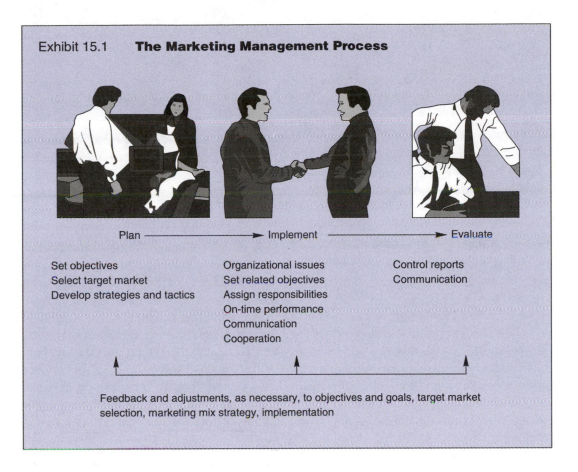

Exhibit 15.1   The Marketing Management Process

Plan ──────────────▶ Implement ──────────────▶ Evaluate

Set objectives	Organizational issues	Control reports
Select target market	Set related objectives	Communication
Develop strategies and tactics	Assign responsibilities	
	On-time performance	
	Communication	
	Cooperation	

Feedback and adjustments, as necessary, to objectives and goals, target market selection, marketing mix strategy, implementation

to develop the best solutions possible for the customer. Selling strategies also often fall to the individual lines, and in some banks, training is the responsibility of the different lines of business—not centralized under marketing or human resources.

Until banks have fully accepted and implemented marketing as the driving force behind the bank's business, and being customer-focused as the key philosophy for success, the placement of marketing within the organization will continue to evolve and shift.

The Centralized Marketing Department

There is a great variety in the way marketing fits in the organizational structure, even in banks where all marketing functions are centralized. Two of the most common structures, however, are the functional organization and the product management organization.

Functional Organization

In a marketing department that is organized functionally (see exhibit 15.2), specialists who supervise various functions, such as advertising, sales promotion, and research, are coordinated by a marketing head. This type of organization has an important disadvantage, especially as the number of products or target markets increases: the essential marketing tasks of product development and pricing are not represented.

This issue raises two questions: (1) Where does the responsibility for product strategy and new product development lie? and (2) How do those functions relate to the marketing department? In some banks that are organized along functional lines, products are developed by whichever operating area is responsible for servicing them. For example, a new personal revolving credit line would be designed and developed by the consumer credit operations department.

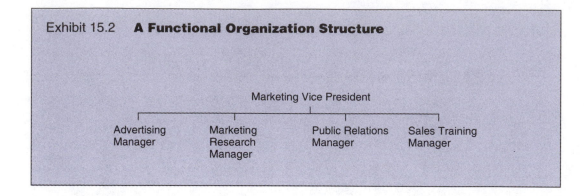

Exhibit 15.2   **A Functional Organization Structure**

Marketing Vice President

Advertising Manager | Marketing Research Manager | Public Relations Manager | Sales Training Manager

That department would work with the computer systems staff to make the programming modifications necessary to offer the product. It would also work with the funds management and accounting areas to determine how the product should be priced. The greatest problem with this approach is that the operations staff who are responsible for product design often have more of a production orientation than a consumer or marketing orientation. Also, this puts the marketing department in the position of having to successfully promote a product that may not be as competitive and marketable as it could have been.

Product Management Organization

This organizational structure is similar to that of the functional organization, except that the bank's marketing department includes another manager or group of managers who have product responsibility. (See exhibit 15.3.) These product managers use the services of the other functional managers in the marketing department, who are marketing professionals.

The concept of product management began in 1927 at Procter & Gamble. The company's Camay soap was not selling well, so one man was given sole responsibility for marketing the product. He succeeded in greatly improving Camay's market position and was later made president of the firm. The product management (or brand management) concept was extended to other products within Procter & Gamble and eventually spread to other firms.[2]

A product manager's job is to develop and enhance products, establish and implement marketing strategies, and measure results. The functional departments (advertising, marketing research, public relations, and sales training) are a resource or staff service available to the product managers.

The principal shortcoming of the product management form of organization in banking is that the product manager has certain responsibilities with respect to a specific product, but generally has no authority over the people on the line whose cooperation and sales efforts dictate the success of the product marketing plan. One way in which some banks have addressed this problem is to develop a form of matrix management in which the product managers report to two people: the marketing head and the respective division head. For example, the retail deposit product manager would report to both the marketing manager and the head of the retail division. In this form of organization, the division head is specifically responsible for the development and enhancement of products as well as for the implementation of product marketing plans. The product manager's responsibilities do not change, but the likelihood that product plans will be implemented is greater.

There are numerous other approaches possible. For example, in a midsize bank in Illinois, five executive vice presidents report to the CEO: retail banking, commercial lending, administration, credit analysis, and marketing and sales. Each of these EVPs has a staff to manage independently.

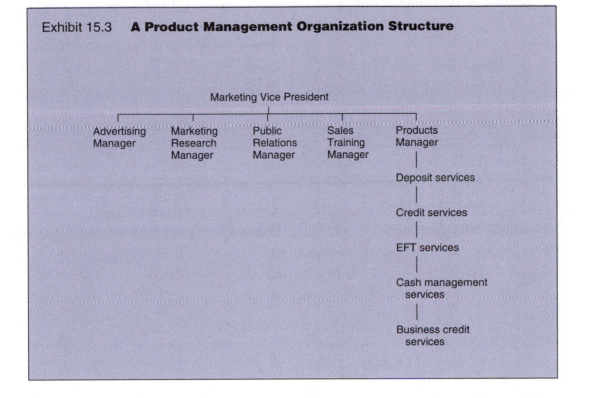

Exhibit 15.3   A Product Management Organization Structure

Marketing Vice President

- Advertising Manager
- Marketing Research Manager
- Public Relations Manager
- Sales Training Manager
- Products Manager
  - Deposit services
  - Credit services
  - EFT services
  - Cash management services
  - Business credit services

It is possible that every bank has a slightly different approach to product management and to organizing staff members to handle these responsibilities. Consider how your own bank is organized compared with the above midsize bank.

The Location of Marketing within the Bank

When a bank has a centralized marketing department, the title and position of the marketing head on the bank's organization chart indicate the bank's level of marketing awareness. For example, if bank management sees marketing as fundamental to the business of the bank, the marketing head of a smaller bank might report directly to the president or chief executive officer and will have the same status as the line division heads.

In a large bank, it is not the title so much as the power of the person to whom the marketing head reports that is important. In a bank that places a high priority on marketing, the head of marketing may report to an executive vice president or a senior vice president. What is important is that, either directly or through the chain of command, the marketing head must be able to mobilize many line and staff areas of the bank (such as systems, operations, and branch administration) to support the marketing plan.

In some banks, marketing is regarded as necessary, but peripheral to the essential operations of the bank. Again, the marketing department head may report directly to the president, the chief executive officer, or some other senior executive, but he or she will not have the same status (or title) as the individuals who head the line divisions of the bank. In this type of organization, the marketing function is not fully integrated into all areas of the bank and is unlikely to be because the attitude of the top management is communicated and expressed to the rest of the organization through the institutional structure.

In still other banks, the marketing head is one step removed from the center of power and authority and has a lower status than in either of the other two organizational structures. The marketing department in this type of organization, because it does not have the strong backing of the bank's management, is especially vulnerable when budget and staff cutbacks become necessary.

The level of awareness and importance of marketing has risen significantly during the 1990s. Even experts from Wall Street call on banks to recognize the critical importance of marketing as a philosophy and an approach to business.[3] As the level of marketing awareness grows and banks become more customer focused, many banks have adopted a decentralized marketing organization.

Decentralized Marketing

Few banks have reached the highest level of marketing awareness in which a customer focus permeates every department of the bank. Increasingly, however, bankers are recognizing the importance of having a customer focus. As this happens and line areas (such as consumer finance, retail banking, and small business banking) become customer focused, these areas take on responsibility for product development and product management.[4] Line staff who have demonstrated a keen marketing awareness are promoted to product management positions. As marketing becomes more integral to the bank, the marketing department may be phased out. Marketing is seen as the business the bank is in. Often, marketing research and promotional functions—such as advertising, sales promotion, and publicity—continue to be handled by a centralized department that handles marketing services and public relations.

The challenge in an organization characterized by decentralized marketing is that it becomes harder to coordinate marketing activities that cross departmental lines. Interdepartmental communication takes on increasing importance since different departments that are designing products for the same market must be aware of one another's activities. Some banks address this problem with yet another type of marketing organization. Rather than having product managers who deal with a specific product line (such as deposits, revolving credit, or mortgages),

they have market managers who analyze specific targeted segments of the bank's market and work to develop and enhance products aimed specifically at each market segment.[5]

With a decentralized marketing department it is critical to ensure there is clear and constant communication between the groups to avoid product duplication. Good communication also enhances cross-selling opportunities and referrals.

Organizing for Marketing in a Holding Company Environment

In bank holding companies, marketing functions may be either centralized or decentralized. The organizational structure depends largely on the size of the subsidiary banks. In a holding company with multiple small banks, marketing is likely to be centralized at the holding company level. In this way, the individual banks can take advantage of economies of scale in the production of advertising and promotional materials. For example, a small bank might pay several cents apiece for its statement stuffers. By consolidating and standardizing advertising efforts, the bank holding company might be able to provide the same materials to its subsidiary banks for one cent or less. Holding company subsidiaries also can draw on research and other marketing expertise available from the holding company, which they would not be able to afford if they were independent institutions.

Another alternative is to establish a centralized marketing function at the holding company level, with a marketing head in each subsidiary institution. This may be the preferred option when the subsidiaries are medium-sized or large banks. Some holding companies are taking this approach one step further. They are creating a marketing strategy at the holding company level, but transferring the great majority of execution and daily decisions to the local level.

The reason for this type of decentralized marketing is to position each bank as a "community bank," a much-envied descriptor. Because marketing is handled at the local level, branches can tailor their efforts to their local markets—which they know far better than the holding company could ever hope to. Numerous banks are finding that positioning themselves as "community and customer-oriented banks" and empowering the local banks to carry out the customer focus (and the marketing) wins over customers.[6]

In some cases, holding companies do not have a separate corporate marketing staff at the parent company level. In this situation, the marketing department of the lead bank may service all the subsidiaries. This type of organization fosters economies of scale, but, in addition to possible operational difficulties, the small subsidiaries may resent being dependent on the staff of the lead bank. They may feel that their interests are not being adequately represented or that they are not receiving their share of the marketing department's time. Clearly, each organizational alternative must be evaluated for its suitability to a particular bank or bank group.

In summary, the organization of the bank and the position of marketing in the hierarchy tell a great deal about the extent to which the bank has adopted a customer-centered marketing orientation. In addition, the way in which the bank is organized to perform marketing functions affects the development and implementation of the bank's marketing strategy.

Relationship of Marketing to Other Departments

In the ideal marketing-oriented bank, all departments and divisions work together toward achieving the goals and objectives set forth in the marketing plan, and all have a solid customer orientation. In the real world, however, few banks have reached this ideal state. Generally, each bank department is run by specialists who have their own particular concerns and ways of viewing their jobs and the business of banking. Often, they fail to see their efforts as part of an overall marketing effort.

Nevertheless the marketing staff constantly interacts with other departments, and the implementation of a marketing plan depends on just about every department in the banking organization, especially the following:

- data processing,
- systems and operations,
- human resources and personnel,
- accounting and finance,
- bank investments,
- legal services,
- auditing,
- line divisions, and
- the branches.

Data Processing

Many bank products exist solely as electronic entries on a piece of magnetic tape. Where exactly is John Doe's checking account? It is stored with thousands of other accounts on a computer tape that can be held in one hand.

Since most bank products are data based, the product specialist must be able to work and communicate effectively with data processing professionals. It is equally important, however, that bank products be designed by the product manager and not by the data processing staff. The objective of the data processing group is to develop systems that accomplish a desired result. In contrast, marketing's objective is to see that all the steps taken along the way are customer-oriented. For example, a checking account statement developed by the data processing department might include everything it is supposed to, but still might be difficult for customers to understand. The responsibility of the marketing department would be to ensure that all of a bank's products (including its statements) are customer friendly.

The data processing department can also provide a vast amount of customer information to the research manager and the product manager. Such information is essential in the evaluation stage of the marketing management process, but it is not automatically available. Not only must the required information be requested, but the desired format must be specified.

Systems and Operations

As a product is being developed, someone must design the forms and write the procedures telling the branch staff how to set up for and service the product. But operations officers are primarily concerned with the smooth, accurate, timely accomplishment of the day's work. For them, customer satisfaction may be secondary to the need to have everything properly documented with checks and balances in place to prevent error, fraud, or other operational problems. Many officers would rather risk causing the customer some inconvenience than risk being found at fault by the bank's auditors or examiners. Marketers who have some experience on the front lines of the banking business may be better able to anticipate and minimize potential clashes in these areas.

Human Resources and Personnel

The human resources department is responsible for recruiting and training employees, establishing salaries and benefits, and monitoring the performance appraisal system. In a truly marketing-oriented bank, the customer orientation should be reflected in the job description of each customer-contact person, and performance appraisals and salary increases should reflect how well the individual has performed in this regard. For example, a customer service representative's job description should include responsibility for instructing the customer about the bank's array of services. The bank marketer must provide the customer service representative with the tools (such as brochures) and sales training and product information needed to do the job. In fact, because sales are now so important, today's banks try to hire people with retail sales backgrounds and a customer-orientation instead of a banking or business background. Many banks have found that they can teach banking to someone, but selling skills require a particular personality.

Because incentive and bonus programs are a form of employee compensation, the human resources staff responsible for compensation should be involved in the design of such programs. The sales and marketing staffs should help structure the incentive and bonus plans, as well as create reliable tracking systems to ensure fairness.

Accounting and Finance

A bank's financial staff often view the marketing staff as extravagant spenders who are not "bottom-line" oriented. Actually, the marketing concept seeks customer satisfaction *at a profit,* so marketers will be profit oriented if they are doing their job well. The more bank marketers do their homework (that is, plan, set measurable objectives, justify the cost of their programs, show results through tracking reports, and report on their progress), the more credibility they will have with the accounting staff.

Marketing staff work with account and finance staff in the development of the marketing budget and in assessing the profitability of the bank's various products. It is essential that bank marketers understand how the bank makes money and know how to interpret the bank's income records and statements of condition.[7] The marketing head should sit in on meetings of the asset/liability management committee so that he or she always fully understands the bank's present and anticipated objectives for deposit acquisition and loan volume and its current investment policy.

Bank Investments

The marketing manager must be aware of, and sensitive to, the bank's long- and short-term goals for its asset and liability structure as well as its cost of funds and rate of return on investments. Deposits that are brought into the bank through marketing efforts must be put to use on the asset side of the balance sheet; similarly, new loans must be funded from the liability side. Therefore, marketing decisions that affect rate setting—for example, offering premium rates to consumers in order to attract new deposits or lowering interest rates for a loan promotion—cannot be made in a vacuum. The marketing staff must obtain rate information from the manager of bank investments and then must demonstrate that the difference between the cost of funds and the use of those funds is sufficient to generate a reasonable margin of profit for the bank.

Legal Services

The large number of regulations banks must operate under is burdensome and costly. Banks are regulated by the Federal Deposit Insurance Corporation (FDIC), the Federal Reserve Board, the Office of the Comptroller of the Currency, state banking departments, and, if publicly held, the Securities and Exchange Commission. Many laws and regulations, such as the Equal Credit Opportunity Act, influence the delivery of bank services. Other regulations, such as Regulation DD (which implements the Truth-in-Savings Act), govern advertising. Bank marketers must be knowledgeable about these regulations so that bank services and ads will be in compliance. In larger financial institutions, an attorney is likely to be involved in the product development process and will be responsible for reviewing all advertising copy for each new service to ensure that it is in compliance.

The marketing department, through its research function, may also participate in the preparation of applications for new branches, mergers, and acquisitions of banks. Since these applications are submitted to banking regulators, the legal department may either coordinate their preparation or at least review them for completeness.

Auditing

Marketing is less involved with the internal auditing department than with most other bank departments. However, because of the substantial volume of billing for expenditures on advertising media, the marketing department may be audited periodically to ensure that proper accounting and record-

keeping procedures are being followed. During the development of new products or services, auditing is involved in the review of plans to ensure that adequate controls are in place and that security is not violated.

Bank examiners are paying increasing attention to bank compliance with consumer protection regulations, especially the Community Reinvestment Act. To make sure a bank is in compliance, they may ask to see a bank's marketing plan and samples of its advertising. Thus it is important that the advertising manager maintain accurate records of what advertising has been produced, including when and how the bank's services were publicized (by keeping samples of newspaper ads and brochures, account terms and condition statements, and any notices to customers of changes in account terms, for instance).

Since customer complaints may come in years after an account was established and may result in court battles, it is critical to keep information that pertains to the original account terms on hand. Having information on account terms, advertising offers, and subsequent changes, with the dates of those changes, helps create an audit paper trail should one be necessary to clear up disputes.

Auditing often will check customer service, too, by periodically sending out notices to randomly selected customers, asking them about their account statements and if they have received any notices of changes. This may lead to questions from customers about account terms that require employees to refer to terms on file. Auditing conducts these random checks to uncover internal and external fraud, especially with dormant accounts or those with "unusual" activity.

Line Divisions

If a bank's marketing function is centralized, its marketing staff will be called on to provide services for the consumer banking, corporate, trust, and international divisions of the bank. If the bank's marketing function consists of the advertising and art department, they will be called on by each line manager to execute the marketing materials the division determines necessary.

These are marketing's internal clients, so to speak. The heads of these divisions must be involved in the marketing planning process because they will be responsible for implementing the plan. Open and frequent communication between marketing and the line divisions of the bank is essential.

Branches

The branches are still a bank's principal retail sales and distribution outlets. A constant flow of information must move in both directions between the branches and the functional areas within marketing. For example, the marketing department gathers a great deal of information on the competition and on customer attitudes that can be useful to the branch staff in their dealings with customers. Similarly, branches have access to firsthand observation of customer reactions and behavior that they should pass on to the marketing department. The advertising department regularly sends point-of-sale advertising, such as brochures, posters, and counter cards, to the branches and relies on them to display them properly. The branches use the services of the marketing department to help them function in their local communities by providing advertising to run in local program books and community newspapers, or by planning local promotions, celebrations, or customer entertainment events.

Retail marketing is highly dependent on the cooperation of the branch staff to support the bank's promotional campaigns. For this reason there must be a very good working relationship between the branch managers and the various functional managers in marketing.

Chief Executive Officer

The marketing head works with and requires the cooperation of all the departments in the bank but has no authority over them. Thus the marketing staff must depend on the president or chief executive officer to be marketing oriented and to communicate that marketing is the bank's priority to other members of the management team. Without support from the top, the organization cannot be marketing oriented in practice, and the implementation of even the best-planned marketing program will falter. That is why it is essential to communicate marketing's contribution to the bottom line to the CEO, to educate the CEO about marketing's activities and accomplishments, to involve the CEO as much as possible in marketing efforts, and to prepare well-thought-out proposals and presentations geared to achieve profits, positive publicity, and increased market share to appeal to CEOs.

Implementing the Marketing Plan

Developing a marketing plan is a necessary element that contributes to marketing success, but it is not the only factor. The marketing plan must also be implemented. Marketing goals will not be attained unless the plan is well thought out and correctly implemented. Implementation is the process that turns a marketing plan, which identifies who, where, when, and how the bank will operate its marketing campaign, into specific tasks to be performed at all levels and in all departments of the bank. Implementation ensures that each step is carried out in a way that accomplishes the plan's objectives.

If the implementation process is poorly executed and managed, the plan will not succeed. However, factors other than faulty implementation may impede achievement of the plan's objectives. If the implementation process has been well executed, failure to achieve objectives will be traceable to a change in the bank's uncontrollable macro-environment or microenvironment or to some problem in objective setting, target market selection, or marketing mix strategy.

The following section explains the importance of proper implementation in the success of a marketing plan.

The Quality Movement and Implementation

In the early 1980s, McKinsey & Co., a management consulting firm, launched a study to identify the secrets to successful business management. The findings of McKinsey's researchers, Thomas Peters and Robert Waterman, Jr., were published in a book that gave impetus to the quality movement in this country: *In Search of Excellence*.[8] Peters and Waterman identified eight attributes that characterize the most successful companies. Many of these can be applied to the successful implementation and evaluation of the strategic marketing planning process as well. Among other attributes, the most successful companies stayed close to the customer by delivering quality products and reliable, responsible service. They also recognized their workers as the source of quality and productivity, involved them in their planning, and empowered them to serve the customer responsively. Additionally, their executives used a hands-on management style and were driven by the companies' key values.

Many of the steps that must be taken by a bank seriously striving for service quality are steps that will also enhance the implementation of marketing plans and facilitate the monitoring and control of results. In 1990, the Bank Marketing Association defined service quality as "performing to standards that meet the objectives of the organization and its strategic business units and fulfill customer needs and expectations."[9]

While each of these definitions of service quality is correct, they don't convey the passion for excellence that banks will need to succeed in the future. The service quality movement in the banking industry has taken on greater meaning than ever before. Now often known as relationship management, target marketing, and one-to-one marketing, service quality has become more demanding.

Its goal is not merely to meet customer expectations but to exceed them. This philosophy can be seen in action as a growing number of banks across the country implement marketing strategies that focus on competing on value and being totally customer-focused.

As was discussed in chapter 1, customers need and expect a bank to provide reliable service, courteous treatment, clear and understandable communications, competent staff, and responsive service. To ensure that they are meeting these needs, customer-oriented banks involve the staff throughout the bank in setting measurable performance standards for reliability and responsiveness. They develop systems for measuring performance relative to those standards, and they take action to continually improve performance. They also survey their customers periodically to measure customer satisfaction with the quality of their services. A bank that is doing all these things is well positioned for success in implementing and evaluating its marketing programs.

Factors Affecting Implementation

Effective implementation of a marketing plan depends on many factors. Two of these factors have already been discussed: how the bank is organized to perform the marketing function and how marketing fits into the bank's overall organizational structure. Other important factors include the following:

- *On-time and accurate performance by marketing staff, agencies, and vendors.* The product management, advertising, and sales promotion staff, the bank's advertising agency, and any other vendors (such as check printers, premium vendors, and printers) must deliver their services according to the specifications in the plan.
- *Clear delineation of responsibility for various elements of the implementation process.* An implementation task list showing each task that must be accomplished and naming the individual responsible is a useful, if not essential, implementation tool.

- *Communication of the plan's objectives, strategies, and tactics throughout the bank.* All areas of the bank, even those that are not directly involved, should be aware of the bank's marketing efforts. Often a corporate banking customer will mention seeing a bank ad for a retail product to the calling officer. That officer is in an awkward position if he or she is not familiar with the ad. Also, it can be very embarrassing to the bank staff if they feel that the customer knows something about the bank that they do not. Of course, any area of the bank that deals with customers who are responding to the marketing program (either in person or by phone) must be notified of the advertising campaign before it is launched and given the necessary training to deal effectively with the customers affected by the campaign to accomplish the bank's sales goals.

- *Cooperation of all areas affected by implementation.* Cooperation is a function of communication and involvement. The establishment of an implementation task force consisting of representatives from each area that will be involved in the implementation will help ensure a smooth implementation process. The individual who chairs the task force (the product manager or the marketing manager) must effectively steer the group toward the desired end.

- *Monitoring of results.* The bank must have a system in place for monitoring the implementation process and its progress toward achievement of the plan's goals. However, evaluation is one of the three elements in the marketing management process and deserves special attention.

Evaluation: Performance Monitoring and Control

As mentioned earlier, conditions change and events rarely proceed as expected; therefore, the marketing plan needs to be adjusted from time to time. The key planning element that enables the bank to recognize deviations from plan and allows this adjustment to occur is performance monitoring and evaluation. If a bank has an adequate system for monitoring results, it will know when it falls short of its objectives and goals, be able to analyze why, take corrective action, and carry on with a revised plan. Conversely, if the bank does not have an adequate system for monitoring results, it will not know that its objectives are not being met, the underlying problems will not be detected, and the plan will fail to accomplish its objectives.

If a marketing plan fails to accomplish its objectives, it may be difficult to persuade management to try a similar marketing plan again. The marketing department may have to propose a whole new strategy, instead of adjusting the existing plan. Furthermore, the staff's morale will have been damaged—those employees who met their objectives will not have been rewarded, and those who failed to meet their objectives will not understand why they failed. As a consequence, there may be little motivation to cooperate again. The only way to keep the plan relevant and on course is to continually monitor its execution to detect variations and to take immediate remedial action. In other words, the plan must be monitored and managed.

The bank must use measurements and monitoring devices to ensure that its objectives are attained or to discover why its objectives are not being reached so that corrective action can be taken. Because we live in a dynamic, changing environment, it is essential to be flexible. Marketing plans are not static—they should be monitored to ensure that they are keeping pace with the changes in the bank's internal and external environments and adjusted when necessary to keep the plan on track.

At times, however, a plan may derail. The environment in which the bank is operating may change. Recall from chapter 2 that the market is an ever-changing entity, affected by the competitive environment and by the external environment of social, economic, technological, natural, and political-legal factors. Or the plan's failure to proceed as scheduled may be due to some situation within the bank. For example, there might be a lack of cooperation at the operating level, or certain departments may not have the resources they need to get the job done. In any event, such deviations should not be viewed negatively or interpreted as a weakness in the plan. Rather, problems should be viewed as opportunities for learning, growth, and improvement.

Some Reasons for Deviations from Goals

Careful analysis of the reasons for a failure to reach goals will generally indicate that corrective action needs to be taken or that changes need to be made to one or more of the four key planning elements: the situation analysis, the objectives and goals, the target market selection, or the strategy and tactics.

Changes in the Situation Analysis

A marketing plan, based on a list of strengths, weaknesses, problems, and opportunities, is derived from a study of the bank's internal and external environments. If any of the major elements in the situation analysis changes, it will likely affect the execution of the entire plan. For example, if the plan assumed that the competitive situation would remain unaltered during the planning period, but a new competitor unexpectedly enters the market, the plan's deposit or loan projections may no longer be attainable. Likewise, the existing competition might introduce a new service that threatens to take away some of the bank's customers. Whatever the new situation is, the bank must respond to it.

Similarly, the economic environment can change. If the plan assumed constant interest rates but, in fact, interest rates change dramatically, the bank's goals might not be attainable. Or there might be a layoff in a major industry in the bank's market area that would affect many customers and make it difficult for the bank to achieve its goals.

Another unanticipated change might occur in the social or political-legal environment, such as the mandatory development of a low-cost basic checking account affecting a bank's product, pricing, and promotion strategies.

Any environmental situation that could possibly affect the attainment of the plan should be part of a bank's monitoring and control process. In this way, changes can be detected before they have an opportunity to hamper the plan seriously, and objectives or strategy and tactics can be adjusted accordingly.

Problems with Goals and Objectives

Goals and objectives may need to be changed either to reflect changes in the situation analysis or to bring unrealistic objectives and goals into line. If objectives are being reached ahead of schedule, the bank might want to adjust them upward for subsequent periods. If objectives are not being reached, the bank needs to understand why. Some of the more common reasons that banks fail to reach their objectives and goals are as follows:

- *The initial assumptions were incorrect.* The bank should review the situation analysis and make adjustments as required. The bank's staff may have some insights into what factors have changed that management might otherwise overlook since the staff is generally closer to the customer and the problem.

- *The resources committed were inadequate.* If the task simply cannot be accomplished with the existing resources (people and money), then the bank must decide whether to lower its expectations or commit additional resources.

- *The tactics were not specific.* If management failed to assign specific tasks geared to the attainment of the goals, objectives will not be met. The solution is to assign tasks, establish a timetable for their accomplishment, and evaluate employees on the basis of how well they perform these tasks.

- *The objectives and goals were unrealistic.* This is a conclusion a bank may be too quick to reach. Before deciding that the bank's objectives were unrealistic, the marketing planning staff should look carefully at the strategy and tactics to determine whether they are ineffective. Perhaps the bank simply lacks internal marketing expertise. This shortcoming can be supplemented by adding marketing talent to the staff or by using outside professional expertise. An advertising agency or bank marketing consultant can help evaluate the effectiveness of existing strategies and suggest alternative ones.

If it is clear, however, that the objectives and goals were unrealistic, then the bank must adjust them. The revised objectives and goals and the reasons for their revision should be communicated to all employees. The lesson learned from the experience will be useful input to the next planning experience.

Problems in Target Market Selection

The failure to achieve objectives might be due to a failure to follow the guidelines for target market selection (see Chapter 8). The bank might have failed to select a target market or may have failed to differentiate itself adequately from the competition. As a result, its offer might hold no special appeal, resulting in a tepid response. Or the bank might have aimed its strategy at a market segment that it did not fully understand. For example, suppose that a bank discovers that the 20 percent of its savings customers who account for 80 percent of its balances are primarily people over 60, and it decides to develop a promotion to attract similar customers from other banks. Its research should have shown that this segment of the population is the least likely to switch banks.

Another possible reason for failure is that the bank selected a target that is not consistent with its image or positioning. Take, for example, the small bank that advertised itself as the region's "leader" in business banking, or the large commercial bank that advertised itself as "the saver's bank" when that position was locked up by the giant local savings bank. Or the bank might have gone after a market that was not consistent with its resources, as when a small, newly established bank attempts to attract the mass market in a large city. Or the bank might have targeted a market that leads to unprofitable volume, as when a bank's consumer loan strategy attracts a market that results in considerably increased application volume but doubles the turndown ratio.

Finally, the bank might have targeted a market that was already saturated with competitors, as when a bank that is the last one to enter a market with a product promotes it as if it were something new. Careful marketing research can help banks avoid many problems involving selection of the target market.

Problems with Strategies and Tactics

When the environmental situation remains unchanged, the objectives appear to be achievable, and an appropriate target market appears to have been selected, the bank must study its marketing strategies and tactics as the possible source of the failure to attain its marketing objectives. The problem might lie in the bank's product strategy, pricing strategy, promotional strategy, or distribution strategy. Fortunately, problems in these areas are generally not difficult to detect. If a product is not generating customer interest, or if the price is out of line with market conditions, this will be immediately apparent. If customers are having difficulty using the service, or if the target market is not being adequately reached, the bank will know it through direct feedback from the customers or the staff.

Weaknesses in promotion strategy, including personal selling, are more difficult to evaluate and are more likely to require primary research. For example, the customer contact staff may need training in how to sell a new service. If so, a shopper study can be undertaken to determine what techniques are lacking. Perhaps the advertising program was developed without considering how to measure its communication effect. Having failed to set measurable goals, management will have to rely on subjective opinions as to whether the advertising was effective. Just as the advertising budget is highly vulnerable when management is looking for ways to trim the budget, advertising may be an easy scapegoat when the marketing team is looking for a place to lay the blame for failure to reach its goals—especially sales goals. The only way to avoid this situation is to set specific, measurable goals, whether in advertising or in other areas of marketing.

The Reporting Process

During the development of the marketing plan, the bank should (1) design whatever forms are required to develop internal secondary data on the attainment of objectives, (2) arrange a timetable for carrying out primary research to get feedback from the marketplace, and (3) identify the external secondary data needed to monitor changes in the economic, competitive, technological, and political and legal environments. Reports that a bank might generate include

- an annual or semiannual telephone survey to determine banking habits and behavior and the share of new business being obtained by each bank in the market,
- a quarterly follow-up study to monitor changes in attitude toward the bank among the target markets,
- an annual analysis of published data on market share,
- quarterly reports from department heads on progress toward reaching their objectives,
- weekly reports of cross-selling activity by the customer service staff, and
- monthly reports to senior management on new-account activity compared with the prior month and prior year.

From this list, it should be clear that the frequency and distribution of reports will vary.

Frequency

Although there is no strict formula for determining how often control reports should be prepared, there is a rule of thumb: the more tactical the object of control, the more frequent the need for reporting activity; the more strategic the object of control, the less frequent the need for reports. The logic for this is simply that operating personnel responsible for the day-to-day tactical activities of marketing plans require more frequent status checks.

For example, the branch manager might collect daily reports on cross-selling. In addition to providing information on a daily operating basis, this also helps stimulate the branch staff to achieve its goals. The manager in turn will compile less frequent statements of status with regard to operating objectives and strategies based on the daily cross-sell and other reports. The branch manager might send a weekly report, including data on cross-selling activity, to the branch administrator; he or she may in turn report monthly on the cross-selling activity of all the bank's branches as part of a larger report to the chief executive.

Distribution

Monitoring reports flow upward through the chain of command. However, these reports should also be distributed downward to the staff members involved in the activity being reported on. In this way, the bank staff can see how their activities fit into the larger picture and how the department is progressing toward the achievement of specific goals. In addition, the employees may be able to explain why performance was better or worse than expected. Making reports available in this way also ensures that the staff understands the importance of the marketing plan and identifies with it.

Finally, reports should be distributed horizontally so that managers can see how the bank as a whole is progressing toward its objectives. Summary reports may be more useful than the full detailed reports. The marketing manager should be on the distribution list for all control reports so that he or she can monitor the progress of the strategy and identify areas needing corrective action.

Content

The monitoring report should be clear, concise, and direct. It should begin with a statement of the objective involved, the time period, the specific goal, the results, and a statement explaining any circumstances that caused better or worse results than anticipated.

Exhibit 15.4 shows a quarterly review of a hypothetical marketing plan prepared by

---

Exhibit 15.4 Marlton National Bank Home Equity Credit Line Product Introduction

Quarterly Review

Marketing Objective: Increase the ratio of interest-sensitive assets in our loan portfolio.

Goals	*Three-Month Progress*
600 accounts opened in 12 months	300 accounts opened in 3 months
450 active accounts (75 percent of total)	240 active accounts (80 percent of total)
Average outstanding balance per account: $20,000	Average outstanding balance: $22,000
Total outstandings in 12 months: $9 million ($6 million average for year)	Outstandings after 3 months: $5.3 million

Comments:

At three months, we have attained 50 percent of our first-year goal for number of new accounts. We are ahead of projection for

- percentage of accounts with credit line in use, and
- average dollar amount outstanding.

With outstandings at $5.3 million, we will clearly exceed our target for average outstandings for the year of $6 million.

Our advertising for this new product broke at a time when competitive banks were not promoting heavily, giving us a higher than normal share-of-voice in the media.

Our direct mail response rate appears to be running ahead of projection. Final results will be available next month.

Marlton National Bank's marketing director. It is a report to management on the bank's progress toward goals relating to the introduction of a new home equity credit line. (For more information on Marlton National Bank's planning activities, see Case B.)

Some Common Problems Encountered in the Planning Process

Performance monitoring and evaluation are appropriate only after the bank has successfully completed the planning process and has begun implementing the plan. However, any number of things can go wrong either before or during the planning process. Some of the more common problems include the following:

- *Cooperation is lacking during the initial development of the plan.* This problem may reflect a lack of understanding of the importance of planning or a fear of the performance evaluation that might result when the plan is implemented. This lack of cooperation can be overcome if (1) top management communicates to all employees its support of the planning process, and (2) management personnel are trained in how to plan. An antidote to the fear of measurement is to emphasize that the evaluation process will be factual and objective and not subject to whim or personal feelings; that good performance will be rewarded; and that the process affords an opportunity for improving one's job performance.

- *The staff is willing but unable to get started with planning.* This may reflect a lack of specific direction or confusion about precisely what needs to be done. This problem can be overcome by assigning specific tasks to individuals.

- *The planning process was started but never completed.* This may reflect a lack of commitment to the planning process by senior management. Failure to complete the process may also result from the managers' failure to understand what is required of

them. Another possibility is that the planning process got bogged down because the staff was trying to accomplish too much. It is better to focus on one or two objectives and to accomplish them than to have far-ranging plans but no results.

- *The planning process was completed too late to be useful.* One must plan ahead for planning. If the bank's annual budget must be submitted in October, the planning coordinator must work back from that date and develop a timetable showing when each stage in the planning process must be completed. For some banks, this means that the planning for the following year must begin in April. Others start in June, while some banks (some people operate best under pressure!) wait until August.

- *The plan was developed but then shelved.* This cannot happen if responsibility for implementing the plan and achieving the goals is assigned to specific individuals and a control system is put into place.

- *The project stalled after situation analysis.* This may happen when the staff is unable to develop specific objectives because the data in the situation analysis are irrelevant, incomplete, or too general. To get back on track, management must identify precisely what data are needed and arrange to collect these data. If the data are adequate, the problem may be that the staff does not know how to interpret them. In this case, the solution may be to seek marketing expertise either internally or externally.

- *Employee morale slumped after setting objectives and goals.* The three most likely reasons for this reaction are that (1) the staff did not participate in the establishment of the objectives and goals, so it feels the plan has been imposed arbitrarily; (2) the objectives and goals are unrealistic, and the staff, recognizing this, loses its motivation; or (3) the resources allocated are not sufficient to do the job. All these problems can be resolved by improved communication and by making some changes in either the objectives or the resources.

- *The bank failed to develop strategies and tactics for achieving its objectives and goals.* This may reflect a lack of creativity or marketing expertise on the part of those assigned the task of formulating strategy and tactics. This problem can be remedied by a program to update marketing talent within the bank or by contracting for such talent on a temporary basis.

- *Enthusiasm is lacking for further planning.* Lack of enthusiasm likely stems from two sources. First, management may have failed to take the time to recognize the contributions of the staff to the planning effort and to the results. If the chief executive officer does not give this recognition to the managers, they will be less inclined to make the effort again. Second, the results of the planning effort may have been disappointing. If a bank followed all the steps outlined in this text and yet results were disappointing, it may be that the planning effort was not adequate to the task. Ideally, the bank's management should get further training in planning or call in experts to help them through the process as a learning experience.

Summary

The marketing management process consists of planning, implementing the plans, and evaluating the results. Implementation of the marketing plan is a critical element in that process, and it is a step that must be well thought out and executed if a bank is to have any chance of realizing its plan objectives. Implementation of the plan may be hindered or helped depending on how the bank is organized to perform marketing functions and the way that marketing fits into the overall organization of the bank. Effective implementation rests on a number of other factors, such as on-time and accurate performance by marketing staff, agencies, and vendors; clear delineation of responsibilities in a formal task list; com-

munication and cooperation throughout the bank; and the monitoring of results. The level of customer orientation in banking directly affects these stages of the marketing planning process by involving all areas of the bank in setting standards, measuring performance, and making adjustments as necessary to improve performance.

To be effective, marketing planning must be an ongoing process. The ingredient that ensures that it will be continual is the element of performance monitoring and evaluation. Since things often don't proceed precisely as planned, systems must be in place to alert management when things are not proceeding as planned. Unless the plan can adapt to change, it will quickly become outdated.

By instituting procedures to continually monitor the situation in which the bank is operating and its progress toward its objectives and goals, the bank is in a position to revise and adapt the plan in response to changing external and internal factors.

If the bank's objectives and goals are not being met, the problem may lie in the bank's situation analysis, its strategies and tactics, its target market selection, or the objectives and goals themselves. The situation analysis may need to be revised to reflect changes in the internal bank environment or the external market environment. The strategies and tactics may not produce the desired effect because of inherent weaknesses or problems in the way they are being implemented. Or the target market may not have been properly selected. The objectives and goals themselves might be unrealistic. Whatever the problem area, the bank must receive timely feedback if it is to recognize the problem and take remedial action.

Project management reports are an essential part of the monitoring process. Their frequency will depend on what is being measured. Their distribution should be in three directions: (1) upward to senior management; (2) horizontal, so that all managers know how the bank is progressing toward its goals; and (3) downward within a department, so that the staff can see how it and the bank are doing. The reports should be clear and concise. They should contain specific information about what is to be accomplished, by whom, and within what time frame, along with results and relevant comments to help management understand why goals have been reached, exceeded, or not met.

Apart from the many problems that might arise in the execution of a plan, there are also a number of problems common to the planning process itself. Planning problems generally revolve around several primary causes: lack of top management support; failure to set specific, realistic, measurable goals; failure to involve staff in the process of setting objectives; failure to assign responsibility to specific individuals; failure to acknowledge and recognize the performance of individual employees; lack of marketing expertise; and failure to communicate results to staff members.

Points for Review

1. Explain this statement: "As banks become more marketing oriented and customer driven, marketing departments will disappear."

2. Explain how the position of the marketing department on a bank's organization chart can indicate the level of marketing and customer orientation at the bank.

3. Describe ways in which marketing interacts with line and staff departments of a bank.

4. Explain how the service quality movement relates to the implementation and evaluation stages of marketing planning.

5. List five factors affecting the implementation of a marketing plan.

6. Why is performance monitoring essential to the planning process?

7. What are some reasons that results may deviate from the plan?

Notes

1. Much of the information in this section was gathered through interviews with bankers in June 1997, including Susan Little Abbott, executive vice president, retail banking, Busey Bank, Illinois; Lance Kessler, senior vice president and director of marketing, Keystone Financial Corp., Pennsylvania; and Lori McCarney, director of brand and merchandising management, Bank of America, California.

2. Kotler, *Marketing Management,* p. 691.

3. Tanja Lian, "Marketing Must Be an Integral Part of Everything the Bank Does," *Bank Marketing,* March 1996, pp. 37ff.

4. Lauryn Franzoni, "Merging Marketing: The Maturing of a Discipline, Not Just A Function," *Bank Marketing,* January 1992, pp. 14ff.

5. *Ibid.,* p. 17.

6. Katherine Morrall, "Home Grown and High Touch: Community Banks Market Their Turf," *Bank Marketing,* February 1997, pp. 51–59.

7. The reader is directed to the many courses offered by the American Bankers Association/American Institute of Banking, including Principles of Banking and Money and Banking.

8. Thomas J. Peters and Robert H. Waterman, Jr., *In Search of Excellence: Lessons from America's Best-Run Companies* (New York: Harper & Row, 1982).

9. *Service Quality Management* (Chicago: Bank Marketing Association, Service Quality Institute, 1990).

16

THE WHOLESALE SIDE OF BANKING

Learning Objectives

After studying this chapter, you should be able to

- define the term *wholesale banking,*
- use primary and secondary research to identify and assess the market,
- describe some ways in which the product mix and product lines for business banking services differ from retail banking services,
- contrast pricing strategies, promotion mix services, and distribution issues in business and retail banking, and
- provide an overview of product, pricing, promotion, and distribution issues facing trust marketing.

Introduction

This chapter will give you a brief overview of business banking and trust marketing and the application of marketing principles to these areas. Business banking and trust marketing are two subsets of the wholesale side of banking, which refers to all banking products and services not aimed at the retail or individual consumer market. Wholesale banking applies to small business banking, corporate banking, government banking, correspondent banking, international banking, corporate trusts, and any other activities directed toward organizations rather than individuals.

Despite their different focuses, the services banks provide to the wholesale and retail banking markets overlap to some extent. For example, trust services may be marketed both to individuals (personal trusts, estate planning) and to corporations (pension fund management). Some corporate banking services, such as demand loans, are sometimes available to individuals (for example, "bridge" loans for home buyers). Exhibit 16.1 lists services for the wholesale market and indicates which of them apply to the retail market as well.

The wholesale side of a bank, particularly the business banking effort, is extremely important to the success of a commercial bank because of the large volume of business (deposits, loans, and fee-based services) capable of being generated from a relatively small number of customers. Commercial accounts typically constitute about 20 percent of total demand accounts, but from two-thirds to three-quarters of total demand balances. On the asset side of the balance sheet, commercial loans typically constitute half or more of a bank's total loans.

Most rates on commercial loans are tied to the prime rate. When rates rise, the yield on these loans rises; when rates fall, the yield falls. It is advantageous for a bank's assets to be rate sensitive (or able to change) since the liability side of the balance sheet (deposits and borrowed funds) is rate sensitive. The once-large core of low-cost, fixed-rate savings deposits has disappeared as a result of deposit interest rate deregulation, and non-interest-bearing demand deposits have declined as a percentage of total deposits and borrowed funds. They are being replaced by market-rate deposits.

Another reason for the importance of the business or commercial side of the bank is that it is less labor-intensive than retail banking is. While large numbers of staff are required to service a bank's many individual customers, each one generating a relatively small amount of deposits or loans, a small number of banking officers can service a handful of business accounts that generate considerable income for the bank. These corporate officers are supported by staff from other areas of the bank, such as corporate cash management and customer service.

The market breakdown for business banking services varies from bank to bank but is usually segmented into the small-business market, the middle market, and the large-corporation market. The small-business market consists of retailers, wholesalers, manufacturers, professionals, and others with sales of less than $10 million annually. In many banks, the branch system has responsibility for calling on this market. Because of the large number of small businesses in most trade areas, this market can be an important source of business for a bank.

The middle market consists of firms with annual sales greater than $10 million but less than $120 million. This market is generally served by a bank's commercial business development officers. The large-corporation market includes companies with annual sales of $120 million or more. Because the size of a bank dictates the maximum amount it can lend to any one borrower, the large-corporation market is usually targeted only by regional or money center banks.

The trust area has potential for sizable account relationships and fee income, but it

Exhibit 16.1 Range of Services Provided to Wholesale and Retail Customers

	Wholesale	Retail
Deposit/Funds-Generating Services		
Checking	X	
Money Market Deposit Account	X	X
Savings Account	X	X
Certificates of Deposit	X	X
IRA/Keogh/401(k)	X	X
Treasury Tax & Loan Account	X	X
Credit/Funds-Using Services		
Term Loan	X	
Line of Credit	X	X
Mortgage Loan	X	X
Lease Financing	X	X
Acceptance Financing	X	X
Installment Loan	X	X
Credit Card	X	X
Overdraft Funding	X	X
Demand Loan	X	X
Export Financing	X	X
Equipment Leasing	X	X
Noncredit Fee-Based Services		
Account Reconciliation	X	
Balance reporting	X	
Zero Balance Accounts	X	
Lockbox	X	
Concentration Account	X	
Depository Transfer Checks	X	
Payable Through Drafts	X	
Direct Deposit of Payroll	X	
Wire Transfer	X	X
Deposit of Credit Card Drafts	X	
Preauthorized Checks/Debits	X	
Controlled Disbursement	X	
Automatic Investment	X	
Investment Services	X	X
International Services		
Domestic & Foreign Collections	X	X
Letters of Credit	X	
International Funds Transfer	X	X
Foreign Exchange Service	X	X

is a highly specialized market with unique marketing challenges. Some banks excel in the trust area. Others have been in it for years with little to show for it on the income statement.

This chapter concentrates on two areas of wholesale banking: business banking and trust marketing, and the application of marketing principles to these areas.

Business Banking

The basic objective of marketing remains the same regardless of the market being addressed—small businesses, the middle market, or the large-corporation market.

Chapter 6 explained how the buying behavior of organizations is affected by environmental, interpersonal, individual, and organizational factors. Furthermore, especially in larger companies, the purchasing process usually involves several persons. Although the behavior of organizational buyers tends to be based more on economic logic than does the behavior of individual buyers, personal and interpersonal factors still play a large part in the marketing of business banking services.

Identifying the Market and Assessing Its Needs

Even more than in the retail banking market, customers in the business market must be sought out. By opening a branch on almost any street corner, the bank will attract some retail customers who find that office convenient. However, a convenient location is unlikely to attract any new commercial lending or business deposit customers. Prospective business customers need to be identified through research and called on by sales officers.

Secondary Research

To develop its commercial business, a bank must identify its prospects systematically. Through secondary data sources, including personal inspection of the trade area, telephone calls, information from the Chamber of Commerce, Dun & Bradstreet reports, and industry directories, the bank can identify firms that are within its geographic trade area. There are also databases and software programs that contain information on companies within a specific area. The Internet also provides a valuable search tool for banks seeking companies in a particular area and of a certain size. Secondary research is conducted before primary research because it generally is faster and cheaper—the bank checks information that already exists (secondary information) instead of commissioning a new survey or research project (primary information), which generally costs more and can take longer to compile and analyze.

For each firm, the bank should note its line of business, annual sales volume, number of employees, and the names of the principal officers. It is also helpful to determine which banks the firm is currently using.

While most small businesses deal with only one bank, most larger firms deal with more than one bank. Their primary bank is the one in which they have their demand account or from which they receive the most services. In most cases, they also have secondary banking relationships with institutions that provide them with auxiliary services. For its existing business customers, a bank should know (1) whether it is the primary or secondary bank; (2) if it is the primary bank, with what other banks the firm has secondary relationships; and (3) if it is not the primary bank, which of its competitors is. The bank should attempt to gather information about the banking relationships of prospective business customers as well.

The purpose of these data is to direct the bank's calling (or selling) efforts. The most productive marketing area for a bank lies in calling on firms with which it already has secondary relationships—the objective being to turn them into primary relationships.

Knowing the secondary banking relationships of customers enables the bank to assess its vulnerability to competition. For example, suppose Bank A knows that it is the primary bank for XYZ Corporation and that Bank B and Bank C have secondary relationships with XYZ. The calling officers at Bank A become aware that Bank C is making a major push to develop new business. Therefore, they would be wise to direct special attention to XYZ and to other customers who deal with Bank C in order to protect their own bank's relationships against Bank C's competitive efforts.

When trying to attract new corporate customers, a bank should know about the firms' existing relationships and as much as possible about the competition so the calling officer can prepare for the call. For example, suppose Bank A's calling officer knows that TUV Corporation is using Bank B's account reconciliation service. The calling officer also knows that Bank A's account reconciliation service has several features that make it more efficient than Bank B's. These features would be points to cover when calling on TUV's financial decision makers.

Primary Research

As is the case with retail banking, primary research can be a useful tool in determining the bank's present situation in the market and the needs of business customers and prospects. For example, through the use of focus groups among small business owners, one midwestern community bank learned that this market had business needs that could be met through personal home equity loans.[1] The bank targeted a home equity loan campaign specifically to small business owners and launched it through print advertising, direct mail, and a follow-up officer call program. Within four months, the bank had generated a substantial volume of new outstandings.

The larger the firm, the more difficult it is to do research by communicating directly with the business-banking decision maker. Many companies have "gatekeepers" that effectively screen out mail and phone calls from banks or other firms that wish to interview the president or chief financial officer.

Since primary research is a specialized field, a bank may wish to hire a consulting firm to conduct research among the middle market (sales of $10 million to $120 million), the large-corporation market, the correspondent banking market, and the corporate trust market. A bank may share in the results of syndicated research, or it may commission a study of its own. The type of information that can be obtained includes the names of banks used for credit and noncredit services, the level of satisfaction with banks used, the ways corporate needs for various banking services are changing over time, the image and market share of the bank, and the strengths and weaknesses of the bank compared with its competitors.

Adapting the Marketing Mix to the Business Banking Market

Since the business banking market is different from retail banking, the marketing mix must be adjusted accordingly. The product, pricing, promotion, and distribution strategies that are effective in the retail area will not necessarily be effective in selling banking services to businesses.

Product Strategy

As exhibit 16.1 illustrates, the product mix for business banking is more diversified than it is for retail banking. In addition to the line of deposit services, banks provide a deep line of fee-based cash management services and a line of international banking services. The line of credit services is also deeper for businesses than for individuals.

Exhibit 16.2 illustrates some of the key differences between retail and commercial banking services. Within a retail product line, such as consumer loans, the various product items (car loans, home improvement loans, personal loans, and so forth) are actually quite similar. Also, their terms are standardized. Conversely, wide differences exist within the product line of business credit. Loans (such as collateral, payback plans, and

Exhibit 16.2 Some Key Differences Between Retail and Commercial Banking Services

	Retail Services	*Commercial Services*
Customers	Individual Customers	Business, Institutions
Nature of product	Similarity within product lines, for example, consumer loans (car loans, home equity loans, lines of credit)	Wide product differences, for example, customized loans, customized product features for large corporate customer
Pricing	Published and applied to all customers (fees occasionally waived but not modified)	Published but negotiable; paid with fees or compensating balances
Promotional mix emphasis	Mass media advertising; point-of-sale promotion; in-bank personal selling	Personal selling supported by advertising and sales promotion
Promotional appeal emphasis	Combination appeal to emotions, economic logic	Appeal to economic logic
Distribution channels	Branches, ATM's, telephone	Account manager, account support staff, Automated Clearing House system, telephone and computer terminal, branches (for some services)

length of time involved) are frequently tailored to a company's specific needs.

Traditionally, a bank's credit services are the key to its success in the business banking arena. By and large, a firm will deal with the bank that provides it with credit when needed.

Many banks use cash management products as a way to gain entry to a larger small business or middle-market firm whose credit needs are satisfied. The larger the company, the more likely the bank will be to lead

with its noncredit products. Cash management products (see exhibit 16.3) are designed to speed up the company's collection of receivables, concentrate its cash, forecast its disbursements, slow down its cash outflow, and provide systems to give the company information and control over its cash position.

Corporate treasurers have become more sophisticated in the management of available funds in order to maximize return for the company. Thus it is increasingly diffi-

Exhibit 16.3   The Cash Management Product Line

Collection Products
Lockbox
Preauthorized checks
Preauthorized ACH debits

Concentration Products
Depository transfer checks (paper or electronic)
Wire transfers

Disbursement Products
Zero balance accounts
Controlled disbursement
Direct payroll deposit
Payable through drafts
Automatic investment (sweep)

Information and Control Products
Account reconciliation plans
Automated balance reporting
Telephone balance reporting

cult for banks to generate the high-balance, interest-free commercial demand deposits of yesteryear.

Technological advances have also been a factor. Using a computer terminal in his or her own office, the corporate treasurer can assess the firm's cash position at any time in order to decide where to put its idle funds for the best return overnight, over the weekend, or until they will be needed.

A side effect of this sophistication is that cash management has become one of the most important financial services in middle-market and large-corporation banking. Although only the largest banks and data processing suppliers have developed their own cash management services, any bank can purchase sophisticated software and provide these services to its corporate customers.

The market for business banking services is dynamic. The successful commercial banks will be those that monitor changing product needs and respond to them in a timely manner.

Pricing Strategy

Many companies pay for business banking services either through compensating balances or through account analysis, rather than through payment of explicit fees. As part of a loan arrangement, for example, the bank may require the borrower to keep a minimum balance in an interest-free demand account at all times to compensate the bank for its services. The bank invests these "free" deposits, thus earning income to pay for its services. With account analysis, there is a stated fee for each of the bank's services, such as for each deposit ticket and deposited item, each check that has cleared, returned checks, night drops, and so on. (See exhibit 16.4.) Each month, the bank totals the services used and computes their total cost for each customer. Then the bank applies to the customer's average daily balance an earnings credit rate that reflects the current cost of funds. If the earnings credit exceeds the month's fees, the customer pays nothing. If the fees exceed the earnings credit, the customer is billed, or the account is debited, for the excess.

When interest rates are high, the potential value of idle funds increases, and many corporate treasurers prefer to put their idle funds into short-term investments and pay a fee for the bank services they use. With more and more corporate treasurers managing their cash positions to maximize income, fewer are using demand balance accounts, and banks have had to move toward explicit pricing for their services.

Distribution Strategy

In retail banking, physical location is an important aspect of distribution for banking services. In corporate banking, physical location is less important. Personal selling plays a much greater role in business banking relationships. For example, making a commercial loan does not require the physical presence of a branch. Similarly, a deposit relationship does not necessarily require physical proximity since the corporate treasurer can use telephone and computer lines to transfer funds. A large company might have its primary demand account in a bank in New York City or San Francisco, with accounts in numerous, smaller local banks that are "swept" every night so that balances can be concentrated in the primary account. The primary reason for maintaining a relationship with a local bank that is convenient to the firm's offices is for the regular deposit of cash receipts or to facilitate check cashing by the firm's employees. Some banks cater to large firms in their marketing area by providing a courier service to pick up noncash deposits.

Since physical proximity of a branch is not required to provide credit services, many U.S. and foreign banks have successful commercial loan production offices scattered across the country.

Promotion Strategy

The numerous tactics that make up the promotion strategy all play a role in marketing wholesale bank services: personal selling, advertising, direct mail, seminars, and entertaining.

Exhibit 16.4 **Fee Schedule for a Business Checking Account with Account Analysis**

Marlton National Bank
Business Checking

Average investable balances earn credit at the current 91-day Treasury bill rate. Earnings credits are offset against the following charges:

Monthly account maintenance	$6.00
Check paid	$ .15
Deposited item	$ .10
Deposit ticket	$ .20

Personal Selling

Although physical location is relatively unimportant, the personal selling element of the promotion strategy is very important in marketing business banking services. Research and experience in the middle market indicate that the quality of a bank's calling officers is of paramount importance to financial decision makers. (See also chapter 12 on personal selling.) Calling officers absolutely must know their products and as much as possible about the company with which they are talking, and have the ability to get the job done—whether that means arranging a loan or providing some fee-based service. (See exhibit 16.5 for an example of an ad in which a bank touts the quality of its calling officers.) It is with good reason that articles and books about business banking consistently stress the importance of developing a formal officer call program. Yet many banks, both large and small, still do not have an organized, systematic method for calling on customers and prospects who have the greatest potential for becoming customers.

An officer call program has two purposes: to acquire new customers and to retain and develop established business. Firms that are satisfied with their present banking relationships are much less vulnerable to the competition than are dissatisfied firms. Meeting the corporate customer in his or her own territory is one way of assessing and maintaining satisfaction with the bank's services and learning about a company's needs for other services.

Small- to medium-sized banks usually involve their entire marketing staff in the calling effort, although some allow only trained corporate banking officers to call on business customers. To be effective, the bank must set goals in terms of number of calls per month per person. The calling officer should prepare for each call by reviewing the customer's present accounts, or if calling on a prospect, by reviewing whatever information has been gathered about the company— such as the nature of its business, the name of the financial decision maker, and the firm's current banking affiliations. The calling officer should have a goal for each call, even if it is just a call to offer advice or to review accounts and update customer information. The calling officer should always be prepared to get a commitment and close a deal unless the service requires the approval of a loan committee.

Advertising

Advertising in the business banking area is largely aimed at paving the way for the calling officer. For a graphic illustration of this point, recall the McGraw-Hill ad shown in chapter 12 (see exhibit 12.1). Since the target audience for communication about the bank's business banking services is a select one, a bank's promotional strategies for addressing this market will be quite different from its retail promotion strategy. Small business owners, corporate treasurers, and presidents of small- to medium-sized firms are not a mass market. Nevertheless, mass media can be used selectively to reach this group.

For example, Case E presents a study of a promotional program for a bank that wanted to communicate a new, updated image to its community and target markets. The bank conducted research on its competition and surveyed its customers to find out what its current position was in the community. Then it carefully analyzed the information and created a new position and a new logo to convey its contemporary image. This case illustrates that market research and strategic advertising can be used effectively to structure an image campaign and reach new and existing markets.

One objective of enhancing the bank's image in its target market is to increase the bank's market share. When the new logo and image are created, advertising is designed to spread the word and to communicate the bank's updated message to its existing customers.

Advertising is also used to generate a response from prospective customers. Mark

Exhibit 16.5

A bank's lenders and calling officers are a critical factor in serving the business market.

Twain Bancshares, Inc., headquartered in St. Louis, Missouri, and having assets in excess of $2 billion, established a financial objective of increasing its loan outstandings by 10 percent to 15 percent during 1993. Through focus groups, Mark Twain uncovered a perception among business customers that banks did not want to lend money. In a sense, the bank needed to change the image of banking in these customers' minds. In considering a strategy for communicating the bank's willingness to lend, the advertising manager and advertising agency determined that making loans to businesses ultimately creates jobs; they built the campaign around that idea. The campaign included television, print, outdoor, direct mail, and point-of-sale merchandising and generated so many telephone calls that a toll-free 800 number was installed to handle them. One of the ads used in this campaign is shown as exhibit 16.6.

Community banks can be very creative in developing advertising strategies to reach their business prospects. One bank has found an effective way of targeting small business owners and professionals while spending very little on advertising. The bank has a 54-member advisory board made up of local businesspeople who meet quarterly to give the bank advice and feedback on its services. Because of their special involvement with the bank, the advisory board members are also the bank's best salespeople, referring numerous other businesses to the bank. Another bank has brought favorable attention to itself by offering a courier service. The bank's van acts as a circulating billboard as it travels around to pick up non-cash deposits from its customers. Another bank has targeted companies that are eligible for Small Business Administration guaranteed loans. It runs newspaper and magazine advertising and periodically puts on seminars for this target market. A southwestern bank surrounded its trade area with 12 outdoor posterboards, each with a different lending theme, which it then followed up with 30-second spots on local radio stations. This promotion was credited with a significant increase in the bank's commercial loans. (See exhibit 16.7.)

When calling on prospective business customers, the calling officer should leave behind some promotional literature describing the bank and its services. A bank's promotional brochure should contain considerable product information, since its objective is to promote understanding of the bank's financial services. However, an equally important objective of the literature is to promote awareness. Leaving a brochure for the prospect to read later is a good technique for reminding the prospect of the call, the calling officer, and the bank. It's also valuable to follow up after a meeting with a telephone call to see if the customer has any questions.

Direct Mail, Seminars, and Entertaining

Direct mail can also be used effectively in the corporate banking market when a bank has a list of firms that it has identified as prime prospects. An attention-getting direct mail piece can pave the way for a follow-up phone call in which the calling officer attempts to set up a meeting with the prospect.

Another useful promotional tool in business banking is the presentation of seminars for business people and professionals, such as attorneys and accountants. The latter are in an excellent position to refer their business clients to a particular bank and, therefore, may themselves be the object of a business development program or advertising campaign.

Finally, entertaining commercial customers and prospects is an effective strategy that can be used as part of the business development effort. It provides an opportunity for financial decision makers to mingle with the senior and executive management of the bank. Such top-level attention from the bank is well received by business people. A Chicago bank has used this strategy to appeal to the middle market. The bank sponsors radio broadcasts of baseball, football, and basketball games and holds monthly breakfasts featuring sports celebrities. As a result of this strategy, research shows increased awareness of the bank among the target market.

Page 304. This well-researched and planned commercial loan advertising campaign generated a large volume of phone calls from prospective borrowers.

Page 305. Outdoor advertising was part of the media mix for this bank's business lending campaign.

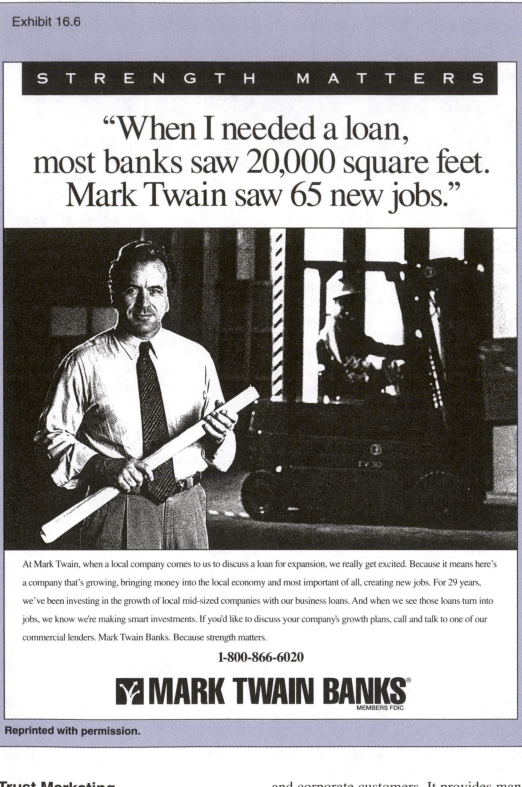

STRENGTH MATTERS

"When I needed a loan, most banks saw 20,000 square feet. Mark Twain saw 65 new jobs."

At Mark Twain, when a local company comes to us to discuss a loan for expansion, we really get excited. Because it means here's a company that's growing, bringing money into the local economy and most important of all, creating new jobs. For 29 years, we've been investing in the growth of local mid-sized companies with our business loans. And when we see those loans turn into jobs, we know we're making smart investments. If you'd like to discuss your company's growth plans, call and talk to one of our commercial lenders. Mark Twain Banks. Because strength matters.

1-800-866-6020

MARK TWAIN BANKS®
MEMBERS FDIC

Trust Marketing

The corporate trust area is another important wholesale banking activity. The trust department, however, services both retail and corporate customers. It provides management services for an individual's investments or an estate, as well as management services for corporate pension funds. That said, the role that corporate and retail trust

Exhibit 16.7

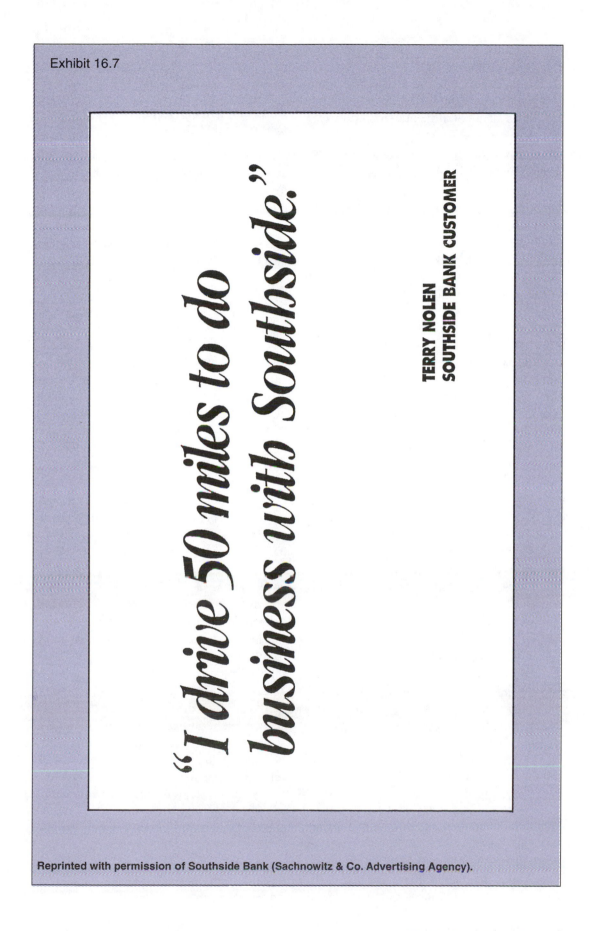

"I drive 50 miles to do business with Southside."

TERRY NOLEN
SOUTHSIDE BANK CUSTOMER

departments play today is far different from their historical role.

The affluent population is growing at five times the rate of the total U.S. population, but banks' share of affluent market revenues has dropped by 50 percent since 1992. There are many reasons for this decline, among them trust's staid image as a department for elderly wealthy people, its resistance to a sales orientation, and increased competition.[2]

As more wealthy customers have moved their assets to investments outside the bank, trust bankers have seen their target markets and their fee income dwindle. To recapture these customers, trust departments in many banks are changing into trust, investment, and private banking departments. Many trust bankers have become talented salespeople with the strong listening skills and patience needed to close a trust sale, which can take a year or more to close. No longer content to wait for referrals or until the customer retires, this new breed of trust marketers now actively seeks younger, wealthy customers and tries to build relationships with customers during their peak earning years—between ages 35 and 55. The goal is to build lifelong relationships with customers instead of a brief relationship at the end of the customer's life.

As with the market for corporate banking services, the market for trust services is a select one. (See exhibit 16.8.) The individuals who make up the market for trust services have significant assets to invest and consequently represent only a small percentage of the total population of a bank's market area—perhaps 5 percent or less. The market for pension fund management is made up of companies of all sizes that have pension funds to invest.

A truly customer-oriented bank will be able to make the most of its trust and private banking department with referrals from other departments within the bank. For example, because of their regular contact with business customers and thorough knowledge of corporate customers' needs, savvy corporate banking calling officers can be important sources of referrals for the trust department.

Adapting the Marketing Mix to the Trust Market

Here again, product, pricing, promotion, and distribution strategies must be adjusted to serve the market for trust services. The marketing mix for trust services bears some resemblance to that of business banking services, but, in several important ways, it differs.

Product Strategy

Strictly speaking, a bank's trust services all relate to the management of assets held "in trust" for another—either an individual or a business. Traditionally, there has been considerably less product innovation in the trust area than in the corporate banking area. Nevertheless, the more aggressive trust marketing banks find ways to repackage existing investment management services for new markets, especially in the face of keen competition for those new markets. Some banks, especially those in mature markets where the personal trust business is no longer growing, have developed services for individuals who have as little as $100,000 in assets to be managed. Other banks have developed investment services for individuals who want to invest in precious metals or collectibles.

The backbone of the trust department is its investment research and its resulting record for earnings on managed funds. The bank's ability to outperform some well-known indicator of stock earnings, such as the Dow Jones Industrial Average, is an accomplishment worth advertising.

Some aggressive bank trust departments sell their investment advisory services for a fee to others, such as insurance companies, brokerage houses, money market funds, and other banks. Although the basic product

The trust market is so specialized that effective trust advertising must convey reliability, strength, and security to capture prospects.

remains asset management, marketing-oriented trust departments are successful at finding new markets for old services and new ways to earn fees.

Pricing Strategy

The trust department is the only area of a bank that earns its income almost exclusively from fees. Fees may be quoted either as direct fees for specific services or as a percentage of the total assets being managed for a customer. In the past, the trust department's services did not, for the most part, generate interest income. Now, as banks work to become customer focused (by providing high-level investment services to customers) and remain profitable, the trust department in most banks is under increasing pressure to produce revenue.

As in retail and corporate banking, trust departments must know the cost of their services and price them accordingly. Although the market for trust services is not highly sensitive to price because it is diffi-

cult for customers to place a value on the quality of the service provided, banks must now call attention to the high value they provide. The expertise of the investment advisers, the level of personal service, and the department's earnings record—all of which are of primary importance to the customer—must now enter the bank's marketing strategy for trust customers. Trust cannot remain quietly in the background if it is to succeed. Banks with the best track record are in a position to demand the highest price, and trust marketers must tell their customers and prospects about the benefits and value the bank provides.

Distribution Strategy

As with corporate banking, the distribution of trust services is less dependent on the physical proximity of the bank. Instead, trust services rely more on personal sales and service to fortify the relationship. However, for the management of personal trusts, the trust officer should be near enough to meet with the client at least occasionally. Some banks, having recognized the importance of maintaining close contact with their trust customers, establish trust offices in areas to which large numbers of their customers have retired. It is not unusual to find a trust office of a northeastern commercial bank in Florida or Arizona. Of course, these banks are not motivated solely by their desire to serve existing customers. Retirement areas are often populated by a high concentration of individuals who are good prospects for personal trust services—namely, senior citizens with substantial assets to be managed or disbursed after their deaths.

Promotion Strategy

One of the tactics the trust department uses to communicate its value and its performance and service record to its customers and prospects is direct mail. But more than the promotional material from any other department in the bank, the direct mail materials the trust department sends out must be very carefully written with keen attention to detail and a highly personal

touch. Prospective trust customers receive numerous solicitations. To make a strong, positive impression, any materials sent must have the potential customer's name, title (if applicable), and address exactly right. Typos and incorrect information are instant turnoffs. Many banks believe a business letter from the president or from the senior trust officer is the best way to go, omitting glossy brochures altogether.

Lists of customers who are potential personal trust prospects can be developed from the bank's records—for instance, by searching for high-balance customers and frequent visitors to the safe-deposit-box area. Lists of firms that might need employee benefit plan management services can be derived from various directories, published by the federal government and by private sources, which list the names and sizes of all companies, unions, and other organizations with pension funds. Attorneys, accountants, and insurance agents can also be valuable sources of referrals.

Once trust service prospects have been identified, the bank should develop a communications program to address them. For the retail trust market, even the smallest bank can buy preprinted brochures explaining the need for, and the operation of, various trust services. Some banks offer personal financial planning courses through the mail, with each part of the course containing an exam that the prospect returns to the bank to be graded. At the end of the course, a computerized financial analysis is provided, and the prospect is encouraged to make an appointment for a consultation with a trust officer.

Some investment management services can be effectively marketed through print advertising in selected newspapers and magazines. Whether the bank has an exceptional earnings record, or is offering a special service (such as a personal financial analysis), or is simply trying to build up its image, an ad in the financial pages or in periodicals read by high-income individuals can be effective. Whenever possible, the ad should include some kind of response device, such as a toll-free number, that the reader can use to request additional information. This provides the trust department with specific leads to follow up on. Because of the potential size of trust accounts, even a low response rate can more than justify the cost of the ad.

Another effective promotional device for the trust area is the sponsorship of seminars for individuals, businesses, and such professionals as attorneys, accountants, and insurance agents. Seminars enable the bank to demonstrate its expertise and provide an opportunity for its staff to mingle with prospects and opinion leaders.

Point-of-sale advertising should be used within the bank, especially in the safe-deposit-box area, the new-accounts area, and the corporate banking area, where it may be seen by business clients.

The officers in the trust department should be active in organizations that are likely to generate leads for new business—for example, service and charitable organizations, municipal boards, cultural groups, and educational institutions. This type of activity provides positive publicity and visibility for the bank, as well as contacts and business leads.

Summary

Business banking and corporate trust services are two of the wholesale banking departments that are commonly found in a commercial bank. These departments and others (correspondent banking, government banking, international banking, and so on) must operate on the same basic marketing principles as outlined previously for retail banking—namely, the satisfaction of customer needs at a profit through a well-planned, well-executed strategy and in a socially responsible manner.

Research, both primary and secondary, is the foundation for understanding the task to be accomplished in the business banking market. Banks must identify and gather information about their best prospects and develop an organized plan for calling on them since it is primarily through personal sales that business services are sold.

The product mix for business banking services is very broad and product lines are deep, with many product items. Products are often customized to the needs of the customer. This market also exhibits rapid product development and frequent product alterations brought on by changing technology and by competition from within and outside banking. Business banking officers must be aware of, and keep abreast of, the ever-changing market. They also must identify areas where income can be generated through fees, especially as idle demand balances continue to diminish in the face of increasing sophistication of corporate treasurers.

The traditional bank practice of pricing business services on the basis of compensating balance requirements is losing ground among larger corporate customers as they recognize the value of investing their idle funds in the money market. Bankers are in the position of having to provide cash management services that compete with, indeed cannibalize, their own demand deposits in order to retain and develop customer relationships. At the same time, high prices (interest rates) for loans are causing corporate borrowers to seek alternative sources of credit.

Advertising in business banking serves to prepare the target audience for the selling effort of the calling officer and to enhance the bank's image in the business banking market. Personal selling and referrals are the leading sources of sales, so promotional efforts are geared to support these. Such promotional efforts often include media advertising, direct mail, informational material, seminars, and business entertainment.

The trust department serves a select market, and its services revolve around its ability to skillfully manage the assets of its customers, both individuals and organizations (profit and nonprofit). Product alterations and pricing are less volatile than in corporate banking, but the more aggressive trust marketers are continually finding ways to develop new markets for variations of trust and investment services.

In both business banking and the trust area, the distribution system relies more on the bank officer servicing the account than on the physical proximity of the bank. Advertising to these markets presents a challenge because the individuals who are decision makers for the trust and business banking services are a relatively small proportion of the total marketplace. Therefore, a bank must seek efficient ways to communicate with them without wasting its efforts on those who are not part of the target market.

In summary, the tactics involved in the marketing of wholesale banking services differ from those used in retail banking, but the overall approach of planning, objective setting, target market selection, strategy formulation, and control is the same. This chapter completes the study of the fields of marketing and public relations as applied to banking. The next chapter looks at where banking may go in the years ahead and what this might mean to bank marketers.

Points for Review

1. What is meant by the term *wholesale banking*?
2. How can banks most effectively use information from primary and secondary corporate market research?
3. How do retail and business banking pricing strategies compare?
4. How does the promotion mix for business services differ from that for retail services?
5. How do distribution strategies differ for business and retail banking?
6. How can adapting the marketing mix to trust marketing help trust departments attract young, affluent customers?

Notes

1. "Kansas Focus Groups Expose New Angle for Home Equity Loans," *101 Marketing Ideas,* volume IV (Chicago: Bank Marketing Association, 1990), pp. 151–152.
2. Tanja Lian, "Turning the Tables on Trust: From Complacent to Competitive," *Bank Marketing,* August 1996, pp. 49–52.

17

THE FUTURE OF BANK MARKETING

Learning Objectives

After studying this chapter, you should be able to

- describe some of the changes taking place in the structure of the banking industry that will affect the nature of competition,
- identify service to customers as the primary focus of bank marketing, and
- discuss the long-term strategic marketing initiatives for the banking industry.

Introduction

Marketing entails managing change. The future of banking, and consequently of bank marketing, will be shaped by changes that are underway or expected to take place in the external macroenvironment and microenvironment in which banks operate. (See exhibit 2.1.) This chapter reviews some of the ways in which the structure of the banking industry in this country is changing, and how these changes may affect marketing. Then it looks at the next iteration in the evolution of the marketing concept and the role that bank executives envision for marketing as we move into the twenty-first century. The macroenvironmental force that is expected to have the most far-reaching impact on the industry is technological change, and some ways in which technological change may affect the marketing of bank products in the future are also considered here. The chapter concludes with some long-term strategic initiatives that bankers have identified as being most important and their potential impact on the marketing of bank products and services.

The Changing Structure of the Banking Industry

In 1980, more than 14,700 commercial banks operated in the United States.[1] The real estate crash, recession, and loan-work-out problems of the late 1980s and early 1990s brought about a number of changes in the structure of banking in this country. Thousands of banks closed or were merged into other institutions. Pressure on profits led many banks to find ways to reduce their non-interest expense and improve productivity. The sheer number of banks had created significant overcapacity in the banking industry. Many banks, especially the larger ones, saw mergers and consolidations as a way to reduce that excess capacity and to improve productivity and, ultimately, earnings.

The number of commercial banks in the United States has diminished by more than 5,000 since 1980, and industry experts expect the total to fall below 8,000 by the year 2000 as consolidations continue.[2] Through consolidation and mergers, the size of some banks has grown tremendously. Now banks with assets over $75 billion are called megabanks, and superregionals have assets between $25 billion and $75 billion.[3] Industry experts anticipate that the number of megabanks and superregional banks will continue to increase through mergers and acquisitions. In 1996, there were 12 megabanks and 18 superregionals.[4]

There is a trend that suggests that the emphasis among larger banks in the industry is shifting from broadening their geographic reach to penetrating more deeply the geographic areas in which they are already located. In other words, they are shifting from a strategy of *market extension* to one of *market concentration* (the measure of total market share held by the market leaders).[5] This trend is especially visible in the Midwest, the Central States, and the South.

In the East, the 1995 merger of Chemical Bank and Chase Manhattan dislodged Citibank from its long-held position as the nation's largest bank. The new bank retained the name Chase Manhattan and had assets greater than $272 billion in 1996. In the West, First Interstate was the target of hostile takeover bids in the mid-1990s and was finally acquired in 1996 by Wells Fargo, making it the fifth largest bank that year. In the South, NationsBank acquired Boatmen's Bancshares, also in 1996, making that bank the seventh largest bank that year.[6] In 1997, NationsBank acquired Barnett Banks, furthering its geographic reach and increasing its assets.

In states where the largest banking companies are pursuing a strategy of market concentration, there will be a few very large and powerful banks and a number of smaller midsize and community banks. The big banks will have the resources to invest in research, product development, and technology and will create healthy competition with one another for innovation and service improvement. Meanwhile, the smaller banks will compete among themselves for their share of the remaining market. The key to success for all banks, however, will be the degree to which they adopt and aggressively implement a marketing strategy and customer focus.

In addition to the phenomenon of market concentration by big banks, industry analysts point to the supercommunity bank as the strategic positioning that megabanks, superregional banks, and large regional banks will adopt.[7] These banks will strive to be like community banks in their proximity to the customer, commitment to customer service and relationship building, involvement in the community, and caring, responsible, personal service. They will empower local branches to make the majority of customer decisions (such as credit approvals) and allow them to tailor their marketing to their local market needs. At the same time, these large banks will be able to offer efficiencies through consolidated back-office functions, high-level technology, and a team approach to the business of banking.[8] With well-trained, knowledgeable staff members who are responsive to customers' needs, banks hope to regain much of the market share that has been lost to other financial services competitors.

Despite consolidation and the growth of very large banks, community banks will continue to have an important role in their communities, too. The number of start-up charters for new banks indicates that the public still wants small, accessible, locally owned banks. Community banks doing business in markets that are also served by megabanks, superregional banks, or supercommunity banks will be challenged to find ways to identify a target market and establish a niche for themselves. They will have to identify and capitalize on the marketing advantages that their smaller size gives them. The use of marketing research, an understanding of the customer's needs and wants, and an emphasis on personal-

ized, quality service will continue to be priorities for community banks. The banks that experts believe are at the greatest risk of being squeezed out, consolidated, or acquired are the midsize banks, which may have trouble carving out a niche between small, intimate community banks and efficient, high-tech superregional banks.

The Next Stage in the Evolution of the Marketing Concept

The role of marketing in the banking industry continues to change. For many years the primary focus of bank marketing was public relations. Then the focus shifted to advertising and sales promotion. That was followed by a focus on the development of a sales culture. Now it is clear, as it has been to other industries for more than the last decade, that the focus must be on the individual customer, meeting and even anticipating his or her needs, and developing trusting, long-term relationships by delivering high-quality, personalized service. (See exhibit 17.1.)

Although all the elements of the marketing concept—customer satisfaction, profit, integrated framework, and social responsibility—will remain important, customer satisfaction must receive the greatest emphasis in the years ahead.

The chief concerns of most bank executives still focus on legal and regulatory issues, according to most surveys. Community banks are particularly concerned with eliminating barriers that give unfair advantages to financial services competitors, such as credit unions.[9] However, another concern pertains to technology: keeping nonbank competitors out of the payment system.[10] For example, software companies such as Intuit and Microsoft made a bid in the mid-1990s for access to the payment systems network by suggesting that all customers would go through a "gateway," such as Quicken (a software product offered by Intuit), to access their financial data and accounts. In return, the software company would collect a small fee. Most banks balked at losing direct contact with their customers, losing fee income, and surrendering customer data as each person passed through the gateway.

When this gateway system was first proposed, access to the Internet was very new and few banks had the resources and knowledge to set up their own direct-access lines for customers. PC banking was also a budding service that few customers had embraced. At this writing, however, customers have shown a growing interest in on-line banking services, and banks have responded by quickly putting in place proprietary sites on the World Wide Web and offering PC banking. Exhibits 17.2, 17.3, and 17.4 are examples of one bank's Web site. Bank of America has created a customer-friendly web site that offers access to numerous products, services, and information.

Not every bank can offer the most up-to-date technology, or proprietary PC banking services, or a Web site, but all are aware of the critical role technology will play in the future of financial services.

The top community banks, for example, are currently investing in improved internal technology. Eighty-eight percent of community banks surveyed reported that PC networks for platform personnel and tellers are either in place or will be in the next three years. And sales tracking software and relational databases are also priority technology investments.[11] Within the next five years, 93 percent of community bank executives surveyed say they plan to offer telephone banking, and 79 percent plan to offer PC banking.

When asked which technology holds the most potential for the future, bank executives identified call centers first.[12] As customers continue the transition into a high-tech world in which they want information and answers more quickly and

The Internet will play a major role in the diversity of banking services. Elements of this home page are revolving messages under the "New and Notable" heading, hyperlinks to other Bank of America web pages, and a direct link to the customer's account information

Exhibit 17.2

Reprinted with permission.

Exhibit 17.3

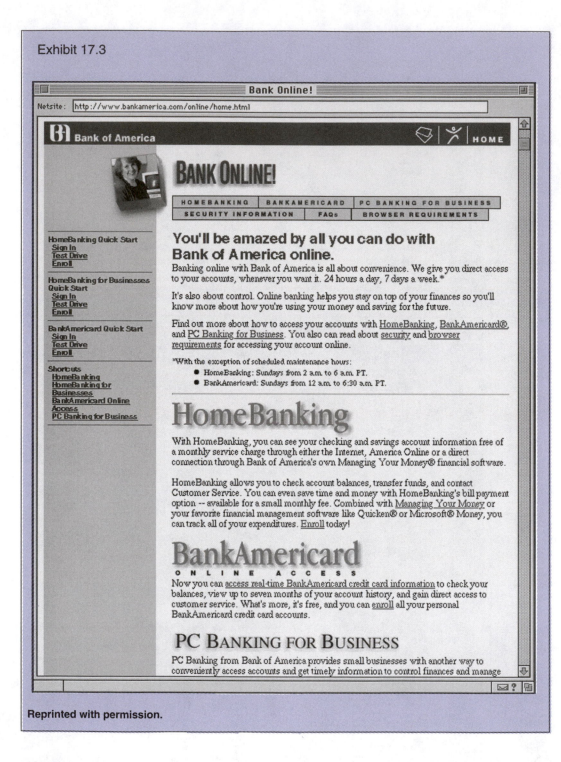

accurately than ever before, call centers offer the ideal bridge. With 24-hour access to either automated information or live operators, customers do everything from check their accounts to apply for a loan. Bank executives also identified PC banking as having the most promise for the future, followed by Internet access and broad-function kiosks.[13]

The Impact of Technology

Technology continues to advance at a rapid pace. The power of personal computers for

Exhibit 17.4

Bank of America HomeBanking

Netsite: https://ihbprod2.bankamerica.com/ihb-bin/ihbcgi?balance_inquiry

Bank of America — *Quick Balance* — SIGN OFF — ?

Account Info | Bill Payments | Transfer Funds | Customer Service

Here are today's balances:

QUICK CODE	ACCOUNT#	BALANCE	CREDIT AVAILABLE
Checking			
HOME ACCOUNT	xxxxx-56789	$3,869.21	
WORK ACCOUNT	xxxxx-98765	$8,211.00	
Savings			
VACATION	xxxxx-98765	$2,103.57	
VISA or Line			
VISA	xxxx-xxxx-xxxx-6543	$1,050.00	$8,950
MasterCard			
MASTER CARD	xxxx-xxxx-xxxx-3456	$93.00	$4,907

Done

Secure Area

Quick Balance | Account Info | Bill Payments | Transfer Funds | Customer Service
Main Menu | Help | Sign Off

Reprinted with permission.

marketing purposes now appears limitless. Banks can connect their personal computers via a local area network (LAN), which allows a group of linked personal computers to talk and share information with one another, permitting various business units within the bank to share data with one another. A LAN consists of a large-capacity personal computer (a server) that serves information down to the workstations. Even more current, however, are companies that have created their own intranets. An intranet taps Internet technology to connect everyone in a company. It allows everyone within the company to have access to applications, information, data, and processes by storing all functions in a single "warehouse" and allowing everyone access using Web servers and browsers. It eliminates the problem of having to convert information to different formats.[14]

To illustrate how an intranet might help

The Bank of America Bank Online! page not only explains the benefits of PC banking, but also helps the customer set up an account online. (left)

When customers have all their services with one bank, they can check all their accounts on one balance sheet, as with this Quick Balance page on the Bank of America Web Site. (above)

with target marketing and sales, consider the following hypothetical case: A prospect file, generated by a research or business development area, is posted on the company's intranet site. A branch manager responsible for business development taps into the file using her PC to identify sales leads in her market area. She then calls up the bank's sales support system, which helps her plan the calls she will make this week in order to maximize her call effectiveness. After each business development call, she files a report with the central information file, and each prospect on whom she called is entered into a tracking system. In this way, both she and her manager can monitor the effectiveness of her corporate calls.

Meanwhile, one of the customer service representatives identifies a CD customer as a potential client for brokerage services. He passes the referral along to the brokerage department via the intranet, then calls it up on his PC a few days later to find out the status of his referral. He sees that a brokerage officer called the customer, opened an account for her, and handled the purchase of some mutual fund shares for her. From this example, one can see how important a role technology can play in the performance monitoring and control aspects of marketing.

Many other technological advances will affect bank marketing.[15] For example, voice-recognition technology will be refined and will replace touch-tone access to telephone customer-information systems. The customer will be able to call the bank's system and say "stop payment," or "account balance," or "transfer funds" and the transaction will take place without having to push any buttons or having to listen to a long list of menu selections. Voice-recognition technology will extend the usefulness of telephone-based services to customers who are unwilling or unable to use the current touch-tone systems.

Image technology will also advance, enabling computers to capture handwritten information from the face of a document rather than being entered via a keyboard. Computer screens will speak to people in a more user-friendly manner with graphics, maps, and animation. Optical storage will be in common use, enabling banks to store images of vast numbers of checks in a very small space. Customers will receive images of checks, rather than the checks themselves, with their monthly statements.

These and other technological advances will affect service delivery systems and the way the customer experiences the bank. Marketing will have the task of communicating to customers the benefits of these new systems and of educating them in their use.

Technology will also assist bank marketing researchers. Many marketing departments already take advantage of geographic information systems that provide color-coded maps to indicate where their customers for various products are located. This type of information has also allowed banks to identify new market opportunities by showing them where they do not have customers and where they do not have a branch, kiosk, or ATM. Knowing these factors while being able to enter additional marketing data has enabled banks to conduct detail market analysis and also ensure that they are complying with the Community Reinvestment Act.

Because computers have become both easier to work with and an integral part of the business of banking, banks now can place more emphasis on hiring workers with good "people" skills instead of hiring workers who are mostly data and detail oriented. By hiring people-oriented employees, banks will continue to move toward espousing a true marketing strategy and customer orientation. Bank employees in customer-contact positions may be expected to have more time for personal sales and service as banks strive to provide quality service and customer satisfaction.

The Challenge Ahead for Bank Marketers

In 1991, when the BMA-MAC Group survey asked bankers to rank long-term strategic initiatives in order of importance, the three top-ranked initiatives were all marketing related: "better service, expanded sales and marketing capability, and more precise customer targeting through market segmentation."[16] These strategic initiatives continue to be implemented. The implications of this finding for those who are engaged in bank marketing tasks are many:

1. *Bank marketing researchers* will need to focus on customers' needs, attitudes, values, and behaviors. With the goal of satisfying individual customer needs, marketing research will be an essential tool. Customer research will help the bank's product development staff understand and anticipate customer needs that can be met through product development or enhancements. It will monitor customer satisfaction with personal service and with automated service-delivery methods in order to pinpoint areas where service quality can be enhanced.

2. *Research staff* will also be challenged to use technology to more precisely identify and segment markets and prospects that can be targeted with a specific offer.

3. *Advertising staff* will be challenged to find the most cost-effective way to reach each target market. Advertising budget dollars will shift from mass media promotion to direct marketing techniques. The mass media will be used primarily for building and maintaining an institutional image, while products will be promoted through more targeted efforts, such as direct mail and telemarketing. Advertising staff will be challenged to account for the cost and results of their programs.

4. *Sales management staff* will be challenged to help build and maintain a customer-focused sales and service culture throughout the bank. As accountability takes on increased importance, systems will be needed to ensure that objectives are set, performance is monitored, and success is rewarded.

5. *Product management staff* will continue to be challenged to listen to the customer and to respond by fine-tuning products and adding benefits, thereby adding value for the customer. The banks that do the best job

of understanding which benefits provide most value to customers, and then provide that value, will be in the best position to price their products profitably.

6. Those who are responsible for the *distribution* of the bank's services will be challenged to find increasingly cost-effective new technologies for making the bank's services available when and where the customer wants them.

In addition to these six points, it is clear the huge impact of the Internet will affect all areas of banking through greater access to research, data, and communication, as well as advertising and marketing opportunities.

Marketing is the business that all businesses are in. Although the banking industry has been slow to adopt this view, it is clear that in the twenty-first century, marketing will at last stop being a department where marketing things are done and become the way banks do business.

Summary

The structure of the banking industry is changing, largely as a result of the economic and financial problems of the late 1980s and early 1990s. The industry is seeing an increase in concentration as a few large banks in many states capture a significant share of total deposits. These banks will compete with one another to be market leaders and innovators. Meanwhile, community banks will strive to differentiate themselves from one another as they compete for their share of the market.

Over the years, the marketing concept and the view of marketing have been evolving in the banking industry. The emphasis in marketing has moved along a continuum from marketing as public relations, to marketing as advertising and sales promotion, to marketing as sales, and now, at last, to marketing as customer satisfaction. As banks recognize the importance of listening to and anticipating the needs of the customer and responding with products and services to maximize customer satisfaction, marketing expertise will be more challenged than ever.

Technological advances not only will enhance the delivery of services to bank customers, but also will enable banks to do a better job of performance monitoring and evaluation. Bank executives will be turning their attention from short-term earnings concerns to longer-term marketing concerns—specifically service quality, sales effectiveness, and targeted marketing. Marketing will, at last, become a business strategy and an integral focus of the business of banking.

Points for Review

1. Describe some of the changes taking place in the structure of the banking industry that will affect the nature of competition.
2. Describe some ways in which technological advances will affect the marketing of bank services in the future.
3. Describe three long-term strategic initiatives for the banking industry that have marketing implications.

Notes

1. *1980 Annual Report of the Federal Deposit Insurance Corporation* (Washington, D.C.: Federal Deposit Insurance Corporation, 1980), Table 105, p. 235.
2. *Statistics on Banking: A Statistical Profile of the United States Banking Industry* (Washington, D.C.: Federal Deposit Insurance Corporation, 1996), Table 105A, p. B-26.
3. "1996 Performance of Top U.S. Banking Companies," *American Banker,* March 26, 1997, p. 15.
4. *Ibid.*
5. This concept and the following information on market concentration are derived from James M. McDermott, Jr., "The Changing Landscape of Banking," *The Stonier Forum,* Fall 1991, pp. 1-3.
6. "Banking's Largest Mergers," *American Banker,* June 20, 1995, p. 4; "Biggest U.S. Bank Mergers," *Washington Post,* August 29, 1995, p. A4; *American Banker,* January 25, 1996, p. 1; *American Banker,* September 3, 1996, p. 9.
7. Katherine Morrall, "Home Grown and High Touch: Community Banks Market Their Own Turf," *Bank Marketing,* February 1997, pp. 50-58.
8. Anat Bird, *Supercommunity Banking Strategies: Winning the War for the Customer Relationship* (Chicago: Irwin Professional, 1997), p. 57.
9. "Small Banks: Limit Nonbanks' Payment System Access," *American Banker,* February 14, 1997, p. 1.
10. *Ibid.*
11. "What the Top Small Banks Buy," *Bank Technology News,* August 1996, p. 16.
12. "Call Centers Prevail," *American Banker,* June 3, 1996, p. 3A.
13. *Ibid.*
14. BES, Inc., *The Intranet Journal,* Web site, June 1997.
15. "Racing into the 21st Century: An Interview with Serge Beauregard," *American Banker,* May 28, 1992, p. 13.
16. Robert B. Hedges, Jr., "Banking in the Year 2015," *Bank Marketing,* September 1991, p. 33.

Part VI

CASE STUDIES

A

Conducting Marketing Research to Assist in a New Product Pricing Decision

We asked the marketing research manager of the fictitious Marlton National Bank to review the steps she followed when conducting a recent marketing research project to evaluate whether the bank should introduce a new low-cost checking account. That review follows.

Market Research Report: Pricing a New Low-Cost Checking Account

Defining the Problem

Our bank (Marlton National Bank) currently offers only one type of personal checking account, priced as follows:

- If the monthly minimum or average balance is $500 or more:

  No charge for checking

- If the monthly minimum or average balance is less than $500:

  Maintenance charge: $3.00

  Each check: $.25

We wanted to add to our product line a low-cost checking account for persons of limited means—that is, an account for individuals who write few checks and keep low average balances. Our marketing department, therefore, sought information that would help us design a new checking account that would appeal to this target audience and yet not reduce our fee income so much as to be detrimental. We determined that marketing research could help us to

- establish a pricing structure that would appeal to the target audience, both customers and noncustomers, and minimize the loss of fee income to the bank;

- estimate what percentage of our own customers might switch to the new account; and

- estimate the number of new accounts that we might expect to draw from our competitors in response to the new product.

Since any pricing decision would surely result in some reduction in service charge income from existing customers, we needed to develop a product that would attract new customers to help offset that loss of income as much as possible.

Planning and Designing the Project

Secondary Data

From internal data, we learned that nearly half of our personal checking accounts (9,204 out of 20,000) had average monthly balances of $500 or less. Although these accounts constitute only 4.5 percent of our total personal checking balances, they account for 100 percent of our personal checking service charge income of $51,750 per month. (See exhibit A.1.)

Primary Data

We wanted to measure the appeal of five alternative pricing schemes among low-balance checking customers by surveying a sample of the target audience. The marketing research department worked with an outside research supplier in the design, implementation, and interpretation of the research.

Selecting a Research Tool

It was determined that a telephone survey would be the most effective method of conducting this research. A questionnaire was developed to gather information on

- the type of checking account currently used by the respondent,

- the number of checks written each month,

- the respondent's stated likelihood of switching banks to save $1 per month in service charges,

- reaction to five alternative pricing schemes, and

- demographic information about the respondent.

We also determined that the best way to compare the relative appeal of each of the five pricing alternatives would be to use the trade-off analysis technique—that is, the potential pricing schemes would be paired, and the interviewer would ask the respondent to indicate which of the two pricing schemes he or she preferred. This would be done for five pairs of pricing schemes. The five pricing schemes to be tested were

1. a $5 flat fee (no charge for checks written),

2. a $1 maintenance fee plus $.35 per check,

3. a $2 maintenance fee, 8 free checks, $.50 each for checks written in excess of 8,

Exhibit A.1 Stratification of Personal Checking Accounts

Average Monthly Balance Range	No. of Accounts	Balances ($000)
0–300	6,443	604
301–500	2,761	966
501–1,000	4,276	3,094
1,001–2,500	4,238	6,549
2,501–5,000	1,387	4,763
5,001–10,000	560	3,819
10,001–20,000	212	2,883
20,00–50,000	90	2,674
50,001–100,000	21	1,436
100,001–250,000	8	1,194
250,001–500,000	2	675
500,001 or more	2	6,548
	20,000	35,205

4. a $1 maintenance fee, 8 free checks, $.50 each for checks written in excess of 8, and

5. $.50 per check (no maintenance fee).

The respondents were asked to indicate a preference among the following five pairs: 1 or 2; 2 or 5; 3 or 2; 4 or 2; and 1 or 5. On the basis of this information, we were able to rank the five pricing schemes in order of appeal to the target audience.

Designing the Sample

We felt we could safely assume that our own low-balance checking customers were typical of other banks' low-balance checking customers. Furthermore, from our own checking account system, we could easily compile the names and addresses of customers with balances under $500. Therefore, we decided to sample only our own low-balance checking customers.

We observed from our secondary data that the number of accounts with balances under $500 were not evenly distributed among the balance ranges from zero to $500. Rather, there were more than twice as many accounts with balances of $300 or less than with balances from $301 to $500. Since these groups were likely to be different from one another demographically and attitudinally, we decided to draw a large enough sample from each of these categories so that they might be analyzed separately.

In determining the size of our sample, we recognized that the larger our sample, the more statistically reliable our data would be, but also the greater our cost would be. We decided that interviewing a sample of 200 customers, half with balances under $300 and half with balances between $301 and $500, would provide us with sufficiently reliable data for our purposes.

Drawing the Sample

Our goal was to obtain 100 completed interviews from each balance category. In drawing the sample, the following facts were taken into consideration:

- Many customers have unlisted telephone numbers.
- Those with listed numbers may be difficult to reach at home.

- Some customers will refuse to participate or will terminate the interview before it is completed.

Therefore, we made the following assumptions:

- Half of our accounts will have unlisted numbers.
- We will be successful in reaching only half of the customers called.
- Half of those reached will complete the interview.

On the basis of these assumptions, we needed approximately 800 customer names and addresses from each balance category, or a total of 1,600 names and addresses. If only half our customers actually did have listed telephone numbers, we would be providing the research firm with four names and telephone numbers for every interview we hoped to obtain.

Knowing that 6,443 customers had balances of $300 or less and that 2,761 had balances of $301 to $500, we prepared instructions for the data processing department to draw a systematic sample as follows:

- For customers with balances of $300 or less, they were to draw every eighth account (6,443 divided by 800 = 8.05), resulting in 805 names.
- For customers with balances from $301 to $500, they were to draw every fourth account (2,761 divided by 800 = 3.45), resulting in 690 names. We anticipated that this would be adequate given our conservative assumptions about unlisted numbers and incomplete interviews.

The sample was drawn by computer and sent to an outside firm that looked up our customers' telephone numbers.

Collecting the Data

We instructed the research firm to conduct the interviews in the evening during the week (from 4 to 9 p.m.) and on weekends (between noon and 6 p.m.). We held a training session with the interviewers during which we reviewed the questionnaire and answered their questions about the study. Participants were not to be told that our bank was sponsoring the research, but rather that they had been selected at random to participate in a banking study. We felt that the respondents might be more honest, especially about their likelihood of switching banks, if they were not aware that they were speaking to a representative of their checking account bank.

Analyzing the Data

Much more data were gathered and tabulated for this project than is reported here. The tables presented here cover the key issues and enabled us to see the differences in response between the very low balance and moderately low balance customers and between four different age groups of customers, as well as for the sample of 200 respondents as a whole. In our analysis of the data, we looked specifically at the following:

Demographics

We asked ourselves if there is a relationship between age of customer and average checking balance. (See exhibit A.2.) We found that about one-fifth of our low-balance customers (balance of $300 or less) were 25 or younger. Only 1 out of 11 customers (9 percent) with balances of $301 to $500 was 25 or younger. Less than half (46 percent) of lower-balance customers were between the ages of 26 and 45, while 57 percent of higher-balance customers were in that age group. As a result, the average age of lower-balance customers was three years younger than the average age for higher-balance customers.

We looked at the relationship between average balance and household income. (See exhibit A.3.) Generally speaking, the higher the income, the higher the balance level. Twenty percent of lower-balance customers had incomes under $15,000, but only 4 percent of higher-balance customers are in this income category. At the other end of the scale, 60 percent of higher-balance customers are in the $25,000 to $49,999 income range, but only 36 percent of the lower-balance customers are in that income range.

Exhibit A.2   Age of Respondents

	No. of Respondents	Balance $0–$300	Balance $301–$500
Total	200	100	100
By Age			
25 or less	30	21	9
26–45	103	46	57
46–60	50	24	26
More than 60	13	6	7
Refused to Respond	4	3	1
Average Age	38.7	37.4	40.0

Likelihood of Switching Banks

We recognized that asking people what they would do "if . . ." has limited value. Asking such questions opens the door to conjecture and to influence by all of the factors that affect customer behavior. Generally, it is better to ask people questions based on their actual past behavior than to ask what they "might" do. Nevertheless, the answers to this question were helpful in determining which groups of customers might be more likely to change banks in reaction to a cost saving.

Exhibit A.3   Household Income of Respondents

	Total	Balance $0–$300	Balance $301–$500	Age 25 or Less	Age 26–45	Age 46–60	Age Over 60
Total Income	200	100	100	30	103	50	13
	100.0	100.0	100.0	100.0	100.0	100.0	100.0
Less than $15,000	24	20	4	9	4	7	4
	12.0	20.0	4.0	30.0	3.9	14.0	30.8
$15,000–24,999	29	19	10	6	19	3	1
	14.5	19.0	10.0	20.0	18.4	6.0	7.7
$25,000–49,999	96	36	60	8	55	25	7
	48.0	36.0	60.0	26.7	53.4	50.0	53.8
$50,000 or more	24	11	13	3	12	8	1
	12.0	11.0	13.0	10.0	11.7	16.0	7.7
Refused	27	14	13	4	13	7	—
	13.5	14.0	13.0	13.3	12.6	14.0	—

Switchers were of concern to us because (1) they are our best prospects among non-customers, and (2) among our own customers, they are the ones we would have the most difficulty retaining in the face of stiff competition from a comparable product.

The question to be answered was, what percentage of total respondents indicated that they are very or somewhat likely to switch to save $1 in monthly fees and which customers are most likely to do so? (See exhibit A.4.) One-third of customers surveyed (33 percent) said they were very or somewhat likely to switch banks for checking to save $1 per month. A larger proportion of customers in the 46 to 60 age group said they were very likely to switch to save $1 a month. Combining those saying very and somewhat likely, customers over 60 appear least likely to switch to save $1 a month, and those between 26 and 60 are most open to the idea. Customers 26 to

60 represent more than three-fourths of customers with balances under $500, so this is a reasonable concern. Not surprisingly, a greater proportion of lower-balance customers say they are very or somewhat likely to switch.

Checking Activity

We asked ourselves how the number of checks written differs among age and balance groups. (See exhibit A.5.) We calculated the average and median number of checks written by each group. However, when we calculated the modal values for each group, we found meaningful differences between groups. More than one-fourth of low-balance customers write only 4 to 6 checks per month, but nearly one-third of the higher-balance customers write 10 to 12 checks per month. Looking at averages, the average customer with a balance under $300 writes about 11 (10.51)

Exhibit A.4   **Liklihood of Switching Banks to Save $1**

Question:

"If another bank in your area had a monthly fee for a checking account that was $1 less than your bank charges, and everything else was the same, how likely do you think you would be to move your checking account to that bank?"

		Balance		Age			
	Total	$0–$300	$301–$500	25 or Less	26–45	46–60	Over 60
Total Income	200	100	100	30	103	50	13
	100.0	100.0	100.0	100.0	100.0	100.0	100.0
Very likely	25	15	10	2	12	10	1
	12.5	15.0	10.0	6.7	11.7	20.0	7.7
Somewhat likely	41	25	16	6	27	7	1
	20.5	25.0	16.0	20.0	26.2	14.0	7.7
Not very likely	62	26	36	11	32	14	2
	31.0	26.0	36.0	36.7	31.1	28.0	15.4
Not at all likely	72	34	38	11	32	19	9
	36.0	34.0	38.0	36.7	31.1	38.0	69.2

Exhibit A.5 **Number of Checks Written Each Month**

		Balance		Age			
	Total	$0–$300	$301–$500	25 or Less	26–45	46–60	Over 60
Total	200	100	100	30	103	50	13
	100.0	100.0	100.0	100.0	100.0	100.0	100.0
1–3	9	9	—	5	—	3	1
	4.5	9.0	—	16.7	—	6.0	7.7
4–6	37	28	9	6	20	7	3
	18.5	28.0	9.0	20.0	19.4	14.0	23.1
7–9	29	12	17	5	15	6	2
	14.5	12.0	17.0	16.7	14.6	12.0	15.4
10–12	51	20	31	5	26	16	2
	25.5	20.0	31.0	16.7	25.2	32.0	15.4
13–15	28	12	16	2	16	6	4
	14.0	12.0	16.0	6.7	15.5	12.0	30.8
16–18	9	5	4	2	4	3	—
	4.5	5.0	4.0	6.7	3.7	6.0	—
19–24	17	8	9	3	13	1	—
	8.5	8.0	9.0	10.0	12.6	2.0	—
25–35	16	4	12	1	9	5	1
	8.0	4.0	12.0	3.3	8.7	10.0	7.7
36 or more	2	1	1	—	—	2	—
	1.0	1.0	1.0	—	—	4.0	—
Do not know	2	1	1	1	—	1	—
	1.0	1.0	1.0	3.3	—	2.0	—
Average	12.14	10.51	13.78	9.86	12.72	13.00	10.54
Median	11	10	12	9	11	11	10
Modal range	10–12	4–6	10–12	4–6	10–12	10–12	13–15

Note: In statistics, the *mode* of a set of numbers is that value which occurs with the greatest frequency. In the chart above, it is the range that contains the largest number of each segment of customers. The *median* is the middle value, or the average (mean) of the two middle values. In the above, where there are 100 customers in the group, the median is the average value for the 50th and 51st customers. Half fall above and half below that value.

checks per month, and the average customer with a balance of $301 to $500 writes about 14 (13.78) checks per month.

Pricing Preference

We asked ourselves what the average customers from each balance category are paying for checking today with Marlton National's current pricing and what they would pay at each of the five pricing schemes being tested. The results were as follows:

	Balance $300	Balance $301-500
Number of checks written/ month (the approximate average for each balance group)	11	14
Charge at current pricing: $3.00/month and $.25/check	$5.75	$6.50
1. $5.00 flat fee	$5.00	$5.00
2. $1.00; $.35/check	$4.85	$5.90
3. $2.00; 8 free checks; $.50/check over 8	$3.50	$5.00
4. $1.00; 8 free checks; $.50/check over 8	$2.50	$4.00
5. $.50/check	$5.50	$7.00

For each of our six customer groups (very low balance and moderately low balance customers plus the four age groups), we wanted to rank the pricing schemes on the basis of the information in exhibit A.6. Starting with the lowest-balance group, we developed the ranking of the five pricing schemes for each of the six groups. (See exhibit A.7.)

Not only were we attempting to provide customer satisfaction with our pricing, but we were also concerned with the "profit" component of the marketing concept. Therefore, we wanted to rank the five pricing schemes from the bank's perspective. We prepared two rankings, one for the customer who writes 5 checks per month and one for the customer who writes 11 checks per month. (These were the modal values for each balance category.) We added this to exhibit A.7.

Developing a Pricing Recommendation

Referring to the grid of eight rankings in exhibit A.7, we used a process of elimination to narrow down the recommended pricing alternatives. The pricing scheme that is one of the most acceptable to the bank ($.50 per check with no maintenance fee) is the least acceptable to most customer groups. Therefore, we eliminated that option. Likewise, the $1 a month with 8 free checks and $.50 per check after the first 8 was least acceptable to the bank but most acceptable to customers, so that was eliminated. The $5 flat fee was unacceptable to customers over 60 and was rated poorly overall by both balance groups. Therefore, we narrowed down our recommendation to two plans: (1) $2 a month with 8 free checks and $.50 per check after the first 8, and (2) $1 a month and $.35 per check, regardless of how many are written.

Although the second alternative had greater income potential for the bank, management chose the first pricing scheme for the new account.

Reporting the Results

After analyzing the data and discussing their implications with our own staff and the research supplier, we wrote the research report. The format that we used is one that management finds most informative and helpful:

The Executive Summary

This was a three-page summary of the key findings and resulting recommendations. The information was presented in bullet-point format rather than in lengthy narrative.

Methodology

In this section, we set forth
- our objectives for the study,
- the background to the questionnaire design,
- how we designed and selected the sample,
- our experience in the data collection phase (number of calls attempted and completed, length of interview, and completion rate), and

		Balance		Age			
	Total	$0–$300	$301–$500	25 or Less	26–45	46–60	Over 60
Total	200	100	100	30	103	50	13
	100.0	100.0	100.0	100.0	100.0	100.0	100.0
A monthly fee of $5.00 and no per-check charge	113	44	69	18	58	30	5
	56.5	44.0	69.0	60.0	56.3	60.0	38.5
A monthly fee of $1.00 and $.35 per check	87	56	31	12	45	20	8
	43.5	56.0	31.0	40.0	43.7	40.0	61.5
A monthly fee of $1.00 and $.35 per check	147	70	77	21	76	39	8
	73.5	70.0	77.0	70.0	73.8	78.0	61.5
No monthly fee and $.50 per check	53	30	23	9	27	11	5
	26.5	30.0	23.0	30.0	26.2	22.0	38.5
A monthly fee of $2.00 and $.50 for each check over 8 with the first 8 free	109	52	57	11	61	29	7
	54.5	52.0	57.0	36.7	59.2	58.0	53.8
A monthly fee of $1.00 and $.35 for each check	91	48	43	19	42	21	6
	45.5	48.0	43.0	63.3	40.8	42.0	46.2
A monthly fee of $1.00 and $.50 for each check over 8 with the first 8 free	120	64	56	16	66	29	8
	60.0	64.0	56.0	53.3	64.1	58.0	61.5
A monthly fee of $1.00 and $.35 for each check	78	35	43	14	36	20	5
	39.0	35.0	43.0	46.7	35.0	40.0	38.5
A monthly fee of $5.00 and no per-check charge	116	48	58	16	61	30	5
	58.0	48.0	68.0	53.3	59.2	60.0	38.5
No monthly fee and $.50 per check	82	51	31	14	41	19	8
	41.0	51.0	31.0	46.7	39.8	38.0	61.5

Exhibit A.6 **Results of Trade-Off Between Pairs of Pricing Schemes**

- information on the statistical reliability of the results.

Detailed Findings

In this, the largest section of the report, we addressed each of the key findings, in order, with the supporting tables and a detailed interpretation of the findings.

The Questionnaire

A copy of the survey instrument is always included as an appendix to the research report so that the reader may see how the questions were worded.

Exhibit A.7	**Rankings of Pricing Schemes**							
	Customer Rankings					Bank Rankings		
	Balance			Age Level			5 cks	11 cks
$1 monthly fee; $.50/check; 8 checks free	1	1	2	2	2	1	5	5
$2 monthly fee; $.50/check; 8 checks free	2	1	5	3	3	2	4	4
$1 monthly fee; $.35/check	3	3	3	4	4	3	2	3
$5 monthly fee	5	4	1	1	1	5	1	2
$.50/check	4	5	4	5	5	4	3	1

Income to Bank for Various Pricing Schemes

		5 checks	11 checks
$1/mo; $.50/check;	8 free	$1.00	$2.50
$2/mo; $.50/check;	8 free	$2.00	$3.50
$1/month; $.35/check		$2.75	$4.85
$5.00 monthly fee		$5.00	$5.00
$.50 per check		$2.50	$5.50

Note: 1 is most preferred; 5 is least preferred.

B

MARKETING PLAN FOR A NEW PRODUCT: HOME EQUITY CREDIT LINE

This is a hypothetical case that presents Marlton National Bank's marketing plan for a new product—a home equity credit line.

Executive Summary

This plan constitutes a recommendation that we introduce an equity-secured revolving line of credit in March of next year. Some key features of the proposed product are:

Line limits	$10,000 to $100,000
Interest rate	Prime (our bank's) plus 1.75 percent, adjusted quarterly
Means of access	Checks and automated teller
Term/minimum monthly	10 years; $50 or 1/120th of outstanding
Payment	Principal plus accrued interest (whichever is greater)
Fees	Bank's cost for appraisal, recording of mortgage, other closing costs (maximum of $350)

We anticipate a first-year profit margin of 2 percent on average outstandings of just over $6 million, and a second-year profit margin of 2.5 percent on average outstandings of $11.7 million. In year two and thereafter, we anticipate a net profit margin of 2.5 percent, based on the assumptions that the bank's cost of funds continues at prime rate minus 1.5 percent, that no increase in staff will be needed in the consumer lending division, and that revenues and expenses are as follows:

Net interest income	3.25%[1]
Insurance income	.10%
Total income	3.35%
Operating expense	(.60%)
Marketing expense	(.25%)
Total expense	(.85%)
Net profit margin	2.50%

We project that at the end of year one, we will have 600 approved lines of credit with the average line being $30,000, or a total of $18 million in approved lines of credit. We expect 75 percent of these lines to be in use, with average outstandings of $20,000, so

that total outstandings at the end of year one will be $9 million. Net first-year profit is projected to be $121,000 on average outstandings of $6.05 million, rising to $292,500 in year two. (See exhibit B.1.)

Introductory promotion of this new product will consist of newspaper advertising, direct mail with follow-up telemarketing to a selected sample of current credit and deposit customers as well as to targeted prospects within our branch trade areas, statement inserts, point-of-sale materials, and personal sales efforts by our customer service representatives.

At 1.75 percent over the prime rate, our pricing is highly competitive, while affording us a profit margin of 2.5 percent in year two. (Our profit margin in year one is narrower because of the high initial cost of product introduction.)

We believe these plans and projections to be reasonable and conservative, and we fully expect to meet or exceed our projection of $9 million in outstandings within 12 months.

Situation Analysis

Economic Data

Second mortgage lending, the foundation of this product, has grown considerably since the early 1970s due largely to the effects of inflation:

- Inflation in the 1970s caused housing values to more than quadruple while mortgage debt grew at a slower rate. As a result, the total value of household equity in the United States grew from $876 billion to $3.5 trillion between 1970 and 1981.

---

1 Difference between cost of funds and yield on this product. With cost of funds at prime minus 1.5 percent and the yield being prime plus 1.75 percent, the interest margin on this product is 3.25 percent (1.5 percent plus 1.75 percent).

Exhibit B.1 Home Equity Credit Line Financial Projections

	Year 1	Year 2
Applications received	1,000	600
Applications approved (60%)	600	360
Total accounts	600	960
Total volume of lines ($30,000 average)	$18 mil	$28.8 mil
Number in use (75% of total approved)	450	720
Outstandings ($20,000 average)	$ 9 mil	$14.4 mil
Average outstandings for year	$6.05 mil[1]	$11.7mil[2]
Income		
Interest margin (at 3.25%)	$196,625	$380,250
Credit life insurance (at 0.1%)	6,050	11,700
Net income	$202,675	$391,950
Expenses		
Advertising & promotion	$ 45,375	$ 29,250
Operations (0.6%)	36,300	70,200
Total expense	$ 81,675	$ 99,450
Net profit	$121,000	$292,500

1 Assumes 400 new accounts within six months.

2 Assumes new accounts are spread evenly throughout the year.

- Record high interest rates in the late 1970s and early 1980s and the recession in the early 1990s caused a tightening of the housing market. Homeowners chose to borrow against the equity in their houses to make home improvements rather than move.

- Also, since the late 1970s, banks have found second mortgages more attractive than first mortgages because their shorter maturities are more desirable when the cost of funds and the future of interest rates is uncertain.

These factors were felt in our own trade area as well as throughout the country.

Demographic Data

Research indicates that the demographic profile of users of equity-secured credit closely parallels the demographics of our own customer base. Users tend to be high-income heads of "full-nest" households, generally males age 35 to 49 years. Credit needs are high at this stage of life, while liquid assets tend to be relatively low. Applicants for this type of credit typically cite their children's education or home remodeling as the purpose for which the funds will be used.

As for the future, we can expect that the market segment most likely to use equity credit lines will grow as the general population matures and as housing values in our trade area continue to increase.

Political/Legal Considerations

The demand for equity-secured credit was stimulated by the Tax Reform Act of 1986. Since then, borrowers have not been able to deduct from their taxable income the interest they pay on most consumer debt. The only consumer debt interest that remains deduc-tible (with certain limitations) is debt secured by the equity in a house. As a result, many borrowers are using equity- secured credit lines and installment loans to pay off other forms of debt in order to retain the interest deductibility. Since the tax benefits of equity-secured credit lines are much publicized each year at tax time (when our promotion will be in full swing), the timing of this new product introduction could not be better.

Social/Cultural Considerations

The social and psychological stigma attached to putting one's home up as collateral for a loan has virtually disappeared in recent years. Homeowners who are the primary target market for this type of credit—namely those with household incomes of $50,000 and more, with housing values in excess of $100,000, and in their peak wage-earning years—are not subject to this bias to the extent that their parents were. However, we are cognizant of the devastation caused by losing a home to foreclosure, and we are prudent in making our loans.

Competitive Analysis

Most major area banks, as well as a number of nonbank competitors, are already offering this type of product. Three of them are aggressively promoting their home equity credit lines, thereby increasing market awareness of, and interest in, the product. In addition, numerous competitors—including banks from neighboring states and two finance companies—have blanketed our trade area with direct mail programs.

Exhibit B.2 compares our product features and pricing with that of our four major competitors. At prime plus 1.75 percent, ours is the best rate in the area. This should help offset the fact that we will lend only up to 70 percent of the available equity in the house, compared with 75 and 80 percent by our competition. With $50,000 in loanable equity, we would lend a maximum of $35,000

compared with $37,500 and $40,000 by our competitors.

A major competitive advantage of our product is the monthly payment: with a repayment period of 10 years and a minimum payment of 1/120th of outstanding principal, our monthly payment at any given loan amount is considerably less than all but one of our major competitors. At the average projected outstanding principal of $20,000, the amount of principal payment required monthly would be only about $167 compared with $278 to $400 by three of our major competitors. (See exhibit B.3.)

Self-Analysis

Good Experience with Equity-Secured Installment Credit

Our bank has been doing second mortgage lending for several years and currently has outstandings of $9 million in fixed-rate second mortgage installment loans. The delinquency rate on this type of credit is low: 0.90 percent compared with 1.94 percent for non-equity-secured installment credit. Furthermore, we have had no charge-offs in this portfolio within the past three years.

Success with Unsecured Revolving Credit

Three years ago, our bank offered an unsecured revolving line of credit to the market, and today we have the dominant share of this business in our trade area. This experience in selling, delivering, and servicing revolving credit will serve us well as we begin offering a secured revolving line of credit.

Need to Be Competitive

We will be the last bank in our trade area to offer an equity-secured credit line. Given the recent and projected popularity of this type of credit, we must offer this product to remain competitive.

Predominance of Fixed-Rate Credit in Portfolio

Even with the popularity of our unsecured revolving credit line, 75 percent of our consumer credit outstandings are at a fixed rate.

Exhibit B.2   Equity Credit Line Competitive Comparison

	Marlton National	Statewide National	Peoples Savings	City National	First National
Interest Rate	Prime + 1.75%	90-day T-bill plus 5.25%	Prime + 3.0%	Prime + 2.0%	Prime + 2.0%
Frequency of Rate Adjustment	Quarterly	Quarterly	Quarterly	With prime change	Monthly
Minimum/ Maximum	$10,000/ 100,000	$10,000/ none	$5,000/ 50,000	$10,000/ 90,000	$10,000/ 100,000
Percent of Equity Loaned	70%	Not quoted	80%	75%	75%
Payment/ Repayment Terms	$50 minimum; 1/120th of principal plus accrued interest	$50 minimum; 1/50th of principal, plus accrued interest	$50 minimum; 1/72nd of principal, plus accrued interest	$50 minimum; 1/180th of principal plus accrued interest	$150 minimum; 1/60th of principal, plus accrued interest
Access Method	Checks/ATM	Checks	Checks; telephone transfer	Checks; premier credit card	—
Minimum to Access	$100	$100	$100	None	—
Fees/ Other Requirements	Actual closing costs; may be funded from credit line	Actual closing costs; paid in cash	Actual closing costs; title insurance required	$300 closing costs; $25 application fee; $25 annual fee	$175 closing cost

Exhibit B.3   Competitive Comparison of Monthly Payments

	Outstanding Principal Balance			
Bank/Principal Due Monthly	$10,000	$20,000	$50,000	$90,000
City National (1/180th)	$56	$111	$278	$500
Marlton National (1/120th)	83	167	417	750
Peoples Savings (1/72nd)	139	278	694	1,250
First National (1/60th)	167	333	833	1,500
Statewide National (1/50th)	200	400	1,000	1,800

In the current relatively low-rate environment, and in light of our corporate goals, it is advisable to increase the variable-rate component of our consumer credit in order to reduce the risk associated with future rate increases.

Current Penetration of Target Market

Our recent customer survey demonstrated what we believed to be the case—namely, that we have an above-average share of suburban households with incomes greater than $50,000 and with household heads in the 35 to 55 age range. This profile closely matches that of the likely equity credit line user, giving us a captive market to tap for this new product and providing us with an opportunity for product expansion.

Ability to Price Competitively

For a variety of reasons, we are uniquely positioned to price this product competitively and still realize or exceed the profit margin required by the bank's corporate goal. We have an excellent computer software package that has been enhanced and tested through several years' experience with unsecured revolving credit. We have an experienced revolving credit operations department that is staffed to handle the expected increase in volume resulting from introduction of this new product. We have lenders experienced in buying a high quality of equity credit. The better the credit quality, the lower the costs related to collection and servicing.

Summary of Problems and Opportunities

Problems

- We are a late entrant to the market for this product.
- Our consumer credit portfolio is still too heavily dependent on fixed-rate assets.

Opportunities

- The annual tax-time consciousness of the nondeductibility of most types of interest is expected to stimulate the market for equity-secured credit just as we are entering the market.
- Our customer profile matches the profile of the target market.
- Our consumer credit systems and operations are experienced in dealing with revolving lines of credit.
- Our customer service representatives are comfortable selling revolving credit, and we can capitalize on this experience.
- We have a proven track record of success in equity-secured lending.
- Our new product is highly competitive in terms of rate and monthly payment amount.

Goals

Corporate Goals

Introduction of the proposed equity credit line is consistent with the following corporate goals as set forth in the bank's five-year master plan:
- We will increase the ratio of interest-sensitive assets in the bank's portfolio.
- We will achieve a profit margin of at least 2 percent on each of our consumer credit products.

Marketing Goals

Our marketing goals for the Equity Credit Line are as follows:
1. We will generate outstandings at the end of year one of $9 million in this variable-rate product.
2. We will generate a total of 600 equity credit lines in the first year, with 450 (75 percent) lines in use.
3. We will price our products to reflect the cost of doing business and generate at least a 2 percent margin on outstandings by generating net revenue in year one of $202,675 and year two of $391,950.
4. We will achieve a net profit of $121,000 in year one and $292,500 in year two (or 2 percent and 2.5 percent, respectively).

5. We will create and maintain an image of our bank as a provider of a full range of consumer banking products by achieving a 30 percent level of awareness among the target market of our bank as a provider of equity credit.

6. We will train customer contact staff during the second and third weeks of February.

7. We will provide customer contact staff with the materials they need to be effective in selling our consumer banking products by providing point-of-sale materials to branches during the last week of February.

8. We will achieve a 1 percent response rate to the direct mail campaign and a 5 percent response rate to the telemarketing program to introduce the Home Equity Credit Line.

Detailed Marketing Strategy and Tactics

Target Market

The principal target market for the Equity Credit Line is high-income heads of "full-nest" households—generally males age 35 to 49 years. Credit needs are high at this stage of life while assets tend to be relatively low. Research indicates that applicants for this type of credit line typically cite children's education and home improvement as the initial purpose for such credit.

We expect many existing customers to become users of this new product. However, we also hope to attract many new customers meeting the profile of the target market.

Product Strategy: Product and Market Expansion

The Equity Credit Line recommended in this plan has been designed to offer features and benefits that meet consumer needs, to be competitively superior, and to comply with all legal and regulatory requirements. This section presents the features of the proposed product, lists the key features and the match-ing consumer benefits to be stressed in product sales, and describes our target market.

Product Description

For a complete description of this product, see exhibit B.4.

Features and Benefits

A chart of features and benefits is presented in exhibit B.5.

Pricing Strategy

We are recommending a penetration pricing strategy that meets the financial goals of the bank (2 percent profit margin on retail credit products) and positions us as the most affordable equity credit line in the city. The latter reflects our relatively low rate (1.75 percent over prime, compared with competitors' rates of 2 percent or more) and our 120-month repayment period. We believe that this pricing will give us the competitive edge needed as a late entrant to this market.

Promotion Strategy

We propose a niche strategy, aiming at a carefully selected target audience from our own customers and from noncustomers within the trade area. Our tactics include advertising, point-of-sale promotion, and direct mail with follow-up telemarketing. Although we will highlight the affordability of our equity credit line in comparison with the competition, we will not adopt a "bargain-basement" approach that would attract unqualified applicants.

Advertising Tactics

(Responsibility: advertising manager)
We propose using limited print advertising in the principal daily newspaper and in the weekly papers in upscale suburban communities. The objective will be to increase general awareness that our bank has introduced this new, competitively priced product. We do not propose the use of radio or television because these media reach too broad an audience for this product.

Exhibit B.4   Product Description for Equity Credit Line

Definition	Variable rate revolving line of credit secured by equity in borrower's primary residence
Target Market	High income heads of full-nest households
Interest Rate	Bank's prime plus 1.75 percent Rate adjusted quarterly Periodic rate (rate divided by 365 days) charged daily against outstanding principal balance
Minimum Line	$10,000
Maximum Line	$100,000
Access Device	Checks Automated teller
Minimum Amount to Access Line	$100
Credit Review	Annual in-house performance review and updated credit bureau report Reappraisal of property every 5 years
Payment Terms	Higher of $50 or 1/120th of principal, plus applicable interest
Fees	Actual costs of appraisal, mortgage recording fee, property search, closing fee, and credit report fee (total up to $350) May be funded from credit line or paid in cash Charged only on approved lines
Insurance	Optional: credit life Required: fire
Late Charges	5 percent of entire billing amount if not paid within 15 days of due date

Point-of-Sale Promotion

(Responsibility: advertising manager)
Our in-branch lobby displays will include posters, counter cards with a "take-one" pocket for the announcement brochure, and rack brochures matching the style of our other product brochures. These materials will be distributed to the branches following the kickoff and training ses-sions to coincide with the first newspaper ad and the first wave of direct mail solici-tation.

Statement inserts describing the product will be inserted in all retail checking and savings statements during the month of March. In addition, computer-printed state-ment messages will tell customers to "Ask about our new Equity Credit Line, the

Exhibit B.5   Equity Credit Line Feature and Benefits

Feature	Benefit
A revolving line of credit	You can use the amount of credit you want when you want it
	No need to reapply every time you need credit
	As you repay your loan, the funds become available to you again
Secured by the equity in the borrower's primary residence	The amount of credit available to you is limited only by the amount of equity in your house (and, of course, your ability to repay)
	The interest you pay is tax deductible
The interest rate is the bank's prime plus 1.75 percent, adjusted quarterly	Your interest rate is lower than the rate on unsecured credit lines and installment loans
	You pay interest only on what you use
	Your interest rate will fall when rates in general fall—you are not locked into a fixed rate
	While the prime might change at any time, your rate cannot change more than quarterly
$100 or more may be accessed by writing a check and through our automated teller network	Obtaining the funds is as easy as getting cash out of your checking account
	No need to reapply every time you need funds
	It is confidential; the people to whom you write checks will not know that you are using credit
Customer may borrow up to 70 percent of the appraised value less the first mortgage (if credit review indicates ability to repay)	You can put the unused equity in your house to work for you
Monthly payment is $50 or 1/120th of outstanding principal, whichever is greater	Very low monthly payment because repayment is spread over ten years
	You can pay the line off faster if you wish — there is no prepayment penalty

affordable way for homeowners to meet all their financing needs."

Direct Mail and Follow-Up Telemarketing Tactic

(Responsibility: sales promotion manager) A direct mail package will be sent to targeted and prescreened customers and noncustomers, as follows:

1. Over the four months of March through June, we will stagger our mailing to the following customer groups:

- Mortgage customers
- Secondary mortgage installment loan former customers
- Other installment loan and unsecured credit line customers meeting certain credit criteria

2. In addition, we will obtain a list of local subscribers to national business publications and professionals at their home addresses. Each of the names generated will be screened through the credit bureau using criteria established by the consumer loan division.

Distribution Strategy and Tactics

We expect a large proportion of applicants for this product to be walk-ins to branches. An essential element of our program will be product knowledge and sales training specifically for the Equity Credit Line. We will accomplish this through the following tactics:

- We will develop a product manual consisting of product features and benefits, forms, and procedures for taking applications and handling loan closing, after approval by central lending. (Responsibility: product manager)
- We will hold a kickoff meeting for all branch managers and assistant managers, and regional and division heads at which the product plan will be introduced. The product manuals for the customer service representatives (CSRs) will be distributed at this meeting. Managers will be instructed to discuss the new product in a staff meeting and to make sure the CSRs review the material in the manual. (Responsibility: product manager)

- We will hold half-day training sessions for CSRs in groups of 12 to 16 over the two-week period before roll-out. Training results will be measured by means of a pretest and posttest. (Responsibility: training manager)
- We will do a special mailing to all commercial account officers explaining the product and suggesting that they discuss it with the executives of the companies in their portfolios. (Responsibility: product manager)

Employee incentives are not being planned for the introduction of this product.

Measurement and Evaluation of Results

In order to monitor the success of this new product introduction from the start and to measure our progress toward our stated marketing goals, the following reports will be generated:

Marketing Goals 1 and 2: The consumer loan division will provide the product manager with a monthly report showing the following end-of-month figures:

- number of Equity Credit Lines
- number of lines in use
- dollar volume of lines approved
- dollar outstandings (amount in use)

Marketing Goals 3 and 4: The product manager will produce an interim revenue and profitability report (using information supplied by the accounting department), which will be submitted to the marketing director six months after introduction of the Equity Credit Line (that is, the report will be due on September 15 incorporating data as of August 31). Subsequently these reports will be produced at the end of each calendar quarter.

Marketing Goal 5: Questions to measure market awareness of our Equity Credit Line will be incorporated into our quarterly advertising tracking research. Marketing research will provide preliminary results to the product manager in early May.

Marketing Goal 6: The training department will provide results of the pretests and posttests conducted during product and sales training of CSRs to the product manager by March 15.

Marketing Goal 7: By copy of the memo accompanying the point-of-sale materials sent to the branches, the advertising manager will inform the marketing director that these materials were distributed on time (before February 27).

Marketing Goal 8: To measure the effectiveness of our direct mail and telemarketing programs, the advertising manager will report the response rates to the marketing director each week. Furthermore, to better understand the market we are attracting, we will do the following:

- The marketing research department will track income, occupation, county of residence, and stated purpose of the loan from approved applications. The first report to the product manager is due May 1; subsequent reports are due quarterly.

- The consumer loan division will report weekly to the product manager on the ratio of approved applications to total applications received.

By the end of the first week of each month, the product manager will provide the marketing director with a memo reporting on the progress of the new product introduction and summarizing the information described above.

C

Sales Techniques

Following are three scenarios that illustrate effective and ineffective selling and customer service techniques:

- new checking customer (effective technique)
- new checking customer (ineffective technique)
- new savings customer (effective technique)

Scenario 1. New Checking Customer—Effective Technique

A customer service representative looks up as a gentleman enters the bank and walks over to her desk.

Customer service representative (CSR) (stands and extends hand to customer): Good morning! I'm Kathy Mayer; may I help you?

Customer: Yes. I need to open a checking account.

CSR: Fine. Please have a seat. May I ask your name?

Customer: I'm Jim Anderson. My wife and I just moved to the area.

CSR: Oh really? From another part of the state or from out of state?

Customer: I've been transferred here from the West Coast.

CSR: That's quite a move. Well, I hope you'll be very happy here. This is my home state and town, and I love it. Now, you're interested in checking. This is going to be a personal household account?

Customer: Yes. This is our first try at getting some banking done. With the move and everything, things get so hectic.

CSR: I know what you mean, Mr. Anderson. We have a number of different checking plans. The one that's best for you and your wife will depend on your account balance and what you want from the account. Generally speaking, what's the approximate balance you maintain in your checking account each month?

Customer: Well, we write a lot of checks—about 30 a month—and I'd say our balance averages around $2,000 a month.

CSR: Well, we have two checking plans that would be good for you. The first is our Interest Checking Account. As long as your average balance for the statement period is $1,000 or more, there's no monthly maintenance fee, no matter how many checks you write. Meanwhile, the balance in your account earns interest every day. If your balance falls below $1,000, there's a $10 fee for the statement period.

While this account would meet your checking needs, I'd like to also tell you about our Select Banking Service. *(CSR opens a brochure titled "Select Banking" and points to the features and benefits as she continues.)* At some point, you will probably want to open some type of savings account, such as a money market account, and Select Banking would give you both checking and savings, plus a lot of additional benefits. As a Select Banking customer, if you maintain a combined balance of $3,000 or more in all your accounts—checking, money market, and any CDs you might open now or later—you get a whole lot of extra benefits. You get a preferred rate on your money market account; plus, you get buyer's protection and an extended warranty on merchandise that you purchase with your personal check. You'll also have an automatic $200 overdraft protection on your checking account, and you can withdraw up to $500 any day from any automated teller in our ATM network. Plus, you pay no transaction fees for using any ATMs in the network. With the first account I described to you, the daily ATM limit is $250 and there's a $1.00 charge every time you use another bank's ATM. So, Select Banking gives you checking, money market savings, no charge for ATM transactions, and a number of other benefits. How does that sound to you?

Customer: I'd need to keep a higher average balance, right? Would I still get interest on checking?

CSR: You'd need to maintain a total of $3,000 in all your accounts to avoid the $10 monthly maintenance fee. But if, as you say, you regularly average $2,000 in your checking account, you'd just need $1,000 in a money market account to get all the benefits of Select Banking. You'd be earning our Select money market account interest rate on the balance in the money market account, and you'd have a regular checking account. To get interest on both the money market and checking balances, you'd need to maintain a combined average balance of $5,000 or more. Those funds could be combined in CDs, your checking account, and your money market account. Which of these options sounds better to you?

Customer: I guess the one that requires $3,000. But I don't have that much with me today.

CSR: No problem. You can open your checking account today with only $50. The minimum opening deposit for the money market account is $1,000. Can you do that today?

Customer: I don't have that much cash available right now with the move and all, but within a week, I'd be able to build up the balance.

CSR: Fine. We'll open your checking account today with $50. Then I'll complete the paperwork to open your Select money market account and keep it here. You can come back next week and we'll open it with your initial deposit. How's that?

Customer: That sounds good.

CSR: Mr. Anderson, I'd also like to call your attention to the fact that, with your Select money market account, the higher your balance, the higher the rate of interest you earn. As you can see from this chart, there's an advantage to building up your balance. Tell me, do you have a savings or money market account at your old bank that you might want to transfer to this account?

Customer: Well, yes, I do, but that will take awhile.

CSR: That's fine. If the time comes that your combined balance is regularly $5,000 or more, please see me and we'll make a minor adjustment so that the balance in your checking account starts earning interest also. Now, before we start filling out the application, I'd like to call your attention to some other benefits of Select Banking. When you need a loan for any purpose, such as a new car or whatever, as a Select Banking customer, you'll get a 1/2 percent discount off our regular rate. Also, for new Select Banking customers, there's no annual fee for the first year when

you apply for our Visa or Visa Gold card. Do you have a Visa card now?

Customer: Yes, so I don't need another one.

CSR: Our rate is quite low *(she quotes the rate),* and after the first year, the annual fee will be only $15. How does that compare with the interest rate and annual fee on the card you have now?

Customer: I think it's about the same.

CSR: I'd like to suggest that you apply for our Visa card and transfer your balance from your current card. That way, you'll still have only one card, you'll save on the annual fee for a year, and you'll have more of your banking business here, close to your new home. Shall I give you an application?

Customer: I don't have the time to fill out an application just now.

CSR: I'll include it with the package of materials I'll be giving you today and you can fill it out at your convenience. Or, you can call me and I'll take your application over the phone. It takes only a couple of minutes. Now, I just have to ask a few questions so we can get you started with a checking account right away.

(They complete the paperwork.)

CSR: It's been a pleasure meeting you, Mr. Anderson. Just mail back the cards with your wife's signature as soon as you can. I've given you an envelope for that. Here's my card, in case you have any questions or if there's anything else I can do for you. Now, is there anything else I can help you with today?

Customer: No, thank you. You've been very helpful.

CSR: Well, thank you for coming by, Mr. Anderson. We're looking forward to serving you. And best wishes getting settled in your new home.

Scenario 2. New Checking Customer—Ineffective Technique

A customer, new to the bank, walks in the door and looks around for the most likely place to open a new account. There are two customer service representatives on the platform, and neither of them has a customer at the desk. The one nearest the door is on the phone, and the one behind him has her head down, apparently buried in her work. No one looks up in the direction of the customer.

The customer, Mrs. Benjamin, moves within view of the CSR at the first desk. He continues talking, obviously completing a personal phone call, without looking up. After several seconds, he says, "I've gotta go. I've got a customer." He hangs up and looks up, saying, "May I help you?"

Mrs. Benjamin takes a seat on her own initiative and tells him that she wants to open a checking account. The CSR reaches for the signature card and service brochure and starts quoting the monthly balance requirement to avoid a service charge on a regular checking account.

Mrs. Benjamin changes direction entirely and indicates her particular interest in "something that offers an overdraft line of credit . . . does the bank offer anything . . . ?"

Clipping her last question, the CSR refers automatically to the cash reserve account and says that it's something customers have to qualify for. He informs Mrs. Benjamin that she'll have to fill out a credit application and that the bank will probably start her off with a $500 line and see how she manages it. Then, after a while she can request an increase if she wants. He asks the necessary questions and completes the paperwork to open the checking account and hands her the cash reserve application, telling her that she can mail it back or drop it off next time she's in the bank. He asks her if she wants an ATM card. She says no, and that's the end of that discussion. She selects her check style, gives him her opening deposit, and finishes the transaction.

As Mrs. Benjamin leaves the bank, she wonders if everyone who works for the bank is as poor in human relations skills as this fellow. She also wonders if she made a mistake by not just walking out after being

told, in essence, that she might not be a good enough customer to qualify for more than $500 of the bank's credit. Well, anyway, she's stuck with them now—for a while at least. She'll wait and see how it goes over the next few months, and she thinks to herself, "If I'm still not comfortable with the bank, I'll shop around and move my account to a bank where the people treat you as if you really matter to them."

Scenario 3. New Savings Account—Effective Technique

CSR: Excuse me, you look like you could use some help. Is there a problem?

Customer: Oh, I'm afraid so. I've been trying to understand these savings accounts, and I think I'm just getting more confused.

CSR: That's understandable. We do have a number of savings plans. Let's see if I can help. Why don't you sit down over here at my desk. By the way, I'm Nancy Stevenson.

Customer: Thank you. My son used to help with my affairs, but he and his family just moved away. I've had some bonds come due, and this time I want the money in the bank so I know exactly where it is.

CSR: I understand. May I ask your name . . . ?

Customer: Oh, of course. I'm Mrs. Frazer. You probably know my son, Henry. He used to come here all the time.

CSR: I'm sure I've met him, Mrs. Frazer. I think the key to planning your savings program is knowing how you want your savings to work for you. You probably should be asking yourself some questions. For example: Do you want to be able to make deposits or withdrawals at any time? Do you want to invest your funds and see them grow? Could you use some additional income each month for living expenses?

Customer: All that's going to help me figure out what kind of savings account I want?

CSR: Yes, it will. Once you tell me how you want to use your savings, and the amount of your investment, then I can recommend a savings plan that will be in your best interest.

Customer: Well, that sounds fine. I need an account that I can add to from time to time. And being on a pension, I could use some extra money each month.

CSR: Many of our retired customers supplement their monthly income with the interest on their savings. Mrs. Frazer, what amount are you planning to deposit?

Customer: I have $25,000 in checks right here.

CSR: That's fine. Now, Mrs. Frazer, we have many types of certificates of deposit that let you earn interest on your funds and give you the option of receiving your interest each month, either by check or by automatic deposit to a checking or money market account here at our bank.

Customer: That would be nice.

CSR: You mentioned that you'd like to have an account that you could add to from time to time. I suggest that you put $2,000 into a money market account. That account pays you a higher rate of interest than a regular savings account, and you can make deposits and withdrawals at any time. You can also write up to three checks to third parties each month. How does that sound?

Customer: I already have a checking account here for paying bills, so I don't need another checking account.

CSR: That's fine. You can simply treat the account like a savings account and use the checks just for taking cash out of the account whenever you need to. If we put $2,000 in a money market account, that leaves $23,000 to invest at a higher rate of interest. Will you be needing any of this money in the near term?

Customer: No, I just need some place to keep it safe and secure.

CSR: Well, right now, interest rates are lower than they've been in a while and there's a good chance that within a few months they'll be going up again. So, I'm going to suggest that we deposit half of your money into a six-month CD. That way, in six months, if rates have gone up, you can either roll it over at a higher rate or put it into a longer-term CD at a rate that is higher than the one you could get today. How does that sound?

Customer: So you're saying I should put $11,500 in a six-month CD and see what the rates are six months from now?

CSR: That's right. Then, I suggest the rest of the money go into a one-year CD. That way, half your money will mature in six months and the other half, six months later—giving you the opportunity to see where interest rates are and perhaps lock some of your money up for a longer time—maybe even five years— if rates go up higher. Meanwhile, you can be getting monthly interest from both of the CDs.

Customer: Yes, that's what I'd like to do.

CSR: Now, we can deposit the interest you earn each month into your money market account or your checking account. That way, it would be right there for you to use and you won't have to go through the trouble of receiving the check and then getting to the bank to deposit it or cash it. Would that be good for you?

Customer: I'd prefer to get the check in the mail. I like to see the income coming in. And besides, I like coming to the bank.

CSR: That's fine. *(She figures out the approximate amount of interest the customer will receive each month, tells her the amount, and opens the money market account and the two CDs.)* By the way, Mrs. Frazer, are you having your Social Security check deposited directly into your checking account?

Customer: No, I like to get it at home.

CSR: I can understand that you like to see that it's arrived, but it's so much safer to have it deposited directly to your account. You never have to worry about whether it's arrived or not, and if you're away or if the weather's bad, you don't have to make a trip to the bank to deposit the check. Wouldn't that be good?

Customer: I suppose it would, but I'm just an old fuddy-duddy. I like doing things the old-fashioned way.

CSR: Well, if you ever change your mind, I'll be happy to help you. Is there anything else I can do for you today?

Customer: No, you've been very helpful. Thank you so much.

D

DEVELOPING A RETAIL PROMOTIONAL CAMPAIGN

The following is an account of the actual introduction of a new product and its related promotional campaign.

Bank of Hawaii Introduces Its Own MasterCard

Background

Bank of Hawaii (Bankoh) celebrated 100 years in business in 1997. With more than 74 branches in Hawaii—more than any of its competitors—and assets of more than $12.5 billion, Bankoh is one of the two largest banks in Hawaii (the other is First Hawaiian).

After a weak economic performance in the early 1990s, Hawaii started experiencing a comeback in 1994 and 1995. The improving economic situation, combined with the new interstate branch banking laws that took effect in 1996, makes it seem likely that out-of-state banks will open branches in Hawaii. Bankoh realized that it needed to safeguard its strong, loyal customer base. Although surveys showed that 7 out of 10 households in Hawaii have a relationship with Bankoh, the bank believed that it would need to offer additional value to its customers to fend off out-of-state banks.

Setting Goals and Objectives

Research showed that Bankoh's bank card portfolio was a strong source of income. Although the bank had only offered Visa Classic and Gold cards in the past, a survey of existing customers revealed they would be interested if Bankoh added a MasterCard to its products. The goal of the campaign was to increase the value of credit card services to Bankoh customers. Greater value would spur greater loyalty and satisfaction, and also increase outstandings to $500,000,000 in five years, a 178 percent increase. Therefore, the bank decided to offer the MasterCard bank card to reach this goal.

To save time and money, Bankoh decided to introduce both the Gold and Standard MasterCard at the same time. The bank had learned through the same customer survey that Visa was perceived as being accepted more widely. To avoid "cannibalizing" their Visa market share, the bank increased the line of credit to existing customers on their Visa cards and offered them the new higher line of credit on their new MasterCards. It also offered customers balance transfer rebates and check writing. The higher credit limits were thought to add enticement to customers.

Strategy and Tactics

Research confirmed that MasterCard would be accepted by existing Bankoh customers. It also showed that by offering MasterCard products, the bank would be able to provide a more complete bank card menu for customers to select from. The benefits of MasterCard customers preferred were an annual fee that is waived if the card is used at least once a year, and a low introductory interest rate.

Product development required the creation of a task force made up of numerous departments in the bank. With the addition of MasterCard bank cards, Bankoh anticipated market expansion outside Hawaii in the future. By offering both cards, Bankoh would have the widest appeal to potential customers both in Hawaii and in other states.

At the time, Bankoh offered five types of Visa:

- Bankoh Opportunities—Visa card with risk-based pricing,
- Bankoh Secured Visa—for those who wish to rebuild credit rating,
- Business Visa—for small business owners,
- Visa Classic—competitively priced low annual interest rate card, and
- Visa Gold—Bankoh's premium card.

By introducing the Gold MasterCard, Bankoh would also be able to offer the product's many travel benefits, such as pre-trip information and planning assistance, MasterAssist Travel Assistance Services (which includes medical assistance), additional travel insurance, and lost luggage matching reimbursement, which set it apart from Visa.

Distribution was achieved primarily through branches. Direct mail and loan by phone were two other avenues of distribution. In-branch merchandising and special product training were implemented.

Design was important to the success of the card. A painting of an island known to all natives and residents, but not as well known to tourists, was selected for the card. The visual appeal of the card accounted for much of the card's success.

Selecting the Media

Bankoh chose to create an awareness of the new product through strong visual imagery in collateral materials to distinguish the new MasterCard from the Bankoh Visa. Direct mail was used to distribute brochures, both black-and-white and four-color print advertising was used to introduce and market the new MasterCard, and in-branch merchandising supported the campaign. In addition, statement stuffers were included in Bankoh DDA and Visa accounts. Radio advertising incorporating the bank's "Smart Money" theme was used to promote the card.

Creating the Advertising

Advertising was the platform that supported the direct mail campaign, the in-branch merchandising, and the sales efforts.

- The bank capitalized on MasterCard's national "Smart Money" theme to improve name recognition and to reinforce the campaign.
- The objective of the advertising was to introduce the gold and standard cards in the summer of 1995, to create awareness of the new MasterCards, and to communicate the product's features and benefits.
- The strategies included developing collateral materials, print ads for both magazine and newspaper, in-branch merchandising, statement inserts, and radio advertising.
- The goal was to position MasterCard not as competition to Bankoh's exist-

ing Visa card, but as a companion to the Visa card, to "give you more of what you want" in a card, plus the advantages (with the Gold MasterCard) of travel benefits.

- The overall response rate to the direct mail for both Gold and Standard MasterCards was 7.93 percent. More than 51,000 pieces were mailed and the bank received 4,045 acceptances.

Developing the Sales Promotion Materials

Branch managers played a key role in the success of the campaign. The advertising generated leads, but many of the sales were closed by branch personnel. The sales initiative was successful due to the in-depth product training and incentive plan the bank developed. The Branch Incentive Award Program (BIAP) had a preestablished point system and had no ceiling on incentive payments. The system worked so well that within 90 days, 5,061 new accounts had been opened.

Internal and External Communications

Since MasterCard is a mature product, Bankoh felt that there was no need to invest in special communications to the news media about the launch. Internal communications, including a "Marketing Alert" flier detailing the product's features and release dates and an in-depth article in the employee newsletter, conveyed the important information staff needed to know to sell the new card.

Monitoring and Evaluating Results

To ensure that the product remains on track, Bankoh set up ongoing analysis of customer behavior and used its marketing customer information file (MCIF) to support the marketing of the MasterCards, track the segmentation, monitor customer profitability, and implement life cycle marketing and product development.

Bankoh also is tracking costs and spending; monitoring competition; and evaluating strategies and tactics to ensure that the bank is on target for retaining customers and will be able to distribute the product outside of Hawaii in the future.

Note

1. Information drawn from Susan K. Moss, *Introduction of MasterCard Bank of Hawaii,* a School of Bank Marketing Marketing Planning Assignment thesis paper, 1996.

E

Developing an Advertising Campaign

Introduction

LaSalle State Bank (LSB) was founded in 1894. Located in Illinois Valley, Illinois, it has a staff of 36 and assets of over $72 million. The bank meets the needs of more than 30,000 people.

The citizens of Illinois Valley have an average annual income of $30,000, are action oriented, have a strong work ethic, and support their schools and community.

The three major employers in the area are agriculture, manufacturing, and services, with services now leading the other industries. Although the population of Illinois Valley declined 10 percent between 1980 and 1990, recent data show an upward shift in population.

The financial institutions in the area are known for being sound and stable. The primary and secondary markets for financial services are saturated, according to the bank's research. With tough competition and a tight market, LaSalle State Bank needed a way to communicate its "bold new image" of being an aggressive, innovative bank. Here is how the bank determined it needed a new logo to launch its new image.

Background

LaSalle State Bank researched the image advertising of its competitors. Exhibit E.1 shows a sampling of the strengths and weaknesses the bank found among its competitors.

By conducting this research about competitors in the market area, LSB was able to pinpoint some of the strengths and weaknesses of its competitors as well as its own strengths and weaknesses. Knowing that another bank is being acquired, for example, helped identify how many competitors LSB was facing and what their status in the marketplace was. Knowing that a bank has high visibility showed LSB that one competitor would be tough to displace from a prominent position in the community.

Exhibit E.1

Eureka Savings & Loan

Strengths
- Well established
- Facility location
- High visibility
- Name/logo not market specific

Weaknesses
- Low profile
- Not known for community involvement
- Logo offers little life

LaSalle National Bank

Strengths
- High visibility
- Very aggressive
- Active in community affairs
- "Cavalier" logo is symbol of community

Weaknesses
- "LaSalle" is market specific
- Poor location
- Fights name identity with LSB
- No consistency

First National Bank of Peru

Strengths
- Good location
- Signage
- Consistency
- Quality advertising

Weaknesses
- Being acquired by large bank
- "Peru" is market specific
- Low profile

Exhibit E.2

LA SALLE STATE BANK

654 FIRST STREET ♦ P.O. BOX 462 ♦ LA SALLE, ILLINOIS 61301-0462
815-223-8800 ♦ FAX: 815-223-8824

Analysis of the LaSalle State Bank's Logo

The bank's intermediate and long-range goals call for geographic expansion through acquisition and possibly through building new branches. Therefore, LaSalle State Bank needed a new identity to allow it to penetrate new markets while adapting to new environments.

The existing logo had positive and negative attributes. The positive included incorporating the bank building as part of the logo, which helped identify the bank with its location. The current logo also helped identify the bank as a cornerstone of the community. (See exhibit E.2.)

On the other hand, the existing logo was difficult and costly to reproduce due to the detailed artwork; looked old-fashioned; was not used consistently in the bank's materi-

als; was easily confused with the bank's competitor, LaSalle National Bank; was not adaptable to new locations outside the current market (because of the LaSalle name and the building); and did not reflect the bold new image the bank wanted to project.

Since the negative elements outweighed the positive, the idea to create a new logo was approved and moved forward. The bank launched the new logo (exhibit E.3) to update its image, create possibilities for expansion, and, in the process, improve its bottom line. Here is how the campaign unfolded.

Marketing Mix

Positioning was a major part of the strategic plan. The bank's goal was to increase customer awareness of the bank and its contemporary products. During the course of the

Exhibit E.3

LSB
LA SALLE STATE BANK

image update, many other elements of the bank's image and culture were addressed as well. Retaining customers and rewarding the bank's employees who provided excellent service were two additional objectives that related to the overall image update. The bank adopted the position that customer satisfaction is the reason for the business's existence.

Goals and Objectives

The bank believed its goal of increasing earnings and shareholder returns would be achieved through improved customer retention and acquisition. The marketing plan therefore included ways to contribute to the bank's bottom line while introducing the new bank logo.

The official objective of the campaign was to promote, in a profitable manner, the inauguration of the LaSalle State Bank's new logo to existing and prospective commercial and retail customers while enhancing the bank's image within the boundaries of LaSalle State Bank's primary and secondary geographically delineated area.

The bank asset and liability committee (ALC) stated that it expected 4 percent growth in consumer installment loans and overall a 25 percent growth objective for the bank's consumer installment loan portfolio. Implementation of the marketing plan drew staff from several departments, including marketing, customer service, the front line, and senior management. Employees learned about the campaign and the bank's expectations through the in-house newsletter and the calendar/newsletter.

The steps involved included creating a marketing plan; developing a logo reproduction handbook with standards and guidelines for the new logo's use; designing and executing a uniform look on all the bank's materials; developing a promotional campaign to raise awareness of the bank among current and potential profitable customers; and identifying potential risks in the campaign.

To create awareness among existing customers, the bank

• sent demand deposit account (DDA) customers one direct mail piece containing a magnet with the new logo printed on it,

• provided wall and pocket calendars, pens, and pencils to lobby and drive-through customers,

• gave customers cubes of note paper with the logo printed on the side,

• created statement inserts and messages,

• developed in-house signage,

• distributed buttons for branch employees to wear that said "Notice Anything Different?" to encourage customers to ask about the new logo and employees to talk about it, and

• designed static stickers (which are plastic and adhere to glass surfaces without stickiness or glue and are easily removed) and distributed them at numerous events.

To create an awareness among potential customers within the target market area, the bank decided to tie the introduction of the logo and the awareness campaign to a predefined bank product. The bank's ALC determined that the new car buyer market would be targeted. The marketing plan contained detailed target dates for print advertisements and radio spots. Throughout the campaign the bank's auto loan rate was advertised, and the bank worked to strengthen its relationship with the local auto dealers. The goal was to increase the indirect lending portion of the consumer installment loan portfolio.

LaSalle State Bank and a local radio station conducted a joint campaign called "Summer of Fun and Prizes," at the end of which a grand prize of a car was awarded. This part of the image campaign was found to be especially effective. In a small town with only a few radio stations to choose from, the chances that customers were listening to either of two stations (one AM, one FM) was very high. The bank asked local merchants to distribute bumper stickers with the new logo printed on them, and the radio stations announced where the stickers could be found. Then, throughout the summer, the license plate numbers of cars sporting the bumper sticker were announced on the radio, and customers had a limited amount of time to call in to win the grand prize. Merchants also appreciated the campaign because of the increased traffic in their stores. Customers enjoyed the competition, and the car was won at the end of the summer. To keep customers interested, the car was on display at festivals and locations throughout the summer and bore the new bank logo.

Monitoring

The bank used a large wall calendar with all the campaign's target dates and events marked to keep everyone focused. A biweekly "special events" newsletter was printed and distributed to all employees to keep everyone up to date.

To ensure that the new logo was treated consistently in all the bank's materials, the marketing department was designated the "gatekeeper." All materials bearing the new logo are sent for approval to the marketing department. The *LaSalle State Bank Logo Reproduction Handbook* contains the guidelines and policies to help ensure that the logo is used consistently.

Evaluation

After nearly two years using the new logo, the bank is very pleased with the increased customer awareness of the bank. Although no formal awareness studies have been conducted, the new image campaign was a catalyst for other marketing efforts that have produced strong responses from customers.

For example, to accompany the contemporary and updated image the new logo helped engender, a series of new products was launched that targeted new markets. The Mighty Bucks program was created to provide a savings program for young families with children. The new image spurred the bank to focus on market segmentation and keener target marketing. Previously, the bank had mostly older customers. The new marketing efforts have brought in a greater number of younger customers and their families.

The logo has also helped the bank achieve its geographic expansion goals. The bank acquired a branch in a neighboring town and found that the new logo helped enter a new market because of its contemporary look. The new logo no longer pins LaSalle State Bank to its original location.

The bank is also planning another location in a different town.

Conclusion

Although it is difficult to pinpoint an exact dollar amount generated by the new logo, the marketing director of the bank believes the new logo helped change the marketing course in the bank considerably.

The bank marketing director says the new logo was an important starting point for additional enhancements in the bank, such as new products (for example, debit cards and bank-by-phone services), attracting new employees to a more contemporary bank, and new advertising campaigns with a sleeker look.

The bank's slogan "Look To Us . . ." works well with the new logo as well.

LaSalle State Bank's new image campaign was considered a success.

Note

This case is drawn from "A Bold New Image," a paper by Daniel D. Lawler. The full paper may be found in the ABA/BMA Center for Banking Information (MP96-2).

F

DEVELOPING A MARKETING PLAN FOR CONSUMERS NATIONAL BANK

This hypothetical case demonstrates the steps in developing a marketing plan for a bank.

Introduction

Consumers National Bank (CNB) is a hypothetical bank with assets of approximately $160 million. It is located in a rural county that has a population of 135,000. All eight of the bank's offices are located in Overland County.

The data presented in the following situation analysis are not all-inclusive, but they illustrate the variety of information that might be gathered and how it might be used.

Situation Analysis

Analysis of the Economic Market Environment

Employment Trends

Exhibit F.1 shows employment trends (nonagricultural) for the county. Not shown is the fact that the county has approximately 250 active farms, employing about 1,900 people, or about 3.5 percent of the workforce. Exhibit F.2 shows total labor force (agricultural and nonagricultural), employment, and unemployment. On the basis of this and other information obtained during our research phase, we observe the following:

- The workforce (nonagricultural) continues to diminish.
- Manufacturing continues to diminish, although the region is still more dependent on it than is the state as a whole. The industries suffering the greatest loss of jobs are glass, apparel, and food processing.
- The only manufacturing growth has been in the "other durable goods" category, primarily in the electronics components and aircraft-related industries.
- While the manufacturing sector has been diminishing, the nonmanufacturing sector has been growing steadily. The area of greatest growth has been retail trade, as shopping centers have opened in the outlying areas.
- Job gains in the services industry are due largely to expansion of health care and medical facilities.

Exhibit F.1 Nonagricultural Wage and Salary Employment Trends: Overland County

	1985	1990	1995
Nonagricultural work force	54,700	54,300	52,600
Manufacturing	19,100	18,100	14,700
Durable Goods	10,700	10,500	9,000
Stone/clay/glass	9,100	8,600	6,500
Other durables	1,600	2,000	2,500
Nondurable goods	8,500	7,600	5,700
Food	2,700	2,500	2,100
Apparel	2,500	2,300	1,800
Nonmanufacturing	35,600	36,200	37,900
Construction	1,700	1,800	1,800
Transportation/communications/public utilities	3,000	3,000	2,200
Wholesale & retail trade	9,100	9,000	10,500
Finance/insurance/real estate	2,200	2,400	2,700
Services	8,200	8,500	9,600
Government	11,500	11,500	11,200

Exhibit F.2 Labor Force, Employment, and Unemployment

Year	Civilian Labor Force (000)	Employment (000)	Unemployment (000)	Unemployment Rate (%)
1993	58.6	50.2	8.4	14.3
1994	56.8	49.3	7.5	13.2
1995	54.5	48.5	6.0	11.0

- The unemployment rate, while declining each year, is still significantly greater than the state's rate of 5.7 percent.

Retail Activity

Exhibit F.3 shows the changes that took place in the retail sector of CNB's trade area. Some of the conclusions that can be drawn from this information are as follows:

- From 1990 to 1995, the number of retail establishments in CNB's trade area declined by 10 percent. Hardest hit were automobile, gasoline, and fuel dealers and businesses affected by the relatively low level of population and income growth (home furnishings and eating and drinking establishments).
- Total retail sales grew by 37 percent over the five-year period, but sales actually declined by 13 percent when adjusted for inflation.

Construction Activity

Exhibit F.4 shows residential construction for Overland County's three major cities, where all of CNB's offices are located, and for the entire county. In 1992, for the first time since 1980, the number of new dwelling units authorized in the county exceeded 300. More than two-thirds of these units were located in Plattville, where the bank has only one office.

The most significant commercial construction in the past few years has been in the health care field, as three area hospitals underwent major expansions. Other commercial construction has been limited to renovations and minor expansions.

Analysis of the Demographic Environment

Exhibits F.5, F.6, and F.7 show population trends and projections and demographic characteristics of the population in CNB's trade area. For the market served by CNB, we can say the following based on these tables:

- While the county's population showed good growth during the 1980s, the area was hard hit by the recession of the early 1990s. Natural increases in population due to the excess of births over deaths were offset by out-migration, causing total population to decrease in 1995.
- Population is projected to increase slightly over the next 30 to 35 years, but at a rate considerably lower than that projected for the state as a whole.
- Other data (not shown here) indicate that 85 percent of the recent gains in population reflect growth in Plattville and Milltown, while the population of Bridgeboro is declining.
- During the 1980s, the population of the area aged somewhat, so that 57 percent of the residents are now 25 years old or older. The educational level and family size also increased during this period.

Kind of Business	Number of Establishments*			Sales ($mil.)		
	1990	*1995*	*Change (%)*	*1990*	*1995*	*Change (%)*
Total	839	759	(10)	426.8	583.7	37
Building materials, hardware, garden supply, mobile home dealers	43	33	(23)	16.9	19.8	17
General merchandise stores	19	17	(11)	49.3	61.4	25
Food stores	114	112	(2)	120.4	165.4	37
Automotive dealers	82	62	(24)	85.0	104.7	23
Gasoline service stations	82	74	(10)	24.6	50.6	106
Apparel and accessory stores	87	80	(8)	22.9	30.3	32
Furniture, home furnishings, and equipment stores	57	44	(23)	16.8	17.8	6
Eating and drinking stores	180	157	(13)	29.4	37.8	29
Drug and propietary stores	19	19	—	12.8	18.9	48
Miscellaneous retail stores	156	161	3	48.7	77.0	58
Liquor stores	21	26	24	8.0	13.2	65
Used merchandise stores	11	10	(9)	1.8	2.2	22
Misc. shopping goods stores	49	54	10	8.7	13.6	56
Nonstore retailers	17	12	(29)	5.1	6.4	25
Fuel and ice dealers	24	18	(25)	21.3	36.0	69
Florists	12	15	25	1.3	2.0	54

*With payroll.

Customer Analysis

Customer Survey

The following results are based on 276 responses to a questionnaire mailed to a representative sample of 914 systematically selected checking account customers of CNB. (The response rate was 30 percent.) They show some effect (but within tolerable levels) of the recent price changes—that is, the service charge on low-balance savings and the increased minimum balance for no-charge checking.

- About one in five of our present checking customers say they have closed some bank account with us within the past year. Only 20 percent of these closings are reportedly due to our pricing changes. It appears that about 5 percent of our present checking customers took some negative action in response to our price changes. Of course, those who left the bank entirely were not measured by this study.

Dwelling Units Authorized by Building Permits

	1992		1994	
	Single Family	Multiple Unit	Single Family	Multiple Unit
Bridgeboro	4	—	1	—
Milltown	44	410	34	—
Plattville	315	448	181	102
Overland County*	490	858	309	108

*Includes all 14 municipalities in the county.

Source: State Department of Labor and Industry.

• The bank has a very large core of long-term customers. Over 57 percent have been with us more than 10 years; 75 percent for more than 5 years.

• While the bank received good ratings on many attributes, those rated lowest were our pricing, drive-in and parking facilities, and speed of service from tellers.

The physical problems at our two old drive-in windows are causing service problems, and parking has long been a problem at two of our busiest offices.

• There is a very high level of usage of other financial institutions by CNB checking customers: 55 percent have an account with another bank.

Exhibit F.5   **Population Trends: Overland County and the State**

	County		State	
	Population	% Change	Population	% Change
1980 Census	121,374		7,171,112	
1990 Census	132,866	9.5	7,365,011	2.7
1994	133,800	0.7	7,430,000	0.9
1995	133,000	(0.6)	7,468,000	0.5

Source: State Department of Labor and Industry.

Exhibit F.6   **Population Projections for Overland County 1990–2020**

1990	132,866
1995	132,900
2000	140,300
2010	151,500
2020	149,900

Source: State Department of Labor and Industry.

Demographic Characteristics of the Population of Overland County

	1980	1990
Total population	121,374	132,866
Percent nonwhite	14.9%	14.2%
Family income		
Total families	30,718	37,962
Mean family income	$26,842	$39,890
Median family income	$21,223	$31,540
Families below poverty level	7.8%	7.8%
Education		
% of population 25 or over	57.0%	59.0%
Median school years completed	11.8%	12.5%
% high school graduates	45.0%	53.0%
Persons per household	3.5	3.7
Housing characteristics		
Number year-round units	38,854	45,590
Built since 1960	21.7%	34.7%
% owner-occupied	57.3%	64.2%
% renter-occupied	30.4%	25.8%
Median value, owner-occupied	$32,700	$78,050
Median rent	$ 225	$ 487
Percent work inside SMSA	81.5%	82.5%

• One-fourth of checking customers opened some type of new account in the past year. However, less than half of all new accounts opened by CNB checking customers within the past year were opened at CNB. No one reason for the use of other banks predominates, although the low balance requirements at savings and loans were mentioned by several customers.

• Nearly two-thirds of our customers express interest in having greater access to automated tellers; 80 percent of those under 35 years of age said they would be very or fairly interested in increased access.

• Other demographic data that characterize our checking customers can be summarized as follows: About one-quarter are under age 24, one-third are between ages 35 and 54, and about one-third are over age 55. Under half (approximately 44 percent) have had at least some college education. Median income is $31,000, with 15 percent making $50,000 or more. Fifty-nine percent of our customers are married; 14 percent are single; and 22 percent are widowed, divorced, or separated.

• Customers rate the bank very highly on most attributes—especially employee familiarity with customers.

- Checking account customers have, on average, 2.67 services with CNB and 0.8 services with another financial institution.

Trade Area Household Survey

Because we conducted such a survey last year, CNB management decided that the cost involved did not justify an update this year. The survey will be redone next year, however, to enable us to measure the effects of our marketing strategies.

New Account Survey

More than half of our new accounts are opened by people who already have some relationship with the bank. Of the new customers, two-thirds are new to the area, and the majority say a friend or relative recommended CNB to them. Records indicate that the average customer opening any new account is sold 1.3 accounts.

Closed Account Survey

Last year, the bank instituted a $2.00 service charge on savings accounts having a quarterly average balance of less than $100. This year, the bank increased its service charges on checking. These actions resulted in some accounts being closed. The following results relate to savings accounts that were closed during the first six months of this year:

- In 25 percent of the account closings, the funds were consolidated with other accounts within the bank or used to open a new account or certificate of deposit at the bank.
- In nearly half of the cases (47 percent), the account was closed for reasons beyond the control of the bank (14 percent moved; 16 percent needed the money; 7 percent died, married, or divorced).
- One in five (21 percent) closed the account because of increased service charges.
- Only 2 customers out of 229 were critical of staff or service.

Analysis of the Bank's Competitive Environment

Operating Statistics

CNB competes with a number of banks in Overland County. However, because of merger activity, many of them have their headquarters in other counties. Because their operating statistics would reflect operations outside Overland County, these banks are not truly comparable to CNB. Therefore, exhibit F.8 compares selected statistics for CNB and our two competitors that are headquartered and located only in Overland County. These data are summarized here:

- CNB is the largest bank (based on asset size) headquartered and located only in the county. However, if current rates of growth continue, Merchants will exceed CNB in assets and deposits within three years.
- The bank's five-year compound growth rate for deposits is not keeping pace with the competition.
- The bank has maintained a consistently high ratio of loans to deposits, and there is little likelihood of increasing this proportion.
- Our loan portfolio is skewed toward consumer loans. The competition is much more active in the commercial sector.
- CNB has a very high proportion of mortgages. These low-yielding, fixed-rate, long-term loans are a disadvantage in a fluctuating rate environment.
- CNB has an unusually large proportion of "other installment loans" because of our consumer banking service package, which includes a line of credit.
- CNB is one of the leading automobile financers because of our dealer relationships.
- Net interest margin as a percent of average assets is lower than the competition.
- Noninterest income as a percent of average assets is well below Merchants'.

Operating Results of CNB and Other County-Headquartered Banks, 1992 and 1997

	CNB		Merchants		Anacola	
	1992	1997	1992	1997	1992	1997
Total assets ($000)	97,085	160,900	673,850	148,000	42,395	103,987
Return on average assets	.69	.75	.79	.84	1.02	1.45
Total deposits ($000)	84,806	141,489	66,036	131,833	37,466	92,632
5-yr. compound growth	4.6%	10.8%	4.6%	14.8%	9.5%	19.9%
Loans/deposits[1]	72.9%	74.3%	78.0%	77.6%	49.7%	48.5%
Total loans	62,887	97,447	46,485	80,917	17,736	46,921
As a % of total loans:						
Auto	17.2	18.5	22.5	23.0	4.4	5.5
Other installment/revolving	16.9	17.5	5.5	5.8	5.3	8.2
1–4-family residential	22.8	20.2	12.1	11.8	19.6	17.6
Commercial/industrial	13.2	15.2	32.2	31.5	28.4	27.8
As a % of average assets:						
Net interest margin	4.38	3.76	4.26	3.87	4.78	3.84
Noninterest income:						
Service charges on deposit accounts	.26	.24	.26	.28	.10	.10
Other service charges	.04	.05	.16	.18	.01	.10
Total noninterest inc.	.43	.44	.59	.61	.17	.25
Operating expense:						
Salaries/benefits	1.45	1.43	1.64	1.65	1.51	1.18
Occupancy	.89	.85	.64	.62	.49	.43
Total noninterest exp.	3.46	3.24	3.35	3.39	2.88	2.36

1. Net loans to total deposits less public funds.

This is primarily because of the income generated by Merchants' large trust department.

• CNB's noninterest expense ratio was the highest of the three banks in 1992, but it has been reduced through reductions in the "other expense" category. Occupancy expense is the highest of the group.

Market Share

Exhibit F.9 shows deposit market share for CNB and our principal competitors. Analysis of these deposit market share statistics reveals the following:

• With regard to transaction accounts, CNB's market share has held fairly steady over the past five years. At least two commercial competitors are losing market share.

• With regard to certificates of deposit, CNB lost share over the five-year period, as did most commercial banks.

• The credit union is becoming an increasingly significant competitor.

• Public funds share is highly volatile. Such funds generally go to the highest bidder, so market share is not relevant. Merchants Bank now has nearly half of this business.

	Transaction Accounts*		Certificates of Deposit		Public Funds		Total Deposits	
	1992	1997	1992	1997	1992	1997	1992	1997
Consumers National	**12.2**	**12.0**	**11.1**	**9.5**	**12.2**	**20.1**	**11.7**	**11.9**
County Federal S&L	13.3	24.1	20.3	20.5	0	0	15.8	21.8
Merchants National	10.3	11.1	5.1	4.2	29.7	48.0	8.9	11.1
Modern S&L	8.4	8.0	12.5	13.8	0	0	9.8	8.9
Traditional Bank	9.3	8.0	6.6	6.5	4.9	7.2	7.6	7.6
Peoples Trust	12.2	6.0	12.4	6.3	26.1	18.1	13.0	6.8
Patriots Bank	9.5	6.0	7.0	6.0	18.0	4.3	8.8	5.9
Anacola National	1.0	2.9	1.1	4.0	0	0.3	1.0	3.5
County Workers C.U.	0.5	3.3	3.9	3.0	0	0	2.0	3.0

Exhibit F.9 **Deposit Market Share Data (Percent of deposits held each year)**

*Interest- and noninterest-bearing transaction accounts, money market deposit accounts, and saving accounts.

- Patriots Bank has lost considerable market share since being acquired by a large state-wide bank that changed local management and policies.

- The inclusion of public funds in total market share masks the fact that Merchants' market share in the basic retail and commercial business has risen from 7.45 percent to 8.8 percent, while CNB's share has fallen from 11.0 percent to 10.7 percent.

Competitive Marketing Strategies

Exhibit F.10 compares retail products and pricing of CNB and our competitors, and exhibit F.11 compares facilities and hours. Our analysis of these data suggests the following:

- CNB's pricing of transaction accounts is among the more expensive. Thrift institutions have priced for volume.

- CNB's interest rates on savings and time accounts are generally competitive and are compounded daily.

- CNB offers longer daily banking hours than any competitor.

- CNB is one of only four banks providing full-service banking on Saturdays.

- CNB is one of only two banks that operate in all major towns of the county.

- CNB is one of the few banks not participating in the regional ATM network and thus not offering the benefit of convenient automated teller access to accounts.

- In random "mystery shopping" of competitors and CNB, we found our staff to be far better informed and more courteous than the staff at the other banks.

- CNB's parking facilities are a competitive disadvantage.

- The physical appearance of the bank's offices is neat but not particularly appealing in comparison with some of our competitors.

- CNB has excellent locations except in the largest city, where the bank does not have sufficient coverage.

Exhibit F.10 Competitive Comparison of Retail Products and Pricing

Institution	Interest Checking	Regular Checking	Overdraft Checking	Regular Savings	Money Market Account	Certificates of Deposit
CNB	$1,500 avg. = free $1,000–$1,499 = $3 Under $1,00 = $5 Compounded daily	$500 avg. = free $400–499 = $1 $300–399 = $2 $200–299 = $3 $100–199 = $4 Under $100 = $5	Advances equal to overdraft amount	Compounded daily, paid quarterly; Under $100 = $2 charge	$2,500 = free Under $2,500 = $5 Compounded daily	$1,000 min. Compounded daily
Peoples Trust	$1,000 min. = free Under $1,000 = $5 Compounded daily	$250 min. = free Under $250 = $3	Advances in $50 multiples	Compounded daily, paid monthly	$1,000 = free Under $1,000 = $2.50 Compounded daily	$500 min. Compounded daily
Patriots Bank	$2,500 avg. = free Under $2,500 = no interest and $5 Compounded monthly	$500 min. = free Under $500 = $5	Advances in $100 multiples	Compounded and paid quarterly	$2,500 = free Under $2,500 = no interest and $5 Compounded monthly	$1,000 min. Simple Interest
Merchants National Bank	$1,000 min. = free Under $1,000 = $3 plus 15¢/ check Compounded daily	$300 min. = free Under $300 = $3	Not available	Compounded and paid quarterly	$2,000 min. =free Under $2,000 =$3 Compounded daily	$50 min. Compounded daily
Anacola National Bank	$1,000 min. = free Under $1,000 = $4 No interest if under $500 Compounded monthly	$200 min. = free $100–199 = $2 Under $100 = $3	Advances in $50 multiples	Compounded daily, paid quarterly	$2,000 min. = free Under $2,000 = $2 Compounded monthly	$100 min. Compounded daily
Traditional Bank	$1,000 min. = free Under $1,000 = $3 plus 20¢/ check Compounded daily	$100 min. = free Under $100 = $1 plus 20¢/ check	Not available	Compounded daily, paid quarterly	$2,000 min. = free Under $2,000 = $3 Compounded monthly	Offer discounted CDs $100 min. Compounded daily
Modern S&L	$500 min. = free Under $500 = $2 Compounded daily	N/A	Not available	Compounded daily, paid monthly	$500 min. = free Under $500 = $2 Compounded daily	$50 min. Compounded daily
County Federal S&L	$500 min. = free Under $500 = $2 Compounded daily	N/A	Not available	Compounded daily, paid monthly	$500 min. = free Under $500 = $2 Compounded daily	$50 min. Compounded daily

Subjective Factors

The following information is drawn from the experience of CNB's officers:

- CNB's staff is at least equal to, and in many cases superior to, the competition's in terms of performance and appearance. There is good morale and low turnover among staff.

- Patriots Bank is having many problems. Many key people have left the bank, leaving many customers—especially business customers—vulnerable to sales efforts by other banks.

- CNB offers no formal sales training program for our retail and commercial customer-contact staff. To the bank's knowledge, none of the competition engages in sales training either.

Self-Analysis

CNB's self-analysis is included in the analysis of our customers and our competitive situation. These sections provide information on how the bank is seen by our customers; how our customers compare with other residents of our market; how our financials compare with those of the competition; and how our facilities, products, and marketing strategies compare with the competition.

Summary of CNB's Problems and Opportunities

- The population of our market area is growing, but much of that growth is in areas where the bank does not have adequate market coverage.

- CNB has a relatively low proportion of commercial loans and a high proportion of mortgages in our loan portfolio. This disproportion between fixed-rate and flexible-rate assets puts the bank at a disadvantage as the cost of funds rises.

- CNB's deposit growth rate is not keeping pace with that of our principal local competitor. At current rates, Merchants will become the dominant bank, outstripping CNB in deposit size within three years.

- While CNB's noninterest income ratio is high, it is still well below Merchants'—suggesting some room for improvement.

- CNB's regular and interest checking prices are high for the market. The $1,500 average balance required to avoid a service charge may be perceived to be higher than the $1,000 minimum balance requirement of other banks.

- CNB's minimum deposit requirement for certificates of deposit is higher than the competition's.

- CNB's parking facilities are a competitive disadvantage.

- CNB is at a competitive disadvantage by not participating in the regional automated teller network.

- The bank's drive-in facilities are inadequate and are a source of customer dissatisfaction.

- Customers are opening more new accounts (including savings, checking, CDs, and loans) at other financial institutions than at CNB. This is an unfavorable trend.

- CNB's cash-reserve line of credit is the most consumer-oriented service of this type in the market. Other banks either do not have the service or advance in multiples of $50, which is detrimental to the customer.

- The bank gets very few complaints about the service given by our staff. In fact, many customers praise our staff very highly, and the level of referrals from customers indicates an excellent reputation.

- Patriots' problems are making its business and personal customers vulnerable to the sales efforts of other banks. (See exhibit F.11.)

Goals and Objectives

Mission Statement and Corporate Goals

1. CNB's mission is to provide quality financial service to individuals and

Exhibit F. 11   **Competitive Comparison of Facilities and Hours**

Institution	24-Hour Banking	Daily Hours	Friday Evening Hour	Saturday Hours	Parking	Appearance of Offices	Locations
CNB	No				Poor at main office; fair at others	Aging but clean	One of only two institutions serving all three major cities; central business districts, except one location on fringe of largest city
Lobby		9–3	6–8	9–1			
Drive-In		8–5:30	5:30–8	9–1			
Peoples Trust	Yes				Limited at city offices	Cluttered with premium merchandise	Largest city: central business district; good locations
Lobby		8:30–3	3–8	9–1			
Drive-In		8:30–5:30	5:30–8	9–1			
Patriots Bank	No				Adequate	Modern, colorful facilities	All good locations in all three major cities
Lobby		9–3	6–8	None			
Drive-In		9–5:30	5:30–8	None			
Merchants National	Yes				Excellent	Beautiful new main office; others aging	Capitol city; central business district and major intersections; all good
Lobby		9–3	6–8	10–1			
Drive-In		8:30–5:30	5:30–8	10–1			
Anacola National	No				Adequate	Modern, neat	Good locations in largest city
Lobby		9–9:30	6–8	None			
Drive-In		8:30–5:30	5:30–8	None			
Traditional Bank	Yes				Limited in cities; adequate elsewhere	Old offices recently refurbished; pleasant	All good locations in two of three major cities (except capitol)
Lobby		9–3	5–8	None			
Drive-In		9–5:30	5–8	None			
Modern S & L	No				On-street or limited parking	Old offices looking rundown	Central business districts of capitol and smallest city
Lobby		9–3	6:30–8	None			
Drive-In		9–3	3–8	None			
County Federal S & L	Yes				Excellent parking facilities	Old offices well maintained	Excellent locations in central business districts and major intersections of largest city
Lobby		9–3	3–8	10–1			
Drive-In		9–5	5–8	10–1			

businesses in Overland County. The bank will attempt to offer the complete spectrum of financial services to meet customer needs (as permitted by law), as long as the bank returns an adequate profit to its shareholders.

2. To the extent permitted by the economic characteristics of the market, the bank will attempt to achieve a balanced service approach between consumer and commercial segments of the market.

3. The bank will pursue deposit growth through product and market expansion but not through merger or acquisition.

4. CNB will attempt to achieve a growth rate in total deposits of 15 percent in the coming year and an increase in pretax profits of 12 percent.

Target Market Selection

On the basis of the situation analysis, the following markets should be targeted in our objective-setting and strategy formulation:

- higher-income individuals, especially managerial and professional workers,
- newcomers to our geographic trade area,
- existing customers,
- residents of Plattville, the fastest growing city in our trade area, and
- the business community.

Selected Marketing Objectives

1. To increase CNB's share of new accounts opened by existing customers from 45 percent to 55 percent during the coming year.

2. To increase the bank's penetration of higher-income segments of the market in the coming year by 2 percent over the penetration found in last year's household survey.

3. To increase to 15 percent the bank's share of accounts opened by newcomers to the area.

4. To increase the bank's share of market for total deposits from 12 percent to 13 percent.

5. To increase consumer and customer awareness of the services currently offered by the bank.

6. To increase community awareness of the locations of the bank's offices.

7. To increase the proportion of commercial loans in the total loan portfolio from 15 percent to 17 percent.

8. To create an image among the business community that CNB is a strong commercial banking organization, and that its calling officers are innovative and have the expertise and authority to meet financial needs in a fast, responsive, and imaginative way.

9. To increase the bank's presence in Plattville by establishing a new branch office there.

10. To evaluate the financial impact of joining the regional ATM network.

Strategy and Tactics (Action Plan)

This section of the plan spells out the specific strategies and tactics that will be used to attain the bank's marketing objectives. It is possible, and indeed likely, that more than one objective might be served by a particular set of strategies and tactics. The following is an excerpt from the action plan, which addresses three of the objectives specified above: increasing the bank's share of new accounts opened by existing customers, increasing its share of the total deposit market, and increasing awareness of the services currently offered by the bank.

Strategy #1

Improve the sales effectiveness of our new-accounts staff.

To help meet the objectives of increasing the bank's share of new accounts opened by customers, its share of total deposits, and customer awareness of the services we offer, we will improve the sales effectiveness of our new-accounts staff in the branches. The specific tactics we will use are as follows: (1) to train new-accounts staff with respect to knowledge of our products and in the skills necessary to interview new customers to identify their needs and to sell the services that will meet those needs; and (2) to develop a product manual, which will be kept up to date, and which will serve as a reference guide for all customer-contact staff.

1. Develop and implement a three-day sales and product knowledge training course.

Responsibility: Training director Laura Brown.

Timetable: Program to be developed from January 1 through March 31 for implementation in April and May with a follow-up in September.

Resource commitment: $1,000 for expenses (refreshments, supplies, visual aids); two consecutive days during April or May for each new-accounts representative; one day in September.

2. Develop a product manual in loose-leaf format, describing each bank product, its features and customer benefits, and the profile of customers most likely to benefit from the product.

Responsibility: Retail product manager John Smith.

Timetable: Manual to be completed by mid-March in order to be incorporated into training program.

Resource commitment: $300 for materials and printing; half of John Smith's time for 10 weeks.

Strategy #2

Increase customer awareness of the availability of need-meeting products through a "Service of the Month" promotional program. Each month, for six months, a specific product will be emphasized.

1. Develop a series of in-bank displays, statement stuffers, and teller handouts promoting auto loans, home equity loans, overdraft protection, money market accounts, IRAs, and CDs.

Responsibility: Advertising director Edith Jones.

Timetable: Development of materials during January and February; program to be implemented from March through August.

Resource commitment: $3,000 for design and printing of materials.

2. Develop an incentive program to motivate tellers and branch service representatives to mention the service of the month to customers with whom they come in contact.

Responsibility: Sales manager Fred Thompson.

Timetable: Details of incentive plan are to be presented to the branch administrator by February 5.

Resource commitment: No out-of-pocket expenses foreseen at this time.

G

EXAMPLES OF BANK COMMUNITY RELATIONS ACTIVITIES

Following are examples of three different types of community relations programs: community development, community support, and community improvement.

A Community Development Project:

Barnett Bank of Central Florida, N.A., Builds Home Ownership[1]

In the early 1990s, Barnett Bank regularly held a Community Homebuyers' Workshop program based on the Fannie Mae Community Homebuyers' Workbook. The program format was very strong, but the bankers came across as stiff and reserved, and very few loans were generated through the program.

In 1991, the bank received some valuable feedback that told them they were not reaching the people they most wanted to help. The bank learned that the minority and low-income community in Florida did not know about the program and that the workshop location was not convenient.

The bank's President and Chief Executive Officer, Tom Yochum, took a personal interest in improving the program and set up a special task force to determine the best way to deliver the workshops effectively.

The task force was called the Barnett Bank Community Group and was made up of five community volunteers and three Barnett employees. Together, they worked to enhance the bank's image in the community, provide housing education to lower-income and minority families, and better understand cultural differences in ethnic communities.

After several meetings, the bank learned the following:

- The bank's credit standards for home loans were too difficult for many lower-income families to meet. Barnett reexamined the criteria it used for loans and began analyzing utility and telephone bills and receipts from rent payments to develop new criteria. This allowed the bank to take into account consistently punctual bill and rent payments as part of an applicant's creditworthiness.

- The workshops should not be held at the bank, but rather in the communities the bank hoped to reach.

- Workshop presenters should dress more casually, not in a tie and coat.

- Members of the community should be asked to help spread the word about the workshops (ministers, merchants, community leaders and organizers, etc.).

The bank's president was so pleased with the work of the group that he committed $7.5 million in residential loans to the program.

In May 1992, the first revised workshop was held in a community church, and 125 people attended. The church's minister had hoped to present his congregation with this type of financial information, and the program fit well with his goals. Four loans were closed and disbursed as a result of that workshop, totaling approximately $195,000.

The Community Group continued to meet and learned more about potential home buyers' needs. They found that there was a demand for the workshops in other languages, such as Spanish and Chinese, as well as among people in other economic brackets. In early 1993, the group changed its named to P.O.W.E.R. House (for Providing Opportunities With Education and Resources) and changed its goals to providing home buyer education to everyone.

As the program continued to develop, more community members joined the P.O.W.E.R. House task force: real estate agents, builders, inspectors, credit agencies, and the Consumer Credit Counseling Service. Each member contributes a unique perspective from a different aspect of home buying, and each also benefits by meeting potential customers at the workshops. Now there are between 25 and 30 volunteers contributing to the program.

In 1993, Barnett hosted 23 P.O.W.E.R. House Workshops, and held them in community centers, churches, and city government offices. By 1994, the project was again looking for ways to expand and held workshops in libraries and on community college campuses. By the end of 1994, 38 workshops had been held, and in 1995, 45 were conducted. As of early 1996, $6 million of the $7.5 million the bank's president committed to the program had been lent through 107 loans. President Yochum said the bank's commitment to the project wouldn't end when the original funding was gone-new funds would be made available.

The bank and the community have found the workshops to be mutually beneficial in many ways. The bank's image and name recognition have greatly improved in a wide variety of communities, and people in all income brackets and from all ethnic communities have a better understanding of what it takes to purchase a home and achieve their goal of home ownership.

Community Support Efforts:

Community Banks Help Battle Floods[2]

During the winter of 1997, record snowfalls were recorded in North Dakota. As the snow began to melt, the imminent danger of floods along the banks of the Red River became apparent. Executive management of the Community First National Bank in Fargo, North Dakota, asked its 250 employees for volunteers to help prepare for the floods. Approximately 200 employees and their family members signed up and began filling sandbags after work.

When the flooding began, the bank's staff joined the other city volunteers placing the sandbags. During the second week of the flooding, the bank reduced its staff during business hours and sent employee volunteers out during the day to help fight the flood. Bank employees contributed more than 650 hours of time to the flood effort, and helped clean up after the river crested.

On the other side of the Red River, in Minnesota, Rural American Bank in East Grand Forks assisted its sister bank in Ada by clearing checks and taking phone calls. The town had lost power for long periods of time and had evacuated many residents.

In Montevideo, Minnesota, the First National Bank not only provided employee volunteers who helped with bagging sand and distributing food, but also created a Disaster Dollars Program. This low-rate loan program was designed to help with storm-related repairs and rebuilding. The bank also created a savings account that accepted donations from others to help flood victims, and it even permitted some loan clients to skip a payment on their loans.

The Bank of South Dakota joined with six other banks to administer the Income Continuation Loan Fund. The fund accepts contributions from individuals and businesses and lends up to $500 in interest-free loans to flood victims. The fund allows up to 12 months to repay the loan.

During this time of crisis in 1997, many banks and their employees made a critical difference in their communities by contributing time and money to flood victims.

Community Improvement Project:

A New Library Revitalizes Small Town[3]

In the mid-1990s, the Peoples State Bank of Velva, North Dakota, saw the need for economic development and a way to attract more people to the tiny town of 950 people. The city administrators wanted a new library, and the bank agreed. A new library would attract new construction, new customers, and new residents to Velva. The bank fully supported the project. It contributed $10,000 cash to the project, as well as computer equipment and books. In addition, the bank purchased almost 50 percent of the bonds floated to construct the new library.

The result of the bank's support is that the new library has been built and is beginning to generate the additional commerce and attract the new residents that had been hoped for. The town's high quality of life and good schools, and now the high-tech library (which is part of the town's public school complex, and one of the two sites in North Dakota to have been granted free Internet access), have attracted about 50 new residents. In addition, two large companies, Archer Daniels Midland Co. and Verendrye Electric Co-op, have made Velva the location of their new plants.

The Peoples State Bank of Velva is given a great deal of credit by the town's citizens for always being involved in and supportive of the town.

Notes

1. Information drawn from Susan J. Blexrud, "Barnett's Workshops Teach Home Ownership," *Bank Marketing,* March 1996, pp. 13–16.
2. Information drawn from *Northwestern Financial Review,* April 19, 1997, pp. 16ff.
3. Information drawn from *The Independent Banker,* February 1997, pp. 69–71.

H

MARKETING IMPLICATIONS OF MERGERS AND ACQUISITIONS

Introduction

Some experts believe the merger/acquisition trend will continue and even increase in the coming years.[1] Among the many causes of mergers and acquisitions are increased competition (the merger pushes one bank out of business or causes a bank to want to expand); a saturated marketplace (a merger reduces redundancy); increased efficiency (from all angles—technology, personnel, reduced number of branches, etc.); legislation allowing interstate banking and branching (there are more opportunities than ever for banks to grow); and opportunities to strengthen the bank (by adding a critical position or additional assets).[2] Mergers require planning, but here's what you need to know to make merger or acquisition a success.

Communication

Internal Communications

Without a doubt, no merger will be a success without careful, consistent, continuous, and relevant communication-both internal and external. To most employees, and to customers, too, a merger signals a reduction in jobs and services. That's a key reason for immediate, clear communication with employees about how the merger will affect them, so they won't worry about losing their jobs and can go on providing top-notch customer service during the merger instead of turning customers against the new bank.

It's important to set up task forces of managers, including branch managers, to allow the best and brightest ideas for handling the details of merging the two companies (such as job assignments, budget concerns, etc.) to be offered and heard.

Banks have handled their communications efforts in numerous ways, but the most successful are a daily or weekly newsletter to the staff, information posted on the Internet or intranet, and regular meetings that include all employees.

External Communications

Since customers tend to leave in droves when they hear that their bank has been bought, it's important to show them that the offices of the acquired bank are open for business and to assure them that their business is very important to the new bank.

The top three reasons people choose a financial institution are the people and the service, the products and pricing, and the location and convenience.[3] Knowing this, it is important to convey to the customers of both banks that they can count on quality service, familiar faces (if possible), the best products and competitive pricing, and continued convenience.

Many banks also install a toll-free number for customers to call with questions. This reinforces the goal of letting customers know they are important to the bank.

Product, Pricing, and Distribution Issues

Any time two banks merge there will be duplication of products and locations (unless the market areas of the banks are entirely different locations). In most cases, this duplication means that product lines are merged and the products are assigned new names. Some products will be eliminated or downplayed, and some locations might be closed down.

Customers will be very sensitive to product and pricing changes, and marketing should be particularly prepared to inform customers of any new prices and policies, as well as any changes in the terms of the accounts; the new bank locations and hours; and alternative delivery methods that will be available to customers to ensure they will still have access to convenient financial services.

Establishing a New Identity

For many banks, merging means losing their identity. Today's mergers try hard to truly blend two successful companies, but sometimes it's not practical to develop an entirely new name. For example, in 1995 the Dime Savings Bank merged with Anchor Savings Bank in New York. The new logo incorporates Anchor but maintains the Dime as the name (as DIME Anchor). When Chase Manhattan and Chemical Bank merged, the two banks conducted research and found that Chase had a higher name recognition internationally and nationally than Chemical. Hence, the name Chase was retained.

Merger Strategies for Customer Retention

The key to a successful merger/acquisition is a high customer retention rate. Here is a 10-step strategy for customer retention:[4]

1. Identify the top business customer base. Remember that 20 percent of your customers most likely generate 80 percent of your profits, and focus on retaining those customers in particular.

2. Develop and distribute marketing scripts to all employees. They will be bombarded with questions about the merger, and it is useful to give everyone the same information, with instructions to be positive and encouraging.

3. Initiate and maintain contact with top customers. You don't want to lose any of your very best customers, so help them feel comfortable.

4. Send business development officers on outside calling assignments. During any merger/acquisition, the flow of new prospects tends to slow down. Business development officers (who normally seek out new prospects) can be made to feel a part of the team by involving them in calls to high-value customers.

5. Stop defections by having early warning systems and emergency defection plans in place. Notice when customers are closing accounts or drawing down their balances, and find out why they are leaving. Empower branch managers to find out why the customer is considering leaving

and to offer the customer valuable reasons to stay.

6. Keep track of why customers are leaving so you can fix the problem.

7. Establish communication networks for employees so all merger concerns and questions can be answered (and any bright new ideas can be considered).

8. Track retention percentages, and communicate the results to all employees. Again, keep everyone involved.

9. Recognize and reward top retainers.

10. Emphasize the support of top management.

Conclusion

Above all, during a merger or acquisition, communication is key. Regularly sending out updates containing relevant information is essential to customer retention and positive attitudes in employees. If customers detect uncertainty among the employees, it will most likely affect their decision to stay with or leave the newly merged bank.

Follow up once the merger is complete with focus groups and consumer surveys to ensure you're still on target with your customer satisfaction initiatives.[5] You'll get lots of valuable feedback that will ensure the new bank's success in the future.

Notes

1. Richard Reece, "Easing the Transition during a Merger or Acquisition," *Bank Marketing*, August 1996, p. 38.

2. Mark Barrett, "Retaining Small Business and Other Customers during a Merger," *The Journal of Lending and Credit Risk Management*, August 1996, p. 27ff.

3. Katherine Morrall, "Managing a Merger without Losing Customers," *Bank Marketing*, March 1996, p. 19.

4. Barrett, p. 29.

5. Karen Kahler Holliday, "Will Bank Mergers Destroy Customer Loyalty?" *USBanker*, October 1995, p. 30.

GLOSSARY

advertising—Any form of communication paid for by a sponsor for the purpose of informing and persuading consumers to buy goods, ideas, or services. By using advertising, an organization can control what is said about its products, and when and where the information appears.

advertising agency—A company that specializes in delivering the services required to design, execute, and place advertising messages in the various press and broadcast media. Ad agencies may also serve as consultants in developing marketing strategies.

AIDAS process—An acronym for the five successive stages of consumer responsiveness in the selling process. The letters of the acronym stand for Awareness, Interest, Desire, Action, and Satisfaction.

audience research—The process of surveying consumers for their recollection of and reaction to an advertisement delivered in print or through a broadcast medium.

bank elasticity—The likelihood that customers will change banks in response to a change in the price of services.

basis point—One-hundredth (1/100) of one percent. Used in connection with interest rates. For example, a yield of 4.06% is 6 basis points higher than a yield of 4.00%.

behavior modification pricing—Setting a price that encourages consumers to alter their buying behavior.

captive finance company—A credit-granting subsidiary whose principal business is to finance consumer purchases of the parent company's products, such as automobiles or major appliances.

channel of distribution—The means through which goods and services move from seller to buyer.

collateral material—Literature in the form of brochures, counter cards, and posters that describes to a customer the range of available products.

community relations—Active participation in and financial support of community projects by an organization for the purpose of fostering goodwill and gaining public esteem.

Community Reinvestment Act (CRA)—A 1977 law requiring financial institutions to meet the credit needs of low- and moderate-income segments of communities they serve and to report on the extent of their investment in the areas they serve. A 1989 policy statement expanded the way regulators evaluate banks' CRA programs.

competitor—A rival business selling identical or similar products in the same market.

concentrated marketing—The practice of designing a single product and marketing strategy to appeal to one market segment.

concept testing—The process of trying out a new product or marketing approach on a selected group of consumers. It measures reactions to an idea rather than actual buying behavior (See also *test marketing*.)

consumer buying behavior—The actions individuals take in deciding which goods and services to purchase.

consumerism—A movement originating in the early 1960s to protect consumers from bad products, poor service, and misrepresentation by businesses about their products and warranties.

control—In discussions of the strategic planning process, the measurement of performance against objectives and the taking of corrective action, if necessary, to stay on course.

core deposits—That portion of a bank's deposits that, despite seasonal and cyclical fluctuations and interest rate changes, is relatively stable and has a predictable cost. Consumer savings and time deposits make up the largest portion of core deposits.

corporate objective—A broad statement that gives direction to the business decisions taken to strengthen an organization's long-term financial position.

credit card—A card issued by a financial institution or company that, when used to make purchases or withdraw cash, debits a line of credit established for the customer.

cross-selling—The practice of promoting financial services in addition to the one currently being used by a customer.

cue—Information that arouses interest—such as an advertisement, unusual packaging, or a product display.

customer profile—A description of the distinctive attitudes and personal characteristics of the typical consumer who buys a product.

customer relations—The policies and practices for the handling of all customer contacts—including one-on-one transactions with employees, complaint resolution, and written communications—in a professional manner that results in a favorable image of the organization.

debit card—A card issued by a financial institution to its customers that, when used to make purchases or withdraw cash, debits a customer's checking or savings account.

demarket—The use of marketing strategy to decrease demand for a product or service.

demographics—The study and analysis of population characteristics such as age, income, education, occupation, sex, and race.

deregulation—The removal or liberalization of legal restrictions to promote competition—such as price deregulation (removal of interest rate ceilings), product deregulation (regulatory approval allowing banks to offer more diversified products and services), and geographic deregulation (removal of restrictions that prohibited expansion across state lines).

differentiated marketing—The practice of designing unique products and specialized marketing strategies to meet the needs of two or more market segments. A variation is to offer one basic product but use distinctive marketing strategies to appeal to each segment.

direct marketing—The promotion and selling of goods and services through the mail, over the phone, and in advertising that includes a customer-response mechanism (such as a coupon or application).

distribution—The process of moving goods and services from the seller to the buyer.

diversification—The development and sale of new products to new markets.

early adopter—A consumer who, after *innovators* but before the *early majority,* accepts and uses a new product before it has established mass appeal.

early majority—Consumers who, unlike *innovators* and *early adopters,* are deliberate and cautious in their willingness to accept and use a new product before it has established mass appeal.

elastic—A condition in which demand changes quickly and dramatically in response to a change in price.

escheat—The reversion of property to the state when it remains unclaimed by the owner for a specified number of years.

exposure—The amount of loss that could be taken should a borrower default, excluding all unnamed amounts, such as finance charges, unpaid premiums, and dealer reserves. Exposure is essentially the net principal amount. Also called loss exposure.

external public—The people outside an organization who have an indirect impact on its ability to do business and achieve its objectives—for example, community organizations, the general public, and the media.

family life cycle—The progressive stages of a typical family's spending and investment behavior.

fixed costs—Expenses incurred regardless of the volume of goods produced or services provided.

focus group—A group of people brought together in an informal setting to be interviewed concerning their opinions of specific products, services, and marketing ideas. Responses may not be representative of a larger, scientifically selected population.

goal—A statement of the specific, measurable result to be achieved in pursuit of an organization's corporate and marketing objectives.

heterogeneity—The degree to which quality of service may vary, depending on who provides the service, in what manner, and at which location.

hierarchy of needs—The theory, developed by psychologist Abraham Maslow, that five levels of need—physiological, sense of security, need to belong, sense of esteem, and self-actualization—motivate human behavior.

hypothesis—A proposition put forth to explain a phenomenon. In marketing research, the researcher proposes one or more hypotheses to explain, for instance, the behavior of a target market. The researcher then designs the research to test whether the hypothesis is correct.

implementation—Putting a plan into action.

incremental cost—The change in expenses as a result of increased production or added services.

inelastic—A condition where demand either changes slowly or not at all in response to a change in price.

innovators—The small number of consumers who are the first to accept and use a new product. Innovators tend to be younger and from higher socioeconomic groups.

internal public—The people within an organization who have a direct impact on its ability to do business and achieve its objectives—for example, employees, directors, and shareholders.

Internet—An international network of computer databases that can be accessed using various technologies called browsers and servers.

interstate banking—The establishment of a banking presence in another market across state lines for the purpose of taking deposits.

Intranet—An intranet taps Internet technology to connect everyone in a company. It allows everyone within the company to have access to applications, information, data, and processes by storing all functions in a single "warehouse" and allowing everyone access using Web servers and browsers.

investor relations—The preparation and presentation of financial reports and programs by an organization for the purpose of fostering goodwill with and gaining esteem from its stockholders and the investment community.

laggard—The small number of consumers who are among the last to accept and use a new product. Laggards tend to be from a lower socioeconomic standing, older, and more conservative.

last majority—Consumers who are likely to accept and use a new product only after the majority of the population has found it satisfactory.

local area network (LAN)—A group of linked personal computers that can communicate and share information with one another, allowing various units within an organization to access the same data-base. It consists of a large-capacity personal computer (a server) that serves information down to the workstations.

macroenvironmental factor—(The prefix "macro" means large or great.) A major trend or force in society that influences market conditions. Macroenvironmental factors, such as the economy, the political situation, and the current state of technology, are beyond a company's control but must be monitored and responded to.

management—The process of planning, staffing, organizing, allocating resources, initiating action, providing leadership, and evaluating performance in the pursuit of specific objectives.

market—All the potential customers for a product.

market aggregation—See *undifferentiated marketing.*

market elasticity—The speed and degree to which total demand for a product will change in response to a change in price.

market expansion—Finding new markets for existing products.

market penetration—Selling more of existing products to present markets.

market profile—A description of the geography, housing, population, and economic activity in the primary area (the densest concentration of customers) and secondary area (a sparser concentration of customers) where a product is sold.

market research—The process of gathering and analyzing factual information about a specific market—its geography, customers, and competitors—to understand better one's own position.

market segmentation—The process of dividing a market into subgroups, each identifiable by its specific preferences or needs, so that distinctive products can be developed and sold profitably to each.

market share—One seller's portion of the total sales of a product, usually stated as a percentage.

marketing—"The process of planning and executing the conception, pricing, promotion and distribution of ideas, goods and services to create exchanges that satisfy individual and organization objectives." (American Marketing Association, *Marketing News*, March 1, 1985, p. 1.)

marketing concept—The philosophy that an organization's profit objectives can best be met by identifying the needs and wants of target customers and meeting those needs and wants through an integrated, efficient, organization-wide effort.

marketing customer information (MCIF)—A software program that can sort and analyze customer information and that can serve as a customer information database.

marketing information system—The people, computers, and procedures in an organization that are responsible for the collection and analysis of market data and the subsequent distribution of this intelligence to marketing management for use in planning and decision making. A marketing information system can be broadly defined as "a framework for the day-to-day management and structuring of information gathered regularly from sources both inside and outside an organization." It is a system that comprises both hardware and software. Because of its broad scope, tremendous capacity, and speedy ability to process great quantities of information, it is often called a universal marketing database or datawarehouse.

marketing intermediary—A third party, or middleman, that helps the seller promote and distribute the product to the consumer.

marketing management—The planning, implementation, and evaluation of programs that sell goods and services in a way that both satisfies a consumer need and results in a profit for the seller.

marketing mix—The combination of four marketing activities—product development, pricing, promotion, and distribution—aimed at creating demand among the target market.

marketing objective—A broad statement giving direction to an organization's short-term product, pricing, promotion, and distribution decisions.

marketing plan—A written statement of the product, pricing, promotion, and distribution strategies that will be implemented to achieve long-range goals.

marketing research—The gathering and analysis of factual information about products, prices, promotion, distribution, and consumers for use in marketing management and decision making.

mass market—A market that has not been differentiated on the basis of geography, demographics, psychographics, or other form of segmentation.

McFadden Act—A federal law enacted in 1927 that prohibits banks from establishing branches across state lines.

media—Means of communication that carry advertising—such as newspapers, television, radio, magazines, outdoor boards, and direct mail.

media relations—A coordinated program of policies, procedures, and written communications to foster good working relations with and favorable news coverage by the media.

media research—The process of identifying the number, characteristics, and buying behavior of consumers who are regularly exposed to a particular advertising medium, such as consumers who read the city newspaper every day or who regularly listen to a particular radio station.

microenvironmental factor—(The prefix "micro" means small.) A key player or other factor in the immediate marketplace that affects a company's ability to do business. Microenvironmental factors are "controllable" to the extent that a company can make business decisions about them—for example, which suppliers of raw materials will be selected, which middleman will be hired to help promote products, and what strategy will work best against a competitor.

micromarketing—The opposite of "mass marketing." It is the identification, usually through the use of a marketing information system, of small (thus micro) markets characterized by similar needs, wants, and preferences. Direct selling, marketing, and sales promotion tactics are then aimed at the micromarkets.

middleman—See *marketing intermediary.*

MIS—See *marketing information system.*

mission statement—A statement of common purpose that explains why an organization exists and what it hopes to accomplish.

motivation—An inner need that causes a person to act, usually toward a specific goal.

multiple segmentation—See *differentiated marketing*.

mutual fund—A company that invests in a diversified portfolio of securities. Customers buy shares in the fund directly, rather than through a stock exchange.

neotraditionalism—The blending of traditional American values (adherence to principles, discipline, patriotism, and the importance of family, friends, and community) with the ethic of the 1980s that emphasizes the importance of self (making one's own decisions, choosing one's lifestyle, and needing time for leisure and self-fulfillment).

new product development—The process of taking ideas for new or enhanced products and developing them into actual goods and services that can be sold profitably. The basic steps in this process include (1) idea generation, (2) weeding out of ideas that are not viable or likely to succeed, (3) a business analysis to forecast sales and profitability, (4) development of a sample, (5) market testing to determine consumer acceptance, and (6) introduction or commercialization of the new product.

nonbank bank—A financial institution owned by a nonbanking company (such as an insurance company or brokerage firm) that avoids being defined as a bank holding company for regulatory purposes by limiting the activity of its bank to only one of the two functions that define a commercial bank (that is, it either accepts demand deposits or makes commercial loans, but not both). Such banks can compete with commercial banks while their parent companies engage in activities forbidden to bank holding companies (such as underwriting corporate securities, underwriting insurance, managing mutual funds, and so on).

objective—A statement of the specific, measurable result to be achieved in pursuit of an organization's corporate and marketing objectives. Used interchangeably with "goal."

observation—A marketing research method in which data are collected by physically observing how consumers use goods and services rather than by questioning them.

organizational buying behavior—The decision-making process used by firms to evaluate and select suppliers of goods and services.

outsourcing—The practice of turning over part or all of a bank's data processing operations to a third-party provider.

Pareto principle—The theory that states that 80 percent of a business's profits come from 20 percent of its customers.

penetration pricing—Setting a low initial price in order to quickly attract a large market share.

perception—The process by which people receive, organize, and interpret sensory information.

personal banker—A program in which a bank employee is assigned to provide personalized customer service to a valued customer. Personal bankers are professionals who understand the unique financial needs of each customer and have the authority to handle their nonroutine banking transactions.

personal selling—One-on-one contact between a seller's representative and a potential buyer for the purpose of arousing interest and convincing the buyer to purchase products. Personal selling lays the groundwork for long-term relationships between the buyer and seller.

physical distribution—The planning, handling, and delivery activities that result in the movement of goods and services from seller to buyer.

place—A synonym for distribution, or the ways in which products move from the seller to the buyer.

planning—The process of setting objectives for the future and deciding on strategies for achieving them. Planning is deciding now where you want to be in the future and how to get there.

point—A fee on a loan or mortgage. One point equals one percent of the amount of the loan.

positioning—The art of promoting a product in such a way as to make a distinctive impression about the product in the consumer's mind.

premium—Cash or merchandise that a business gives away or sells at discount as an incentive to purchase a product.

pretesting—The process of evaluating the likely effectiveness and acceptance of a new advertising campaign by presenting it first to a representative group of consumers.

price—The amount of money one must pay to own a product or use a service.

price sensitivity—The degree to which changes in price will affect the demand for a product.

primary data—Data collected directly from original sources. The findings based on answers to questionnaires administered to individual customers or prospects are an example of primary data.

product—A tangible good that has both physical and psychological characteristics that make it desirable to the consumer. Often this term is used in a broader sense to refer to anything (goods, services, places, people, events, or ideas) that satisfies a consumer need.

product expansion—To increase demand by selling new products to current markets.

product item—A specific version of a product.

product life cycle—The successive stages of a product's sales volume. The four stages, which vary in length from product to product, include introduction (low sales), growth (rapid growth in sales), maturity (constant level of sales), and decline.

product line—A group of products that have similar characteristics or serve related functions. In banking, the savings product line would include passbook, statement, and money market savings accounts.

product management—The assignment of an individual or department to be responsible for introducing, marketing, and ensuring profitable sales of a product or product line.

product manager—An employee who is given responsibility for successfully introducing and managing the profitable selling of a product or product line.

product/market expansion—See *diversification*.

product mix—All the goods and services offered for sale by a company.

promotion—Activities that increase customer awareness and demand.

promotion mix—The unique combination of four promotional activities—advertising, sales promotion, publicity, and personal selling—that results in a profitable demand for products.

promotional material—See *collateral material*.

psychographics—The study and analysis of the attitudes, interests, and opinions (AIO) that influence buying behavior.

public relations—A coordinated program of policies, conduct, and communication designed to foster goodwill and gain esteem.

publicity—Any form of unpaid communication about goods or services that informs and persuades consumers to buy. The media reports publicity at no cost to the seller because it is judged to have news or human interest value. As a result, consumers find publicity a more credible source of information than paid advertising. For the issuing organization, the disadvantage of publicity is the loss of control over how the information is edited, and when and where it appears.

qualitative research—A research method in which information is collected by in-depth, interactive interviewing of a small number of consumers. This method is effective for determining basic needs, desires, and reactions to new product concepts and for identifying issues to be measured with quantitative research.

quantitative research—A research method in which data are collected by presenting a sizable sample of consumers with carefully prepared questions, either verbally or in writing. The result is statistical data about consumer attitudes and buying behavior.

rate sensitivity—The exposure of assets or liabilities to changes in interest rates. Rate sensitivity analysis involves reviewing company assets and liabilities to determine net exposure.

redlining—The illegal practice of intentionally or unintentionally eliminating residents of certain geographic areas from eligibility for credit (mortgages, loans) because the area is considered a poor risk.

reference group—One or more persons whose attitudes and opinions influence the actions of others.

regional banking—The establishment of a banking presence in nearby states either by merger, acquisition, or new charter. Regional banking occurs when reciprocal laws are passed allowing bank holding companies in one state to acquire or establish a bank in another.

Regulation DD—The Federal Reserve Board regulation that implements the Truth-in-Savings Act.

Regulation Q—A Federal Reserve Board regulation that prohibits the paying of interest on demand deposits, sets rules for advertising deposit accounts, and until recently set the maximum rate banks could pay on savings and time deposits. The Depository Institutions Deregulation and Monetary Control Act of 1980 mandated the gradual phasing out of interest rate ceilings between 1980 and 1987.

relationship pricing—To set prices that provide an incentive for consumers to use multiple products.

sales promotion—Any device, other than advertising, publicity, and personal selling, that provides incentive to the consumer to purchase goods or services—for example, cents-off coupons, premiums, and in-store displays.

sample—A small number of individuals, scientifically selected from the general population, whose opinions, preferences, and characteristics are representative of the group as a whole.

secondary data—Data collected by a third party and made available for others to use. The U.S. Statistical Abstract is an example of secondary data.

segmentation—See *market segmentation*.

selective distortion—A tendency to alter or interpret information so that it is consistent with one's prior beliefs.

selective exposure—A tendency to notice only information that is needed, expected, or exceeds expectation.

selective retention—A tendency to remember only the information that supports one's current attitudes or beliefs.

selectivity—The process of filtering information from the environment so that only what is important is received and retained.

service—An intangible activity or benefit performed by a business that satisfies a consumer need. In banking, this term is often used interchangeably with *product*.

service packaging—The practice of marketing a group of services as a single product.

service shopping—A marketing research method for collecting information about competitors' products and services by having an employee pose as a potential customer. This technique can be used to measure how well an organization's own employees understand and market services.

single-segment marketing—See *concentrated marketing*.

situation analysis—The process of evaluating one's position in relation to the internal and external environments to identify strengths, weaknesses, and future courses of action.

skimming pricing—To set a high initial price for a product in order to attract the "cream" of the market—that is, consumers who will buy regardless of the price.

snipe—A brief marketing message placed in an unexpected location, such as across the face of the outer envelope of a direct mail piece or across the corner of a billboard or print advertisement. It is usually used to communicate urgency (for example, "Important news about your accounts" or "Only five days left to get this great rate!").

social responsibility—The obligation of a company to conduct business activities in a way that does not adversely affect its customers or the community as a whole and to devote a portion of its resources to civic improvement efforts.

societal marketing concept—The philosophy that an organization's profit objectives can best be met by identifying the needs and wants of target customers; meeting those needs and wants through an integrated, efficient, organization-wide effort; and carrying out this effort in a socially responsible manner.

source market—The market that provides the raw materials that enable a company to make and offer products to another market. In banking, consumers who deposit funds in checking or savings accounts are a source market because they provide the funds that can be loaned to or "used" by other customers, who are known as the *use market*.

specialties—Small, useful novelties such as calendars, pens, and matchbooks that carry advertising messages and can be given free of charge to customers.

spread—The difference between the income earned in using funds and the cost to the bank of those funds. The goal is to maximize that spread, also called the "net interest margin."

strategic marketing planning—The process of identifying an action plan for attaining long-range marketing goals, of implementing that plan, and of measuring and evaluating its success.

strategy—A plan for achieving a desired result.

superregional bank—A bank with assets between $25 billion and $75 billion at year end.

survey research—A marketing research method in which data are collected by asking consumers a series of questions, either orally or in writing, about their attitudes and buying behavior.

systems selling—Selling products and the associated services that support them as a comprehensive response to multiple customer needs.

tactic—A specific action taken to attain a goal. Tactics determine who will do what, when, and at what cost.

target market—A preselected group of buyers for whom a product is created and to whom a marketing campaign is directed.

telemarketing—Promoting and selling products by telephone.

test marketing—The process of selling a product on a limited scale in several representative markets to measure the actual buying behavior. The feedback from consumers, dealers, and competitors enables the marketer to predict acceptance of both the product and the marketing campaign in national markets. See also *concept testing*.

Truth-in-Savings Act—A law governing the disclosure of rates and terms on interest-bearing deposit accounts. It was implemented through Federal Reserve Board Regulation DD on June 21, 1993.

undifferentiated marketing—The practice of designing a single product and marketing strategy to appeal to the greatest possible number of customers.

use market—The customers who use a company's end product when they buy goods and services. In banking, consumers who apply for personal loans are "using" the resources supplied by depositors, who constitute the *source market*.

value pricing—To set a price for a product based on its perceived value to the consumer, not on the basis of its cost to the producer.

variable costs—Expenses that vary in amount depending on the volume of goods produced or services provided.

SUPPLEMENTAL RESOURCE GUIDE FOR FINANCIAL SERVICES PROFESSIONALS

Journals

(in addition to the newsletters and journals cited in the endnotes to the chapters):

Financial Advertising Review
Bank Advertising News
Bank Marketing

Advertising

Burns, Thomas J., *Effective Communications and Advertising for Financial Institutions*. Prentice-Hall, 1986.

Dru, Jean-Marie, *Disruption: Overturning Conventions and Shaking Up the Marketplace*. John Wiley & Sons, 1996.

Geller, Lois K., *Response! The Complete Guide to Profitable Direct Marketing*. Free Press, 1996.

Griffin, Jack, *The Do-It-Yourself Business Promotions Kit*. Prentice-Hall Trade Publications, 1995.

Janal, Daniel S., *Online Marketing Handbook: How to Promote, Advertise and Sell Your Products and Services on the Internet*. Van Nostrand Reinhold Trade Publications, 1997.

Shaver, Dick, *The Next Step in Database Marketing: Consumer Guided Marketing: Privacy for Your Customers, Record Profits for You*. John Wiley & Sons, 1996.

Vitale, Joe, *Cyberwriting: How to Promote Your Product or Service Online (Without Being Flamed)*. AMACOM, 1996.

Business (of Banking, and General Business)

Bollenbacher, George M., *The New Business of Banking*. Irwin Professional, 1995.

Brown, Albert J., Jr., *The High Performance Bank: Insights and Advice on How to Make Your Bank a Consistent Top Performer*. Probus, 1994.

DeBonis, J. Nicholas, and Roger S. Peterson, *AMA Handbook for Managing Business to Business Marketing Communications*. NTC Business Books, 1997.

Drucker, Peter F., *Management: Tasks, Responsibilities, Practices*. Harper & Row, 1974.

Goldstein, Douglas, and Joyce Flory, *The Online Business Atlas: The Best Online Sites, Resources and Services in: Management, Marketing and Promotion, Sales, Entrepreneurial Ventures*. Irwin Professional, 1996.

Hunter, Victor L., and David Tietyin, *Business to Business Marketing: Creating a Community of Customers*. NTC Business Books, 1997.

Levinson, Jay Conrad, *Guerrilla Marketing: Secrets for Making Big Profits from Your Small Business*. Houghton Mifflin, 1993.

McArthur, C. Dan, and Larry Womack, *Outcome Management: Redesigning Your Business Systems to Achieve Your Vision*. Quality Resources, 1995.

Peters, Thomas J., and Robert H. Waterman, Jr., *In Search of Excellence: Lessons from America's Best-Run Companies*. Harper & Row, 1982.

Wing, Michael J., *The Arthur Andersen Guide to Talking with Your Customers: What They Will Tell You about Your Business When You Ask the Right Questions*. Upstart, 1997.

Distribution Strategies

A Guide to Selecting Bank Locations. American Bankers Association, 1968.

Bennett, Rex O., *Bank Location Analysis: Techniques and Methodology*. American Bankers Association, 1975.

Komenar, Margo, *Electronic Marketing*. John Wiley & Sons, 1996.

Littlefield, James E., G. Jackson Burney, and William V. White, *Bank Branch Location: A Handbook of Effective Technique and Practice*. Bank Marketing Association, 1973.

Seibert, Paul, *Facilities Planning and Design for Financial Institutions: A Strategic Management Guide*. Irwin Professional, 1996.

Future of Banking

Hamel, Gary, and C.K. Prahalad, *Competing for the Future: Breakthrough Strategies for Seizing Control of Your Industry and Creating the Markets of Tomorrow*. Harvard Business School Press, 1994.

Marketing Planning

Bayne, Kim M., *The Internet Marketing Plan: A Practical Handbook for Creating, Implementing and Assessing Your Online Presence*. John Wiley & Sons, 1997.

Hensel, James S., "The Essential Nature of the Marketing Management Process: An Overview," in Leonard L. Berry and L. A. Capaldini, eds., *Marketing for the Bank Executive*. Petrocelli Books, 1974.

Hodges, Luther H., Jr., and Rollie Tillman, Jr., *Bank Marketing: Text and Cases*. Addison-Wesley, 1968.

Joselyn, Robert W., and D. Keith Humphries, *An Introduction to Bank Marketing Planning*. American Bankers Association, 1974.

Ries, Al, and Jack Trout, *Marketing Warfare*. McGraw-Hill, 1997.

Ries, Al, and Jack Trout, *The 22 Immutable Laws of Marketing: Violate Them at Your Own Risk*. HarperCollins, 1993.

Solomon, Michael R., and Elnora W. Stuart, *Marketing: Real People, Real Choices*. Prentice-Hall, 1996.

Stanton, William J., and Charles Futrell, *Fundamentals of Marketing*, 8th edition. McGraw-Hill, 1987.

Marketing Research

Berry, Michael J.A., and Gordon Linoff, *Data Mining Techniques: For Marketing, Sales and Customer Support*. John Wiley & Sons, 1997.

Heslop, Janet (editor), *American Marketplace: Demographics and Spending Patterns*, 3rd edition. New Strategist Publications, 1997.

Pol, Louis G., and Richard K. Thomas, *Demography for Business Decision Making*. Quorom Books, 1997.

Pope, Jeffrey L., *Practical Marketing Research*. American Marketing Association, 1993.

Schoner, Bertram, and Kenneth P. Uhl, *Marketing Research, Information Systems and Decision Making*. John Wiley & Sons, 1975.

Smith, J. Walker, and Ann S. Clurman, *Rocking the Ages: The Yankelovich Report of Generational Marketing*. HarperBusiness, 1997.

Positioning

Ries, Al, and Jack Trout, *Positioning: The Battle for Your Mind*. McGraw-Hill, 1986.

Trout, Jack, *The New Positioning: The Latest on the World's #1 Business Strategy*. McGraw-Hill, 1997.

Vandermerwe, Sandra, *The Eleventh Commandment: Transforming to 'Own' Customers*. John Wiley & Sons, 1996.

Pricing

Moebs, G. Michael, and Eva Moebs, *Pricing Financial Services*. Dow Jones–Irwin, 1986.

Product Development

Bobrow, Edwin E., *The Complete Idiot's Guide to New Product Development*. MacMillan General Reference, 1997.

Effective Bank Product Management: How to Be Profitable in a Competitive Environment. Bank Administration Institute, 1988.

Patrick, Jerry, *How to Develop Successful New Products*. NTC Business Books, 1997.

Thygerson, Kenneth J., *Product-Line Performance Evaluation Systems for Financial Depositories*. Quorom Books, 1997.

Public Relations

Shiva, V.A., *The Internet Publicity Guide: How to Maximize Your Marketing and Promotion in Cyberspace*. Allworth Press, 1997.

Selling and Sales Management

Alexander, James A., and Michael C. Lyons, *The Knowledge-Based Organization: Four Steps to Increasing Sales, Profits and Market Share*. Irwin Professional, 1995.

Baron, Gerald R., *Friendship Marketing's Salt Principles: Seasoning the Business of Life*. Quest Enterprise Institute, 1997.

Berry, Leonard L., David R. Bennett, and Carter W. Brown, *Service Quality: A Profit Strategy for Financial Institutions*. Dow Jones–Irwin, 1989.

Bly, Robert W., *Secrets of Successful Telephone Selling: How to Generate More Leads, Sales, Repeat Business and Referrals by Phone*. Henry Holt, 1997.

Crosby, John V., *Managing the Big Sale: A Relational Approach to Marketing Strategies, Tactics and Selling*. NTC Publishing Group, 1996.

Sales and Marketing. Harvard Business School Press, 1996.

Graham, John R., *203 Ways to Be Supremely Successful in the New World of Selling*. Simon and Schuster MacMillan, 1996.

Khandpur, Navtej, and Jasmine Wevers, *Sales Force Automation Using Web Technologies*. John Wiley & Sons, 1997.

Lewis, Herschell Gordon, and Robert D. Lewis, *Selling on the Net: The Complete Guide*. NTC Business Books, 1996.

Maslow, A.H., *Motivation and Personality*. Harper and Brothers, 1954.

McCloskey, Larry A., and Bryan Wirth. *Selling with Excellence: A Quality Approach for Sales Professionals*. American Society for Quality, 1992.

Peppers, Don, and Martha Rogers, Ph.D., *Enterprise One to One: Tools for Competing in the Interactive Age*. Currency/Doubleday, 1997.

Peppers, Don, and Martha Rogers, Ph.D., *The One to One Future: Building Relationships One Customer at a Time*. Currency/Doubleday, 1997.

Sterne, Jim, *Customer Service on the Internet: Building Relationships, Increasing Loyalty, and Staying Competitive*. John Wiley & Sons, 1996.

Stowell, Daniel M., *Sales, Marketing, and Continuous Improvement: Six Best Practices to Achieve Revenue Growth and Increase Customer Loyalty*. Jossey-Bass, 1997.

Webster, Frederick E., Jr., and Yoram Wind, *Organizational Buying Behavior*. Prentice-Hall, 1972.

Strategic Marketing and Planning

Beemer, C. Britt, and Robert L. Shook, *Predatory Marketing: What Everyone in Business Needs to Know to Win Today's American Consumer*. William Morrow, 1997.

Hall, Robert E., *The Streetcorner Strategy for Winning Local Markets*. Performance Press, 1994.

Kerin, Roger A., and Robert A. Peterson, *Strategic Marketing Problems: Cases and Comments*. Prentice-Hall, 1997.

Kremer, John, and J. Daniel McComas, *High Impact Marketing on a Low-Impact Budget: 101 Strategies to Turbo-Charge Your Business Today*. Prima, 1997.

Lewis, T.G., Ph.D., *The Friction-Free Economy: Marketing Strategies for a Wired World*. HarperBusiness, 1997.

Lovelock, Christopher H., *Services Marketing*. Prentice-Hall, 1996.

McKitterick, J.B., *The Frontiers of Marketing Thought*. American Marketing Association, 1957.

Vavra, Terry G., *Aftermarketing: How to Keep Customers for Life through Relationship Marketing*. Irwin Professional, 1995.

Violano, Michael, and Shimon-Craig Van Collie, *Retail Banking Technology: Strategies and Resources That Seize the Competitive Advantage*. John Wiley & Sons, 1992.

Target Market Selection/ Segmentation

Best, Roger J., *Market-Based Management: Strategies for Growing Customer Value and Profitability*. Prentice-Hall, 1997.

Gerber, Jerry, Janet Wolff, Walter Klores, and Gene Brown, *LifeTrends: The Future of Baby Boomers and Other Aging Americans: The Compelling Analysis of What They Will Have, Want and Need*. Stonesong Press, Macmillan, 1989.

Morgan, Carol M., and Doran J. Levy, Ph.D., *Segmenting the Mature Market: Identifying, Targeting and Reaching America's Diverse, Booming Senior Markets*. Probus, 1993.

Ritchie, Karen, *Marketing to Generation X*. Lexington Books, 1995.

Sharp, Kevin, and Daniel Johnson, *Know Thy Customer: How to Follow Marketing's First Commandment*. Dartnell, 1997.

Stanley, Thomas J., *Marketing to the Affluent*. McGraw-Hill, 1997.

Rossman, Marlene L., *Multicultural Marketing: Selling to a Diverse America*. AMACOM, 1996.

Trivers, Jonathan, *One Stop Marketing*. John Wiley & Sons, 1996.

Marketing Financial Services Organizations

Advertising Mail Marketing Association
1333 F Street NW, Suite 710
Washington, DC 20004-1108

Advertising Research Federation
641 Lexington Avenue
New York, NY 10022
212-751-5656

American Advertising Federation
1101 Vermont Avenue NW, Suite 500
Washington, DC 20005
202-898-0089

American Association of Advertising
    Agencies
405 Lexington Avenue
New York, NY 10174-1801
212-682-2500

American Bankers Association
1120 Connecticut Avenue NW
Washington, DC 20036
202-663-5000

American Marketing Association
250 South Wacker Drive, Suite 200
Chicago, IL 60606
312-648-0536

Bank Marketing Association
1120 Connecticut Avenue NW
Washington, DC 20036
202-663-5422

Business Marketing Association
150 North Wacker Drive
Chicago, IL 60606
312-409-4262

Direct Marketing Association
212-768-7277

Marketing Science Institute
617-491-2060

Media Dynamics
18 East 41st Street
New York, NY 10017
212-683-7895

National Automated Clearing House
    Association
607 Herndon Parkway, Suite 200
Herndon, VA 22070

Promotion Marketing Association of Amer-
    ica, Inc.
257 Park Avenue South, 11th Floor
New York, NY 10010
212-420-1100

Public Relations Society of America
212-995-2230

Sales and Marketing Executives
    International
Statler Office Tower, Suite 977
Cleveland, OH 44115
770-661-8500

Web Site Resources

http://www.ffiec.gov/nic/default.HTM
National Information Center of Banking
    Information

http://www.banksite.com
BankSITE Global Directory

http://www.bankweb.com
BankWeb

http://www2.ari.net/cirm
Creative Investment Research

http://www.orcc.com/banking.htm
Online Banking and Financial Services
    Directory

http://www.qualisteam.com
Qualisteam

Search Engines

http://www.altavista.digital.com
Alta Vista

http://www.excite.com
Excite

http://www.hotbot.com
HotBot

http://www.infoseek.com
Infoseek

http://www.lycos.com
Lycos

http://www.mckinley.com
Magellan

http://www.webcrawler.com
WebCrawler

http://www.yahoo.com
Yahoo

Bank Directories

http://www.aaadir.com
AAAdir World Banks

http://www.cybertechnic.com/eye-on/
    yAlphaBanking.html
Eye-On Banking

http://192.147.69.47/drs
FDIC Institution Directory System

http://www.financial-net.com
Financial Net

http://www.findex.com
Findex

http://www.ffiec.gov/nic/default.HTM
National Information Center of Banking
    Information

Directories of Bank Web Sites

http://www.aba.com/abatool/showme_rel.
    html?location=membanks.html
American Bankers Association, ABA
    Member Bank Web Sites

http://www.banksite.com
BankSITE Global Directory

http://www.bankweb.com
BankWeb

http://www.orcc.com/banking.htm
Online Banking and Financial Services
    Directory

General Directories

http://www.tollfree.att.net/index.html
AT&T Toll-Free Internet Directory

http://www.bankersmart.aba.com
BankersMart

http://www.bigbook.com
BigBook

http://www.finweb.com
FINWeb

http://www.FOUR11.com
Four11-the Internet White Pages

http://www.mastercard.com/atm
The MasterCard/Cirrus ATM Locator

http://www.nfsn.com
National Financial Services Network

http://www.smart-card.com
Smart Card Resource Center

Related Trade Associations

http://www.acbankers.org
America's Community Bankers

http://www.aba.com
American Bankers Association

http://www.aiadc.org
American Insurance Association

http://www.bannister.com/aft
Association for Financial Technology

http://www.bai.org
Bank Administration Institute

http://www.bmanet.org
Bank Marketing Association

http://www.bsanet.org
Bank Securities Association

http://www.bankersround.org
Bankers Roundtable

http://www.efta.org
Electronic Funds Transfer Association

http://www.fiia.org
Financial Institutions Insurance Association

http://www.fma.org
Financial Management Association

http://www.fstc.org
Financial Services Technology Consortium

http://www.fwi.org
Financial Women International

http://www.ibaa.org
Independent Bankers Association of
America

http://www.mbaa.org
Mortgage Bankers Association of America

http://www.nahb.com/
National Association of Home Builders

http://www.realtor.com/homepage.htm
National Association of Realtors

http://www.nasd.com
National Association of Securities Dealers

http://www.nacha.org
National Automated Clearing House
Association

http://www.obanet.org
Online Banking Association

http://www.sia.com
Securities Industry Association

http://www.smartcrd.com
Smart Card Forum

State Bankers Associations

http://www.arkbankers.org
Arkansas Bankers Association

http://www.capcon.com/cba
Colorado Bankers Association

http://www.ctbank.com
Connecticut Bankers Association

http://www.webbanker.com
Florida Bankers Association

http://www.gabankers.com
Georgia Bankers Association

http://www.ilbanker.com
Illinois Bankers Association

http://www.inbankers.org
Indiana Bankers Association

http://www.iabankers.com
Iowa Bankers Association

http://www.ink.org/public/kbank
Kansas Bankers Association

http://www.kybanks.com
Kentucky Bankers Association

http://www.lba.org
Louisiana Bankers Association

http://www.massbankers.org
Massachusetts Bankers Association

http://www.mibankers.com
Michigan Bankers Association

http://www2.minnbankcenter.org/mba
Minnesota Bankers Association

http://www.mobankers.com
Missouri Bankers Association

http://www.nebankers.org
Nebraska Bankers Association

http://www.nh.com/banking/nhbank.html
New Hampshire Bankers Association

http://www.obanet.com
Ohio Bankers Association

http://www.oba.com
Oklahoma Bankers Association

http://www.oregonbankers.com
Oregon Bankers Association

http://www.pabanker.com
Pennsylvania Bankers Association

http://www.scbankers.org
South Carolina Bankers Association

http://www.tnbankers.org
Tennessee Bankers Association

http://www.txbanc.com
Texas Bankers Association

http://www.wvbankers.org
West Virginia Bankers Association

http://www.wisbank.com
Wisconsin Bankers Association

Bank Statistics

http://www.fdic.gov/databank
Data Bank

http://www.ffiec.gov/nic
NIC-National Information Center

Economic Statistics

http://stats.bls.gov
Bureau of Labor Statistics

http://www.conference-board.org/
products/c-consumer.cfm
Consumer Research Center

http://www.lib.umich.edu/libhome/
Documents.center/stats.html
Statistical Resources on the Web

http://www.cob.ohio-state.edu/dept/fin/
osudata.htm
The Financial Data Finder

http://www.hsh.com
HSH Associates, Financial Publishers

Current Mortgage Information

http://www.ramresearch.com
RAM Research

Demographics

http://www.demographics.com
American Demographics/Marketing Tools

http://www.bls.census.gov/cps/cpsmain.
htm
Current Population Survey Main Page

http://tiger.census.gov
Census TMS (TIGER Map Service) Home
Page

http://stats.bls.gov:80/csxhome.htm
Consumer Expenditure Survey

http://www.census.gov
U.S. Census Bureau

Financial Institutions Resources

http://www.ncua.gov
National Credit Union Administration

http://www.access.gpo.gov/ots/index.html
Office of Thrift Supervision

http://www.occ.treas.gov
Office of the Comptroller of Currency
(OCC)

http://www.sbaonline.sba.gov
Small Business Administration

Business and Financial News

http://www.bloomberg.com
Bloomberg

http://www.businesswire.com
Business Wire
http://cnnfn.com/index.html
CNNfn

http://www.newspage.com
Late Breaking News

http://www.nytimes.com/library/cyber/
reference/busconn.html
New York Times Business Connections

http://wsj.com
Wall Street Journal Interactive Edition

http://www.edgar-online.com/
EDGAR Online

Journals and Newspapers

http://www.banking.com/aba
ABA Banking Journal Online

http://www.americanbanker.com
American Banker Online

http://www.bmanet.org/n-copy-1-back-
home.html
Bank Marketing

http://www.kiplinger.com/magazine/
maghome.html
Kiplinger Online

On-line Databases

http://www3.elibrary.com/search.cgi
Electronic Library

http://usserve.us.kpmg.com/fs
KPMG Financial Services—Banking and
Finance

INDEX

Personality symbol, communicating message through, 239
Personal selling, 75, 208–223, 228
  AIDAS formula in, 215
  in business banking market, 301
  characteristics of successful salesperson in, 212–216
  comparison to marketing, 208–212
  designing training programs in, 220–222
  as element of customer service, 208–209
  executing training programs in, 222–223
  importance of, in banking, 209–212
  managing selling process in, 216–220
Peters, Thomas, 283
Philip Morris, 153
Physical distribution, 75
Physiological needs, 99
Piaget, Jean, 143
Plastic cards, 203–204
Plus Network, 181
PNC Bank, 204
Point-of-purchase merchandising, 248
Point-of-sale advertising, 309
Political environment, 36–37, 65
Population characteristics, and location selection, 197
Positioning and marketing segmentation, 142–143
Postpurchase feelings, 110–111
Posttesting, 246
Potential product, 149
Premiums, 249–250
Prepurchase activity, 108, 110
Press conferences, 261–262
Press releases, 262–264
Pretesting, 246
Price
  awareness of differences in, 176
  definition and role of, 172–173
  duration of differences in, 176
  estimating customer response to changes in, 178–179
  initiating changes in, 182–183
  sensitivity to, 175
Price elasticity of demand, 174–179
  at market and firm levels, 177–178
Pricing, 75
  decisions, responsibility for making decisions on, 185–186
  and income generation, 172
  and primary data, 178
  reactions to, 186–187
  responding to regulations affecting, 184
  and secondary data, 178–179
Pricing strategies, 148
  in business banking market, 299–300

for new products, 179–182
  in strategic market, 52–53
  in trust market, 307–308
Primary data and pricing, 178
Primary research
  designing sample for, 124
  selecting tool for, 123–124
Primary sources, 120
Problems and opportunities, analysis of, 76–77
Procter & Gamble, 153, 164, 276
Producers and suppliers, 40–41
Product, modification of, 152–153
Product adopter categories, 158–159
Product advertising, 227–228
Product contraction, 152
Product development, 163
Product elimination, 166
  benefits of, 166–167
  industry resistance to, 167
Product expansion, 87, 152
Product failures, 165–166
Production orientation, 20
Product item, 149
Productivity, improved, 211
Product knowledge, 221–222
Product life cycle stage, 230–231
Product life cycle strategies, 154–158
Product line, 149
  extension of, 161
Product management, 164–165
  challenge for staff in, 319
  organization for, 276–277
Product/market expansion matrix, 86
Product marketing plan, applying strategy to, 90–92
Product mix, 149–150
  strategies for, 152–154
Product orientation, 18–20
Products, 75. See also New products
  approaches to selling specific, 221
  changing price of existing, 182–186
  definition of, 148–149
  importance of, 148–152
  modification of existing, 159, 161
  quality of, in setting price, 172
  repositioning, 153–154
  versus services, 150–152
Product screening, 161–162
Product strategy, 52
  in business banking market, 297–299
  in trust market, 306–307
Profit, 174
  earning by bank, 173–174
  in marketing concept, 8
  in setting price, 172
Promotional activity, 75
Promotional campaign, 250
  developing retail (Case study D), 351–354
Promotion mix, 227
  relative use of elements, 228–231

Promotion strategies, 53, 148. See also Advertising; Personal selling; Sales promotion
  in business banking market, 300
  in trust market, 308–309
Proprietary PC banking services, 314
Psychographics, 108, 137
Psychological factors, and consumer behavior, 104–106
Public relations, 254
  activities not covered under, 257, 259
  benefits of broader perspective for, 267, 269
  definition of, 228, 255–257
  position of, in organization, 259–260
  role of, 260–269
  tasks in, 260–267
Publics, 42, 76
Purchase, significance and frequency of, 177
Purchase decision, 110

Q

Quaker Oats Company, 137
Qualitative data, 124
Qualitative research, 163
  on pricing, 178
Quality movement, 283
Quantitative data, 123
Quantitative research, 163
  on pricing, 178
Questionnaire, designing, 125–126
Quicken, 313

R

Recruiting in selling process, 216
Redlining, 11
Reference group influence, 103
Regulations
  bank advertising, 247
  effect on pricing, 184
Regulatory environment, 36–37, 65
Reinforcement, 105
Related marketing and advertising efforts, 220
Relationship management system, 85
Relationship pricing, 181
Reliability, 23
Research. See also Marketing research
  advertising, 246
  audience, 246
  challenge for staff, 319
  media, 246
  qualitative, 163, 178
  quantitative, 163, 178
  survey, 75
Response, 105
Responsiveness, 22–23
Retail activity, 64
  developing promotional campaign in, 351–354

Return on investment (ROI) in setting price, 172
Revlon, 153
Rewarding results of sales effort, 219–220
Roles, 103
Rolex watches, 85

S

Sales
  declining, 12, 14
  evaluating efforts in, 219
  rewarding results of, 219–220
  techniques in (Case study C), 210, 213, 345–350
Sales management staff, challenge for, 319
Salesperson, characteristics of successful, 212–216
Sales promotion, 247–248
  contests in, 249
  definition of, 228
  incentives in, 248
  point-of-purchase in, 248
  premiums in, 249–250
  seminars in, 248
  specialties in, 248
Samples of products and services, 220
Scientific evidence, communicating message through, 241
Secondary information, 120
  bankers use of, 122–123
  and pricing, 178–179
  searching, 123
Securities and Exchange Commission (SEC), 36, 281
Security and safety, need for, 99
Selective distortion, 101
Selective retention, 101
Self-actualization, need for, 100
Self-administered questionnaires, 124–125
Self-analysis in situation analysis, 61–63
Self-concept, 107, 108
Selling
  differences between marketing and, 208–212
  as element of customer service, 208–209
  importance of, in banking, 209–212
  managing process of, 216–220
  skills in, 213–216
Selling orientation, 20–21
Seminars
  in banking market, 303
  in sales promotions, 248
  sponsorship of, 309

Service industry, distribution in, 192–194
Service quality movement, growth of, 111
Services
  approaches to selling specific, 221
  versus products, 150–152
Service shopping, 75–76
7-Up, 143
Signature, 245
Single-segment marketing, 142
Site location decisions, 196–197
Situation analysis
  changes in, 285
  conducting, 50–51
  four elements of, 61–67
  reasons for formalizing, 60–61
  self-analysis in, 61–63
Skimming pricing, 179
Slice-of-life technique, communicating message through, 237
Smart Card Forum, 204
Smart cards, 203–204
  challenge of, 204
Social and cultural environment, 33, 36, 65
Social class, 104
Social factors and consumer behavior, 103
Social responsibility in marketing concept, 10–12
Specialties, 248
Specific site analysis, 199–201
Status, 103
Status quo in setting price, 172
Strategic marketing planning, 43
Subculture, 104
Supercommunity bank, 313
Supporting objectives, 80
Survey method, selecting, 124–125
Survey research, 75
Survival in setting price, 172
Swatch, 85
Systems, 159
Systems and operations, relationship to marketing, 280

T

Tangibles, 23
Target markets
  characteristics of, 220
  and market segmentation, 85–88
  problems in selecting, 288
  selecting, 51–52, 140–142
Tasks, public relations, 260–267
Tax Reform Act (1986), 65
Technical expertise, communicating message through, 239
Technological environment, 37, 39, 65

Technology, impact of, on banking, 316–318
Telephone interviews, 124–125
Telephones and call centers, 202
Testimonial evidence, communicating message through, 241
Test marketing, 163
Time-saving services, growing need for, 33, 36
Timex watch, 85, 136
Tone of ad, 241
Total company effort in marketing concept, 8, 10
Tracking, advertising, 245
Trading down, 154
Trading up, 154
Training program in personal selling, 216–217
  content of, 221–222
  designing, 220–222
  executing, 222–223
Trust market, adapting marketing mix to, 306–309
Trust marketing, 294, 304, 306
Truth-in-lending regulations, 37
Truth-in-Savings Act, 11, 37, 187–188, 188, 247, 281
Twain Bancshares, Inc., 302–303
Tylenol, 142

U

Undifferentiated marketing, 141
Unilever, 153
Union Bank, 86
U.S. Time Company, 136
University National Bank & Trust Co., 9
Unsatisfied needs, 108–109

V

Variability
  and distribution of bank services, 195
  and new product development, 151
Variable costs, 184
Virtual branches, 204
Visa, 143
Volume segmentation, 137

W

Wachovia, 204
Wal-Mart, 36
Waterman, Robert, Jr., 283
Web site, 314
Wells Fargo Bank, 159, 312
Wholesale side of banking, 294–309